ANTISEMIT

Antisemitism: A History

Edited by
ALBERT S. LINDEMANN
RICHARD S. LEVY

OXFORD
UNIVERSITY PRESS

Great Clarendon Street, Oxford ox2 6DP

Oxford University Press is a department of the University of Oxford.
It furthers the University's objective of excellence in research, scholarship,
and education by publishing worldwide in

Oxford New York

Auckland Cape Town Dar es Salaam Hong Kong Karachi
Kuala Lumpur Madrid Melbourne Mexico City Nairobi
New Delhi Shanghai Taipei Toronto

With offices in

Argentina Austria Brazil Chile Czech Republic France Greece
Guatemala Hungary Italy Japan Poland Portugal Singapore
South Korea Switzerland Thailand Turkey Ukraine Vietnam

Oxford is a registered trade mark of Oxford University Press
in the UK and in certain other countries

Published in the United States
by Oxford University Press Inc., New York

Editorial matter and arrangement
© Albert S. Lindemann and Richard S. Levy, 2010
Chapters © the various contributors

The moral rights of the authors have been asserted
Database right Oxford University Press (maker)

First published 2010

All rights reserved. No part of this publication may be reproduced,
stored in a retrieval system, or transmitted, in any form or by any means,
without the prior permission in writing of Oxford University Press,
or as expressly permitted by law, or under terms agreed with the appropriate
reprographics rights organization. Enquiries concerning reproduction
outside the scope of the above should be sent to the Rights Department,
Oxford University Press, at the address above

You must not circulate this book in any other binding or cover
and you must impose the same condition on any acquirer

British Library Cataloguing in Publication Data
Data available

Library of Congress Cataloging in Publication Data
Library of Congress Control Number: 2010933149

Typeset by SPI Publisher Services, Pondicherry, India
Printed in Great Britain
by
Clays Ltd, St Ives plc

ISBN 978–0–19–923503–2 (Hbk.)
978–0–19–923502–5 (Pbk.)

1 3 5 7 9 10 8 6 4 2

Contents

Preface	vii
List of Maps	viii
List of Contributors	ix
Introduction	1
1. The Jewish Question *Albert S. Lindemann*	17
2. The Ancient Mediterranean and the Pre-Christian Era *Benjamin Isaac*	34
3. Jews and Christians from the Time of Christ to Constantine's Reign *Philip A. Cunningham*	47
4. The Middle Ages *Alex Novikoff*	63
5. Antisemitism in the Late Medieval and Early Modern Periods *Ralph Keen*	79
6. Antisemitism in the Age of Mercantilism *Jonathan Karp*	94
7. The Enlightenment, French Revolution, Napoleon *Adam Sutcliffe*	107
8. Political Antisemitism in Germany and Austria, 1848–1914 *Richard S. Levy*	121
9. Antisemitism in Modern France: Dreyfus, Vichy, and Beyond *Richard J. Golsan*	136
10. Antisemitism in the English-Speaking World *William D. Rubinstein*	150
11. Antisemitism in Russia and the Soviet Union *Heinz-Dietrich Löwe*	166
12. Antisemitism in the Nazi Era *Doris L. Bergen*	196

vi   *Contents*

13. Anti-Judaism and Antisemitism in the Arab
    and Islamic World Prior to 1948   212
    Norman A. Stillman

14. Antisemitism in Eastern Europe (Excluding Russia
    and the Soviet Empire) Since 1848   222
    István Deák

15. Israel and Antisemitism   237
    Meir Litvak and Esther Webman

    Conclusion: Not the Final Word   250

    Glossary of Terms   264
    Index   273

Preface

The central goal of this volume is to offer a readable overview of a daunting topic, trying to gain some distance from the polemics and apologetics that are in danger of becoming predictable and unproductive, especially on a popular level. As editors we sought out a wide selection of recognized scholars, asking them to include the most important new developments in their fields, as succinctly as possible. We have done our best to trim the familiar but at times off-putting conventions of scholarly apparatus and style, while striving to retain the accuracy, rigor, and open-mindedness of the best scholarly traditions.

While we have worked to assure thematic unities in the volume, we have by no means sought to enforce any one interpretive perspective. The scholars represented here do not agree with each other on all points, but they do recognize that conflicting viewpoints of a scholarly nature should get a fair hearing.

As editors we each contributed one of the articles. We collaborated on the Introduction and Conclusion, but they reflect differences of approach and contrasting nuances of interpretation, the Introduction being primarily the work of Albert Lindemann, the Conclusion of Richard Levy.

This work is affectionately dedicated to the memory of John Doyle Klier, who died on September 23, 2007, before he could make his contribution to this volume. The scholarly world is a sadder, poorer place without him.

ASL

RSL

List of Maps

1. Europe and the Mediterannean from ancient times to
   the end of the Middle Ages   x
2. Europe, 1871–1914   xi

List of Contributors

Doris L. Bergen, Chancellor Rose and Ray Wolfe Professor of Holocaust Studies, Department of History, University of Toronto

Philip A. Cunningham, Professor of Theology, Director of the Institute for Jewish-Catholic Relations, Saint Joseph's University, Philadelphia

István Deák, Seth Low Professor of History, Emeritus, Columbia University

Richard J. Golsan, Distinguished Professor of French, Texas A&M University

Benjamin Isaac, Lessing Professor of Ancient History, Tel Aviv University

Jonathan Karp, Associate Professor of History and Judaic Studies, Binghamton University, SUNY

Ralph Keen, Associate Professor of Religious Studies University of Iowa

Richard S. Levy, Professor of History, University of Illinois at Chicago

Albert S. Lindemann, Professor of History, Emeritus, University of California, Santa Barbara

Meir Litvak, Associate Professor of Middle Eastern History, Tel Aviv University

Heinz-Dietrich Löwe, Professor of East European History, Heidelberg University

Alex J. Novikoff, Assistant Professor of Medieval History, Rhodes College, Memphis

William D. Rubinstein, Professor of History, University of Aberystwyth

Norman A. Stillman, Schusterman/Josey Chair of Judaic History, University of Oklahoma

Adam Sutcliffe, Senior Lecturer in European History, King's College London

Esther Webman, Dr., Senior Research Fellow, Dayan Center for Middle Eastern and African Studies, and Stephen Roth Institute for the Study of Antisemitism and Racism

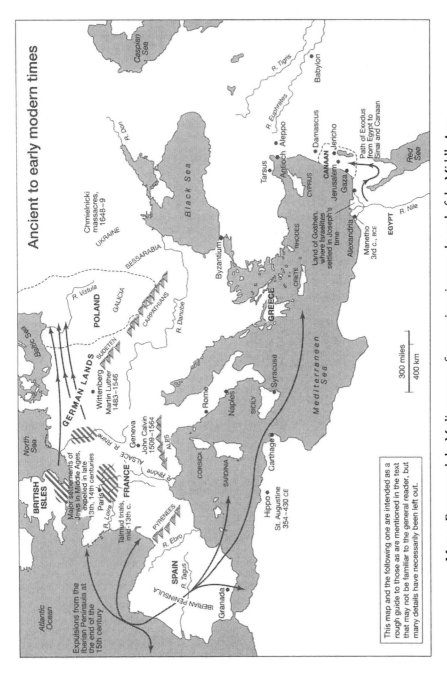

Map 1. Europe and the Mediterranean from ancient times to the end of the Middle Ages

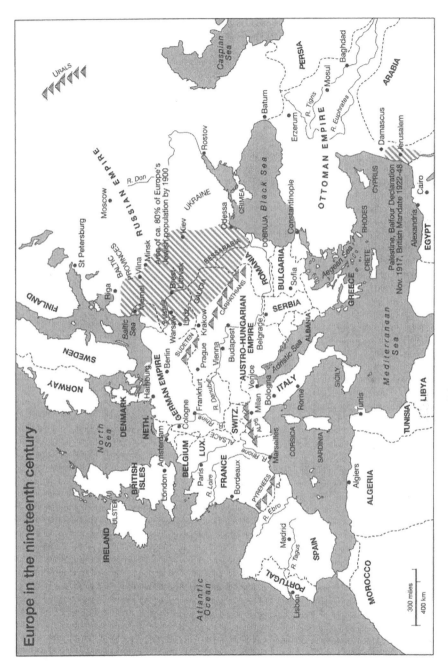

Map 2. Europe, 1871–1914

Introduction

> If only it were all so simple! If only there were evil people somewhere insidiously committing evil deeds, and all that was necessary would be to separate them from the rest of us, and then destroy them. But the line dividing good and evil cuts through the heart of every human being.
>
> Alexander Solzhenitsyn

The subheadings of this Introduction touch on themes that each of the volume's authors has been asked to address. The goal in this Introduction is to alert the reader to key concepts, thus serving as a general overview, posing productive questions without attempting to resolve them. They will be taken up again in the Conclusion in an ampler and less tentative form.

ANTISEMITISM: WHAT IS IT? HOW CAN WE BEST UNDERSTAND IT?

Antisemitism is a complex term, in many ways oddly so. Boundless difficulties arise in attempting a definition of it, especially one that is more than a redundancy (hatred of Jews) and that points to its causes and nature. Much the same may be said about the wider, related term racism. Those using the terms antisemite and racist today often have transparently political agendas and are typically innocent of the terms' tangled histories. Problems of this sort are not uncommon with ideological terms—fascism and liberalism are other obvious examples—but it does seem that what is implied by antisemitism is even more elusive, perhaps uniquely so. It is instructive that even self-proclaimed antisemites have long differed with one another over what the term really means or should mean.

There are those who report that they know antisemitism when they see it, much as with pornography, even if they find it difficult to pin down with words the nature of their recognition. The comparison with pornography is suggestive in that some believe the mere viewing of it to be dangerously corrupting, whereas others believe that it is the already corrupt personalities (or dangerous tendencies in all personalities) that are attracted to pornography. Some, in turn, see antisemitic ideas as mysteriously potent, dangerously corrupting those who have

2   *Albert S. Lindemann and Richard S. Levy*

contact with them; others believe simply that already corrupt personalities are attracted to antisemitic ideas.

There is the associated problem with the term antisemitism, to quote Ian Buruma, that "this particular whistle has been blown so often and with such shrillness that exaggerated anxiety sometimes impairs serious discussion" (*The New Republic*, September 4, 2006, 23). Antisemite has become one of the most feared of today's abusive epithets, along with racist. That problem is yet again linked to the issue of determining the genuine importance of antisemitism and evaluating the way that Jews have defined themselves in relation to it: Are they somehow, in their very nature or by God's design, a suffering people, crucially defined by the hatred they have faced throughout history? Is it possible to imagine a Jewish identity separate from what has been disparagingly termed *Leidensgeschichte* (suffering history, in German), the centuries-old vulnerability and powerlessness of the Jews? Are Jews inclined to dramatize antisemitism, in history and in the current scene, downplaying other factors? Conversely, are non-Jews prone to minimizing the role of Jew-hatred, avoiding the self scrutiny that a realistic appreciation would involve?

Analyses of the causes of antisemitism in history have fallen into several broad categories. At one extreme, it has been argued that the nature of Jews and the actions flowing from that nature are to blame for the hatred they have encountered. Jews must then change their ways if that hatred is to cease. At the opposite extreme, hatred for Jews has been described as being generated from within the non-Jewish world, reflecting its pathologies but lacking any significant relationship to the actual activities or real nature of Jews. Anti-Jewish hatred from this second perspective is defined as essentially a Gentile problem, not a Jewish problem, and is to be solved by Gentile introspection and reform. At any rate, Jewish reform will not change the minds of genuine antisemites; they will always find fault in Jews, whether it is abundant or trivial. Revealingly, the suggestion that both Jews and non-Jews need to change their ways if the hatred is to disappear has been rejected by both sides, often angrily. (The broad history of both sides, in the Jewish Question and a corresponding Gentile question, is explored in Chapter 1.)

A more transcendent view of anti-Jewish hatred is that it reflects God's will: Throughout history He has used the Gentiles to punish the Jews for their failure to live up to the covenant at Sinai. From this perspective, Gentile hatred is to be interpreted not only as divine punishment for Jewish transgressions but as part of God's plan to preserve Jewish separateness—to uplift, purify, and ennoble the Jews through suffering. This general perspective is not limited to those who see a personal God intervening directly in history; as Nobel Prize winning author Isaac Bashevis Singer once put it, "only in exile did the Jews grow up spiritually" (Douglas Villiers, ed., *Next Year in Jerusalem*, London: Viking, 1976, 8). In other words, the centuries-long experiences, both negative and positive, of Jews in being driven from their promised land into exile have deepened their spiritual

Introduction 3

sensibilities and broadened their intellectual horizons, rendering them in some sense unique or at least highly unusual among the peoples of the world.

Conceptualizing antisemitism as generated from within Gentile society has suggestive parallels with the view that criminal personalities reflect inborn character, and not primarily environment. Similarly, in the proposed solutions to criminality and to antisemitism there are parallels in the notions of punishment versus rehabilitation. Some see antisemitism much as others see criminality; both are deeply, even mysteriously rooted and largely incurable. Antisemites, like hardened criminals, must be met with force, not sympathetic understanding; they need to be punished, incarcerated, or rigorously isolated. Efforts to understand them sympathetically will be thankless—and dangerous, much like efforts to appease dictators.

Whichever position one favors, the far-reaching implication of the different power of Jews and non-Jews in history is a crucial consideration. Lord Acton famously commented that power tends to corrupt and absolute power to corrupt absolutely, an observation that might be considered fundamental to Gentile-Jewish relations, insofar as Gentiles have been corrupted by their power over Jews. Yet fundamental to the Judeo-Christian worldview is the belief that power-lessness, suffering, and oppression ennoble. There is the contrary but also deep-set idea that oppression tends to corrupt the oppressed, pushing them toward criminality or other psychic disorders. The many ramifications of these positions will be pursued in subsequent chapters, but virtually all observers agree that the powerful and the powerless see the world in radically different ways, and they compose narratives about themselves in similarly contrasting ways.

The first of the above two interpretive stances (connecting hatred for Jews to Jewish belief and action) is often considered the basic antisemitic position, or that of the Gentile powerful. The second (placing blame on the non-Jewish world) may be seen as that of Jewish defensiveness, or that of the Jewish power-less. The third of the above interpretations, stressing divine will, must be accepted in some sense by all believers in an omnipotent, omniscient, and just god. However, it is not the kind of explanation that modern historians consider adequate. Even for believers it presents some daunting interpretive challenges. At any rate, after the Holocaust to view Jewish suffering as just punishment for Jewish sins is widely dismissed as abhorrent.

In broader application, blaming the victim is taboo today, but beyond the facile way that phrase is sometimes used are some substantial issues, since blame or responsibility, especially when speaking of groups or collectivities, are concepts with remarkably blurred edges. Blaming the Christian world collectively for its centuries of oppression of Jews has long been an element of Jewish self-definition. Similarly, an element of Christian belief has long been that Jews collectively hate them, their savior, and all that Christianity stands for in terms of genuine human equality before God. Obviously the finger-pointing in each direction cannot be termed exactly comparable, again because of the issue of power: The historic powerlessness of Jews, their small populations, and the undeniable reality of their suffering over the centuries give a substantially different tenor to the mutual charges. The countercharge that Jews historically have oppressed and exploited Christians is dismissed by many Jewish observers as an antisemitic canard.

What scholarly balance might mean in regard to these heated exchanges is not easy to say. Many recognized scholars, Jewish and non-Jewish, implicitly accept that Jews have been responsible to some extent for the hatred they have encountered—and even that they have often exaggerated the extent of that hatred in a manipulative way. But such acceptance is usually accompanied by careful qualifications concerning how responsibility is to be defined and how dramatization of Jewish suffering has been an understandable tool of self-protection. A central tenet of Zionism, amply expressed in the writings of Theodor Herzl and other leading Zionists, is that historically Jews, in order to survive in *galut* (exile), acquired character traits that were "objectively detestable." Jews similarly assumed social positions, such as moneylending, that were inherently precarious and tension-creating. The only realistic or long-term remedy to these ills, from the Zionist perspective, is separation from Gentiles and the restoration of sovereign power to Jews in their own modern nation state.

The Zionist form of finding defects in Jewish character easily moves toward the suggestion that the antisemites' point of view has some justification. Herzl repeatedly marveled at how much support he got from the antisemites of his day, while most Western Jews regarded him with deep suspicion. But today the suggestion that Jews were responsible in any sense for antisemitism is widely and often summarily dismissed, especially on a popular level, as a misapplication of the notion of balance and as a failure to understand Jews and their history as they deserve to be understood. Many who have written about the history of antisemitism have operated on an underlying conviction that antisemites are self-evidently bad people who believe bad things. Period. The main task of the historian, then, is to describe antisemites and their ideas amply. That description should be quite enough to reveal how fundamentally evil, groundless, and dangerous Jew-hatred is.

This kind of moral clarity, more amply explored in a separate section below, leaves unresolved the crucial issue of exactly how antisemites are to be identified. Is antisemitism indeed self-evident and is it unitary in nature, as contrasted with being a hatred with a wide range of intensity and causes? In one interpretive direction, Anthony Julius, prominent lawyer and academic, has argued in favor of including as antisemitic all types of "emotional distancing" from Jews, from mild to fierce. In his view, even those non-Jews who express sympathy for Jewish suffering, or who oppose hostile measures against Jews, still must qualify as antisemitic if they distance themselves emotionally from Jews as a collective category. Julius cites instances of "casual anti-Semitism" or "pseudo-philo-Semitism" that he believes qualify as genuinely antisemitic because, in his words,

Introduction

they do not "welcome... [Jews] into those private spaces in which members of a society lead their lives" (David Kertzer, ed., *Old Demons, New Debates: Anti-Semitism in the West*, New York: Holmes and Meier, 2005, 68).

By this definition the majority of non-Jews, even in modern liberal societies such as the United States, have been and are now antisemitic. This definition also implicitly touches on the issue of power, since the exclusion of Jews from the private spaces of the powerful has unquestionably had wide-ranging negative implications for Jews throughout history. But such a sweeping definition has some awkward aspects, for it seems to place those Jews who do not welcome non-Jews into Jewish private spaces in a category of bigotry comparable to that of antisemitism. There is again the important complicating factor of power, but Jewish identity over the ages has notably involved a cultivation of Jewish private spaces, linked to an emotional distancing from non-Jews. Jewish religious leaders in the past prohibited the attendance of Jews at non-Jewish festivals and ceremonies, and the rules of *kashrut* limited socialization with non-Jews even at meals.

IDENTITY, DISTINCTIVENESS, TOLERATION

Ruth Wisse, Harvard Professor of Yiddish Literature, has written that "from earliest days, Jewish sources distinguished 'good' nations from 'evil' according to whether they could tolerate Jewish distinctiveness" (*Jews and Power*, New York: Schocken, 2007, 18). Distinctiveness is another amorphous concept, as is tolerance, but central to modern notions of identity is a recognition of the value of distinctiveness in the sense of various ethnic and religious private spaces. Modern multicultural and multireligious societies affirm the right, indeed the solemn duty, of their members to cultivate an identity that preserves significant differences from others. Those differences are by no means all invidious (and many modern Jews as well as other ethnic groups have obviously sought to minimize them), but some forms of identity are more far-ranging, separatist, and intolerant than others; some establish ampler private spaces, physical and psychological. Some are inclined to define others as morally inferior, if not intolerable. Such radically separatist and morally supremacist identities have existed and continue to exist among both Jews and non-Jews. (There has also long been a tendency, from earliest days, in non-Jewish sources to distinguish good Jews from evil ones, according to whether they are perceived to have malevolent or benevolent attitudes to non-Jewish society.)

However, if the intolerance linked to preserving identity tends in its extreme forms to move toward bigotry, in its opposite direction it meshes with widely agreed-upon standards of moral uprightness. We are proudly intolerant of child molesters and stock market criminals, to say nothing of murderers and rapists. Moral choice inevitably involves not tolerating—indeed taking action against—certain kinds of behavior. But precisely how do we determine which behaviors are tolerable and which are not? That is where consensus begins to come apart even in modern societies, at times explosively.

Adherents of monotheistic religions, including Judaism, Christianity, and Islam, have historically believed in their own superior moral standards. References like those of Wisse to Jewish distinctiveness have clearly been made with such beliefs in mind. Revealingly, the term discrimination is similar in its ambiguity to toleration, in that it can suggest either prejudicial attitudes or penetrating observation. Much the same can be said about the term inclusion, which does not usually mean that Holocaust deniers should be included in scholarly conferences, or that Flat-Earthers should be given a place of respect in scientific discussions of planet Earth. Inclusion must be discriminating.

Throughout history there have been those who have concluded that Jewish identity is *dangerously* different and thus not to be tolerated. They have formed the firm opinion that Jewish distinctiveness involves something inherently destructive to those among whom Jews live. Such conclusions have been especially prominent when Jews are seen to be growing rapidly in numbers, wealth, and influence. It was precisely in those regards that the modern term antisemitism came into common use in the 1880s, with a somewhat novel but hardly original notion of Jews as a material body, a race, rather than as a community of belief. Antisemites of those years, again in a novel but not completely original way, offered various programs of action to deal with the perceived threat from Jews. Anti-Jewish action was considered to be not only a matter of urgent self-defense but also one of moral probity.

In contrast, those in the late nineteenth century, both Jews and non-Jews, who did not accept such anti-Jewish perceptions began to use the new term antisemitism to indicate an *unjust* attitude to Jews, based on false perceptions of their nature and activities. Some defenders of Judaism and secular Jewishness insisted that Jews, rather than being threats, benefited the societies in which they lived.

The traditional Christian position might be considered a variety of that position, with the crucial difference that Christians believed that Jews had lost God's favor by crucifying His son. Still, the prevailing Christian position was not that Judaism was entirely evil. Christian morality was unmistakably influenced by Judaism. Christians recognized that Christ and his original disciples were all Jews, limiting the potential demonization of Jews as a physical entity. The prevailing Christian goal was to convert the Jews, not to destroy them physically.

It is thus a striking paradox that imagery derived from Christianity is blamed for the unique demonization of Jews in Western civilization, whereas mainline Christian doctrine saw Jewish survival as useful and indeed as a reflection of God's will. The ways that modern racial antisemites came to regard Jews as evil in nature involved, in many instances, a switching of the metaphor of their being Christ killers to their being spreaders of disease and disorder. That switch can be considered a kind of return to ancient metaphors, but it also provided the

Introduction

foundation for the concept of a complete physical elimination of Jews—in the way that science was seeking a final solution to syphilis or cholera. Many opponents of antisemitism have themselves resorted to metaphors or similes of disease, describing antisemitism as akin to cancer or spreading as do pandemic viruses—thus the need for them to be wiped out.

Most modern secular defenders of the Jews in the nineteenth century actually accepted the notion, in a sense similar to that of the Christians, that the Jews of their day had fallen into bad times, becoming useless if not positively harmful to modern societies, and were thus in urgent need of reform. A fair number of Gentile observers offered the "salt in soup" analogy: A little salt enhanced the flavor of soup; too much ruined it. A few Jews might be beneficial to a society, but too many undermined it. Even those who most insistently defended the Jews in the nineteenth century rarely if ever denied that dismayingly large numbers of them had acquired antisocial or parasitical traits. Those defenders nonetheless believed that the antisemites of their day exaggerated the problem, failing to see Jews in a just and balanced fashion, and making them all guilty for the failings of some.

THE ISSUE OF UNIQUENESS
AND DEMONIZING IMAGERY

In defending the Jews, the issue of the uniqueness of Jew-hatred again arose, in that the defenders emphasized how the unjust or exaggerated visions of Jews somehow conjured up a uniquely toxic brew of related emotions—hatred, fear, jealousy, contempt—which over the course of Christian history had been embellished with grotesque images, and that imagery somehow infected believers with a curious (or unique) tenacity of belief, a striking resistance to contrary evidence, and ultimately an inclination to violence.

Those historically accumulated images of Jews require special scrutiny. Some of them may be termed normal in that they resembled the imagery applied to other groups (e.g., Jews and Gypsies are secretive; Jews and Germans are arrogant). The more potent anti-Jewish images, however, were distinctly abnormal. Included among them was the Jews' alleged proclivity to practice cannibalism, poison wells, and spread plague, or to drain the blood of non-Jewish children for various Jewish rituals. Jews have been charged—to enter fully into the peculiarly mystical symbolism of it all—with deicide (killing Christ), not only in having orchestrated the original Crucifixion, but in ritually rehearsing and rejoicing over it since then. Jews were charged with transforming their Purim narrative about the killing of Haman (the evil vizier) by the Jews of Persia into a thinly veiled yearly celebration of the killing of Christ. In a similarly mystical vein, a belief spread among Christians that Jews surreptitiously stole Eucharist wafers, tortured and defiled them, thus ritually reenacting the Crucifixion.

8 *Albert S. Lindemann and Richard S. Levy*

Some of the most influential definitions of antisemitism, those offered by such distinguished modern historians as Saul Friedländer and Bernard Lewis, have in common a special attention to the fantastic and mystical, to the peculiar demonization of Jews in antisemitic belief. Friedländer uses the term "redemptive antisemitism" to emphasize how the Nazis claimed to be standing up for godliness, for justice and humanity, against the demonically destructive Jews. Historian Bernard Lewis uses the term "cosmic evil."

Lewis in particular differs from Anthony Julius by warning against the perils, similar to those of crying wolf, of an overly broad or promiscuous use of the term antisemitism. In his opinion, it should not be used to describe *any* dislike of Jews. Ordinary frictions and hostilities that do not entail describing the Jews as a cosmic evil he dismisses as not appropriately termed antisemitic ("The New Anti-Semitism," *The American Scholar* 75[1], Winter 2006: 25–36). He notes that in past centuries Islamic law treated Jews as inferior to Muslims but still treated them as humans, not as a cosmic evil. Muslims did not regularly invite Jews into their private spaces, but the Islamic world only became antisemitic by Lewis's definition when it began to import the uniquely Christian demonization of the Jews.

We arrive at a widely accepted if often inarticulate position: Antisemitism is in some deeply significant sense a hatred like no other—the longest hatred—and the most tenacious and mysterious in human history. The historical depth of that hatred, of that endlessly reemerging antipathy, offers further evidence of its mysterious potency. Ostensibly for such reasons the term Jew-hatred came to appear inadequate to many observers in the late nineteenth century; antisemitism suggested more effectively the uniquely dangerous mystery of it all.

There are problems with this more focused definition, as with the more all-encompassing one, most obviously in its tendency to exclude as antisemitic those hostilities arising from real or ordinary conflict between Jews and non-Jews. In fact, a very large proportion of what is now or has been termed antisemitic does not have to do with demonization but rather with objective conflicts, arising from normal economic competition or social snobbery. Many of those who were called antisemites in the late nineteenth century did not demonize Jews any more than premodern Muslims had.

Wilhelm Marr, the patriarch of modern antisemitism and the man credited with giving the new term wide publicity, emphatically rejected Christian demonization of Jews. Much the same might be said of Heinrich von Treitschke, the celebrated German professor who is credited with giving antisemitism respectability and whose name is associated with the slogan, later taken up by the Nazis, "The Jews are our misfortune!" Whatever his ire at the Jews of his day, Treitschke did not make a cosmic evil of them or advocate physical action against them. He did not even support demands that their recently acquired civil equality in Germany be withdrawn. Moreover, he described many Jews as praiseworthy German citizens. What he was demanding was that some of them

Introduction 9

reform themselves, and he implicitly believed it possible (whereas if Jews were to be considered demons, they could not be reformed). Treitschke's charges were no doubt unfair, but in Lewis's terms they were not antisemitic.

ANTISEMITISM AS A RELIGION, JEWS AS CHOSEN

The term antisemitism was coined in the nineteenth century along with many other modern "isms" that came into broad use (e.g., liberalism, socialism, conservatism). However, given its status as a snarled emotional response to the presence of Jews rather than a reasoned and balanced conclusion based on cogently examined evidence, it sits in awkward company with the other isms or modern ideologies of the nineteenth century. Those who used the term in a favorable sense in the 1880s, such as Marr, claimed that they were relying on measurable, material evidence, on the scientifically verifiable facts of race, not religious dogma or inherited prejudice. But such claims finally failed to persuade many if not most Europeans, and a measure of consensus, especially among the educated and those of liberal inclinations, emerged that, rather than being scientific and rational, this particular ism had something uniquely primitive or atavistic about it.

What is increasingly uncontested today is that race in its nineteenth-century usage was a pseudoscientific concept, one that in practice was applied in amazingly undisciplined and even contradictory ways by racists, including self-described antisemites. Even in the late nineteenth century, many observers dismissed what antisemites claimed as rationally gathered evidence as nothing more than facts assembled tendentiously, to bolster what came down to something like faith, an emotional need (or cynical political ploy) that was remotely if at all related to a disinterested scrutiny of evidence. Stated in other terms, antisemitism was seen to be less about factual evidence about Jews and more about pre-existing attitudes, frames of mind, or psychic states of non-Jews.

Although it is often asserted that antisemites of the late nineteenth century were ignorant, ill-educated people, such was probably no more the case than with the followers of other major ideologies. Psychic serenity, high levels of education, and tolerant liberal values are only tenuously related. Even granting that the leading theorists of antisemitism were of mediocre intellectual stature, many antisemites were (and are) by no means unintelligent or unschooled. Indeed, many of them studied evidence about Jews assiduously and knew far more about Jews in a strictly factual sense than those Gentiles who defended them. Religious belief, too, has a tenuous relationship to intelligence, formal learning, and factual evidence—and much to do with social conditioning and psychic inclinations.

The elusive, faith-based aspect of antisemitism parallels and is suggestively related to the elusiveness of Jewish identity, which might well be termed the

10   *Albert S. Lindemann and Richard S. Levy*

longest identity in history, at least in Western history, and in modern times it has remained much more than what is commonly understood as a modern religious identity. Definitions of that Jewish essence (Yiddish: *dos pintele yid*) have been endlessly if inconclusively debated by Jews themselves. Nonetheless few observers have maintained that there is *no* content whatsoever to Jewish identity (even if Jewish defensiveness at times implicitly makes it seem that such is being claimed).

A familiar conclusion is that Jews have been hated (feared, envied, denigrated) because of their peculiar separatist identity, itself based on their belief that as a people or nation elevated by God they are essentially distinct from the rest of humanity. Nobel Peace Prize winner Elie Wiesel has described this separateness, this *romemut* (Hebrew: elevation), as central to Jewish identity. In his words, the Jews are "ontologically" different from others, that is, different in their essential being (Irving Abrahamson, *Against Silence*, New York: Holocaust Library, 1988, 1:153). His assertion connects with the rabbinical definition of Jews as a *goy kadosh* (holy nation) and an *am nivchar* (chosen people), commanded by God to remain distinct from others, both physically and spiritually. Jews are descended from the Patriarchs, Abraham, Isaac, and Jacob, whereas the *goyim*, (the [Other] Nations) are descended from less hallowed forefathers. Jewish prayers and rituals in most varieties of Judaism to this day connect in one way or another to the concept of Jewish *romemut*. The *havdala* (differentiation) prayer, recited at the end of the Sabbath, links Jews to holiness and light, while the Other Nations are considered ordinary, not holy—and often evil.

That outrage over Jewish pretensions to divine favor and essential separateness from others might be the most fundamental emotion in antisemitism finds a symbolic corroboration in Genesis: "Now Israel [Jacob] loved Joseph more than any other of his children... But when his brothers saw that their father loved him more than all his brothers, they hated him and could not speak peaceably to him" (Gen. 37:3–4).

When Joseph described his dream of his sheaf standing high and the sheaves of his brothers bowing down, his brothers hated him all the more: "Are you indeed to reign over us?" they asked angrily. If the Children of Israel hated their own paternally favored brother enough to try to kill him, it is not a long reach to conclude that the Other Nations have similarly hated and resented the Jews as God's favorite.

Modern interpretations of Jewish tradition have resisted much of the above reasoning; their counterarguments imply that the difference between Jews and non-Jews, far from being ontological, is nominal or minimal, especially insofar as the two groups share a common humanity or souls equal in the eyes of God. Even more, modern interpretations of the difference associated with Jewish identity insist that it does not imply the superiority, physical or moral, of Jews to others. Jews have hardly been immune, individually or collectively, to the *yetzer hara* (inclination to evil), as is amply documented in the Hebrew Bible and

Introduction

emphasized by rabbinical tradition. Modern Jewish wags of a secular bent have characterized Jews as "just like everyone else—only more so."

Modern Jews remain complexly divided on these issues, as on so many others. Judaism, like Christianity, has been and continues to be characterized by competing, seemingly irreconcilable traditions. One Jewish observer has distinguished an Ezra tradition from a Ruth tradition. The first insists not only on the divine elevation of the Jews but on the irreducible otherness (physical and spiritual) and greater inclination to evil of the non-Jew. For those most attracted to the Ezra tradition, "Judaism is not essentially a matter of faith or ethics or ideology but... of mysteriously inherited traits" (Harold Schulweis, *In God's Mirror*, Hoboken, NJ: Ktav, 1990, 200 ff). The opposing tradition celebrates Ruth the Moabite, a woman from an enemy tribe who joined the Jewish tribe ("whither thou goest I will go"), underlining the option of all peoples to become Jewish and thus the fundamental universalism of Judaism.

Self-declared antisemites have actually agreed with those Jewish voices that insist on a unique Jewish identity based on an ontological difference. Frequently antisemites have even seen Jews as more intelligent than non-Jews, or certainly more clever. The essential difference, as antisemites have seen it, lies not in Jews being God's Chosen but rather in their being agents of evil in history, engaged in a mission of destruction of other peoples, with the ultimate goal of ruling over them. Even many of those who reject such demonization as repellent find Jewish claims to universalism a bit Orwellian. ("All animals are equal but some animals are more equal than others", George Orwell, *Animal Farm*.)

Other observers have deemed Jewish claims, whether to *romemut* or to genuine human equality, to be unconvincing but nonetheless tolerable in the way that other religious and ethnic claims are, since in modern multicultural and multireligious societies the awkward details and implications of the beliefs of others are not usually emphasized—or at least are no longer found to be as threatening as they were in centuries past (and for the most part remain unknown). Similarly, in modern liberal societies the extremist views of members of a given religious or ethnic group are not usually accepted as characteristic of the entire group, even if they get the most publicity.

HARD TIMES AND GREAT MEN, ANTISEMITIC IDEAS AND ACTION

Modern historians, as observed above, are not satisfied with historical explanations that rely on the role of divine intervention. The historical profession has also moved away from explanations that focus on great men as the movers and shakers of history. However, insofar as antisemitism has been conceptualized as produced by impersonal forces, there is a parallel with notions of divine predestination—and a similar paradox, in that predestined or historically conditioned

Albert S. Lindemann and Richard S. Levy

decisions are difficult to work into historical narratives that feature moral judgments as primary (a tendency that has been prominent in many if not most histories of antisemitism). We then return to the question: How are antisemites in history to be conceptualized, and what is the proper role of moral judgments in historical narrative?

Scholars accept that hard times—plagues, wars, revolutions, economic depressions, natural disasters—have constituted, along with a perception of Jews growing in numbers and power, a common background to the most important episodes of antisemitic passion and violence. The very nature of modern historical explanation tends to work in the direction of minimizing personal responsibility and maximizing the role of impersonal forces. But how far should this be taken? Is Hitler understandable—and thus in some sense forgivable—because of his unhappy childhood? The question points toward an obvious slippery slope and the point previously made: Toleration and inclusion must be discriminating. Distrust of historical explanations that emphasize the importance of broad historical forces has moved in several directions. One has been back toward an earlier tendency to emphasize the role of famous historical personalities, either great thinkers or great men of action, who somehow have pulled the general population into their visions and ambitions. Lord Acton added to his well-known quip (that power corrupts and absolute power corrupts absolutely) the following observation: "Great men are almost always bad men." In that spirit, many of the standard modern histories of antisemitism have focused attention on great antisemites throughout history, men who are often associated with or believed to personify a tribe, people, or nation. Jewish rabbinical tradition has focused on *Haman ha-rasha*, Haman the Wicked, in the Book of Esther, as a symbol of absolute evil, along with his biblical forebears, Amalek and the Amalekites. In regard to such enemies, no sympathetic understanding is possible, nor is toleration advisable. On a more historically verifiable level, the many other Hamans of Jewish tradition have included Saint John Chrysostom, Martin Luther, and Bogdan Chmielnicki—each of whom have historically been revered by Catholics, Protestants, or Ukrainians, who read their own history in a different way than do most Jews. It is often the case that one people's villain is another's hero.

The issue of sympathetic understanding has emerged with particular acrimony in efforts to understand the Third Reich and the Holocaust. Germany lost millions of its young men in World War I, and was unjustly blamed for having sole responsibility in starting it. Germany's economy was subsequently thrown into chaos, its institutions undermined, its people humiliated. Can we conclude that Germans, particularly the common people, were victims of impersonal forces they did not understand and certainly did not control? Or are they more aptly characterized as active agents, "willing executioners," to borrow a term used in a bestselling book on Nazi Germany by Daniel Goldhagen? (The popularity of that book among English-speaking readers had in part to do with

Introduction

growing resentments about how modern historians, in putting Nazism into historical context, were perceived as playing down issues of personal and national guilt: *Hitler's Willing Executioners: Ordinary Germans and the Holocaust*, New York: Vintage, 1997).

A thought-provoking contribution to this discussion was offered by Milton Himmelfarb, in an essay entitled "No Hitler, no Holocaust." Without Hitler, he argued, there might well have been serious anti-Jewish action in Germany in the 1930s and 1940s but not a systematic program to murder all Jews. Hitler's will—his irrational and irreducibly *evil* will—and his unshakable belief in his mission to save the world from the Jewish peril, were crucial to the Final Solution of the Jewish Question (*Commentary*, March 1984).

Hitler looms as the greatest Haman of all history. It seems only natural that his life story would offer us valuable insights about how antisemitic convictions are formed. Was he criminally inclined at birth, or were unfortunate life experiences crucial to his perverse adult personality? Can he be considered a great thinker, in the way that Karl Marx or John Stuart Mill are usually considered to be? The very notion of an ideology that is essentially "anti," based on hatred, suggests that the antisemitic personality, with Hitler as a prime example, is driven by narrow resentment, fear, and envy, without a broader or more positive vision. The conclusion is familiar: Antisemites, leaders and followers, have been fearful and paranoiac, insecure losers venting their frustrations about their own inadequacies, or the inadequacies of their people, on the convenient scapegoat, the Jews.

However, the conclusion that antisemites have been petty losers, while certainly part of the truth, sits awkwardly with the fact that so many great men in European history have expressed anti-Jewish ideas. Similarly, Hitler was a man of greater intellectual abilities—and even of impressive learning in given areas—than has been commonly recognized (Frederick Spotts, *Hitler and the Power of Aesthetics*, New York: Overlook, 2003). The following chapters offer many examples of the often puzzling disconnect between antisemitic attitudes and anti-Jewish action. Thought and action are naturally assumed to have an integral relationship, but it goes too far to describe all those harboring anti-Jewish ideas as lowbrow losers, since such ideas have been embraced by many successful people and quite a number of impressively subtle intellects. A long list of such figures could be composed for modern times alone. In fact, it would be difficult to make up more than a short list of famous or successful figures who did not have some sharply critical things to say in the public or private spheres about Judaism and Jews.

Did antisemitic ideas somehow fatally infect the personality of these great men, as a disease infects a healthy body, or was it simply, to return to an earlier point, that their personalities were corrupt and thus attracted to antisemitism? A close examination of the lives of such men gives only feeble confirmation to either hypothesis. It is revealing that some of the mostly highly esteemed Righteous

14 *Albert S. Lindemann and Richard S. Levy*

Gentiles of modern times often made statements that qualify as antisemitic even by Lewis's demanding standards. A few of the most obvious examples are Lord Balfour, Winston Churchill, Franklin Delano Roosevelt, and Harry Truman, all of whom are famous for taking friendly actions of great importance to Jewish interests in the twentieth century—yet who have also been denounced as antisemites, based on various comments they made or attitudes they harbored. Churchill: "the Jews have created another system of morality...saturated with hatred as much as Christianity is with love." Truman: "The Jews...are very, very selfish.... When they have power...neither Hitler nor Stalin has anything on them for cruelty or mistreatment to the underdog" (Michael J. Cohen, *Churchill and the Jews*, London: Frank Cass, 1985; Allis and Ronald Radosh, *A Safe Haven: Harry S. Truman and the Founding of Israel*, New York: Harper, 2009).

Perhaps the most celebrated Righteous Gentile in modern times, Oskar Schindler, was a Nazi Party member, by all accounts a man of easy morals and corrupt business practices—to say nothing of being a drinking buddy with some of the worst Nazi thugs. Yet Schindler risked life and fortune to save hundreds of his Jewish workers. Less known today is the story of Georges Picquart, who risked his career by making public the unreliability of the information used to convict his fellow officer, Alfred Dreyfus, in the famous Dreyfus Affair of the late 1890s. Picquart was widely admired as a highly principled person—indeed viewed by Jews at the time as a hero—but his opinion of Jews in general and of Dreyfus in particular remained deeply disdainful, both before and after the Affair.

It is tempting to dismiss the examples of men and women who spoke ill of Jews yet acted courageously in their defense as no more than bizarre exceptions to the rule, but they are too numerous to be so easily put aside. Solzhenitsyn's words in the opening epigram ("the line dividing good and evil cuts through the heart of every human being") certainly apply in analyzing the relationship of antisemitic thought to action. The behavior of these people, moreover, suggests the need to qualify significantly the assertion that anti-Jewish ideas have an irresistible ability to overwhelm other feelings or moral sentiments, that antisemitic beliefs reflect fatally flawed personalities, or that such beliefs will inexorably result in hostile acts toward Jews.

Contrasting but also revealing examples of the disconnect between action and pre-existing ideas could be cited in regard to people of liberal sentiments who had previously shown friendship toward Jews but who then turned against them, ostensibly prompted by opportunism, greed, fear, or cowardice. Perhaps even better known than Schindler today is another Nazi Party member, Adolf Eichmann. His story, as presented in Hannah Arendt's controversial book, *Eichmann in Jerusalem*, has given rise to the current use (and abuse) of the term "the banality of evil." Arendt observed that before he had joined the Nazi movement, Eichmann had not been notably hostile to Jews; he even seemed to have had

Introduction 15

substantial reasons to be friendly to them. His participation in mass murder was almost certainly not prompted by powerful pre-existing antisemitic convictions but rather by personal ambition, unquestioning respect for his superiors, and a related concern to show himself faithful to their Nazi ideals (to say nothing of an utterly breathtaking moral obtuseness). If Eichmann had been ordered by his superiors to come to the aid of Jews—and especially if he had believed doing so was necessary to the advancement of his career—there is much reason to believe that he would also have followed those orders faithfully. Eichmann was normal (or banal) in other regards, with no previous signs of psychosis, sadism, blood-lust, or criminality. If he had lived in another country, he would have followed other norms, as set by his recognized superiors, so long as they conformed to his self-interest.

Hitler's case stands in stark contrast, since he was not taking orders but giving them, and, in his early career, he had taken great risks in assuming positions that both questioned authority and stood outside respectability. Nonetheless, even in his case there are little-appreciated enigmas about how he acquired his passionate convictions and especially about the connection between those convictions and his actions between 1919 and 1945. His towering hatred of Jews by the eve of World War II seems beyond serious question, but precisely when or how he acquired that degree of hatred is less obvious. At the beginning of his political career, he does not seem to have had a coherent program in regard to the Jews (whatever his flights of vicious rhetoric against them). Even more than Eich-mann, before 1919 Hitler had had a number of friendly relationships with Jews. Again, on the basis of what we know about Hitler's personal experiences with them, it seems that he had far more palpable cause to be friendly or grateful than full of hatred, since several of them helped him in significant ways (Brigitte Hamann, *Hitler's Vienna: A Dictator's Apprenticeship*, New York: Oxford Univer-sity Press, 1999).

The examples of the above-mentioned men are more complex in their details and ambiguous in meaning than can be explored here. But if Churchill or Truman had experienced the disasters and humiliations of Germans or Russians, and if antisemitic traditions had been stronger in their countries, the ambiguities they felt about Jews might well have taken other directions. In both Churchill's and Truman's cases, Jewish support, financial and in terms of prospective votes, in their political careers plausibly played a role in the decisions they made. Churchill wavered rather dramatically in his attitudes, especially in crisis periods, but he was more inclined to see the "good" Jews as more typical than the "bad." Simi-larly, although Truman at times privately expressed fierce irritation with "the Jews," the main object of his ire was certain Jewish leaders and not all Jews (among whom he counted close, lifelong friends and concerning whom he retained benevolent intentions).

Many Nazi leaders recognized that there were a few good Jews but insisted that most were destructive. Even Hitler, in private conversations, recognized that perhaps a few Jews were good, but he believed the bad ones were far more typical. Had Germany been victorious in World War I, Hitler's attitudes might well have developed in different directions, his friendly or admiring contacts with Jews given greater meaning. It is even more likely that without World War I and the Bolshevik Revolution, Hitler would have remained a pathetic Austrian misfit, unknown to history.

History may have lessons for us, but the historical record is also something easily—one is tempted to say usually—misused, its supposedly clear lessons applied in simplistic or crudely tendentious ways, ironically leading to new disasters. A fitting parallel observation to Solzhenitsyn's, concerning the line between good and evil, might be made concerning the inspirations granted to us by Clio, the muse of History: If only it were all so simple.

1

The Jewish Question

Albert S. Lindemann

The history of the Jewish Question overlaps but is not synonymous with the history of antisemitism or the history of Jewish-Gentile relations. The overlaps are nonetheless instructive; the debates about the position of Jews in modern society have been deeply colored by the history of previous relations and historical expectations. The specific term, the Jewish Question (sometimes the Jewish Problem), came into wide usage in the early nineteenth century, as part of a characteristic reforming mood and an optimism about how a series of problems could be solved reasonably, prominent among them the Irish Question, the German Question, the Social Question, and the Woman Question. To state what is obvious but at times unappreciated, most of those who offered proposals to solve the Jewish Question believed in that possibility, implicitly accepting Jews into the human family and not considering them a mystically separate and unchangeable branch of it.

That optimistic attitude about reforming Jews went contrary to centuries-old traditions in Christian Europe but also nonetheless connected with Christian universalism (insofar as Christians accepted Jewish converts). That some of the nineteenth-century discussions of the Jewish Question moved not toward a reasonable resolution but rather toward antisemitism, that is, to a raging, demonizing hatred—and ultimately toward a "final solution"—reminds us again of the issue of Jewish uniqueness. No comparable final solution was seriously entertained in regard to the other questions listed above. Indeed, the Holocaust marked a significant stage in the modern conceptualization of the mystical uniqueness of the Jews, insofar as it has been claimed that the mass murder by the Nazis was fundamentally unlike any other, rendering it in some sense beyond human comprehension, thus connecting the Holocaust with the most mystical definitions of antisemitism.

In Europe up to the last years of the eighteenth century, Jews, women, and the lower orders did not enjoy full civil equality; their inferior legal status was linked to a long-standing belief that they were inferior in other regards. Reformers began to ask: Should they now be given the vote and awarded other equal legal rights? The character and habits of the Irish and the Jews were widely viewed in negative ways, and debates raged throughout the nineteenth century about what could be done to improve them, to transform them into productive and law-abiding citizens. Overlaps in the debates also existed with the Social and Jewish questions, in that it was widely predicted that emancipated Jews would benefit from capitalism and liberal institutions, whereas the emerging free-market factory system was believed to be potentially dangerous to the well being of the laboring classes. What then would be the repercussions of granting civil equality and the vote to Jews (or to workers)? Similarly, was it desirable to let the Irish have their own nation state, a notion that was being discussed for the Italians and Germans?

To repeat, "the" Jewish Question refers specifically to a modern secular issue and discussions of practical political, economic, and social reform, asking if the Jews had the capacity or the desire to become fully emancipated modern citizens, with equal rights and responsibilities. However, "a" Jewish question or problem of a broader nature existed long before the modern period. At the same time, an enduring—if sharply alternating—strain of veneration for Jewish values can be traced, especially insofar as Christianity and Islam based themselves on Judaism. From an entirely different perspective, Jews were often found useful and thus protected, even granted important privileges by non-Jewish authorities. Without that enduring if highly ambiguous respect, paired with a recognition of the Jews' usefulness in practical terms, it is hard to account for their survival over the centuries. This positive side to the relationship is easily overlooked, and any volume of this sort, explicitly focused on the negative aspects of Jewish-Gentile relations, risks giving an unbalanced impression of historical reality. Still, an implicit mandate of historical inquiry is to study historical problems with the belief that in understanding them we can, in some sense, resolve them, or at least live more comfortably with them.

A profound ambiguity about the Jews certainly characterized the Christian Middle Ages in Europe. The increasingly negative attitude toward them in that thousand-year period, however, had more to do with combating Jewish ideas deemed threatening to Christianity than with physically destroying all Jews. There were a number of ugly, violent episodes, and by the late Middle Ages expulsions of Jews from Christian realms were frequent. Still, these fell far short in scope and thoroughness of the mass murder of the twentieth century.

Long before the Christian period, "a" Jewish question also existed, in that many non-Jewish rulers considered the Jews to be a bizarre, irksome, or unruly people, presenting problems that needed to be addressed, and were, at times violently. Conversely, it could be said that, in the brief periods in ancient times when Jews themselves exercised political power to one degree or another, they faced a Gentile question: How were Jews to deal with the non-Jews among them? The answers to that question ranged from methodical physical extermination (Joshua's program, according to the Bible, for Canaanite idolaters), to rigorous separatism (Ezra's solution after the Babylonian captivity), to forced conversions (in the Hellenistic period), to complex mixtures of exclusion and toleration.

The Jewish Question   19

Still, Jewish rulers and religious leaders kept firmly in view the differences between the *goy kadosh*, the Holy Nation, and the *goyim*, the [Other] Nations. The modern ideal of equal rights and dignity for all citizens was not one embraced by premodern rulers, Jewish or non-Jewish, although there were some rough parallels in the Hellenistic and Roman periods. (The problem of granting equal rights to non-Jews has of course arisen as a major one in modern times for the state of Israel, to be addressed below.)

The issue of power and powerlessness, as discussed in the Introduction, is crucial in evaluating these various periods and realms. Non-Jews have ruled over Jews for many centuries. Jews have only rarely ruled over non-Jews. The identities of each in relation to the other have been decisively influenced by their different experiences of power. A perceived rise in the power of Jewish minorities has repeatedly evoked hostile reactions by non-Jews. Jews themselves, even when a politically weak minority of the population, had, in a sense, to deal with a Gentile question; intricate rules regulating relations of the *goy kadosh* with the *goyim* grew up over the centuries, always concerned to preserve the Jewish sense of separateness and to avoid as much as possible the perceived pollutions and corruptions of close contact with non-Jews. Jewish leaders were also concerned with survival, and that concern inevitably entailed many convoluted compromises in dealing with Gentiles, a point all the more relevant for the ordinary population of Jews, often living as a tiny minority among non-Jews.

PHARAOH'S JEWISH PROBLEM

Throughout history both Jews and non-Jews have developed self-affirming narratives about themselves and disparaging counter-narratives about each other. These dueling narratives were often based on the same biblical texts, but each group found remarkably different meanings in them. The Book of Exodus contains an account of what might be termed the first time that Jews became a major problem for a non-Jewish ruler. It is also a founding biblical text for Jewish "suffering history." Exodus is obviously a mythic narrative, distantly if at all related to actual historical events, but it (or endlessly evolving reinterpretations of it) nonetheless has served as one of several key narratives in the evolution of Jewish identity. It has similarly exercised a wide-ranging historical influence in terms of how others have composed narratives about the Jews, whether admiring or derogatory. "Judaism teaches," a modern Orthodox Jew has observed, "that the biblical stories didn't just happen once, never to be repeated. Instead, they set patterns that history will follow down to the end of history" (David Klinghoffer, "Redeeming Ishmael," *Forward*, September 22, 2006, 15). Within Christianity comparable teachings have long existed, as is the case with Islam. All three have shown no little creativity in their interpretations of biblical stories, usually moving far beyond what is obvious from the bare text. Traditional Christian and

20 *Albert S. Lindemann*

Islamic readings have anachronistically been termed antisemitic, but modern racial antisemites, too, have often cited biblical texts to corroborate their hostility to Jews.

An important element of modern Jewish consciousness is a belief that defenseless Jews have been unjustly persecuted or irrationally hated throughout history by the Other Nations. In that light, the Passover holiday commemorates each year the events described in Exodus. Yet the bare text of Exodus leaves open, to say the least, many other interpretive directions. For example, Exodus's opening verses emphasize Pharaoh's legitimate concern about the Israelites' growing numbers and unstoppable, potentially dangerous power. "The Jews are stronger than we are," Pharaoh warned. It was therefore necessary to "outsmart them," to take measures to prevent looming disaster should the Israelites side with Egypt's enemies. Jews were thus put under strict control and set to burdensome tasks.

This notion of Jews as real enemies—not simply the figments of the fevered imagination of non-Jews—is central to the controversies that surround the history and nature of antisemitism. In those controversies, contrasting interpretations of the raw verses of Exodus have been possible not only because of pre-existing agendas but because those verses cannot be easily reduced to the sort of coherent narrative that satisfies modern secular requirements. To modern scholars, the odd lacunae and baffling logical inconsistencies of the verses of Exodus stand out. More than four centuries are unaccountably skipped over—the 430 years since the period when Joseph had served as an Egyptian vizier (high official) and when his policies had rescued Egypt from disaster. He had then been invited by a grateful pharaoh to settle on Egyptian land, with his aged father (Jacob/Israel), his siblings (the Children of Israel) and their various spouses, offspring, slaves, livestock, and other retinue. Inexplicably, centuries later the new pharaoh, as well as his immediate successor and all other high officials, had forgotten Joseph's services in saving Egypt from catastrophe. Over those four centuries, too, the god of the Israelites seemed to have forgotten his chosen people—and only suddenly "heard their groaning and remembered his covenant with Abraham, Isaac, and Jacob" (Exod. 2:24–5).

It further remains unclear from the biblical text how much the Israelites, after the passage of some eighteen generations in Egypt, continued to remember and honor their god. It is only natural to ask how much they had begun to blend into the surrounding population, intermarrying, absorbing non-Jewish ways, and worshipping non-Jewish gods. The account of the Israelites in Sinai after they escaped from Egypt leaves little room for doubt that they believed in the power of gods other than Yahweh.

There is another apparent glaring paradox: If the Israelites had remained, over those four centuries, faithful to their god as the only true god, genuine fidelity to any Egyptian god was impossible. (Cf. Gen. 8:25: "we [Israelites] . . . sacrifice to the Lord our God offerings abominable to the Egyptians.") To be sure, exactly what "sacrificing to our . . . God" entailed before the covenant at Sinai cannot

The Jewish Question   21

be ascertained. Possibly in Joseph's day, the fidelity of the Children of Israel to their own tribal god over any Egyptian god was considered no threat by the pharaoh, since they were but a forlorn tribe, numbering around a hundred. But if they had subsequently increased their population to something like two million, as the biblical account states, the fear the Egyptians felt seems only natural.

If the Egyptian reaction is to be considered a model of subsequent anti-Jewish feeling (establishing a pattern "down to the end of history"), it is worth noting that the driving emotion is presented in Exodus as an understandable dread about the Jews' growth in numbers, linked to their dubious fidelity to the pharaoh and the likelihood of their joining Egypt's many enemies. Of all the examples of biblical "stories that didn't just happen once, never to be repeated," and from which lessons are to be learned, this one of a threatening Jewish rise, against which initial measures seemed futile, must surely rank high.

Another interpretive puzzle in the Exodus account arises in the description of how the god of the Israelites was able to manipulate Pharaoh's mind (or "harden his heart"), making of him essentially a puppet. This seems to imply that the Hamans of history are to be viewed ultimately as acting under divine supervision—that, in other language, antisemitism is embedded in the nature of reality, an expression of an omnipotent god's inscrutable will. The Jewish god's use of evil to accomplish good is often noted in the Hebrew Bible, as for example in Genesis 50:20, when Joseph explains to his fearful brothers (who had earlier plotted to kill him): "You meant evil against me, but God meant it for good," in order that the Children of Israel should eventually come to Egypt, proliferate, and fulfill God's plan for them. (The German philosopher Hegel, in the early nineteenth century, developed kindred notions of evil in his "cunning of Reason.")

Of the many non-Jewish interpretations of the events in Exodus, one of the most influential was that of Manetho, an Egyptian priest-historian of the third century BCE. He indeed went further than reinterpreting the bare text; he dismissed it as simply false in its main assertions. Pharaoh's expulsion of the Israelites, he wrote, was a matter of public hygiene, since they were an unwanted and troublesome band of foreign immigrants who had intermarried with the slave population and moreover were afflicted with contagious diseases.

What we might today term illegal immigration was a common problem for the Egyptian empire, and to that extent Manetho's account has some plausibility as actual history, although modern historians rely mostly on Josephus, a Jewish historian who lived in the first century CE for what they know about Manetho, and Josephus may have significantly edited Manetho's history. At any rate, Manetho's account, as presented by Josephus, and similar texts no longer extant were picked up by non-Jewish observers and reworked in many versions in the ancient world, typically featuring the contagious diseases of the Jews. The Exodus account, according to such perspectives, was a transparently pathetic effort to disguise the Jews' debased and diseased origins. The real reason for their original separation from the rest of humanity was not divine election but disease.

Manetho's counter-narrative might be termed a classic one in the history of antisemitism, in the sense that it radically reversed the Jews' claims to holiness and divine favor, making them both loathsome and dangerous. His account is further noteworthy in that the Egyptians were described in the Bible as a particularly scorned Other Nation. Thus, Manetho's counter-narrative may have reflected specifically Egyptian resentments, since Jews were numerous in Egyptian Alexandria, when Manetho lived there (some thousand years after the Exodus period). By that time they constituted a more affluent and privileged part of the population than the native Egyptians. In short, Manetho may have been rehearsing a contemporary drama, or contemporary tensions, in his rendition of events in Egypt a thousand years earlier. Such a playing-out of contemporary conflicts via biblical texts would be a prominent trait of anti-Jewish writings in the ensuing centuries.

HAMAN'S JEWISH PROBLEM

Manetho has been termed the first antisemite, but a better candidate, especially in terms of associated symbolism and lessons of history down through the centuries, might be Haman. Traditional Jewish interpretations of the biblical text in the Book of Esther and a simple reading of it again point in remarkably contrasting directions, offering ample material for anti-Jewish narratives. In a simple reading, the anger of Haman over the failure of the Jew Mordecai to bow before him seems hardly surprising. What seems incomprehensible is how (or why) Mordecai dared to insult the vizier of a Persian potentate in such a fashion. Haman's subsequent complaint to his sovereign that the Jews of the realm were disrespectful and disloyal ("their laws are different from those of every other people, and they do not keep the king's laws") might be explained simply as personal pique, but it also could be seen as understandable if indeed the Jews did observe laws that went contrary to the laws of the Persian king.

However, in the Book of Esther the actual content of the beliefs of the Israelites, aside from their being "different," is not described; the specific ways in which the Jews allegedly did not keep the king's laws and were thus a danger are left unexplained. At any rate, as in Exodus, the Jews emerge victorious: Mordecai, Esther, and the Jews of Persia outmaneuver Haman, gain favor with the king, and then put Haman, his family, and thousands of his followers to death. For Jews in their centuries of powerlessness, this tale has obviously served as a fantasy of vengeance; for antisemites it has been cited as proof of Jewish guile—and of their ruthlessness once they gain power.

Any number of other narratives of the Hebrew Bible presents comparable interpretive paradoxes and contradictory lessons. One of the most symbolically

The Jewish Question 23

rich is that concerning the twin brothers, Esau and Jacob in Genesis. A literal reading of the story seems to point to the conclusion that Jacob, urged on by his mother, was a conniving scoundrel. He deceived his blind and aged father, Isaac, and was thus able to gain the blessing that Isaac had intended for the elder twin brother, Esau (Gen. 25:19 ff.). Similarly, Esau's anger at Jacob seems justified, hardly the result of baseless fantasy.

Of course, in traditional Judeo-Christian narratives, Jacob stands as a patriarch, the hallowed father of all Jews, whereas Esau is the forefather of the classic enemies of Israel, the Edomites and Amalekites, down to Haman, the Romans, the Christians, Chmielnicki, and Hitler. The story of Esau and Jacob, at an even deeper level, again suggests a divinely predestined hatred, in that the twins were already fighting in the womb, and the Lord announced to their mother, Rebekah: "Two nations are in your womb, and two peoples, born of you shall be divided."

Without the correct initial mindset or emotional predisposition, the texts of the Bible, Old and New Testament, are notoriously prone to what believers, Jews or Christians, dismiss as dangerous misinterpretations. A properly informed initial mindset guides believers along the path of recognizing what should be emphasized and what is to be passed over or explained away. They recognize Jacob's good qualities (above all, the signs of his being chosen by God) and Esau's bad ones (his physicality and brutishness). The key theme of today's Passover ceremony is not that "we Jews grew to two million and scared the daylights out of the Egyptians." It stresses rather that "we were once slaves," cruelly oppressed, and because of our undeserved sufferings, we sympathize with the oppression of others. The authors of the Exodus account seem most of all to have been concerned to emphasize the power of the Israelites' god in relation to the gods of the Egyptians, not his justice and mercy, or his love for all of humanity. Those emphases would come later.

THE CHRISTIANS' JEWISH QUESTION

The early Christians radically reinterpreted the texts of what they came to call the Old Testament, though not as radically as Manetho, since they retained that testament in their Holy Bible and accepted God's elevation of the Jews. Martin Luther yet again reinterpreted various passages of the New Testament, rejecting much of the Catholic reading of them. Interestingly, he was at first confident that he was returning to an originally correct interpretation, close to that long held by the Jews, and he expected that they would welcome his rebellion. When that turned out to be a mistaken expectation, he turned against them with a vengeance—again a familiar syndrome in the subsequent history of antisemitism.

During the three or four centuries immediately following the death of Christ, when Jews and Christians were in hot contention with one another and the foundations for the later Christian demonization of the Jews were being laid, Jewish counter-narratives of Christian texts also emerged. There has been much debate among scholars about the actual content of these texts and even more about the extent to which Jews considered them binding or relevant in later periods. But Christian authorities, especially by the high Middle Ages, came to consider them blasphemous, since they allegedly described Mary as a prostitute and Christ as an errant student of the Torah, a sorcerer and idolater, deserving of the death penalty.

THE FIRST STAGES OF THE JEWISH
QUESTION IN MODERN TIMES

An initial point to keep in mind in approaching the discussions of "the" Jewish Question in the eighteenth and nineteenth centuries is that previously accepted interpretations of the Bible, especially those respecting its divine inspiration, had been subjected to yet another series of counter-narratives, in the form of a searing rationalist scrutiny by the leading figures of the Enlightenment. The so-called *philosophes*, the enlightened thinkers of the age, constructed narratives in which not only the divine inspiration of the Bible but the elevation of the Jews and the sacred status of the Christians were all questioned. Men like Voltaire were inclined to view the Hebrew Bible in particular as a source of evil. With its morally confused tales of tribal cruelty, deception, and mass murder in the name of the Lord, it was deemed the basis of the bigotry and intolerance of the Jews, qualities that had then been passed on to the Christians, as well as to the Muslims, resulting in untold death and destruction in the name of the one true god.

A second and more obvious point is that for centuries Jews had thought of themselves as indissolubly bound together as a mystical collective body by the covenant at Sinai, and as such explicitly forbidden by their god to mix intimately with the Other Nations. This belief by Jews that they were a separate people (that is, a different physical entity) and not simply the upholders of separate religious ideals, was taken seriously by many non-Jews. Even those Christians who were open to the idea of full modern citizenship for Jews often doubted that a people so long culturally apart and so tenaciously committed to physical separation from others could now become one with non-Jewish peoples, blending both bodies and spirits in universalist union. In short, the deeply entrenched notion, as mentioned in the Introduction, that Jewishness is finally "not a matter of faith or ethics or ideology but... of mysteriously inherited traits" (Schulweis) remained an enduring one even in the nineteenth century. Modern racial antisemites refashioned this idea with a hostile "scientific" gloss, using the term *race* to describe those mysteriously inherited traits or separate physical differences (but adding elements to the notion of physical difference that were not part of Jewish tradition).

The Jewish Question

On the other hand, there were growing numbers of Jews, primarily those of the wealthier classes living in the major cities of western and central Europe, who not only aspired to become full members of modern nation states but who went so far as to lament their Jewish origin, yearning to become like non-Jews. Heinrich Heine, the celebrated German-Jewish poet, observed that Judaism could be considered a religion in the way that being a hunchback was a religion. Bernard Lazare, a prominent French-Jewish intellectual, commented that "Everywhere, up to the present time, the Jew has been an unsociable being. . . . The Jewish nation [has been] . . . demoralized and corrupted by an unjustifiable pride" (Albert S. Lindemann, *The Jew Accused*, New York: Cambridge University Press, 1991, 61–2).

Those Jews who wanted to become part of the modern world as equal citizens yet who also continued in some sense to cherish their Jewishness—always a larger group than those who wished to escape from it entirely—agreed that much was repellent and primitive about traditional Jewish beliefs and existing Jewish culture. Various efforts were made by Jews themselves to reform or modernize Judaism and to curb those traits of the general Jewish population that offended others or that seemed to prevent them from becoming full-fledged modern citizens.

For another large part of the Jewish population in the nineteenth century, especially the Jews in eastern Europe, where the overwhelming majority of the Jewish population lived, the modernizing Jews were seen as the problem. They were denounced by Jewish religious leaders as heretics, dangerous in their respect for reason over revelation and rabbinical tradition, to say nothing of their desire to blend into the nations of Europe. Thus, the Jewish Question, while best defined as an issue of what the powerful Gentiles considered necessary to reform the powerless Jews, had also a strictly Jewish dimension, one of Jews versus Jews, tradition versus modernism.

Voltaire and later antisemites, such as Wilhelm Marr, claimed to feel sympathy for the Jews, but that sympathy was based on Jews as victims of Christian bigotry and not because they were considered admirable in their present state. In the discussions of the Jewish Question in the early nineteenth century this Voltairean perspective played a key role, particularly in the assertion that the majority of Jews in Europe had somehow become frozen in a historically remote stage of development, remaining stubbornly attached to backward, irrational ideas and antisocial habits.

Insofar as it was argued that Jewish defects were the result of Christian oppression, reformers urged that Christian oppression be removed. Such reformers were confident that if the humiliating special laws long applied to Jews were abolished, the Jews would then move quickly to improve themselves. The lament of the celebrated Jewish reformer, Moses Mendelssohn, "They bind our hands and then complain that we do not make use of them," was a guiding motto for those in favor of a rapidly introduced Jewish emancipation.

But that motto was not accepted as valid by many others, Jews and non-Jews. The non-Jews objected that if Jews were granted immediate civil equality and personal freedom, their long-established deviousness, vengefulness, and destructive proclivities would simply be unleashed. The opponents of immediate full emancipation for Jews, moreover, believed that those dangerous proclivities were essential to Jewishness, deriving mostly from those Jewish religious dictates that instilled contempt for non-Jews. Thus many reformers believed that certain controls over Jews had to be retained, to be removed only gradually, if at all. It would require a firm hand over many years to transform Jews from blinkered parasites into useful citizens willing to work with others as equals. And, just as important, it would also require many years for non-Jews to grow to trust them.

The universalistic optimism of those who believed the Jewish Question could be rapidly solved was accompanied by a faith in unending progress. Similarly, the notion of how the "major" European peoples benevolently should absorb the "minor" ones was widely accepted in the nineteenth century. Even such prominent liberal spokesmen as J. S. Mill could not fathom how such minor peoples could even *want* to retain a traditional identity, with all its narrowness and backwardness, when they were offered the option of embracing sophisticated, more civilized, clearly superior identities. The Jews, like other minor peoples, needed to abandon their language and culture for the clearly superior cultures and languages of such leading countries as France, Britain, and Germany. In fact, growing numbers of Jews began to do just that.

THE DECLINE IN OPTIMISM REGARDING
THE JEWISH QUESTION

In most European countries, this confidence in the superiority of Western civilization prevailed up to the eve of World War I, although it had begun to fray at the edges during what was then called the Great Depression (in the 1870s and 1880s), when capitalism and liberal values faced questioning. A renewed appreciation of the realm of the nonrational was then expressed by such influential writers as Fyodor Dostoevsky and Friedrich Nietzsche. It became ever more widely recognized that religious values persisted even in those who no longer considered themselves religious. Such was allegedly the case with the Jews more than others, since religion in its traditional Jewish form represented an especially totalistic or all-embracing style of life, one that entailed much more than beliefs about God and the world to come.

By the eve of World War I, Henry Wickham Steed, a prolific and well-known author, traveler, and editor of the influential *The Times* of London, stated that the Jewish Question was "one of the greatest problems in the world"; no one, he added, "can be considered mature until he has striven to face it squarely on its

The Jewish Question

merits." Reactions to his reflections on Jewish matters were revealing. Many Jews denounced him as ignorant, ill-informed, or prejudiced against them. Many non-Jews, on the other hand, considered him soft or naive on the subject of Jews.

NATIONAL DIFFERENCES: FRANCE AND RUSSIA

In broad national and geographical terms, again two contrasting approaches to the Jewish Question can be distinguished, the French (the most progressive) and the Russian (the most reactionary). A third approach might be distinguished in the United States, where a Jewish question comparable in significance to that of Europe failed to arise, in large part because the nation's founding constitution already granted Jews civil equality, but perhaps even more because during the first century of the new nation's existence the population of Jews was extremely small.

In France, in late 1791, after nearly two years of acrimonious debates in the revolutionary national assembly, civil equality was granted to the country's approximately 30,000 Jews (the total population of France was approximately 20 million). Between 1791 and 1815, France's revolutionary armies conquered large areas of central and southern Europe, and Jews in those areas were granted civil equality. In 1806, the Emperor Napoleon obtained from a specially convoked Assembly of Jewish Notables a formal affirmation that French Jews were committed to embracing modern citizenship and French nationality. These were large steps for Jews, so much so that some thereafter referred to a new covenant, replacing the one at Sinai. By mid-century, it seemed to many observers in France that the Jewish Question was well on its way to be being resolved, and that France could stand as a model for others.

The nature of the Jewish Question in the economically backward and politically despotic tsarist empire was revealingly different, in large part because of rapidly growing numbers of Jews there (nearly 1.5 million at the beginning of the century, 5 million by its end), and their far greater poverty. Another difference was the great diversity of populations and the sprawling territories of the tsarist empire, making integral nationalism and monoculturalism of the French model impractical. The Russian empire had long been ruled with a despotic hand, and a change to Western democratic models was seen as both unworkable and undesirable by Russia's leaders.

The Jewish Question overlapped with other questions in Russia even more than in the West. A primary worry for Russian officials was that political and economic liberalization would benefit the Jews but put the Christian lower orders in jeopardy of being exploited. Jews in a liberal state and economy could be expected to take advantage of the simple peasants. Indeed, such issues had been a concern almost as soon as Russia had taken over the lands formerly ruled by the Polish Commonwealth, with its large Jewish population, in the late eighteenth century.

More than was the case for most western European countries, the Jewish Question was but one of many daunting questions facing Russia's rulers, most of which related ultimately back to the issue of how or whether tsarist rule could survive the challenges of modern times. The ever-rebellious Poles were far more of a worry than the Jews; the restive peasants were an even larger concern. While most European states had feared Russian expansion in the early part of the nineteenth century, by the end of the century, the situation had become reversed: The tsarist regime had come to fear rising Western nations, rapidly industrializing Germany and Britain above all. To the east, the expanding and modernizing Japanese empire profoundly humiliated Russia in the Russo-Japanese War of 1904–5.

If ever there was an example of the events of the Bible seeming to repeat themselves, it was in Russia by the turn of the century: The tsars, like the pharaohs, faced a rapidly growing and restive Jewish population, one that Russia's leaders feared might collaborate with the Jews in enemy countries. The tsars feared the Jews as a growing internal danger as well; they became highly visible among the revolutionary populists and assassins of tsarist officials from the 1870s onward. The Bolsheviks and their competitors, the Mensheviks, numbered many Jews in their upper ranks, much beyond the Jewish proportion of the general population.

The explosive growth of the population of the culturally distinct *Ostjuden* (eastern Jews) was viewed with growing alarm outside Russia, since they were known to be even more uncivilized than the Jews in the rest of Europe. By the 1880s they had begun moving out of their east European areas of concentration by the millions, bringing, in the eyes of their detractors, disease, corruption, and revolutionary doctrines to other countries. This mass exodus was a reaction primarily to economic hardship and population growth, but also to popular anti-Jewish violence and what Jews perceived as legal harassment by tsarist officials. A growing part of Russia's Jewish population concluded that its future under the tsars was bleak and that foreign lands, especially the United States, offered brighter prospects. Russian officials, too, saw mass emigration as one way that their Jewish Question could be mitigated. Granting the Jews civil equality was long resisted as simply too dangerous.

NATIONAL DIFFERENCES: THE HABSBURG EMPIRE, GREAT BRITAIN, GERMANY

In the neighboring Austria-Hungary, another multinational empire second only to tsarist Russia in the number and proportion of Jews within its borders, extended discussions of the Jewish Question led finally to the granting of civil

The Jewish Question

equality in 1867, a year of massive internal reforms that included the creation of the Dual Monarchy, or the Austro-Hungarian state form. There was interestingly little pressure on Jews by Habsburg authorities to cast off the traditional national element of their Jewish identity since modern nationalism was considered a grave threat to the survival of the multinational empire.

Nonetheless, significant numbers of Jews in the Habsburg empire, again those mostly of the upper and middle classes in large cities, enthusiastically embraced the language and culture, especially the high culture, of the ruling Germans and Magyars. Here too Jews constituted a scattered and diverse population, but most of the modernizing Jews in the Habsburg empire did not yearn to live in a modern German nation state, even though they enthusiastically associated themselves with German high culture and language. They preferred a multicultural country that protected their human and civil rights but that did not expect that they so alter their Jewish identity as to blend into another national group.

Partly for such reasons, Jewish relations with Habsburg authorities were more harmonious than was the case with Russian authorities of these years. The Emperor Franz Joseph was widely revered by those he affectionately referred to as "his" Jews. Still, popular hostility to Jews in the form of political antisemitism grew into a major issue, as the election of the antisemitic Karl Lueger as mayor of Vienna (1897–1910) demonstrated.

In the rest of Europe the French model was admired by liberals but only cautiously applied. Britain's approach to the Jewish Question as to other political issues was proudly gradualist. That a man of Jewish origin (though converted to Christianity as a child), Benjamin Disraeli, became prime minister was one indication of a more open atmosphere than was the case on the Continent. Still, he was widely regarded by members of the ruling class as unlike them, unchangeably exotic. His own trumpeting of the significance of the Jewish race and its role in Europe's high civilization—indeed the role of Jews in exerting power behind the scenes or in fomenting revolution—provided fodder for many antisemites.

The French model was problematic for Germans, since they tended to define themselves in contrast to the French, especially after the Napoleonic empire fell in 1815. Still politically divided in the first half of the nineteenth century, the thirty-odd German states dealt variously with the Jewish Question but generally preferred caution and incremental improvements in the status of Jews. German Jews who had experienced civil equality under Napoleonic rule often faced a return of various discriminatory laws when Napoleon fell.

Nonetheless, the culture and intellectual life of German-speaking lands were influenced by Jewish genius more impressively than anywhere else in the world. Similarly, the exploration of the Jewish Question, *die Judenfrage*, by German-language thinkers, Jewish and Gentile, in the late eighteenth and early nineteenth centuries was unusually influential. Full civil equality for German Jews came only with the formation of the German Reich in 1871, but in that Reich, as in the Habsburg empire, modern political antisemitism soon challenged the wisdom of granting civil equality to the Jews, spreading alarm about the negative implications of rising Jewish power.

Perhaps the most influential of the earliest German writers on the Jewish Question was the Prussian official Christian Wilhelm von Dohm, whose book *On the Civic Improvement of the Jews* appeared in the early 1780s. Typical of the German enlightened civil servants of the day, Dohm was optimistic but prudent. He observed that the tragic experiences of these "Asian fugitives" had made them devious in their intercourse with non-Jews. The Jews of the biblical past were guilty of murderous hatred of others, he observed, but he concluded that most present-day Jews no longer felt any "commandment to hate and insult members of other faiths." The moral failings of Jews would diminish if they were allowed to enjoy civil equality and if Christians offered them fair and compassionate treatment. Dohm drew the line, however, at allowing Jews to hold public office; that could come only after they had reformed themselves adequately to earn public confidence.

Another German contribution was *On the Jewish Question* (1844) by the young Karl Marx, who was of Jewish origin but like Disraeli formally Christian, since his father had converted to Christianity. Marx was not raised as a Jew, and he married a Gentile, as did Disraeli. But whereas Disraeli held an admiring if not grandiose view of Jews, Marx portrayed them as the archetypical greedy capitalists, so obsessed with money and accumulation of material goods that they had lost their humanity. Only a revolution that would destroy capitalism could solve the Jewish Question. Marx's essay was cast in the impenetrable philosophic jargon of the day, and the exact meaning of many of its passages remains open to question. Still, there is little doubt that Marx's attitude to Jews was profoundly negative, and his essay was later put to antisemitic purposes.

The declining optimism about solving the Jewish Question toward the end of the century was fed, as noted, by a growing critical scrutiny of enlightened ideals in general. Such was true even in France, where the Dreyfus Affair sent shock waves across the country and beyond. An even deeper pessimism about the likelihood of a rational and humane solution to the Jewish Question emerged after the catastrophic decade of war and revolution between 1914 and 1924. For a few years, the German Weimar Republic seemed to offer hope that Jews and Gentiles could work harmoniously and productively together, but that hope collapsed with the Great Depression. The Bolshevik takeover in the fall of 1917 was accompanied by claims that at long last the Jewish Question in Russia was being solved through Communism, but the Communist solution to the Jewish Question implied, following Marx's lead, an eventual disappearance not only of Judaism (and all religions) but of Jewishness as a significantly separate identity. Even more ominous for the future of the Jews, the birth of the Soviet regime and the concept of Marxist world revolution gave life to the new charge of Judeo-Bolshevism, revivifying visions of Jewish destructive conspiracies and plans to

The Jewish Question

31

rule the world—key charges in the Nazi worldview and accepted by many who were not Nazi, even by those strongly opposed to the Nazis.

THE JEWISH QUESTION AFTER 1945

After World War II and the Holocaust, the specific term "the Jewish Question" came to have a dated feel, no doubt largely because Jews had achieved formal civil equality everywhere in Europe and America. The more elusive issue of Jewish social and cultural adaptation became less divisive because of spreading toleration of the concept of Jewish separateness, related to a generally more sympathetic understanding of Jewish tradition and the fact that most Jews reduced the overt markers of their distinctness. A Jewish state was created in 1948, with its own claims to a solution of the Jewish Question. In the United States Jews prospered and felt at home as rarely before in their history, a particularly significant development in that the United States replaced Russia as the country with the largest population of Jews in the world. It also emerged as the world's most powerful state, with Jews strongly represented in many areas of prestige and influence in the country.

The extraordinary paradoxes of the twentieth century and the Jewish Question were epitomized, on the one hand, by its proclaimed and horrific final solution in Nazi Germany, and on the other, by the dazzling accomplishments and successes of Jews. Many of these accomplishments were of obvious value to non-Jews and thus effectively countered the charge of Jewish destructiveness and parasitism. The rise of the Jews in the twentieth century was so remarkable that a historian at the University of California, Yuri Slezkine, described that century as the "the Jewish Century," that is, a century marked by the embrace of Jewish values in Europe, America, and much of the rest of the world.

By the end of the first decade of the twenty-first century, this rise of the Jews was widely celebrated. An ironic development emerged: the issue of excessive Jewish political power, exercised by well-financed, expertly run, and unapologetically assertive Jewish lobbies, came to be taken even more seriously than before by respectable observers in the United States and elsewhere. That this Jewish rise in the United States did not provoke significant antisemitism in the country—and indeed was a source of admiration in those quarters on the far Right previously known as being unfriendly to Jews—underlines the extent to which historical precedents are only suggestive not rigidly predictive. On the other hand, in much of the rest of the world, especially where Islam remained the dominant religion, the rise of Jews in America, linked to the United States' support of the state of Israel, helped to provoke what came to be termed a "new anti-Semitism." Insofar as the Jewish Question retained a visibility or urgency in the second half of the twentieth century, it was reformulated in terms of that new antisemitism in Islamic lands and the hostility to the state of Israel by some on the Left in Europe and America.

After 1948 the new Jewish state faced a Gentile problem that seemed in some regards more intractable than the Jewish problem that had so stymied the tsars. The criticisms of the state of Israel throughout much of the world come back to the Jews' long-standing Gentile question—not, in this instance, in how to deal with the ruling majority but rather with a minority of around 20%, restive and resentful of living as second-class citizens in a state officially declared to be Jewish. The proposed solutions inside Israel to this Gentile question have had suggestive if inexact parallels with various programs of non-Jews to deal with Jewish minorities over the centuries. These range from expulsion to granting full citizenship to non-Jews, *de jure* and *de facto*. Expulsion is entertained mostly by the Israeli radical Right today. Granting full citizenship seems to threaten the end of the Jewish state, or at least the end of a state that preserves a centrality and significantly privileged status for Jews.

The new antisemitism is for the most part a variation on familiar themes in the history of the Jewish Question, with the focus not on Jewish civil equality but the equality of a Jewish state and its acceptance by the rest of the world. This obviously involves the toleration by that world of Jewish uniqueness or distinctiveness. The problem is that many observers believe such toleration inevitably entails, if traditional Jewish religion governs the laws of the modern Jewish state, unfair treatment of those who do not follow that religion or do not have forebears who did.

Those opposing the state of Israel, especially in the areas of large Arab and Muslim populations, have picked up some of the more fantastic and demonizing imagery of European antisemitism. They also denounce Israel from what could be termed a leftist modernizing perspective—that is, in the extent to which racism (defined as the privileges granted to those of Jewish ancestry) characterizes the laws and *de facto* practices of that state and its Jewish population. But the Left, while often intemperate in language, has generally avoided the more fantastic imagery of the old European Right that has been picked up by Islamic activists. The much-denounced double standard (judging Israel harshly for actions that, when done by other states, are often ignored) does not seem to derive from a view of Israelis as a demonic force but rather to reflect a disorientation in dealing with Jews who are not patently righteous victims, a disorientation that in turn is related to a disillusionment on the Left about the modern state of Israel. Some of its founders spoke of Israel as a modern light unto the nations. However, its citizens have turned out to be human, all too human, not notably better or worse than the other nations (which, in fact, was all that some of its founders claimed Jews to be). The double standard can be seen as a backhanded compliment to Israelis—as well as an implicit put down of the states surrounding them—since leftist critics of Israel obviously expect more of its citizens, and of Jews in general, than of the citizens of Arab or other Muslim states.

The Jewish Question   33

If the solution to the Jewish Question has had ultimately to do with Jews and non-Jews sincerely agreeing to regard each as equal in rights and dignity, the failure of the Israeli state to treat its non-Jewish residents in a way that is accepted as just by most of the rest of the world is a paradoxical and sad development in a history filled with many paradoxes and much sadness.

RECOMMENDED READINGS

Auerbach, Rena R. (ed.), *The "Jewish Question" in German Speaking Countries, 1848–1914: A Bibliography* (New York: Garland, 1994).

Bein, Alex, *The Jewish Question: Biography of a World Problem* (Rutherford, NJ: Fairleigh Dickinson University Press, 1990).

Erspamer, Peter R., *Elusiveness of Tolerance: The "Jewish Question" from Lessing to the Napoleonic Wars* (Chapel Hill: University of North Carolina Press, 1997).

Klier, John D., *Imperial Russia's Jewish Question, 1855–1881* (Cambridge: Cambridge University Press, 1995).

Ungvári, Tamás, *The "Jewish Question" in Europe, the Case of Hungary* (New York: Columbia University Press, 1994).

2

The Ancient Mediterranean and the Pre-Christian Era

Benjamin Isaac

TERMINOLOGY

Definitions of antisemitism are many, and, of course, the word did not exist in the ancient world. For the purposes of this chapter, it is briefly defined as a proto-racist set of ideas, a collective prejudice with delusional aspects. We can speak of antisemitism if it attributes to the Jews, as a collective group, negative traits that are unalterable, the result of hereditary factors. Anti-Judaism and antisemitism can be distinguished, in that the one is hostility based on religion, the other on race. When Jews convert to another religion and are accepted by the members of that religion, the attitude to them can no longer be termed antisemitic, since the Jews could, if they chose, cease to be Jews and be accepted by others. Anti-Judaism can be considered a form of intolerance but not racial intolerance. If Jews are regarded with hostility whatever they do, simply because they are Jews, then it can be considered racist (or proto-racist) intolerance. The conceptual difference is significant, and it is possible to find both varieties in the ancient world. In short, modern racial hatred of Jews, while in some regards peculiar to modern times, has more significant roots in the ancient world than many scholars have recognized.

HELLENISTIC EGYPT

Classical Greece of the fifth and fourth century BCE is not relevant, since the Greeks ostensibly became familiar with the Jews only in the Hellenistic period, after the death of Alexander of Macedon (323 BCE). Hostility toward Jews did develop in the Hellenistic period, and for a proper understanding of it we need to consider separately (a) authors in the city of Alexandria, Egypt; (b) Hellenistic, non-Egyptian authors; and (c) Roman literature.

The Ancient Mediterranean and the Pre-Christian Era

The historically significant features in the works of authors living in Alexandria on Jews and Judaism stem from several factors. To begin with, Jews formed a significant part of the population of the city and were from the earliest period of its existence involved in fierce conflicts with other population groups there. In other words, normal urban hostility existed in Alexandria, prompted by proximity and ensuing social friction. A more intriguing factor was that Egypt played a large and negative role in evolving traditions concerning the origins of Jews and their early history as a people.

The surviving Alexandrian texts provide an alternative version of the Exodus story, asserting that the Jews, rather than being God's chosen, were descendants of a group of polluted outcasts, suffering from leprosy and other diseases. They were expelled from Egypt, and then marched to Judea under Moses, who was responsible for building a society that was misanthropic and atheist. (The charge of atheism in the ancient world differed from the modern sense of the word. It did not mean that Jews denied the existence of any god at all but rather that they rejected the legitimate and commonly recognized gods of civilized society.)

The surviving references to the alternate Exodus narrative range from the third century BCE (Manetho) to the first century CE (Apion, Chaeremon, and Lysimachus). The only Latin author to repeat these assertions was the historian Tacitus (first–second centuries CE), whereas the geographer and historian Strabo (in the reigns of Augustus and Tiberius) offered a related, but entirely positive version. Clearly, the origins of the Jews was a subject that concerned the Egyptians far more than the Greeks and Romans. Tacitus, who for whatever reason obviously disliked Jews, used the subject for his own purposes, but no other Greek or Latin author did in this negative form. Moses in the negative accounts is said to have prescribed religious customs and a lifestyle that were the opposite of those of the Egyptians, including a rule that they were permitted to have sexual intercourse only among themselves. Interestingly, this is the sort of general accusation leveled at Egyptians as a whole by Greek and Latin authors, from Hecataeus of Miletus (c.500 BCE) onward (Isaac 2004, Ch. 7).

In the Alexandrian texts Jews were also accused of practicing human sacrifice and cannibalism. In antiquity cannibalism was among the most serious accusations leveled at foreign peoples, questioning their humanity and comparing them to animals. Two Alexandrian authors maintained that the Jews practiced ritual slaughter of foreigners. One was Damocritus, of uncertain date but probably the first century CE. The second was Apion, as cited by Josephus, in the first part of the first century CE. The cannibalistic practice was allegedly repeated annually at a fixed season. The Jews would kidnap a Greek foreigner, fatten him up for a year, and then convey him to a wooded area, where they would slaughter him, sacrificing the body in a customary Jewish ritual. They then ate his burnt flesh, swearing an oath of hostility to all Greeks. The remains of the victim were thereafter thrown into a pit (Stern 1974–84, 2:385 ff).

36   *Benjamin Isaac*

In these accounts, then, we have two of the most hostile and enduring traditions from antiquity that are clearly attributable to Alexandrian circles. There is another feature found once in Hellenistic sources that does not recur in Roman literature, namely a call for the total eradication of the Jewish people. Diodorus Siculus, a Greek historian writing in the first century BCE, reported that the advisors of the Seleucid king, Antiochus Sidetes, urged him "to make an end of this people completely, or, failing that, to abolish their laws and force them to change their ways" (Stern 1974–84, 1:181–5). The reason given was that Jews were xenophobic and had perverse laws imposed by Moses, but it is worth noting that Diodorus approvingly observed that the king rejected the advice offered him.

Another clearly Alexandrian theme, taken up below, was the assertion that the Jews worshipped a donkey (Stern 1974–84, 1:100).

HELLENISTIC, NON-EGYPTIAN

An interesting and enduring charge against the Jews that appeared in a number of authors is found first in the work of Apollonius Molon, an influential orator from Asia Minor, in the first century BCE. The Jewish historian Josephus indignantly quotes him as saying "we [Jews] are the most witless of all barbarians, and are consequently the only people who have contributed no useful invention to civilization" (*Contra Apionem* 2:148; Stern 1974–84, No. 49). The charge is found in Apion, a Graeco-Egyptian author of the early first century CE, who claimed that the Jews "have not produced any remarkable men, for instance inventors in the arts and crafts or men remarkable for their wisdom" (*Contra Apionem* 2:135; Stern 1974–84, No. 175). Similar assertions occur in the writings of Celsus, as explored below (Stern 1974–84, No. 375), and, with a different emphasis, in those of the Roman Emperor Julian (Stern 1974–84, No. 481a), but this particular idea is actually not found in the central works of Roman literature; it originated in Hellenistic circles, was taken over by Alexandrian authors, and then recurs in the writings of a second-century Middle-Platonic philosopher (Celsus) and a fourth-century emperor (Julian) who had a mostly Greek education. Since it occurs four times over a lengthy period it must be considered significant. The accusation that the Jews do not contribute to civilization is familiar in the works of modern antisemites, but it is of Greek origin and did not catch on notably in Latin or Roman circles.

The Jews were similarly accused of cutting themselves off from the rest of humanity. This charge is originally attributed to Hecataeus of Abdera (Stern 1974–84, No. 11), which makes it a relatively early tradition (around 300 BCE). The means by which the Jews kept themselves apart were related to their bizarre customs, especially not sharing meals. The charge recurs in two parallel passages, in which it served as an argument for the extermination of the Jews. A variant appears in Philo's work, in the first century CE, where he defends the Jews against

The Ancient Mediterranean and the Pre-Christian Era 37

such hostile claims (*De Virtutibus* 141). As noted, Apollonius Molon, according to Josephus, called the Jews atheists and misanthropes. Apollonius was from Alabanda in Caria (the southwest of modern Turkey) and later established himself at Rhodes. He does represent the Hellenistic but not the Alexandrian tradition, where we have already encountered such accusations. Apollonius adds the charge, later prominent in modern antisemitism, that the Jews were cowards, characterized by temerity and reckless madness (Stern 1974–84, No. 49).

Classical Greek and Latin authors considered sociability an indispensable feature of a civilized people. Aristotle stated that "The man who is isolated—who is unable to share in the benefits of political association, or has no need to share because he is already self-sufficient—is no part of the polis, and must therefore be either a beast or a god" (*Politics* 1253a, trans. Ernest Barker). Strabo and Diodorus considered it characteristic of remote barbaric peoples to be completely cut off from others, but they were speaking of wild and distant peoples, which the Jews were not.

One of the most peculiar Jewish customs in Greek and Roman opinion was the keeping of the Sabbath. The first known author to comment on this practice was Agatharchides, in the second century BCE, who wrote about the conquest of Palestine and the capture of Jerusalem by Ptolemy I Soter in 302, which succeeded, in his view, because the Jews foolishly refused to fight on the seventh day (Stern 1974–84, No. 30a).

To sum up, an especially strong Alexandrian form of hostility may be distinguished in the sources, in the hostile rewriting of the origins of the Jewish people, and in the accusations of human sacrifice and cannibalism. The Hellenistic, non-Alexandrian tradition included the claim that the Jews provided no useful contribution to civilization. The assertions that the Jews cut themselves off from humanity, and that they were misanthropic and atheistic, are represented in both traditions. The confrontation between Jews and Egyptians was between large groups in an urban setting where Jews constituted a significant minority, whereas the conflict between Seleucids and Jews occurred where Jews formed a majority in a province (their former homeland) of a kingdom ruled by the Seleucids. The former confrontation was marked by constant tension and occasional large-scale violence; the latter saw clashes between long-term Jewish inhabitants and Seleucid rulers.

ROMAN LITERATURE

The importance of religion in Roman evaluations of other peoples should not be underestimated, especially insofar as other religions were seen to undermine Roman religion and society. "For men wisest in all divine and human law used to judge that nothing was so potent in destroying religion as the replacement of native sacrifices by foreign ritual" (Livy, 39.16.9). Foreign cults were usually

38 *Benjamin Isaac*

regarded as a potential threat to the stability of the state, and in principle for Roman citizens to practice foreign rites was punishable as a criminal act, even if the law was not always upheld in fact (Tacitus, *Annals* 13.32.2). Cicero held that the practice of Jewish religion was incompatible with Roman institutions (*Pro Flacco* 26.69), for the organization of rites "is not only of concern to religion, but also to the well-being of the state" (*de legibus* 2.12.30).

A distinction should be made, however, between Roman attitudes toward religions and cults in Rome and Italy and those that were actively practiced only in the provinces. The local religions in the annexed provinces were left alone, provided there was no human sacrifice and the religion did not question Roman authority. The antiquity of cult practices in particular made them respectable in Roman eyes, the reason that Josephus devoted so much of his work against Apion to the citation of records demonstrating the antiquity of Judaism. Foreign cults that attracted attention in Roman society because they were a presence clearly in evidence inside Rome, such as Judaism and various Egyptian cults, were regarded in a different light from those known only through indirect sources as provincial phenomena.

Roman feelings about Jews were often hostile, as is clear from the language used: *sceleratissima gens* ("a most villainous people," according to Seneca, a first-century author of philosophical and literary works); *taeterrima gens* ("a most disgusting people," according to Tacitus); *perniciosa gens* ("a pernicious people," in the words of Quintilian, a rhetorician of the first century CE); "much lower than reptiles," according to Cleomedes, an astronomer. Most of these writers belonged to the mainstream of Latin literature and are representative of a broad section of Roman upper class opinion. In trying to understand these attitudes, one must keep in mind that there was a substantial presence of Jews inside the city of Rome. When the empire became Christian by the early fourth century, an even stronger hostility toward Jews became the norm. The Emperor Constantine referred to the Jews as "bloodstained men who are...mentally blind," "a detestable mob," a "deadly...nefarious sect."[1] The fourth-century bishop Synesius called them *genos ekspondon*, "a graceless people" (Stern 1974–84, No. 569).

SOCIAL CRITICISM

The Hellenistic insistence on the lack of sociability of the Jews was, like other themes of that period, taken up by Tacitus. He wrote, "To establish his influence over this people for all time, Moses introduced new religious practices, quite opposed to those of all other religions. The Jews regard as profane all that we

---

[1] A letter of Constantine, in Eusebius, *Life of Constantine* (Oxford: Clarendon Press, 1999), 3.18.2; 3.18.3.

The Ancient Mediterranean and the Pre-Christian Era 39

hold sacred; on the other hand, they permit all that we abhor" (*Histories* 5.4.1). It was an established tradition among the Romans to claim that those whose religion they did not respect adhered to a moral system that was not worthy of respect either. Thus Tacitus observed that the Jews, while maintaining strict loyalty toward one another,

> feel hostility and hatred toward all others.... They instituted circumcision to distinguish themselves from other peoples. Those who are converted to their way of life accept the same practice, and the earliest habit they adopt is to despise the gods of others, to renounce their country, and to regard their parents, children, and brothers as of little consequence. (5.5.1)

Tacitus emphasized the importance of the Jews' dietary laws, diet being a traditional criterion of ethnicity, and to circumcision, but he also introduced a discussion of sexual customs. Concerning the latter he combined the ideas of unsociability and moral corruption: "Jews keep themselves apart, even in their sexuality, but have no morals among themselves, in contrast to the incorrupt but uncivilized Germans, who maintained the sanctity of marriage and of the relationship between husband and wife" (*Germania* 17, 18). In this connection it is noteworthy that Tacitus, whatever he thought of the Jews, never called them barbarians.

The idea of unsociability was repeated in rather similar terms by Celsus, a polemicist against Christianity, writing toward the end of the second century CE (Stern 1974–84, No. 375, 256). Revulsion over Jewish unsociability was expressed in a particularly fierce form by Philostratus in the third century:

> For the Jews have long been in revolt not only against the Romans but against humanity; and a people that has made its own a life apart and irreconcilable, that cannot share with the rest of mankind in the pleasures of the table nor join in their libations or prayers or sacrifices, are separated from ourselves by a greater gulf than divides us from Susa or Bactra or the more distant Indies. (Philostratus, *Vita Apollonii* 5.33. Loeb edition)

Philostratus's conclusion that it would have been better not to have annexed the Jews is new and relatively rare. It is found also in a much later statement (fifth century) by Rutilius Namatianus (Stern 1974–84, No. 542, 2:664).

Tacitus twice remarked that proselytes to Judaism were the worst, for they were traitors to the religions of their birth, to their native countries, and to their original families. In accepting the foreign cult they thus abandoned all the social obligations that every decent man respects. Conversion, interestingly, was a subject that played no role in the earlier Hellenistic commentaries on the Jews, despite the large-scale efforts by the Jewish Hasmonaean rulers in the second century BCE to convert neighboring peoples. In Tacitus's case, however, we are dealing with responses to the presence of Jews in the city of Rome. The idea that Jews were exclusively loyal toward each other occurs first in Cicero's work (Cicero, *Pro Flacco* 66 ff), where he explicitly asserts that there were large

40 Benjamin Isaac

numbers of Jews in Rome who were hostile to the aristocracy and could influence public meetings. The issue of conversion clearly is a new one that disturbed Roman authors, for Jews were regarded as disloyal elements in society, and non-Jews who converted to Judaism were therefore deemed to be traitors.

In the reign of Augustus, the poet Horace wrote: "This is one of those lesser frailties I spoke of, and if you should make no allowance for it, then would a big band of poets come to my aid—for we are the big majority—and we, like Jews, will compel you to become one of our throng."[2] It is likely that Horace, like Cicero, is referring to the political pressure that Jews could exert thanks to their mutual loyalty.

The issue of loyalty and conversion came up again in the work of the poet Juvenal, in the late first to early second century CE, who attacked proselytes along similar lines: "Having been wont to deride Roman laws, they learn, follow, and revere Jewish law and all that Moses passed on in his secret volume, prohibiting to point the way to anyone not following the same rites, and leading none but the circumcised to the desired fountain."[3] This part of Juvenal's satire was aimed at Jewish proselytes, but there are several characteristics Juvenal believed these proselytes shared with born Jews, the most important of which being that they derided Roman law while honoring Jewish law; in becoming Jewish, Romans cut themselves off from civilized Roman society. There is a significant background here, in that the fear of other foreign secret cults was already strong in republican Rome.

Again, all these texts reflect reactions to the presence of Jews as a tolerated minority. They are not vague feelings about a distant peoples but direct responses to a significant element in Rome's population. The presence of Jews living according to their own customs in Rome was tolerated by Augustus and Tiberius, although from time to time efforts by the state were made to halt the spread of Judaism in Rome. The socio-historical position in Rome was clearly different from that in the Hellenistic world, where the Jews were also accused of being misanthropic and unsociable, but the matter of conflicting loyalty did not come up because the Hellenistic kingdoms did not represent integrated empires. As noted, the Jews formed an unusually significant minority in Alexandria and were the focus of violent conflict, but in Rome it was their alleged collective loyalty (and thus disloyalty to Rome) that attracted particular attention. In this respect opinions about the role of Jews in Rome resembled the arguments of later centuries and into modern times.

The suspicion of dual loyalty could develop into something worse—the fear of being taken over by the subject people. Seneca, for example, considered Jewish influence in Rome to be dangerously subversive. He lamented that "the customs

---

[2] *Sermones* i, 4. 139–43, Stern 1974–84, No. 127, 1:321; 323.
[3] Juvenal, 14.100–104, Stern 1974–84, No. 301.

The Ancient Mediterranean and the Pre-Christian Era 41

of this accursed race have gained such influence that they are now received throughout all the world. The vanquished have given laws to their victors."[4] Juvenal's attack on proselytes, cited above, in combination with his well-known assertion that the Syrian river Orontes was flowing into the Tiber, indicates that he harbored similar sentiments. Cassius Longinus warned in 61 CE that foreign cults were even penetrating the households of Roman magistrates (Tacitus, *Annals* 14.44.3.).

The Emperor Domitian (ruled 69–96 CE) is reported to have gone to great lengths to identify Jews for the sake of the special tax on them. He focused special attention on two categories: non-Jews who lived as Jews without publicly acknowledging it, and born Jews who concealed their origin. Domitian is also recorded as having put to death his relative Flavius Clemens and his wife, on the charge of atheism. According to Cassius Dio, this was a charge on which many who were attracted to Jewish customs were condemned.[5] Elsewhere Cassius Dio, who is unusual in his fairly tolerant description of the Jewish god, refers to both Jews by birth and proselytes as *Ioudaioi*, commenting,

I do not know how they obtained this appellation, but it applies also to other people, even if they are of alien descent, who adopt their customs. This group also exists among the Romans, and although it has been repressed often, it has increased very much and has succeeded in obtaining the right of freedom in its way of life.[6]

The passage is notable in its explicit recognition that there was an increase in the number of proselytes by the early third century, "different from other people in virtually their entire way of life."

In an address assigned by Dio to Maecenas, the latter advises Augustus

to hate and punish those who are involved in foreign cults, not only for the sake of the gods—for if they do not respect them they will not honor any other being—but also because such people preferring new gods persuade many to adopt strange cults and this leads to conspiracies, factions, and political societies which do not profit the monarchy in the least.[7]

The Jews were exceptional in being allowed to assemble for religious services, whereas other foreign religions were forbidden to do so, at least in Rome during the reigns of Caesar and Augustus. It seems then that Dio did not regard the Jews as practicing one of those foreign cults that he wanted suppressed. It may be relevant that Dio was not a native of the city of Rome but of Nicaea in Bithynia, Asia Minor. (The idea that the vanquished were coming to dominate the victors recurs in particularly hostile form in the work of the fifth-century author Rutilius Namatianus, referred to earlier.)

---

[4] Cited by Augustine, *De Civitate Dei*, 6.11; Stern 1974–84, No. 186, 1:431–2.
[5] Dio 67.14.1–3; Stern 1974–84, No. 435.   [6] Dio 37.17.1.   [7] Dio 52.36.2.

42   *Benjamin Isaac*

These anti-Jewish feelings by Roman authors stretched over a period of some five hundred years and therefore may be regarded as a representative feature of the trends in Roman attitudes toward the Jews. The reasons for the feelings are obvious: Romans believed that a superbly successful empire should be superior in every respect, not just through arms and politics, and it should not be influenced at all by its subjects in cultural and religious matters. But it is hard not to conclude that this sensitivity was to some extent irrational. (I firmly disagree with scholars, such as Sherwin-White, who tend to interpret such Roman attitudes toward the Jews as primarily rational and justified by reality.)[8]

In any case, there are enough texts to conclude that there was a marked sensitivity to a perceived presence of Jewish proselytes in Rome, in response to the novel forms of religious and social choice exhibited by some Roman citizens. Roman citizens were abandoning the traditional religion and the community of loyal citizens and committing themselves to a different concept of religion and a separate community.

OTHER TOPICS: MONOTHEISM, DIETARY RESTRICTIONS, SABBATH, CIRCUMCISION

More than anything else it was the exclusive monotheism of the Jews with the concomitant absence of a cult statue in the Temple in Jerusalem before its destruction that struck Roman authors.[9] Several authors approved of Jewish monotheism, but many disapproved, regarding the Jewish concept as a bizarre aberration. Some saw the Jews' concept of a single, jealous God as consistent with their antisocial attitudes: "Their god refused to associate with other gods" (Stern 1974–84, No. 367). The Greeks and Romans rejected unsociability in other peoples and had a similar attitude toward their divinities. However, the particularly hostile Hellenistic tradition that the Jews worshipped a donkey, whose statue stood in the Temple, did not play a significant role in Roman texts about Jewish religion.

The dietary restrictions of the Jews also appeared frequently, notably the abstinence from pork. It was not in itself remarkable for peoples to have their own specific diet, and the Jewish diet was not in itself a subject of criticism. What was criticized fiercely was the idea that the Jews would not share meals with non-Jews.

[8] Adrian Nicholas Sherwin-White, *Racial Prejudice in Imperial Rome* (Cambridge: Cambridge University Press, 1967), 87 n 2.

[9] Varro (116–27 BCE); Schäfer 1997, 34–65; Tacitus, *Histories* 5.5.4; Plutarch, *Quaestiones Convivales* 4.6 (Stern 1974–84, No. 25); Cassius Dio 37.17.2.

The Ancient Mediterranean and the Pre-Christian Era 43

As mentioned earlier, the Jewish Sabbath was ridiculed already by Agath-archides, in the second century BCE. It was mentioned as a well-known institution, without negative emphasis, by several poets in the reign of Augustus,[10] yet another indication that Jews in Rome in this period were plentiful enough for their customs to be familiar in broad circles. Some later authors considered the Sabbath wasteful and a proof of the idleness of Jews.[11] A favorite illustration of the absurdity of the Sabbath was the above-mentioned assertion that Jerusalem was conquered because the Jews would not defend themselves on that day.[12] Plutarch listed observing the Sabbath as one of the bad barbarian customs being taken up by Romans. Several authors in the reign of Augustus and afterwards referred erroneously and some-times ironically to the Sabbath as a fast day. A curious attack is found in a letter from Synesius to his brother, in which he describes how a Jewish skipper and his Jewish sailors stopped functioning at sunset on Sabbath eve and almost allowed the vessel to sink (Stern 1974–84, No. 569). It cannot be said that such mockery of Sabbath practices amounted to serious hostility. It was simply one of the numerous customs and habits that were seen to characterize the Jews.

An unusual accusation found in the writing of fifth-century author Rutilius Namatianus (Stern 1974–84, No. 542) is that the Jewish god was soft or effemi-nate, because he rested on the seventh day. Here again criticism of the Jewish nation and its Sabbath is extended or attributed to its god. However, the Jews together with the Parthians were the two eastern nations not normally regarded as soft or effeminate by Greek and Roman authors. Others definitely were, such as the Syrians and various peoples in Anatolia (Isaac 2004, 63, 65, 209, 307–8).

Finally, there is the topic of circumcision, the essential mark of the Jewishness of males and the final step taken by a convert. It was usually mentioned with great disapproval by Romans, as we have seen already in the case of Tacitus. Strabo referred to it as one of the evil customs of the Jews that were typical of their decline, adopted when "superstitious men were appointed to the priest-hood, and then tyrannical people" (Stern 1974–84, No. 115). There were other peoples who also practiced circumcision, but they were not present in such numbers in Italy, and thus Jews could be referred to as simply "the circum-cised."[13] The satirical author of the first century, Petronius, listed it among other remarkable or even ludicrous physical characteristics of foreign peoples (*Satyr-icon* 102.14). The poet Martial repeatedly mentioned circumcised Jews, each time from the perspective of his persistent preoccupation with their sexuality (Stern 1974–84, No. 243, 245).

---

[10] Tibullus, 1.3.15–18, in Stern 1974–84, No. 126; Horace, *Serm.* 1.9.67–72, in Stern 1974–84, No. 129; Ovid, *Ars Amatoria* 1.413–416, in Stern 1974–84, No. 142.

[11] Seneca, *De Superstitione* ap. Augustine, *De Civitate Dei* 6.11, in Stern 1974–84, No. 186; Tacitus, *Histories* 5.4.3, in Stern 1974–84, No. 281, comments in 2:37 f.

[12] Dio 37.16.2, in Stern 1974–84, No. 406; Frontinus, *Stratagemata* 2.1.17, in Stern 1974–84, No. 229, with comments 1:510 f; Plutarch, *De Superstitione* 8, in Stern 1974–84, No. 256.

[13] Horace, *Serm.* 1.9.70, in Stern 1974–84, No. 129; Persius, *Sat.* 5.184 in Stern 1974–84, No. 190.

44 *Benjamin Isaac*

A later satirical reference to circumcision appeared in a fourth-century text: "At this time the Jews started a war because they were forbidden to mutilate their genitals." This statement became famous because it is the only source stating explicitly that the cause of the Bar Kokhba war was a prohibition of circumcision, a much debated subject.[14] It is worth noting that the text does not use the word circumcision, but mutilation. The implication was that the rebellion was ludicrous, for who in his right senses would go to war because he was forbidden to mutilate himself? The equation of circumcision with mutilation is found also in the work of the famous third-century CE Christian author and early father of the Church John Chrysostom: "Watch out for the dogs, watch out for the evil-workers, watch out for those who mutilate the flesh. For we are the true circumcision, we who worship God in spirit" (*Homilia adversus Judaeos*, *PG* 48. col. 845).

Nonetheless Judaism was legally permitted in Judea, in Rome, and in the provinces. Again, despite the negative feelings that it evoked in some quarters, it was permitted largely because the Jews had the status of a recognized people and therefore had the right to their religion, whatever it was. A recognized people, however, did not have the right to accept foreigners into its midst, and when that happened countermeasures were sometimes taken. The Romans no doubt seriously restricted freedom of religion, since they considered religion an inseparable part of ethnic and social identity. Children had the right to practice the religion of their parents (indeed were obliged to), but no one had an automatic right to embrace the religion of another people, since that was considered a politically significant act. In the case of Roman citizens it was also regarded as a serious breach of loyalty to Rome.

Under the empire, the cult around the emperor became part of this complex of expectations. Rome continued to accept that the Jews had a peculiar fanaticism, making it impossible to demand of them what was demanded of everybody else. They were tolerated as an exception, since the Romans were aware that Jews would face death rather than revere a mortal ruler as if he were a god. For the same reason Jews were exempted from army service and other duties that impinged upon their customs. The Romans succeeded in building an empire in part because they were realists. They did not attempt to enforce the unenforceable.

CONCLUSION

In evaluating ancient Greek and Roman attitudes to Jews, it is well to remember that, as with modern antisemites, pre-existing attitudes and emotions, elusive in their nature and origin, played a key role. Those who cherish their antipathies

---

[14] Benjamin Isaac, *The Near East under Roman Rule* (Leiden: Brill, 1998), 220–52, 233 ff.

toward other nations, groups, or minorities typically claim that their dislike is based on objective realities. In this, the ancients were certainly no exception. Those who dislike Jews in the present easily conclude that there were objective reasons for the Greeks and Romans to dislike them, but the truth is less simple.

One difficulty in understanding the relationships of Jews and non-Jews in antiquity properly is that we have little reliable numerical information. There is no way of accurately knowing how many Jews there were in the various provinces and in Rome, or how many proselytes to Judaism. However this may be, it is clear that people of every period are guided more by emotions than by numbers and facts when thinking about other social groups. It is obvious that most of the ancient authors discussed in this chapter were not guided primarily by rational considerations in their judgments, to say nothing of how frequently they integrated fantastic or delusional elements into those judgments.

We have now reached the point where we can productively address a number of fundamental questions, ones that are of broad relevance in the history of Jew-hatred over the centuries. Perhaps the most basic question has to do with whether Greek and Roman hatred of the Jews was somehow unique or essentially different from the hatred of Jews expressed by non-Greek and non-Roman groups. That hatred does seem to have been noteworthy if not unique, with only a few qualifications (see Isaac 2004, 4–12). There was an old tradition that Egypt was different in every respect from the rest of the world, but the totality and quality of hostile attitudes to the Jews are far greater; the insistence on their unique social attitudes and religious practices has no real parallel.

Greek and Roman hatred of Jews differed from Hellenized Egyptian or Alexandrian hatred, particularly in the latter's efforts to prove the inferior origin of the Jewish people with a counter-narrative of the Exodus story. This version was repeated in hostile form only by Tacitus and did not become a major feature of attitudes toward the Jews in the Roman world. Similarly, the accusations concerning human sacrifice and cannibalism, so prominent in Alexandrian sources, played no role in non-Egyptian Hellenistic and Roman literature, nor did the claim that the Jews worshipped a donkey.

And what was the impact of wars and revolts in the ancient world, as far as hostile attitudes to the Jews are concerned? While it is easily assumed that there was a connection between specific periods of violence and the attitudes of Greeks and Romans toward Jews, the evidence is mixed. As noted earlier, when the advisors of the Seleucid king Antiochus Sidetes urged him do away with the Jewish people completely, those urgings were obviously connected with a war being waged at the time. The particular hostility of the Alexandrian authors Apion and Chaeremon in the first half of the first century CE was probably connected with the serious tension and violent clashes between Jews and non-Jews in Alexandria in that period. It is less easy to point to a direct connection between the statements of specific authors and the major Jewish revolts against Rome. An exception would seem to be Cassius Dio's extraordinarily bloody descriptions. But the authors in the city of Rome appear to have been more influenced by the urban social relationships in the city than by events in the provinces.

Which common antisemitic stereotypes of later periods were absent in Greco-Roman antiquity? The blood libel clearly belongs to a later period, although accusations of cannibalism are found in the Alexandrian tradition. Another feature absent in this period was the idea of the wandering Jew (Ahasverus), the eternal, cosmopolitan foreigner or, perhaps more relevant for antiquity, the idea that the Jews were and remained in essence a nomadic people. Yet another idea that one might expect to find in Roman literature is that of the Jew as a typical Oriental or Asiatic. However, in fact, it nowhere occurs in any of the sources.

No stereotype has been more pervasive during the past centuries than that of the Jew as a grasping, materialistic trader, but it is not to be found in Greek and Latin literature. The typical devious traders in Greco-Roman traditions were the Phoenicians who, incidentally, were also among those described as stereotypically oriental. An obvious reason for this missing stereotype is that relatively few Jews were engaged in trade before the Middle Ages. In Rome the more familiar stereotype, as we have seen, was that of impoverished Jews hanging around synagogues.

Finally, the charge that the Jews were rootless conspirators who aimed to gain world domination through secret machinations was absent in Greek and Latin literature. It is true that there was a fear in Rome that the provincial subjects, including the Jews, were gradually taking over the empire from below, as it were, which was different from the notion that there was a far-reaching plot by a Jewish elite to take over the world, so characteristically developed in the nineteenth century.

RECOMMENDED READINGS

Gager, John, *The Origins of Anti-Semitism* (New York and Oxford: Oxford University Press, 1983).

Isaac, Benjamin, *The Invention of Racism in Classical Antiquity* (Princeton: Princeton University Press, 2004).

Schäfer, Peter, *Judeophobia: Attitudes toward the Jews in the Ancient World* (Cambridge, MA: Harvard University Press, 1997).

Schürer, E., *The History of the Jewish People in the Age of Jesus Christ*, 4 vols. (Edinburgh: T. & T. Clark, 1974–87).

Stern, Menahem, *Jews and Judaism in Greek and Latin Literature*, 3 vols. (Jerusalem: Israel Academy of Sciences and Humanities, 1974–1984).

3

Jews and Christians from the Time of Christ to Constantine's Reign

Philip A. Cunningham

It is a widely held belief that Judaism and Christianity became separate and fundamentally opposed religious communities shortly after the lifetime of Jesus. For centuries, some have traced this intergroup hostility back to Jesus himself, depicting him as an opponent of an allegedly legalistic and heartless post-exilic Judaism. Others linked the parting of the ways to a specific event: the Crucifixion of Jesus (*c.*30 CE), to the activities of the Christian apostle Paul of Tarsus (35–60 CE), or to the first Jewish-Roman War in which the Second Temple in Jerusalem was destroyed (66–70 CE).

Historical research of the past several decades has rendered such simple constructions extremely doubtful. There has been a paradigm shift toward the model of a complex, irregular, and very gradual separation and delineation of Christianity from rabbinic Judaism. The boundaries between Jews and Christians were quite unclear for centuries, and defining differences emerged for diverse reasons in widely scattered places. Hindering an accurate reconstruction of the early relations between the two groups is a tendency to retroject later circumstances, teachings, and conflicts back to the time of their respective origins.

This chapter will sketch the gradual differentiation between Judaism and Christianity, devoting special attention to the emergence of hostile attitudes between them. An underlying question in the development of this antagonism is whether it can properly be labeled *antisemitism*, or if it should be designated by another term.

LATE SECOND TEMPLE JUDAISM

It has become almost axiomatic in recent studies to describe Judaism in the century or so before the destruction of the Second Temple in 70 CE as extremely diverse. Indeed, one prominent scholar has often referred to late Second Temple

Judaisms. There certainly was a common Jewish agreement that God had chosen the people of Israel to participate in a covenant centered on the Torah whose commands the people were to follow, on the Land where God permitted them to dwell, and on the Temple where God was to be worshipped. However, there were many competing interpretations about the details of covenantal life beyond these basics. These diverse understandings gave rise to many different Jewish groups in this period, many of which we cannot clearly identify or tell apart two thousand years later.

One source of diversity within the Jewish world was geographic in nature. It appears that there were more Jews living outside the land of Israel than within it for centuries before the time of Jesus. Second Temple era Jews, for example, responded to the overwhelming influence of Greek culture and to their domination by a succession of imperial regimes in various ways. As is typical among subordinated peoples, some Jews assimilated into the wider culture, some rejected it utterly, and most fell somewhere between the two extremes. Although there is not much detailed information available to us, clearly Jews living in close contact with Greek culture and at a great distance from Jerusalem would live out their religious traditions in ways different than those of their brethren in Israel. Gentiles reacted diversely to their diaspora Jewish neighbors. Some wrote disparagingly of Jewish "clannishness" and their "stubborn" refusal to respect the gods of all peoples. But others admired Jewish solidarity, their ancient ethical code, and their monotheism.

In 63 BCE, the Roman general Pompey conquered Jerusalem and Jewish lands became subject to Roman tribute. A generation-long period of instability followed as rival Roman armies, competing Jerusalem aristocrats, and Parthian (Persian) forces devastated the region. In periodic campaigns, Roman armies burned entire towns, crucifying or enslaving the residents.

In these circumstances, a certain fatalistic attitude manifested itself in different ways among many Jewish groups. Known as *apocalypticism*, this perspective can be broadly defined as the conviction that the world had become so lawless that God would have to intervene to rout the forces of chaos and establish a divine reign of justice. Jews speculated about how this divine intervention would occur. Some wondered whether God would use agents, human or angelic, to assert divine authority. Others pondered the fate of the Gentile nations and peoples, some concluding that God would punish those guilty of idolatry but the righteous among the nations could be included in the kingdom of God. Yet other Jews thought about the form of Jewish self-government in their own Land in the Age to Come, some picturing an ideal king like David of old, some a perfect teacher like Moses, and others a superlative priest who would lead the people in worshiping God in a renewed Temple, cleansed of corrupt clerical regimes. There were also some who expected that the righteous dead would be resurrected into the bliss of God's sovereign rule.

JESUS, A GALILEAN JEW

A series of charismatic prophetic figures arose in this turbulent situation. Some of these individuals we know only by name, but the activity of Jesus from Nazareth in Galilee was to have the greatest historical impact. Known as a popular teacher and healer, he traveled around Galilee and Judea. By means of illustrative parables, welcoming fellowship meals, healings, and symbolic deeds, he announced that the Reign of God was breaking into the world and that Israel was being restored.

Eventually, he brought this kingdom-centered message to Jerusalem during the always tense Passover season, a time when Jews from around the Mediterranean gathered to commemorate the festival of Jewish freedom from foreign domination. Roman authorities tried to avert the demonstrations against their rule that often erupted at Passover time. If unsuccessful in preventing unrest they were poised to restore order forcefully. Some days before Passover, Jesus caused a disturbance in the Temple courts, apparently a prophetic protest against the widely perceived corruption of the priestly leadership (whose chief priest was effectively appointed by the Roman prefect). This incident sparked or reinforced concerns among the Romans and their clerical agents that Jesus might be intending to foment a Passover riot.

Pre-emptive action would seem to account for the Roman execution of Jesus just before Passover began. Crucifixions at prominent sites were used both to torture perceived insurgents and also to deter their followers. By taking the popular Jesus into custody under cover of darkness (Mark 14:2) and quickly dispatching him to a cross, a potential uprising would be blocked and a gruesome warning issued. The fact that Jesus was publicly crucified and not simply made to disappear supports this logic. Moreover, his mode of execution and the capital charge of "king of the Jews" show that his activities on behalf of God's Reign or Kingdom were perceived by Roman overlords as seditious. The priestly elites—not unreasonably as later events would prove—feared for the existence of the Temple if major turmoil erupted (John 11:8).

The preceding paragraphs represent a fairly centrist consensus of current historical Jesus research. In particular, it should be noted that such reconstructions depict Jesus as thoroughly immersed in the life of Second Temple Judaism. His activities were welcomed by some of his Jewish contemporaries and feared by others, but there is no question that he operated well within the range of acceptable Jewish diversity. Some might have challenged his statements, actions, or authority, but his Jewishness was not in question. As will be discussed later, this present-day portrayal understands New Testament passages that suggest a rupture between Jesus's followers and other Jews as anachronistic, actually reflecting the controversies of several decades later. No split between a monolithic Judaism and

50   *Philip A. Cunningham*

the Church occurred in the lifetime of Jesus: first, because Judaism was not so
uniform; and second, because the Church did not yet exist.

THE BIRTH OF THE CHURCH[1]

Jesus of Nazareth was one individual among the thousands and thousands of
Jews crucified by Roman forces. What sets him apart in terms of historical
impact stems from the assertions that his followers, all of them Jewish, began to
make about him shortly after his death. These Jews claimed to have experienced
the crucified one as raised by God to transcendent life. This divine exaltation of
an executed prophet convinced them that the eschaton, the time for the
inbreaking of God's Reign, was indeed commencing just as Jesus had declared.
The idea of an eschatological general resurrection of the dead was adapted to the
unexpected situation of a singular resurrection of a righteous individual, who
would soon usher in the wider resurrection: "[Jesus] the first fruits, then at his
coming all those who belong to [him]," as Paul of Tarsus put it about twenty
years later (1 Cor. 15:23). Since Jesus had been executed as a pretender "king of
the Jews," his followers saw his resurrection as divine confirmation that Jesus
was indeed an anointed agent or messiah of God, just as the anointed Davidic
kings of old. Jesus was hailed as Messiah, in Greek "Christ," but in a particular
sense: he was the one sent by God, faithful even to the point of death, raised to
glory, and soon to return to complete the implementation of God's rule.

The followers of Jesus began to read the scriptures of Israel with different
eyes, searching its passages for texts that would explain their current experiences
to themselves and to other Jews. They continued to gather for the fellowship
meals that had been a characteristic of Jesus's activity, but now transformed into
memorial meals, celebrating the one who had been crucified and raised. Hymns
to God's Wisdom were adapted in praise of Jesus Christ, and they began praying
to him as God's Son and as the Lord who would share in God's power of final
judgment at the eschaton. Their eschatological enthusiasm appears to have
spread quickly to diaspora Jews visiting in Jerusalem and through them out into
the wider eastern Mediterranean region. Local Jewish assemblies called in Greek
ekklesiai (churches, identical in meaning to *synagogai*) formed in many places
and were centered on Jesus the Raised One.

All of these occurrences made the Jewish churches distinctive in comparison
with other Jewish groups, presaging the eventual differentiation of Judaism and
Christianity into separate religious communities. However, idiosyncratic practices, claims, or modes of interpreting the scriptures were not unusual in the

---

[1] I will use church with a lower case "c" to denote local communities of believers in the resurrected Christ and Church with an upper case "C" to refer to all such communities collectively. No
centralized authority is implied in the latter case.

Jews and Christians from the Time of Christ   51

diverse world of late Second Temple Judaism. In these early decades, the churches were still Jewish, not just demographically, but also because they fell within the range of acceptable variety during this period (note the participation of the Jerusalem church in Temple rituals in Acts 2:46–7).

Another development with huge consequences transpired when early preachers (apostles) sought to spread their good news of Christ crucified-and-raised in diaspora synagogues. Perhaps to their initial surprise, their proclamation greatly interested some Gentiles who had already admired Judaism and who were to some degree accepted in local Jewish communities. Some of these "God-fearing" Gentiles had actually received circumcision and been fully incorporated into Jewish life as converts, but others, unwilling to take that step, seem to have informally adopted some Jewish dietary practices and participated marginally in synagogue liturgies. Hearing the apostles of Christ, these God-fearers saw a way of becoming more closely involved in Jewish life and inquired about the possibility of joining the emerging churches.

Although the Jewish apostles probably saw this Gentile interest as further confirmation that the eschaton was approaching, a defining controversy erupted within the churches. Given the inclusive nature of Jesus's own activities, there does not seem to have been much resistance to the idea that Gentiles might be admitted into the Jewish churches, but there was considerable disagreement about admission requirements. The extreme options among the Jewish churches' leaders were, on the one hand, to require circumcision and total observance of the Torah by both Jews and Gentiles in the churches, to on the other hand, the radical eschatological perspective that the Torah's authority had expired now that God's Reign was approaching and need not be observed by anyone in the churches, Jew or Gentile. Various intermediate positions required some minimal ethical standards (no adultery, murder, or idolatry) among Gentiles in the churches, or that the dietary laws be observed at community fellowship meals.

This dispute raged for many decades with different practices operative in different churches. Thus in Gospel of Mark, written around 70 CE, Jesus is said to have eliminated kosher laws by declaring "all foods clean" (7:19), while in Matthew's Gospel, composed around 80–90 CE, Jesus declares, "whoever breaks one of the least of these commandments [of the Torah], and teaches others to do the same, will be called least in the Kingdom" (5:19). While the churches observed various customs in regard to Gentile members, gradually more and more Gentiles participated, becoming the majority in some places. This phenomenon was another wedge that would contribute to the separation of an originally entirely Jewish eschatological movement from its origins among the people of Israel.

As the leaders of the original Jewish churches debated the issue, they mounted arguments about the authority of the Torah that would be read quite differently in later social contexts. Most influential in the long term was Paul of Tarsus, whose letters to diverse early churches, written in the decade of the 50s in the first century CE, are the earliest books in the New Testament. An advocate of admitting Gentiles without requiring circumcision or Torah observance, Paul addressed in his letters specific issues or controversies in particular circumstances that we cannot fully discern. He often tried to convince his opponents with a scattershot series of arguments of varying degrees of persuasiveness that became difficult for later generations of readers, unfamiliar with Paul's immediate context, to understand. Recent Pauline scholarship stresses that he was writing mostly to newborn Gentile churches and so was more interested in the Torah's applicability to Gentiles, rather than in its observance by Jews or its inherent value. He seemed particularly disturbed by opponents, possibly Gentile converts to Judaism who treated circumcision as a magical ritual that automatically put one right with God, but who had little interest in the entirety of the Torah (for example, Gal. 5:3). When his contentions were afterward read in a thoroughly Gentile Christianity that had become alienated from Judaism, Paul's words were used to support a caricature of Judaism as a futile and legalistic effort to earn God's favor through the strict, heartless observance of impossible commandments.

BETWEEN TWO REVOLTS: GROWING ESTRANGEMENT

The first of two Jewish revolts against the Roman empire effectively ended with the destruction of the Second Temple in 70 CE. This trauma had enormous repercussions for all contemporary Jewish groups, giving rise to potent forces that accelerated the differentiation of the followers of Jesus Christ from other Jews. The appearance of the term *Christian* to denote both Jewish and Gentile church members is a sign of this dynamic.

There is some evidence, for instance, that the churches generally did not join in the Great Revolt of 66–70 CE. Their belief that returning, glorified Christ would be the one to establish God's Reign would naturally deter their participation in an insurgency against the empire led by others. Moreover, the persecution of Christians in Rome by the Emperor Nero between 64 and 66 CE, during which two prominent Jewish church leaders, Peter and Paul, were probably executed, demonstrated the new movement's vulnerability and weakness, arguing for its quiescence. The destruction of Jerusalem led to the demise of the mother church, hastening a growing shift in authority from Jewish churches to Gentile ones. At the same time, the disappearance of the eyewitness generation triggered the composition of narratives of the life of Jesus, called gospels, which as part of the New Testament would in time supersede Israel's scriptures as the normative Christian textual authorities.

The destruction of the Second Temple also upset the equilibrium that had existed among the diverse Jewish groups. Although some expected the rapid rebuilding of the Temple (perhaps after seventy years as had happened after the loss of the first Temple centuries before), the surviving Jewish leadership competed for influence in the decades after 70 CE. Among the rivals were some

Jews and Christians from the Time of Christ 53

churches, such as the community in which the Gospel of Matthew was composed. This narrative portrayed Jesus as definitively interpreting the Torah that God now expected all Jews to follow. As leadership in the post-Temple Jewish world tried to coalesce, there seems to have been an effort to limit the diversity of movements and opinions that had characterized late Second Temple Judaism. In such an environment, the idiosyncratic views of Jews in the churches tended to marginalize them in the eyes of other Jews.

Gentile Christians, too, were subjected to conflicting forces in terms of the Church's relationship to Judaism. God-fearing Gentiles already had some conflicted feelings. Although attracted by the Jewish tradition's monotheism, ethics, and venerability, the aversion many felt toward circumcision would have inclined them to be selective about which Torah commandments they would observe. This ambivalence was exacerbated after 70 CE.

On the one hand, Jews in the Roman empire were exempt from worshiping the emperor as a deity, a privilege that Gentiles in the churches sought to claim as well. On the other hand, after the Great Revolt the Romans levied a "Jewish tax" of two drachmas a year on Jews. At first it was ethnically based, but under the Emperor Domitian (ruled 81–96) it was extended to Gentiles who claimed some allegiance to Jewish customs (God-fearers and Christians). This would have encouraged Gentile Christians to deny that they were in any way Jewish and so not liable to this tax, although in times of persecution they would be motivated to claim association with Jewish privileges in order to avoid being forced to worship the emperor.

It was in this environment of war, uncertainty, and shifting identities that the Christian gospels were composed. Written in different church contexts and with different Christian audiences in mind, these narratives of the life and signifi-cance of Jesus shared a common purpose. Their writers, known today as the evangelists, all sought to promote faith in Christ as the divine Son who was appointed to bring about God's Rule. The story of his death and resurrection was, of course, key to their proclamation, but powerful social forces converged in shaping the ways in which they related this crucial episode.

In a Church subject to occasional imperial persecution, the fact that Jesus had been found guilty of sedition by a Roman prefect could not be stressed. It was important to convey not only that Jesus historically was innocent of such charges, but also—despite all the evidence to the contrary—that Roman authorities at the time were not terribly concerned about the kingdom-preacher from Galilee. In different ways, the Gospels depicted the Temple leadership, widely unpopular among Jews before the Great Revolt, as the prime movers behind Jesus's execu-tion. At the time of the composition of the Gospels, the surviving Temple priests were bereft of the physical site of their authority, a vivid testimony in the eyes of many to divine anger with them. At the same time, portraying the Crucifixion of Jesus as another instance of Israel rejecting prophets sent by God enabled the evangelists to appeal to their fellow Jews to believe in the one whom God had

54   *Philip A. Cunningham*

vindicated by raising him from the grave. Luke's Gospel repeatedly describes Jesus in such rejected prophet terms, while Matthew's Gospel offers the residents of Jerusalem, doomed to destruction by Roman legions in the Great Revolt, as negative models of those stained with blood for the death of God's chosen agent.

Thus, the foundational Christian scriptural narratives related the central story of the death and resurrection of Jesus in ways that minimized Roman culpability and accentuated the role played by Jewish figures. Motivated by the complex interplay of internal post-Temple Jewish rivalries with life under an overpowering imperial authority, the evangelists authored texts that were later used in very different social circumstances to justify hostility against Jews and Judaism per se. For instance, the effective social situation would radically change three centuries later when the Roman empire would cease to persecute Christianity and indeed actually embrace it.

However, at the time of the evangelists in the first century, Roman authorities had difficulty distinguishing among Jews, God-fearers, Gentile converts who had been circumcised as Jews, Christian Jews, and Christian Gentiles. In some cases, they may have consulted with known synagogue leaders about the claim to Jewishness of other groups, and, depending on the local circumstances in the particular town, some synagogue leaders may have denounced Jewish or Gentile Christians as not authentic Jews. Such a scenario may lie behind the epithet "synagogue of Satan" found twice in the New Testament Book of Revelation (2:9; 3:9), a work widely thought to have been written during a Roman persecution of churches in Asia Minor in the 90s CE. Similar circumstances may underlie scattered but hard to substantiate claims of Jewish violence against Christians here and there.

Why would Jewish leaders gradually come to view the Church as an increasingly marginal sect, and eventually as beyond the borders of acceptable Judaism? Several factors were at work, which once again played themselves out differently in different times and different places.

First, despite the range of views in the internal Church debate about Gentile admission, some Christians (first Jews then also Gentiles) argued against the continued validity of the Torah. Jews, for whom the Torah remained central regardless of the variety of interpretations of it, would have found this assertion unacceptable.

After the first Great Revolt, and especially after the second, Bar Kokhba revolt (132–5 CE), Jewish leaders became increasingly wary of messianic fervor. Simon ben Kosba, who led the insurrection, was popularly hailed as God's anointed agent of restoration and given the messianic nickname of *bar Kokhba*, the son of the star. Christians, of course, rejected anyone other than Jesus Christ as messiah, but after the disastrous end of this second revolt Jewish leaders also became more cautious about such zealotry. Thus, they viewed with greater suspicion eschatologically enthusiastic movements such as the Church.

Jews and Christians from the Time of Christ 55

In addition, as the first century ended, more churches were becoming entirely Gentile in composition. It would be difficult for local synagogue leaders to view such Christian communities—with their own emerging and independent leadership structures—as in any way Jewish, despite their appeals to Jewish scriptures and traditions.

Finally, theological developments in emerging Christianity increasingly differentiated believers in Jesus Christ from other Jews. Certain churches, such as those that produced the Gospel and Letters of John, stressed the need for belief in Christ's divine status. Although by no means desiring to venture into polytheism, the originally Jewish Johannine community so emphasized the equality of the Father and the Son that to outside Jewish ears this amounted to a rejection of the central truth of Judaism, that God is One. Thus, in the Gospel of John, written near the end of the first century CE, believers in Jesus are portrayed as being thrown out of the synagogue (9:22; 12:42; 16:2). This situation is impossible in the time of Jesus; instead it reflects the recent history of the Johannine community whose Jewish members had been shunned by the local synagogue.

Angered by this expulsion, the author persistently uses the term *the Jews* in the Gospel as unbelieving opponents of Jesus, even though almost every character is Jewish, including Jesus's followers. This literary device sarcastically conveys the alienation experienced by Johannine Jews who, from their perspective, have been cast from their Jewish heritage by so-called Jews. The factor that precipitated the expulsion is clearly what Johannine Jews had been saying about Jesus. In the Gospel, the Jews seek to kill Jesus: "It is not for a good work that we are going to stone you, but for blasphemy, because you, though only a human being, are making yourself God" (10:33, also 5:18). Such a perceived breach of Jewish monotheism was intolerable to the synagogue and difficult for the evangelist to defend against before the doctrine of the Trinity had been developed.

It is hardly surprising in this rapidly changing and varied atmosphere at the turn of the first century, in which loyalties were in flux and in which wars and persecutions raged, that the separating Jewish and Christian communities would begin to define themselves oppositionally, one against the other.

SUPERSESSIONISM AND THE INSTITUTIONALIZATION OF JEWISH AND CHRISTIAN ANTIPATHY

Recalling that these developments occurred without any uniformity in widely scattered locations, and that neither Jews nor Christians were governed by an authoritative central body that could enforce religious decisions, it is still possible to discern a growing separation between the two groups in the second century CE. This trend was founded on a zero-sum posture toward the other: in order for one community's beliefs to be valid, the other's had to be wrong. Such an attitude was evident as early as the letters of Paul; however, in his context, it was one group of Jews, those who held Jesus to be God's Christ, who were discrediting other Jews. In the new century, it was increasingly Gentile Christians and non-Christian Jews who contended. As the Christian "Letter of Barnabas"—a pseudepigraphal epistle written around the year 100 CE that is not part of the New Testament—shows, the logical possibility that both communities could regard each other as in a distinctive and legitimate covenantal relationship with the same God of Israel was rejected: "do not be like certain persons who pile up sin upon sin, saying that our covenant remains to them also" (4:6).

However, just because some Christian writers felt this way does not mean that their views were shared by the vast majority of Christians. For quite some time many Christians associated with their Jewish neighbors as if indeed the "covenant remains to them also." Even as the increasingly Gentile Church was delineating its theological self-understanding, it did so in the presence of a reinvigorated and influential Judaism reconstituting itself after the calamities of the two revolts.

In the years after the destruction of the Temple, the study of the written Torah and the reinterpretation of its commandments for a world in which the sacrificial rituals could not be performed gradually became the central activity of Jewish life. Scholars known as rabbis began to put into writing debates and traditions of interpretation that had been circulating for some time. A body of rabbinic literature developed that used the scriptures of Israel as the starting point for a reconstituted way of Jewish life. The rabbis stressed the need for Jews to walk according to the commandments or *mitzvoth* of God as interpreted through their legal and narrative traditions of discourse. Jewish seasonal festivals of thanksgiving, recommitment, penitence, and renewal became centered in the home and local community, and the observance of the *mitzvoth* was understood as replacing the sacrificial rites of the Temple. As the centuries passed, the rabbis' way of being Jewish would eventually become normative for all the descendants of ancient Israel.

Thus, nascent Christianity and emerging rabbinic Judaism were simultaneously defining their distinct identities by drawing upon more or less the same scriptural traditions, but interpreted in radically different ways: the Church through the lens of the coalescing New Testament and Judaism through the lens of the developing rabbinic literary corpus.

Although they shared this textual commonality, there was an enormous social disparity between Jews and Christians in the Roman empire in the second and third centuries. Jews were legally recognized as a legitimate religious association and continued to be exempt from worshipping Roman deities. Some Diaspora communities undertook extensive synagogue-building projects, sometimes prominently located on main city streets. Jews achieved positions of civic influence in many parts of Greece and Asia Minor, and were vital participants in the life of their towns and cities.

Even though localized anti-Jewish violence flared from time to time, some Gentiles, including many Christians, continued to be strongly attracted by Jewish traditions. This fascination not only led these Gentiles to adopt some Jewish customs in an informal way, but also encouraged a significant number of Christians—both Jews and Gentiles—to continue some degree of Jewish practice within church communities. Such "Judaizing" Christians, as they were sometimes called, could cite those New Testament texts written in first-century churches that had insisted on some measure of Torah observance for incoming Gentiles. Especially important for Jewish-oriented Christians were sayings of Jesus such as Matthew 5:17–18: "Do not think that I have come to abolish the law or the prophets; I have come not to abolish but to fulfill. For truly I tell you, until heaven and earth pass away, not one letter, not one stroke of a letter, will pass from the law until all is accomplished." It appears that for centuries some Christians would frequent synagogue functions as well as local church liturgies. The boundaries between the two groups remained quite porous for a considerable period.

On the other hand, Christians had a low social status in the empire. The Church had no imperial legal recognition and was subject to periodic persecution and popular disdain as a religion of slaves and women. Roman intelligentsia cast Christianity as a superstitious and heretical mutation of Judaism. The polemicist Celsus, for instance, writing toward the end of the second century, used a fictitious Jewish character to mock Christian claims that they understood the scriptures of ancient Israel better than did Jews: "Well, who is to be disbelieved—Moses or Jesus? Perhaps there is a simpler solution: perhaps when the Father sent Jesus he had forgotten the commandments he gave to Moses, and inadvertently condemned his own laws, or perhaps sent his messenger to give notice that he had suspended what he had previously endorsed" (*On True Doctrine*, IX).

Church leaders had to respond to such charges and to combat Judaism's appeal to its own members. Taking polemical passages from the New Testament, which had mostly arisen as part of an inner Jewish debate, and reading the internal criticisms of the Hebrew prophets as evidence of constant Jewish failures, Christian teachers attacked Judaism's respectability using the rhetorical customs of the time. These included litanies of the rival's alleged failings, phrased in the most extreme terms, such as these accusations from within a certain Greek philosophical movement: "They are ignorant, boastful, self-deceived, unlearned and deceptive by their words, evil-spirited, impious, liars and deceivers, preaching for the sake of gain, glory and only their own benefit; flatterers and charlatans, mindless, boastful and shameless, deceiving others and themselves, demagogues."

The Roman destruction of the Second Temple and the Gospels' apologetic enlargement of the Temple priesthood's role in Jesus's Crucifixion provided especially potent ammunition. Thus, Melito, bishop of Sardis in Asia Minor,

58   *Philip A. Cunningham*

would around the year 175 seek to counter the allure of Jewish Passover observances, at first moderately. But his efforts turned vitriolic when he adduced the Crucifixion:

And where was [Jesus] murdered? In the very center of Jerusalem! Why? Because he had healed their lame, and had cleansed their lepers, and had guided their blind with light, and had raised up their dead. For this reason he suffered.... Therefore, the feast of unleavened bread [Passover] has become bitter to you [Jews] just as it was written: "You will eat unleavened bread with bitter herbs." Bitter to you are the nails which you made pointed. Bitter to you is the tongue which you sharpened. Bitter to you are the false witnesses whom you brought forward. Bitter to you are the fetters which you prepared. Bitter to you are the scourges which you wove.... Bitter to you are your hands which you bloodied, when you killed your Lord in the midst of Jerusalem.... You [Jews] forsook the Lord; you were not found by him. You dashed the Lord to the ground; you, too, were dashed to the ground, and lie quite dead. (*Peri Pascha*, 4, 72, 93, 99)

A slightly earlier, but less polemical text similarly tapped into the New Testament Crucifixion narratives to challenge Judaism's social superiority. In his *Dialogue with Trypho*, Justin Martyr recounts a (probably fictitious) conversation with a Jew named Trypho in which he scripturally argues for the superiority of Christianity:

For after that you had crucified Him, the only blameless and righteous Man... when you knew that He had risen from the dead and ascended to heaven, as the prophets foretold He would, you not only did not repent of the wickedness which you had committed, but at that time you selected and sent out from Jerusalem chosen men through all the land to tell that the godless heresy of the Christians had sprung up, and to publish those things which all they who knew us not speak against us. So that you are the cause not only of your own unrighteousness, but in fact of that of all other men. (17)

Here Justin somewhat dispassionately uses the Septuagint (Greek version) of Israel's scriptures and selected Gospel passages to argue with a Jewish interlocutor over the correct interpretation of the sacred writings. Recent historical studies offer tantalizing glimpses of such early scriptural debates between Christians and Jews, and raise the possibility that such exchanges further accelerated the growing separation of the Church and rabbinic Judaism in their formative decades. More research is needed, especially on the question of how much normative Christian and Jewish teaching was shaped by this oppositional dynamic.

On the Christian side, a helpful synthesis of the various elements of its emerging anti-Jewish theology is provided by Origen, a scholar writing around 248 CE in Caesaria against the contentions of Celsus:

For [the Jews] committed a crime of the most unhallowed kind, in conspiring against the Savior of the human race in that city [Jerusalem] where they offered up to God a

Jews and Christians from the Time of Christ

worship containing the symbols of mighty mysteries. It accordingly behooved that city where Jesus underwent these sufferings to perish utterly, and the Jewish nation to be overthrown, and the invitation to happiness offered them by God to pass to others,—the Christians, I mean, to whom has come the doctrine of a pure and holy worship, and who have obtained new laws, in harmony with the established legal systems in all countries.

(Contra Celsum, IV, 22)

Here the contours of the widespread Christian response to invidious comparisons with Judaism are clear: God's covenant with the Jewish people always symbolized the promised coming of Christ and the Church, Jerusalem was accursed and destroyed because of the Jewish rejection and Crucifixion of Jesus, and as a result the divine covenant was transferred to Christians. Christians have been given new, universal laws and rituals that replace the temporary and preparatory Law of Moses. The reason that Jews do not recognize these truths, demonstrable from their own sacred writings, is because, again according to Origen, they do not read "Scripture according to its spiritual meaning, but interpret it only according to the bare letter" (*De Principiis*, 9). This theological delegitimization of Judaism has been called supersessionism because it is premised on the claim that the Church has superseded the Jewish people as covenantal partners with God.

Supersessionism was born out of the vulnerable situation of Christians in the Roman empire, especially in comparison with the more respectable Judaism. Its presuppositions circulated widely in the churches and are evident in the writings of virtually all the influential Christian writers of the early centuries. In addition, these developments occurred simultaneously with defining doctrinal debates about the nature of Christ's divinity and his relationship to the Father that reverberated throughout the Christian world. Thus, in the words of one scholar of the period, "Christian beliefs are so deeply rooted in attitudes toward Judaism that it is impossible to disentangle what Christians say about Christ and the Church from what they say about Judaism" (Wilken 1971, 229). A theological stance became embedded in Christian thought that would not be seriously critiqued until after the Shoah in the twentieth century.

From its advantageous social position, rabbinic Judaism did not need, at least early on, to develop a similar opposing theological system. As long as Christianity was weak and marginal in imperial society, Jewish leaders were content to warn their communities about the novel scriptural interpretations of Christians and to assert in various ways the Oneness of God in the face of Christian claims about the divinity of Jesus. It is very unclear whether later medieval Jewish polemical writings against Christianity, such as the *Toledot Yeshu*, have roots any earlier than the fourth century. This makes sense given Judaism's high social status and the comparative impotence of Christianity in the second and third centuries. There is some evidence of mutual admonitions to avoid close contact with the members of the other community, for example prohibitions of

60 *Philip A. Cunningham*

intermarriage, but based on extant writing it appears that Judaism did not feel as threatened by Christianity as Christians did by Judaism.

The dwindling numbers of Jewish members of the churches were in an increasingly untenable position. Their degree of Torah practice and preference for less exalted claims about Christ made them suspect in the eyes of the Gentile Christian majority. On the other hand, their association with Gentiles who appeared to non-Christian Jews as idolaters or polytheists would tend to make Christian Jews unwelcome in Jewish communities. Such people were trapped in the growing rift between the two groups.

Nonetheless, it must be stressed that despite the widening influence of supersessionism, ordinary Jews and Christians in the empire regularly engaged in social interaction. Indeed, it was this day-to-day contact that prompted efforts by their respective leaders to discourage too close an association, but this occurred differently in each local situation. Of interest in this regard are two canons passed by the church council held in Elvira, Spain around 306 CE, one threatening expulsion if landlords allowed Jews to bless their crops (Canon 49) and another prohibiting cleric or laypeople to eat with Jews (Canon 50).

Clearly Christians, at least in this part of Spain, were habitually asking Jewish friends to bless their crops and were regularly dining with them, or church leaders would not have felt the need to try to discourage these interactions.

EARLY CHRISTIANITY AND ANTISEMITISM

During the fourth century CE, the relative social positions of Jews and Christians in the empire reversed. In 313, the Emperor Constantine declared that Christianity would be tolerated in the empire. He followed this up during his long reign (until 337 and his deathbed acceptance of baptism) with imperial patronage of the Church, which gave Christian leaders unprecedented influence. Although some emperors after Constantine were hostile to Christianity, or embraced deviant forms of it, in 380 Theodosius I made Christianity the preferred state religion, giving Christians considerable access to the power of the Roman legal system. One possible result of being freed from the constant fear of state harassment was an increase in the incidents of Christian attacks against Jewish synagogues during the fourth and fifth centuries, even though imperial authorities at first sought to punish the miscreants. As time passed, Christian leaders promoted the passage of laws that curtailed the privileges of their Jewish rivals, leading ultimately to the marginalization of Jews in the medieval Christendom that arose after the collapse of the Roman empire in the West. But, again, this too was a gradual process, most evident in hindsight, whose full implications could not be foreseen.

This narrative of the gradual separation and mutual opposition between Christianity and rabbinic Judaism leads to the question: when, if ever, during

Jews and Christians from the Time of Christ

this process can antisemitism be said to have appeared? The answer to this question will largely be determined by how antisemitism is defined, and in the case of the New Testament period by how Judaism is defined.

If antisemitism is technically defined as a racialist hatred of Jews simply for being alive, then such antisemitism cannot be said to have existed during the first through fourth centuries CE. In comparison to racial antisemitism, the delegitimization of Jewish traditions represented by Christian supersessionism is more properly termed anti-Judaism—opposition to Jewish religious tenets and practices. Even anti-Judaism is difficult to ascribe to those earliest Jewish church leaders who debated fiercely with Jewish contemporaries. They understood themselves to be part of an eschatologically empowered Jewish community and contended with other Jews who disbelieved this. Their polemical assertions assumed a more anti-Jewish character when reiterated and assembled by later Gentile Christians. The question is therefore very complicated because of shifting identity definitions and communal boundaries.

If antisemitism is more broadly defined as animosity to Jews because of their different customs in comparison with other peoples, then such an antisemitism existed before the appearance of the Church among those Gentiles who belittled diaspora Jews as clannish, elitist, and unreasonable and hostile to mankind for clinging to a single deity while dismissing all others. Such rhetoric was taken up when later Christians competed with Jewish rivals for influence in the imperial world.

On the other hand, such an antisemitism directed against Jewish difference was accompanied, as we have seen, by a philosemitism held by Gentiles who admired Jewish solidarity, venerability, monotheistic spirituality, and ethics. The appeal that Judaism held for a significant number of Gentile God-fearers partially accounts for the rapid inroads made in the Mediterranean world by the Jewish apostles of Jesus Christ.

Philosemitism was also taken up as the Church became more Gentile in its composition. The efforts of many Christians to observe Jewish customs to some degree, their frequenting of local synagogues, and their positive interactions with Jewish neighbors are all signs of this.

Nonetheless, social circumstances fostered the rapid dominance of a theologically based antisemitism (in the broader sense of animosity to Jewish difference) that became entwined with emergent Christian self-understanding: the Church has supplanted Judaism, which has now become obsolete. It is important to appreciate the unique social and historical contexts that gave birth to a distinctively Christian religious antagonism toward Jews and Judaism. Although always latently present in medieval European Christendom, flaring into violence against Jews in times of economic and social turmoil especially after 1000 CE, anti-Jewish perspectives are not religiously intrinsic to Christianity per se. The widespread post-Shoah Christian rejection of the allegation that Jews were divinely cursed for killing Jesus has shaken supersessionism at

62 Philip A. Cunningham

its roots, generating ongoing efforts to express Christian faith in ways that affirm ongoing Jewish covenantal life.

RECOMMENDED READINGS

Bieringer, R., D. Pollefeyt, and F. Vandecasteele-Vanneuville (eds), *Anti-Judaism and the Fourth Gospel* (Assen, The Netherlands: Royal Van Gorcum, 2001).

Davies, Alan T. (ed.), *Antisemitism and the Foundations of Christianity* (New York: Paulist Press, 1979).

Dunn, James D. G., *The Partings of the Ways: Between Christianity and Judaism and their Significance for the Character of Christianity* (London: SCM Press; Philadelphia: Trinity Press, 1991).

——(ed.), *Jews and Christians: The Parting of the Ways, A.D. 70 to 135* (Grand Rapids, MI/Cambridge, UK: Eerdmans, 1992).

Efroymson, David P., Eugene J. Fisher, and Leon Klenicki (eds), *Within Context: Essays on Jews and Judaism in the New Testament* (Collegeville, MN: Liturgical Press, 1993).

McKnight, Scot, *A Light among the Gentiles: Jewish Missionary Activity in the Second Temple Period* (Minneapolis: Fortress Press, 1991).

Meeks, Wayne A., and Robert L. Wilken, *Jews and Christians in Antioch in the First Four Centuries of the Common Era* (Ann Arbor, MI: Scholars Press, 1978).

Nickelsburg, George W. E., *Ancient Judaism and Christian Origins: Diversity, Continuity, and Transformation* (Minneapolis: Fortress Press, 2003).

Richardson, Peter, with David Granskou (eds), *Anti-Judaism in Early Christianity*, vol 1: *Paul and the Gospels* (Waterloo, Ontario: Wilfrid Laurier University Press, 1986).

Saldarini, Anthony J., *Pharisees, Scribes, and Sadducees in Palestinian Society: A Sociological Approach* (Wilmington, DE: Michael Glazier, 1988).

Schwartz, Seth, *Imperialism and Jewish Society, 200 BCE to 640 CE* (Princeton/Oxford: Princeton University Press, 2001).

Smiga, George M., *Pain and Polemic: Anti-Judaism in the Gospels* (New York/Mahwah: Paulist Press, 1992).

Wilken, Robert L., *Judaism and the Early Christian Mind: A Study of Cyril of Alexandria's Exegesis and Theology* (New Haven, CT: Yale University Press, 1971).

Wilson, Stephen G. (ed.), *Anti-Judaism in Early Christianity*, vol 1: *Separation and Polemic* (Waterloo, Ontario: Wilfrid Laurier University Press, 1986).

4

The Middle Ages

Alex Novikoff

The Christianization of the Roman empire that resulted from Emperor Constantine's conversion after 313 CE and Emperor Theodosius's decision to make Christianity the official religion of the empire in 391 CE provoked a cultural revolution destined to have profound consequences for the Christian encounter with Jews and Judaism. Two of the most important issues confronting Christians during this transitional period of late antiquity were the competing interpretations of Christ's nature and the precise relation between Christianity and its mother religion of Judaism. Church councils during the fourth and fifth centuries dealt principally with the former by establishing the doctrine of the Trinity and distinguishing heresy from orthodoxy, while the writings of the Church Fathers, and Saint Augustine in particular, helped to fix a solution to the latter by offering an eschatological conception of the world that drew from, and yet manifestly surpassed, Christianity's Jewish and classical inheritance. Any understanding of the role of antisemitism in the Middle Ages must begin with Saint Augustine of Hippo and give special care to distinguish antisemitism from its theological forerunner: anti-Judaism.

Saint Augustine's writings, like his peripatetic career, responded to the circumstances that he faced living in the Roman empire on the eve of its collapse. In 410, an army of Visigoths under Alaric entered and sacked the city of Rome, dealing a humiliating blow to its proud population who thought the city to be both eternal and invincible. The clear and present danger felt by Christians throughout the Roman empire during these violent times and the doubts about the Christian religion that were raised by many of them compelled Augustine to write the *City of God*, a voluminous work that took over a decade to complete. In this vastly erudite and massively influential work of historical theology Augustine succeeded more than any other author of late Antiquity in formulating a vision of the world in which Rome's destruction at the hands of pagan barbarians was explained as part of God's providential plan, rather than against it, a grandiose cosmogony in which the heavenly City of God (embodied by the Church) is destined to triumph over the sinful City of Man (embodied by Rome). Among the peoples whom Augustine had to account for in his historical theology were

64 *Alex Novikoff*

pagans (who saw themselves vindicated by the Visigothic sack of Rome), other Christian groups whose beliefs deviated from the official teachings of the Church, and Jews. Much like other Christian apologists who came before him Augustine placed Jews in a special position because they alone were the original recipients of God's law. Augustine's novelty (and eventual influence) lay in his pronouncements on what meaning the Jewish presence in society held for Christians and their attainment of the heavenly City of God.

Augustine's understanding of the Jewish presence in society has become known as the doctrine of Jewish witness. This term has the misfortune of belying the complexity of what is meant by it while simultaneously suggesting that Augustine's concern for Jews can be separated from his broader theological concerns, which, recent scholars concur, it cannot. In essence, according to Augustine, the Jews survive as living testimony to the antiquity of the Christian promise. They will eventually convert at the end of time, but until that time comes they should not be harmed or forced to convert because their social degradation and Diaspora serve to confirm the supremacy of Christianity. Indeed their presence in society preserves, represents, and, in fact, embodies the literal sense of the Bible and the material reality of earthly experience. At precisely what point in his career Augustine completed his formulation of the doctrine of Jewish witness remains a subject of debate, but it features prominently in the *City of God*, when he provides an exegesis of Psalm 59:12 and addresses the primal topic of Christian salvation and redemption:

For there is a prophecy given previously in the Psalms...where it is written..."Slay them not, lest at any time they forget your law scatter them in your might." God thus demonstrated to the church the grace of his mercy upon his enemies the Jews, because, as the Apostle says, "Their offense is the salvation of the Gentiles." Therefore, he did not kill them—that is, he did not make them cease living as Jews, although conquered and oppressed by the Romans—lest, having forgotten the law of God, they not be able to provide testimony on our behalf in this manner of our present concern. Thus it was inadequate for him to say, "Slay them not, lest at any time they forget your law," without adding "scatter them." (Augustine, *De civitate Dei* 18:46, CCSL 48: 644–645; translation after Jeremy Cohen, *Living Letters of the Law*, 33)

It is not only that the phenomenon of Jewish survival fulfills divine prophecy, a claim that harkens back to Pauline theology; Augustine interprets the divine prophecy of Jewish survival as a mandate for the faithful in his own day and age: "Slay them not to ensure their survival and that of their Old Testament observance, and scatter them in order to guarantee that the conditions of their survival demonstrate the gravity of their error and the reality of their punishment" (Cohen 1999, 33). For Augustine, the Jews of this world have for Christians a divine, historical, and functional purpose in the ongoing quest to achieve the heavenly City of God, a purpose that necessitates their survival and protection amidst Christians.

The Middle Ages   65

Another aspect of Augustine's doctrine of Jewish witness that holds significance for later Christian attitudes toward Jews involves his depiction of Jews as stagnant practitioners of an outmoded religion. Such a portrayal hinges on the notion that the religion and customs of the Jews, while instructive to living Christians, represents the living testimony of a people unchanged since the first coming of Christ. Ancient, unconverted, and stationary in time, the Jews are a people fixed, as he puts it, "in useless antiquity." There is little if any evidence to suggest that Augustine's writings on Jews and Judaism resulted from face-to-face interactions or disputations with Jews, as was the case with his encounters with Christian heretical groups such as the Manicheans and Donatists. Augustine's conception of the Jew, being an intellectual engagement with Jews as he imagined them to be, has thus been termed the "hermeneutical Jew" (Cohen 1999, 3). This interpretive schema had a powerful resonance in the centuries to follow, as many other theologians in the medieval West found it theologically important and even necessary to contribute to an image of the Jew that was more imaginary than real.

If Augustine broke new ground in first articulating the doctrine of Jewish witness, Pope Gregory I (ruled 590–604) was the first head of the Apostolic See to deal extensively with Jews. Often described as the first medieval pope, Gregory the Great was a key figure in helping to establish the primacy of the papacy in the West and certainly the most influential and prolific pontiff of the early Middle Ages. Broadly speaking, Gregory's teaching concerning the Jews can be differentiated between the executive rulings of his papal correspondence and the doctrinal pronouncements of his biblical commentaries. In the realm of his correspondence Gregory is known to have written over two dozen letters in which he addresses the subject of the Jews and their communities. From these letters one learns that on at least six occasions Gregory intervened to prevent violence against Jews, their synagogues, and their religious practices. In March 591, for instance, a Jew named Joseph complained to the Pope that Bishop Peter of Terracina had repeatedly expelled the Jews of that town from their places of worship. Gregory admonished the bishop for his deeds and urged him to exercise restraint, explaining that those who disagree with the Christian religion should join the faith by means of clemency, kindness, warning, and persuasion rather than by threats and fear.

Similar incidents of coercion occurring later in the decade elicited similar responses from the Pope, most famously in 598 when Gregory wrote to the bishop of Palermo, against whom the Jews had earlier lodged a complaint. "Just as the Jews should not have license in their synagogues to arrogate anything beyond that permitted by law, so too in those things granted them they should experience no infringement of their rights" (Gregory, *Epistolae* 8.25, CCSL 140A: 546–7; Schlomo Simonsohn, *The Apostolic See and the Jews: Documents, 492–1404*, Toronto: Pontifical Institute of Medieval Studies, 1988, 15–16). Known to

66 *Alex Novikoff*

posterity by its initial words *Sicut Judaeis*, this executive ruling, or papal bull, had a major impact on ecclesiastical policy toward the Jews in later centuries. In the period between 1198 and 1254, for instance, when the influence of the medieval papacy was at its height, the bull was reissued no fewer than five times.

Gregory's opposition to baptizing Jews under duress or expelling them from their places of worship acknowledged the legality of their presence in Christian society, but unlike Augustine there is little evidence that he deemed that presence a necessity. In fact, Gregory's correspondence alludes to the necessity of actively undermining the Jewish presence in society through their conversion to Christianity, a theme notably absent in Augustine's doctrine of Jewish witness. To facilitate this effort, Gregory frequently prescribed that baptized Jews receive special protection and financial rewards.

Gregory's corpus of exegetical work is the second major source for locating his attitude toward Jews. In his biblical commentaries, and especially in his *Moralia* on Job, Gregory made frequent reference to Jews and Judaism, often repeating and elaborating traditional patristic anti-Jewish motifs. For instance, he reaffirmed the Augustinian instruction that the blindness of the Jews in Jesus's day had resulted in their persecution of him and that such blindness, then and now, constituted divine punishment for their sin. Consistent with Pauline theology, Gregory believed that the end of days would bring about the complete conversion of the Jewish people. Gregory was evidently also convinced that the devil still abides among the Jews and that the bonds between Antichrist and Judaism continued to undermine the integrity of Christendom and threaten its future. For this reason a mandate for missionary preaching to the Jews entailed an urgency not yet encountered in Christian writings on Jews: "Is it not an awful shame to preach futilely to hard hearts, to take the trouble to demonstrate the truth, but to find no compensation for one's efforts—in the conversion of one's listeners? Nevertheless, the ensuing progress of their listeners is a great comfort for preachers" (Gregory, *Moralia in Job* 35.14.24–34, CCSL 143B: 1791–2; translation after Cohen, *Living Letters*, 81–2).

Just as Job finally received true consolation for his suffering from his brethren, so will Christ and His Church take comfort in the spiritual faith of carnal Israel. The apparent ambiguity, therefore, between Gregory's stated protection of Jews on the basis of legal precedent, on one hand, and his exhortation to campaign actively for their conversion despite their obstinacy, on the other, coalesce to form and indeed exemplify, as one commentator has put it, "the new, distinctive mentality of early medieval Latin Christendom" (Cohen 1999, 85).

The writings of Augustine and Gregory constitute the pillars of the early Latin Church's policy toward Jews and Judaism. In the Romanized Germanic kingdoms of the early Middle Ages, two other influential Church writers addressed with urgency the question of the Jewish presence in society, now in the broader context of both theology and royal policy: Isidore of Seville and Agobard of Lyons. Isidore of Seville (d. 636) exerted an especially great and

The Middle Ages 67

wide-ranging influence on the medieval world. A native of southern Spain, Isidore made his contribution to the Christian treatment of Jews on two fronts. First, his polemic *On the Catholic Faith against the Jews* was the most extensive anti-Jewish treatise since the early third-century apologist Tertullian. The opus echoed many established anti-Jewish motifs, such as Augustine's exegesis of Psalm 59:12 and Gregory's assertion of the allegiance of the Jews to Antichrist, but also went beyond either of them by emphasizing the historical enmity between Jews and Christ and highlighting its relevance for his own society. Isidore forecast that the conversion of Jews would, and must, take place not at some distant point in time, but in the proximate future, since this would usher in the seventh and final stage of history, although he fell short of calling for the forced conversion of Jews. On the other hand the work was composed precisely at the time of King Sisebut's decree (614–15) that did call for the forced baptism of Jews and many of Isidore's ideas were formulated in coordination with Visig-othic practice. Secondly, in his capacity as archbishop of Seville and chief prelate of the Spanish Church, Isidore played a pivotal role in formulating and legis-lating ecclesiastical policy, one that echoed and upheld the stringently anti-Jewish policies of the Visigothic kings. Isidore presided over the Council of Seville (624), which called for policing the Jews whom Sisebut had ordered must baptize their children, as well as the Fourth Council of Toledo (633), which forbade Christians of Jewish origin from holding public office and emphatically upheld the validity of those forced conversions that resulted from King Sisebut's edict. For the first time in the medieval West royal policy and the policy of churchmen coalesced to bring about and justify the immediate conversion of the Jews, a policy that led many Jews to migrate to the neighboring northern land of Gaul.

The writings of the Carolingian reformer and controversialist Agobard of Lyons offer another glimpse of the interaction between ecclesiastical and royal policies. Compared to the Jews in Visigothic lands, the Jewish communities of the Carolingian empire enjoyed considerable privileges and protection, even if such had not always been the case under earlier Frankish kings. Under emperors Charlemagne (ruled 768–814) and Louis the Pious (ruled 813–40) Jews were permitted to live according to their own law and practice their own religion; merchant activity was encouraged and Jews were used in the military service and as diplomatic envoys. It was in protest against these privileges and after clashing with the Jewish community of Lyons, where he was made bishop in 816, that Agobard campaigned. His immediate cause for complaint was his struggle, what he saw as his duty, to convert to Christianity the pagan slaves owned by Jews before the latter converted them to Judaism. He also called for the enforcement of canon and secular laws passed during the later Roman empire that restricted Jews from possessing or owning Christian slaves. After failure and humiliation in his hearing at the palace court of Louis the Pious, Agobard embarked on a vigorous program of polemical writing aimed at changing imperial policy. Agobard and

68 *Alex Novikoff*

his supporters sent no less than five works to the emperor and other clerical confidants at his court with the purpose of demonstrating the Jewish menace in society.

Taken collectively, Agobard's anti-Jewish program is intriguing because it offers yet another instance of the reception of and departure from traditional themes of the patristic *Adversus Iudaeos* works. On one hand Agobard had profound respect for his predecessors in the Church: he acknowledged and maintained the Augustinian principle of "Slay them not," affirmed the property rights of the Jews, and offered to compensate them for those slaves who chose baptism. On the other hand he focused on contemporary Jews as killers of Christ and classified them in relation to Muslims and heretics. He vehemently expressed his horror over indications that Jews enjoyed a social status superior to Christians, particularly as reflected in the Christian purchase and consumption of Jewish food. And in rather exceptional fashion he subjected the religious practices and writings of the Jews, including post-biblical Jewish traditions, to scrutiny and attack, concluding that the Jews were persisting in their contrivance of new superstitions and groundless absurdities concerning God and scripture. However, unlike his predecessors, Agobard provided little in the way of a broader theology or statement of principles. He also failed to bring about any meaningful changes in Carolingian policy.

Perhaps none of the churchmen or princes of the early medieval world could have anticipated the religious violence unleashed on the Jewish communities of western Europe as a consequence of the Crusading movement (1095–1291). From the earliest days of the First Crusade in 1096 and continuing throughout the twelfth and thirteenth centuries, when the Crusading movement reached its maturity, Jews repeatedly found themselves the victims of violent attacks, sometimes by armed knights and sometimes by urban rioters—not infrequently by both. The most famous episode in this grim chapter of Jewish-Christian relations was the first, when an army of Crusaders led by Count Emicho traversed the Rhineland en route to the East. Fired up by the stated goal of freeing the Holy Land from sacrilegious Muslims and Turks, some of the Crusaders concluded that it was proper that they should also help rid their own Christian kingdoms of a people they wholeheartedly believed to be the enemies of Christ. After all, a long tradition of Christian teachings had portrayed Jews as killers of Christ who actively campaigned to undermine Christian society. Violence erupted when the Crusaders arrived at the principal urban centers perched along the Rhine valley where Jewish communities had taken root.

It says something of the relatively steady relationship that Jews in the city of Mainz had enjoyed until this moment that many of them were given safety behind the fortified walls of the archbishop's palace and that the gates of the walled city had been closed by the archbishop and the municipal authorities, who feared for the well being of their town and for the endangered Jewish community. Yet it also says something of the distrust and animosity that resided

The Middle Ages 69

beneath the surface that sympathetic townspeople opened the outer walls to the Crusaders and that men in the service of the archbishop then fled the palace where the Jews were sequestered, leaving the Jews helpless against a well-armed band of Crusaders and angry townsfolk. Presented with the alternatives of conversion or death many Jews took their own lives and chose martyrdom in the name of God instead, a rare but not unprecedented decision in the annals of Jewish history (the same occurred at Masada south of Jerusalem in 73 CE). A few chose to resist the Crusaders with force; fewer still survived the violent ordeal. These, at any rate, are the facts as they are recorded in the accounts of Christian eyewitnesses and Jewish survivors (Peters 1995, 109–39). Similar incidents took place at Worms a few days earlier and at Cologne a few weeks later.

Medieval and modern commentators on 1096 agree: the brutality and tragedy of the attacks against Jews were unprecedented. Modern scholarly opinion, however, has diverged sharply on the interpretation of the larger meaning of these events and the reliability of some of the surviving accounts. Some historians have seen 1096 as a watershed moment in the history of Jewish-Christian relations and a clear marker in the rising tide of antisemitism, while others have played down the overall importance of the events and pointed out that Jewish communities continued to live and prosper in the Rhineland and elsewhere in northern Europe despite the pogroms. Similarly, some historians view the Hebrew accounts of the attacks as reliable historical documents while others have insisted that they are post-factual dirges that have as their chief purpose the memorialization of the deceased and therefore cannot be taken at face value. Others still have sought a middle ground asserting a more nuanced reading of the sources and a less positivistic interpretation of the events (Cohen 2004).

These academic debates do not detract from the fact that large-scale anti-Jewish violence had become by the high Middle Ages a recurrent, if sporadic, feature of Jewish-Christian relations. During the recruiting efforts of the Second Crusade in 1146 mobs stirred up by the frenzy of a new Crusade attacked local Jewish communities in France and Germany, even as the leading cleric of the day Bernard of Clairvaux denounced such violence (but praised the intentions of the rioters). During preparations for the Third Crusade in 1188, a near riot was averted in Mainz only because of the swift action taken by officers of Emperor Frederick I and local bishops. In 1189 and 1190, there were more riots and killings throughout England, the most notorious being in York where local barons were heavily in debt to Jews and took advantage of the widespread attacks to rid themselves of both their debts and their creditors. There was renewed persecution in western France in 1236 at the time that another Crusade was being preached and as late as 1320 the masses of the second so-called Shepherds' Crusade claimed they were exacting vengeance for the Crucifixion as they forced baptism on Jews over large parts of southern France. Indeed nearly all the major Crusading expeditions to the East were accompanied by anti-Jewish violence, a phenomenon that the foremost historian of the Crusades has recently suggested

70 *Alex Novikoff*

can best be explained by the tendency of holy war to turn inwards, the appeal introspective violence appears to have had for lay men and women at the time, and the failure of church leaders to control public emotions (Riley-Smith 2002, 3–20).

The twelfth century occupies a place of special importance in understanding the deteriorating image of Jews in medieval Christendom. Long known to medievalists for the renaissance of culture and learning that developed in the urban centers of northern Europe, culminating in the founding of the first universities, the twelfth century also witnessed a transitional moment in the intellectual engagement with Jews and Judaism and in the opening up of several new lines of polemical attack. The Italian-born monk Anselm of Bec exerted an especially influential role in the Jewish-Christian controversy, as well as in the development of Catholic theology more generally. He was for a time head of the monastic school at Le Bec in Normandy where he cultivated among his students a spirit of learning through dialogue that led him to write several important works that reflect his pedagogical approach to theology. Confident that any reasonable person who was presented a clear explanation of the truths of the faith would accept them, Anselm took a bold leap and aimed to demonstrate by recourse to reason alone many essential doctrines of Christianity. In *Why God Became Man* Anselm applied the same insistence on logic and reason to explaining the incarnation and other Christian concepts to non-believers, framing the discussion as a dialogue between himself and his inquisitive student Boso. At the conclusion of the work Boso congratulates Anselm for having succeeded so well in his endeavor that his arguments would "convince both Jews and Pagans by the mere force of reason" (Anselm, *Cur Deus homo*, in *St. Anselm Basic Writings*, ed. and trans. S. N. Deane Chicago: Open Court, 1962, 301).

It remains unclear the extent to which Anselm was truly interested in refuting Jewish objections to Christianity, but Anselm's own pupil Gilbert Crispin, who became abbot of Westminster, clearly took the matter more seriously. In 1092 or 1093, he wrote his own *Disputation between a Jew and Christian*, which he dedicated to Anselm. The pretext for this work was a real debate that he allegedly had in London with a Jewish merchant from Mainz, a pretext familiar to the history of the Jewish-Christian controversy, but one that cannot be dismissed so easily as a mere literary trope. The description of the encounter does not contradict what is known about Jewish socioeconomic patterns at the time, and the unusually civil tone that is taken between the two disputants has led a number of commentators to accept that an actual debate may indeed be at the origin of the work. This is significant because, if true, one is tempted to conclude that intellectual exchanges on matters of faith between Jews and Christians were by the turn of the twelfth century becoming more commonplace. No less significant is the fact that Gilbert clearly tried to accommodate Anselmian principles into his defense of Christianity, including a strong reliance on rational proofs of the incarnation so that the Jew, he explains, may then be able "to accept it

The Middle Ages 71

on rational terms or to reject it on rational grounds" (Gilbert Crispin, *Disputatio Iudei et Christiani* 93, in *The Works of Gilbert Crispin, Abbot of Westminster*, ed. Anna Sapir Abulafia and G.R. Evans, London: Oxford University Press, 1986, 31).

Even greater reliance on Anselmian reasoning marks Gilbert's other polemic work, the *Disputation between a Christian and a Pagan*, wherein Gilbert proposes to demonstrate the rational basis for Christian belief without even the aid of scriptural authority. There is no evidence that any Jews or pagans (in the unlikely event that there were any pagans in England) converted as a direct result of Gilbert's polemics. On the other hand the *Disputation with a Jew* survives in more than thirty medieval manuscripts, at least two-thirds of which date to the twelfth century (Abulafia 1995, 81). The considerable success achieved by Gilbert's writings is an important indicator that the disputational genre and the Anselmian approach to justifying faith by reason alone provided strong undercurrents in the evolution of twelfth-century thought.

The century following Anselm and Gilbert witnessed a remarkable proliferation of anti-Jewish (*Adversus Iudaeos*) treatises, many of them in dialogue form and many of those purporting to be the product of actual disputations. About 1110, the Jewish convert to Christianity Peter Alfonsi composed his own *Dialogues against Jews*, a series of twelve conversations between his former self, Moses, and his new identity, Peter. The work broke new ground in that it was the first to introduce to Christian audiences the post-biblical writings of the Talmud, prompting Peter and others after him to accuse Jews of the additional crimes of blasphemy and heresy. Alfonsi's *Dialogues* survive in nearly eighty manuscripts, making it a veritable bestseller by medieval standards. Around 1130, France's leading schoolman and medieval Europe's most notorious paramour, Peter Abelard, composed his own *Dialogue between a Philosopher, a Jew and a Christian*. Two conversations, not one, form the basis of this enigmatic work set in a dream vision: the first between a philosopher and Jew and the second between the same philosopher and a Christian. Civility and politeness also characterize these exchanges, with the Jew even offering a touching description of the social and economic hardships faced by Jews and the philosopher at times appearing more rational than the Christian. Around 1142, the Sephardic Jew Yehuda Halevi gave the first counterpunch along similar lines. His *Kuzari* is a religious disputation set at the court of the Khazar kingdom in which Judaism prevails over the respective claims of Christianity, philosophy, and Islam, thus providing an intriguing comparison to its contemporary Christian polemical counterparts (Novikoff 2007).

The upshot of the twelfth-century focus on reason and disputation was not more civil interfaith discussions but rather a devastating attack on the very humanity of Jews. Around 1147, the illustrious monk Peter the Venerable, the Benedictine abbot of Cluny, concluded that because humans are rational creatures and Jews refuse to accept the rational proof of Christianity, Jews must

Alex Novikoff

therefore be less than human. "I do not know whether I am speaking to a man," Peter writes in his scathing polemic *Against the Inveterate Obstinacy of the Jews*, "I know not whether a Jew is a man because he does not cede to human reason, nor does he acquiesce to the divine authorities which are his own" (Peter the Venerable, *Adversus Iudaeorum inveterum duritiem*, CCCM 58: 127). The faculties of reason being absent among them, or "extinguished" as he pointedly put it, Jews are akin to animals and immune to any spiritual aspirations whatever: "Why are you not called a brute animal, why not a beast, why not a beast of burden? Consider the cow or, if you prefer, the ass—no beast is more stupid...The ass hears but does not understand; the Jew hears but does not understand." Beastly stupidity, irrationality, blasphemy, and an implacable carnality are all charges against Jews that gain currency in the course of Europe's twelfth-century renaissance (Abulafia 1995).

The proclivity for real and imagined disputations in the twelfth century made the *disputatio* a central feature of the new thirteenth-century university curriculum. Yet the university was one of only several institutions to emerge as powerful forces in thirteenth-century society. Pope Innocent III (ruled 1198–1215), the most influential pontiff since Gregory I, was instrumental in helping to bring the University of Paris into being, in establishing the new mendicant orders, and in setting new precedents in the Church's directives against Jews. The Fourth Lateran Council that Innocent convened in 1215 enacted several canons against "Jewish perfidy," one of which expressed concern lest Christians "by mistake" have intercourse with Jewish or Muslim women. To prevent this troubling scenario the council mandated that Jews be distinguished from Christians by the quality of their clothes. England was apparently the first country to decree that Jews actually wear a badge.

In 1217, Henry III ordered that Jews wear a representation of the tables of the Ten Commandments made either of white linen or parchment on the front of their outer garments. As part of a series of discriminatory regulations, the Council of Oxford in 1222 ordered that Jewish men and women wear a linen patch of different color than their clothes, two fingers in width and four in length. This was the first regulation that prescribed a specific size. In France the wearing of the badge was not widely established until 1269, under the reign of Louis IX, although various local counts and provincial councils had attempted to enforce Pope Innocent's legislation earlier in the century. In German lands, for reasons that remain unclear, the wearing of the badge appears not to have been widely practiced until well into the fifteenth century. And in Spain, which is often the exception in matters of interfaith relations, a somewhat remarkable story is that of Bishop Rodrigo Jiménez de Rada of Toledo who not only protested the anti-Jewish decrees in Rome, where he was a delegate at Lateran IV, but actually defied the pope's orders on repeated occasions following the council. When in 1219 Pope Honorius III temporarily suspended the requirement of the badge in Castile, Bishop Rodrigo persisted in his defiance and signed a concordat with

The activities of the two mendicant orders approved by Pope Innocent III, the Dominicans and the Franciscans, also played an important role in the church's increasingly aggressive attitude toward Jews. Unlike earlier monastic orders, the mendicant friars preached their sermons in the open and campaigned in town and country to win over the hearts and minds of Christian heretical groups, Muslims, and Jews. The Order of the Preachers, as the Dominicans were officially called, were especially active in this regard, owing largely to the fact that since its earliest days Dominic and his brethren had been involved in disputations with alleged heretics in southern France. The bloody Albigensian crusade (1209–29) that aimed at eradicating these heretics, also called by Innocent III, resulted in the establishment of an inquisitorial office approved by the papacy and directed by highly educated Dominicans who employed the word and the law, rather than the sword, to enforce Catholic orthodoxy. By the mid-thirteenth century the Dominicans had also absorbed under their jurisdiction the duty of preaching sermons to Jews, to which various papal bulls and royal decrees required that they listen. By the end of the thirteenth century Dominicans were learning Hebrew and Arabic for their missionary purposes in Europe and beyond. While generally speaking more energy was spent prosecuting Christian heretics and missionizing among Muslims, several Dominican preachers took up with considerable zeal the task of converting Jews. A notable example was the Catalan-born Ramón Martí who wrote several important anti-Jewish polemics based on his reading of Jewish sources. His highly charged *Daggers of Faith* (1278) is the first serious effort by a Christian to penetrate Jewish thinking through the scrutiny of Hebrew sources and provides a range of theological and practical points on which to controvert Jews and Judaism. It has been described as representing "the high watermark not only of the mid-thirteenth-century missionizing effort but, in many ways, of medieval Christian proselytizing argumentation against the Jews altogether" (Chazan 1989, 137). In 1278, in part as a consequence of the efforts of Martí and other Dominicans, Pope Nicholas III formally made preaching to Jews part of the apostolate of both the Dominican and Franciscan orders.

A dramatic example of the confluence of thirteenth-century institutions in the evolution of anti-Judaism is the so-called Talmud Trial of 1240 in Paris. In 1236, a Jewish convert named Nicholas Donin wrote a letter to Rome accusing the Talmud of containing calumnies against Christians. Pope Gregory IX responded by sending a letter to all the princes of Europe requesting that copies of the Talmud be seized and removed from circulation. Louis IX of France was the only monarch to respond to the papal request. In 1240, various leaders and exegetes of the Jewish community were summoned to the royal court, where, in the presence of the queen mother, Blanche of Castile, they were required to answer Donin's accusations. Other officials present included several members of the Dominican order and the chancellor of the University of Paris, Odo of Chateauroux. This trial, or public disputation of sorts, effectively combined many of the most influential institutions of thirteenth-century society: the French monarchy, the Dominican order, a university official, and papal direction from Rome. The result was the condemnation of the Talmud and the burning of several wagonloads of Hebrew books in Paris in 1242.

Directly or indirectly related to the new intellectual thrusts of the twelfth and thirteenth centuries and the Crusading violence against Jews in western Europe during the same period is a third level of anti-Jewish hostility that takes the form of popular accusations cast against Jewish religious practices and traditions. In the English town of Norwich in 1144, a Christian boy named William was found dead with stab wounds during the Easter season. In short order the Jewish community stood accused of murdering the child in a ritualized fashion. An account of the life and miracles of William by the monk Thomas of Monmouth embellished the story to accuse the Jews of murdering the child in reenactment of their historic crime of Crucifixion. The legend became something of a cult, with William acquiring the status of saintly martyr and crowds of pilgrims bringing wealth to the local church where it was believed the child's body performed miracles. A similar incident occurred at Blois in northern France in 1171, when the Jewish community was also accused of the ritual murder of a Christian child. Thirty Jews were convicted and executed for the crime, despite the community's ardent appeal to the archbishop and despite the inconvenient fact that no body was ever produced.

During the thirteenth century the accusations of ritual murder evolved into two other separate but related accusations, even as ritual-murder charges continued to be made into the fifteenth century. The better known of these two new accusations is the blood libel, the charge that Jews use the blood of Christian youths to perform rituals associated with the Passover celebration, specifically its central wine rituals. First appearing in Germany about 1235, this particular accusation shifts the focus from the Christian celebration of Easter to the more mysterious (to Christian observers) festival of Passover and has proved remarkably alluring and enduring in the popular imagination, even if church and secular authorities have not always been persuaded by the charges and in some cases specifically condemned them. Indeed the blood libel has manifested itself in nearly every century from the thirteenth century to the present, with curious and disturbing variants appearing in Russia and the Middle East in more recent years (Cohen 2007, 109–17).

The second of the two new thirteenth-century allegations was the charge of host desecration in which Christians claimed that Jews, again because of their historic hatred of Christianity, reenacted the crime of deicide by venting their spleen on the host wafer, which contained the body and blood of Christ. A possible source for the development of this charge is the elevation of the doctrine

The Middle Ages

of transubstantiation to a role of central significance in thirteenth-century Christian theology, although if correct this would again signal a Christian fear predicated on the ignorance of Jewish beliefs since transubstantiation was a doctrine that medieval Jewish polemicists consistently labeled as one of the most perverse deficiencies of the Christian faith. Images of misshapen Jews murdering Christians, draining their blood and/or desecrating the Eucharistic wafer are prevalent in late medieval narratives and iconography (Rubin 2004).

The compound influence of Crusading violence, polemical and institutional attacks, and defamatory popular charges—as well no doubt as other resentments such as against Jewish usurers and moneylenders—yielded some of the most famous manifestations of late medieval anti-Jewish legislation: municipal and royal expulsions. Between the late twelfth century and the end of the fifteenth century Jews were repeatedly expelled from various towns and cities and from entire countries, most notably in France, England, and Spain. Shortly after his coronation in 1180, Philip II Augustus of France, influenced by an accusation of ritual murder, ordered the arrest of all of the Jews in the royal domain, finally confiscating all their goods and expelling them in 1182. Most of the Jews went to the neighboring county of Champagne, from which they were eventually recalled in 1198. Local expulsions in France during the thirteenth century included Brittany (1240), Poitou (1249), Gascony (at the order of Edward I of England in 1288), Anjou and Maine (1289), the county of Nevers (1294), and the town of Niort (c.1296). A much vaster expulsion from all royal lands came in 1306 under the secret instructions of King Philip IV of France, under whom the kingdom included the Ile-de-France, Poitou, Anjou, Champagne, Normandy, and Languedoc (Jordan 1989, 200–38). A succession of temporary recalls and further expulsions over the course of the thirteenth century culminated in a different type of royal expulsion in 1394, one that was based upon a royal decree, invoked certain motives, and in principle did not rob those being expelled. Although many Jews eventually returned to French lands, it prefigured the absolute model of medieval expulsion decreed by Ferdinand and Isabella of Spain in 1492.

Only one expulsion from England is known, in 1290, although this proved to be more lasting than any of the expulsions from France. Throughout the twelfth and thirteenth centuries Jews living in England enjoyed considerable freedom of activity, although their position as moneylenders made them subject to higher taxes and special imposts, especially beginning with the reign of King John (ruled 1199–1216). Proselytizing began on a systematic basis in 1232 with the establishment of the first *Domus Conversorum* (House of Converts) outside of London. In 1275, Edward I effectively put an end to the long tradition of moneylending in England with the promulgation of a statute forbidding Jews to lend money on interest. Other restrictions were also imposed, including the obligation that all Jews over the age of seven wear a felt yellow badge. Jews twelve years of age and older were required to pay a special three-pence tax at Easter (Mundill 1999, 291–3). Finally, in 1290, Edward ordered the expulsion of all the Jews from his lands. All outstanding debts owed to the Jews, along with their real estate, including cemeteries and synagogues, were seized by the Crown. This was in sharp contrast to the expulsion from Spain in 1492, when Jews were allowed to sell their property and collect debts, even after they had left the country. Jews would not return to England until the seventeenth century.

The Middle Ages were decidedly not monolithic. How Jews were conceptualized and treated by Christians and how they fared as an autonomous community depended absolutely on time and place. Absolutely, therefore, it would be erroneous to suggest that a single feature of the medieval mind can explain the violence and persecution that occurred, just as it would be profoundly simplistic to attribute later manifestations of antisemitism directly to aspects of the medieval experience. Yet a steady evolution in the medieval construction of the Jew—the hermeneutical Jew—and the myriad examples of anti-Jewish legislation and harassment on local, royal, and ecclesiastical levels demand the attention of any student of antisemitism and indeed of anyone interested in understanding the complexity of medieval European society. It will also be noted that virtually every modern stereotype of Jews and Judaism can also be found in medieval Europe: the Jew as antiquated and stubborn; the Jew as blind and irrational; the Jew as the enemy of Christ and of Christians; the Jew as ritualistic and cannibalistic; the Jew as greedy moneylender; the Jew as physically deficient; the Jew as less than human; the Jew as a menace to society. How does one comprehend the larger meaning of these images in a premodern age? What implications do they have for better understanding the medieval world, and the modern? Several interpretive models have been put forward to help answer these questions.

One of the most significant voices in the recent historiography of antisemitism has been Gavin Langmuir. A medievalist, Langmuir began in the 1960s by criticizing the state of historiography for failing to account adequately for the Jewish experience in textbooks and other studies of medieval Europe, explicitly suggesting that the lack of proper historical analysis of the subject contributes to false beliefs about Jews and that as a consequence of such silences historians give tacit authorization to the perpetuation of those beliefs. What followed was a series of penetrating articles delineating specific aspects of anti-Jewish beliefs and behavior in the Middle Ages, culminating in two important volumes published simultaneously in 1990: *Toward a Definition of Antisemitism* (which includes many of his earlier articles), and *History, Religion, and Antisemitism* (which explores more generally the nature of religious thought and prejudice). An essential component of Langmuir's definition of antisemitism is the idea that by the thirteenth century Christian perceptions of Jews had evolved beyond theological differences and societal boundaries and had become unsubstantiated irrational fantasies he terms "chimerical." Furthermore, these chimerical fantasies were fundamentally the same in medieval and modern times: "to me at least, it seems clear that, already by the end of the thirteenth century, many Christians in northern Europe were manifesting the same kind of completely irrational

The Middle Ages 77

hostility toward Jews that Hitler would express much more devastatingly six centuries later" (1990, 14–15). The Middle Ages, in short, gave birth to the same antisemitism that led to the Holocaust.

Langmuir's particular definition of antisemitism has not gone unchallenged, but his central thesis has been at least partially corroborated in several equally influential works. Jeremy Cohen's study on *The Friars and the Jews* (1982) focused attention on the role played by the mendicants, arguing that their attacks on rabbinic literature in the thirteenth century contravened the hitherto prevailing Augustinian view and that their efforts to disseminate the new ideology—as missionaries, professors, itinerant preachers, and inquisitors—set the stage for the rise and rapid acceptance of anti-Judaism. R. I. Moore widened the focus with *The Formation of a Persecuting Society* (1987), arguing that the period 950–1250 saw the development of a concerted effort to eradicate minority groups (Jews among them) and that this in turn helped to give Europe its distinctive identity as a "persecuting society." And Anna Sapir Abulafia has continued a line of investigation first opened by Amos Funkenstein in arguing that it is within the polemical and disputational literature of the late eleventh and twelfth centuries that the most noticeable rise in anti-Judaism is to be found. Many other works, including especially those by Robert Chazan, have helped to elucidate the complex nature of medieval anti-Judaism and antisemitism. Predictably, a few have pushed back either to posit a more nuanced understanding of medieval persecutory violence or to rethink altogether the long list of unpleasant acts committed against Jews that the historian Salo Baron once pejoratively called the "lachrymose conception of Jewish history" (Nirenberg 1996; Elukin 2007). For medieval Spain a particularly tendentious historiography has sought, not always helpfully, to characterize the coexistence (or *convivencia*) of Christians, Muslims, and Jews as an era of either "tolerance" or "intolerance" (Novikoff 2005).

It is admittedly difficult to treat a subject as sensitive as antisemitism in a period as distant as the Middle Ages when the horrid memories of recent past still so shape our worldview and color our historical interpretations. Still, medievalists are committed to their labor in the hope that the fruits of judicious historical inquiry will continue to enlighten our understanding of the past and inform our present—for what is the alternative, except the sin of despair?

RECOMMENDED READINGS

Abulafia, Anna Sapir, *Christians and Jews in the Twelfth-Century Renaissance* (London: Routledge, 1995).

Chazan, Robert, *Daggers of Faith: Thirteenth-Century Christian Missionizing and Jewish Response* (Berkeley: University of California Press, 1989).

——*European Jewry and the First Crusade* (Berkeley: University of California Press, 1987).

Alex Novikoff

Chazan, Robert, *Medieval Stereotypes and Modern Antisemitism* (Berkeley: University of California Press, 1997).

Cohen, Jeremy, *Christ Killers: The Jews and the Passion from the Bible to the Big Screen* (Oxford: Oxford University Press, 2007).

—— *Living Letters of the Law: Ideas of the Jew in Medieval Christianity* (Berkeley: University of California Press, 1999).

—— *Sanctifying the Name of God: Jewish Martyrs and Jewish Memories of the First Crusade* (Philadelphia: University of Pennsylvania Press, 2004).

Elukin, Jonathan, *Living Together, Living Apart: Rethinking Jewish-Christian Relations in the Middle Ages* (Princeton: Princeton University Press, 2007).

Fredriksen, Paula, *Augustine and the Jews: A Christian Defense of Jews and Judaism* (New York: Doubleday, 2008).

Jordan, William Chester, *The French Monarchy and the Jews: From Philip Augustus to the Last Capetians* (Philadelphia: University of Pennsylvania Press, 1989).

Langmuir, Gavin, *Toward a Definition of Antisemitism* (Berkeley: University of California Press, 1990).

Mundill, John R., *England's Jewish Solution: Experiment and Expulsion* (Cambridge: Cambridge University Press, 1999).

Nirenberg, David, *Communities of Violence: Persecution of Minorities in the Middle Ages* (Princeton: Princeton University Press, 1996).

Novikoff, Alex, "Between Tolerance and Intolerance in Medieval Spain: An Historiographic Enigma," *Medieval Encounters* 11 (2005): 7–36.

—— "Reason and Natural Law in the Disputational Writings of Peter Alfonsi, Peter Abelard, and Yehuda Halevi," in Michael Frassetto (ed.), *Christian Attitudes toward the Jews in the Middle Ages: A Casebook* (London: Routledge, 2007).

Peters, Edward (ed.), *The First Crusade*, 2nd edn (Philadelphia: University of Pennsylvania Press, 1995).

Pick, Lucy, *Conflict and Coexistence: Archbishop Rodrigo and the Muslims and Jews of Medieval Spain* (Ann Arbor: University of Michigan Press, 2004).

Riley-Smith, Jonathan, "Christian Violence and the Crusades," in Anna Sapir Abulafia (ed.), *Religious Violence between Christians and Jews: Medieval Roots, Modern Perspectives* (Hampshire: Palgrave, 2002), 3–20.

Rubin, Miri, *Gentile Tales: The Narrative Assault on Late Medieval Jews* (Philadelphia: University of Pennsylvania Press, 2004).

5

Antisemitism in the Late Medieval and Early Modern Periods

Ralph Keen

INTRODUCTION

When bubonic plague brought terror and death to Europe's mercantile cities in the middle of the fourteenth century, Christians responded, as they had since the Crusades, with expulsions of Jews. Fear of divine wrath provoked new movements of religious cleansing, or pogroms. The failure of such efforts to reduce the spread of plague exacerbated medieval Judeophobia, while the lingering of the epidemic intensified anxieties over divine displeasure with the state of Christendom (Foa 2000, Ch. 1). The notion that at least part of that displeasure was caused by the continuing presence of Jews goes back to the patristic era of the early Church Fathers (Wilkin 1983).

Christian anti-Judaism was so thoroughly woven into the fabric of late medieval culture that the Jew was the perennial other in a world otherwise short on certainties. Among religious beliefs, one certainty was that Christianity was a new divine-human covenant, successor to the old one and exclusive of those persons who adhered to the prior covenant by continuing to hope for redemption and restoration. Ever since the first centuries of Christianity, the coexistence of covenants was considered a theological impossibility (Langmuir 1992; Parkes 1979, 95–106). This conviction endured persistently during an age of unprecedented change in religious thought.

Without much cost to historical exactitude, European Jewish communities in the late medieval and early modern periods can be categorized according to the forms and degrees of instability that they experienced. The succession of dislocations beginning in England in the 1290s and ending with the Iberian expulsion of the 1490s had intensified a sense of vulnerability present since the Roman conquest of Judea. After the outbreak of the plague, the migrations of the late fourteenth century were for many of the Rhineland or Ashkenazic communities a new Diaspora, one in which a measure of mercantile prosperity was replaced with near subsistence conditions of the east European *shtetls*. In the sixteenth and seventeenth centuries, Sephardic communities displaced from the Iberian Peninsula found refuge in the mercantile cities of the North and along the Mediterranean, with some intentionally Messianic settlements in Palestine, geographically closer to Zion but chronologically just as far from redemptive restoration (Werblowsky 1997). "Tenuous" may generally describe diasporic existence over the centuries, but the interpreter of Jewish history during this era of seismic change at the end of the Middle Ages and the beginning of the early modern era must address the factors that made Jewish life in early modernity not merely insecure but unprecedentedly precarious.

Shifting cultural conditions notwithstanding, attitudes and policies toward Jews during the Reformation era were grounded more deeply in religious anti-Judaism than in other constructions of difference. As a result, forms of anti-Jewish sentiment in the sixteenth and seventeenth centuries were determined in large part by the ways in which the mainstream cultures understood their Christianity. Since the early modern period is marked by new efforts to understand the meaning of the church, it follows that the boundaries between Christianity and Judaism were likewise in flux during the Reformation era.

ON THE EVE OF THE REFORMATION

The conventional image of medieval Christendom is not entirely an historical fiction, but it is not the entire truth either. Beneath overarching structures like the Roman Church and the Holy Roman Empire lay regional differences that determined in large measure how each territory defined and treated outsiders. Urban commercial centers differed widely from agrarian communities; and monarchical rule operated far differently from civic republicanism. These variegations are perhaps obvious, but it is important to note that one's membership in a given community was tied in some way to what kind of a community it was.

That being said, Jews collectively held an image in the Christian imagination that had endured almost as long as the Church itself. Religious anti-Judaism rested in apostolic and patristic portrayals of Christian beginnings, in which the first-century Jewish community willfully rejected the Messianic redemption they had been seeking for so long. Holding the Jewish community accountable for the Crucifixion, although a separate idea with its own context, complemented that reading of the New Testament sources. Whatever the archaeology of the idea and no matter how false in its selection of evidence, Jews were generally seen as repudiators of Christianity rather than as outsiders adhering to a positive religious choice regarding redemption. For those who assumed that the Covenant divinely initiated with Abraham had been continued yet transformed with Christianity, adherents to the Old Law were members of a covenant now rendered false (Bonfil 1994).

Antisemitism in the Late Medieval and Early Modern Periods   81

Given the dominance of Christianity, both normatively and descriptively, Jews in the early modern period might at best have enjoyed toleration, but even there the grounds of survival were fragile and the limited freedom often short-lived. In point of fact, the sixteenth and seventeenth centuries were a time of Christian definition and consolidation; relations with Jews were determined by how the dominant communities defined themselves as Christian social organisms.

By the fifteenth century, antagonism toward Jews had extended beyond religious exclusivity to the economic and cultural terrains, fueled in part by condemnations of Jewish moneylending (canon law had prohibited such commerce among Christians) as well as by rumors of anti-Christian propaganda and recurrences of the blood libel. With anxiety over divine wrath at fever pitch during these decades of plague, Jews were readily available scapegoats and often were subjected to punitive civil restrictions and in many cases expulsion—usually to regions equally inhospitable.

By the end of the fifteenth century, the Catholic Church (not "Roman" in the conventional sense until later) was unified more in theory than in fact. Ideally it was uniform throughout its religious jurisdiction, hierarchical in organization, and—according to its own claims—the sole means toward eternal salvation. In practice, on the other hand, regional differences in relations between the secular and ecclesiastical powers accounted for a fairly wide range of policies toward how inclusive or exclusive a given territory might be. We should also recognize that the disciplinary activities of the Church were intended to correct here-sies, that is, errors in Christian belief and practice, rather than convert those outside the Christian fold. It was only when rulers sought to ensure total Catholi-cism in their lands that the Church turned its efforts outward. The notorious instance of such Christianizing of a nation state was the expulsions of Jews from Spain in 1492 and from Portugal in 1497 (Edwards 1988, 11–38).

Whatever the intentions of these Catholic rulers, the effects of the actions by the unified Castilian-Aragonese monarchy were to dislocate a people inhabiting that part of the Mediterranean since before the dawn of Christianity. The Iberian dislocation drove many Jews to regions unprepared for the influx, prompting in some cases new expressions of resistance to a Jewish presence. In Spain itself, a number of prominent Jewish converts or *conversos* became intensely pious Cath-olics, to the point of sharing in the Christian anti-Judaism so prevalent in the West for a millennium. While such antagonism may have been a shibboleth of acceptance in a Christian environment, in point of fact such zeal did not still the fears of Christians. The sheer number of *conversos* led Spain to institute Pure Blood Laws, relegating the convert population to subordinate status alongside the old Christians of Gentile blood (Friedman 1987).

Several Mediterranean Jewish communities were transformed as a result of other factors. In the wake of the fall of Constantinople in 1453, migrations of Greek scholars and rabbis from the East opened vistas into the long eclipsed legacies of classical and Judaic antiquity. Christian scholars gave fresh attention to ancient Judaism, valued not in itself so much as for being the precursor to Christianity (Rummel 2006). Humanists from northern Europe traveled to Italy to study with rabbis, learning not only scripture but Talmud and parts of the medieval liturgical and mystical traditions. There are no reports that these relations were anything but amicable, but they set the stage for confrontations among Christians. One of these conflicts has been seen as a flash-point in Christian attitudes to Judaism (Overfield 1984, 247–97).

The antagonists in the confrontation were Johann Pfefferkorn (*c.*1469–*c.*1522), a converted Jew with little learning but with supporters among the Dominicans, and Johann Reuchlin, a Christian humanist and jurist, a layperson (he would enter the Augustinian order in 1516) in the Württemberg court who had studied Hebrew with the court physician, Jacob ben Jehiel Loans, and later in Rome with Obadiah Sforno, a rabbi of almost legendary fame. Reuchlin was also the leading Christian kabbalist north of the Alps, and a humanist who found mystical value in the Hebrew text. Pfefferkorn, with his convert's zeal, sought to burn all the available copies of talmudic literature and compel Jews to attend Christian services (Kirn 1989). Reuchlin, who (like most Christians at the time) hoped that Jews would eventually convert to Christianity, vigorously defended the preservation of Jewish books, appealing, in order to make his case, to imperial law protecting private property (Reuchlin 2000). Reuchlin's Jewish contemporaries lauded his support as heroic, and the episode has been called a noble one in the history of tolerance. Even so, the dramatic episode did not lead to a major breakthrough in Jewish-Christian relations, which afterward remained largely unchanged. Reuchlin's concern was for the preservation of Jewish books, and his reasons were religious and academic ones: such material was necessary first of all for understanding Christian origins, and secondly for effective missionary work. The rights of individual Jews needed protecting because they, if no one else, would be reliable guardians of their written heritage.

REFORMATION FOUNDATIONS

The Reformation was a reaction to the practices of the Roman Church, but scholars tend to gloss over the fact that the reformers saw their relation to the dominant Catholicism as parallel to the relation the earliest Christian apostolic community bore to Second Temple Judaism as they understood it. Martin Luther was an heir to the medieval struggle for righteousness before God, but also an innovator in conceptualizing grace as the promise of forgiveness for the inability to fulfill the divine demand. Constructing their understanding of Christian origins from an interpretation of certain New Testament books, the reformers, led by Luther's reading of St. Paul, saw the Christian gospel as a nullification

Antisemitism in the Late Medieval and Early Modern Periods   83

(or in some senses a fulfillment) of the Old Law, with the implied correlate being that any subsequent form of legalism was a denial of Christ.

It is a commonplace among historians of early Protestantism that the reformers saw themselves as the new evangelists against Roman legalism, reprising the role of Jesus and the first Christians against the Pharisees of the first-century Temple cult. Superficially, the parallel holds up, but it masks some complex assumptions about the early church and its relation to the religious soil in which it took root. While scholars would now find it unacceptable to hold that Christianity began as a rebellion against Second Temple Judaism, in the early modern period the state of historical knowledge was limited enough to allow humanists and reformers to portray Church and Temple in mutually adversarial terms. And let us not be naïve: the reformers' opposition to the Roman Church conditioned their reading of the early Christian texts; what they confronted in the sixteenth century, they read back into the narratives of the apostolic era.

Thus *Judaizing* and related terms were applied to the Catholic Church rather than to the Jewry of the Reformation era, and their rhetorical force was fueled by a caricature of Jewish legalism more than by any actual comparisons between Romanism and either ancient or contemporary Judaism. The covenant of works, which Paul contrasted with the Christian covenant of faith, became the basis for a latter-day contrast between the Catholic emphasis on works and the reformers' concentration on faith alone as the necessary condition for salvation. Rhetorical fervor, Paul's as well as Luther's, intensified the polarity, so that the Romanists' Judaizing became equated with Catholic works-righteousness. By contrast, the reformers' "gospel" became associated with "solafideism," the doctrine that only faith is the source of salvation. The antithesis was surely exaggerated, and Catholics and Protestants in later decades sought to correct it; but polemically it proved effective indeed.

The Jews of early modern Europe sustained collateral damage from the reformers' polemics, even though they were not the intended objects of early Protestant invective. The success of the anti-Romanist agenda depended on maintaining, even intensifying, a specific Jewish stereotype: scrupulous in the material details of purity and ritual, fearful of a law-giving deity rather than receptive to a redeeming one, and overly trusting in the authority of a priestly caste. This third characteristic, intended as an indictment of the Catholic hierarchy's claims to divine power, suggests that Diaspora Jewry has been a rudderless ship, a tradition without the leadership to give it coherence and direction, but with the healthy skepticism to resist obeying the Roman papacy.

One question that confronts interpreters of Reformation thought is whether the caricature of Judaism preceded the view of the Roman Church or the other way around. The reformers identified Catholicism with Judaism so consistently that whatever stereotype of Judaism was already present in the popular imagination was powerfully reinforced by their polemics against Rome. As we noted, at the dawn of the Reformation the pejorative that stuck to the Roman Church was "Judaizers." And all, presumably, knew that that had referred to *conversos* who continued to practice their law privately (Yerushalmi 1970).

For the reformers, what it meant specifically was undue confidence in humanity's ability to fulfill the commands of divine law. In the minds of the reformers, original sin had so incapacitated the human faculties that the ability to know—much less to fulfill—the divine will was compromised beyond human aid. Revealed law was in one respect a remedy, insofar as the Decalogue prescribed conduct necessary for social survival, but in another respect was meant to confound rather than embolden the people to whom it was revealed. Scrupulous attention to the demands of the law, when driven by fear of divine wrath, was the antithesis, so the reformers felt, to the original purpose of revealed law. The proper purpose of divine law, in their view, was to guide the confounded and humbled person to the grace of divine forgiveness promised in the gospel.

It is important then to recognize that, however negatively first-century Judaism is portrayed in early Reformation literature, Protestant views of its late medieval heirs were ambivalent. While theological anti-Judaism remained strong, the Jews' resistance to the Catholic Church counted in their favor. Hence Luther at the beginning of his reforming work saw the Jews as both a witness against Romanism and as a people potentially receptive to his evangelizing efforts. However, the residual anti-Judaism and neo-Pauline denigration of outward works—the latter a critical component of Protestant anti-Romanism—would have posed strong obstacles to any proselytizing initiatives, had any been attempted.

Two factors hindered even the beginnings of such efforts. One was surely the anti-Judaism of Jewish converts to Christianity, who in their converts' zeal described their ancestral people as obstinate despisers of the Church in either its Roman or its Evangelical manifestation. They might not have meant this; in fact, there is room for believing that these ostensibly anti-Jewish sentiments were actually a tactic to inhibit the evangelization of the Diaspora communities. The second hindrance to conversion lay in the political alliances the reformers forged with their secular rulers. In particular, the theologians held that civil government had sole coercive power within their territories, and from the 1520s onward, and especially in the second half of the century, this power extended in various degrees over religious life and practice. In practical terms, even more ambiguous than the theories at work, Christian monarchs might be able to compel total conformity to a single rule of faith, or at the other extreme to allow a multiconfessional coexistence, whereby a Jewish presence would enjoy a measure of toleration. Instances of the latter were rare and became rarer still with the rise of Absolutism, the political doctrine that granted secular rulers absolute control over their subjects' religious lives.

LUTHER AND THE JEWS

Jews were the indirect casualties of Luther's polemic against Catholicism. Martin Luther is not the whole Reformation but he often represents it when early modern anti-Judaism is the topic (Kaufmann 2006; Lindberg 1995, 15–35). Luther's writings have been blamed for the rise of German antisemitism, and in the middle of the past century he became an Aryan icon. (Lutheran churches have issued formal apologies to Jewish congregations around the globe.) While some biographers have attached substantial weight to Luther's anti-Jewish writings (Marius 1999, 372–80), others have attempted to minimize or at least to contextualize them (Oberman 1989, 292–7; Edwards 1983, 115–42). Although getting to the heart of the matter would require a hefty volume in itself, it may still be useful to ponder some of Luther's own statements about Jews and Judaism.

As the agent of a new "Pauline turn" in Christian history, Luther accentuated the contrasts between the externals of the Mosaic covenant and the inwardness of the Christian one. Scholars during the past few decades have come to recognize that Paul's dichotomy of covenants was exaggerated; during Luther's time the parallels between the Roman Church of his time and the Temple cult of Paul's went largely unquestioned. Luther's (and Paul's) choice of circumcision as symbolic of the external ritual of the Mosaic covenant accentuated the contrast between the Old Law and the New. Reaching into the Patriarchal narrative, Luther in his 1517 *Lectures on Romans* asserted that Abraham's righteousness was his faith in the divine promise and not in his acquiescence to the demand to sacrifice Isaac (LW 25:35–7). Luther held Abraham to be the spiritual progenitor of the covenantal people, the "father in faith," with his descendants being Jews and Gentiles alike. Luther saw that the Gentiles (who had no Old Law from which to be liberated) embraced the message, but the Jews, to their damnation (so he felt), did not.

Luther's characterization of Judaism has specific anomalies, such as the apparent confusion of the ritual and purity laws of revelation on Sinai with the anthropological condition of sinfulness from which the Christian gospel is the promise of liberation. In particular, Luther seems to conflate the ritual legalism of externally scrupulous Judaism with the bondage to the flesh that he describes as the common property of all persons. The gospel, for Luther, signifies freedom from bondage; but whether that bondage was to the human condition or to the impossible demands of the divine law was a function of his rhetorical intent at any given moment. With some certainty we can say that when the target was the legalism of the Catholic Church, the Jews were the demonized proxies for the priestly cult of the Roman "Temple."

Jesus was born a Jew: few statements are less controversial than that from the standpoint of history. Whether he also died as one, however, is a question to which faith, rather than history, claims to hold the answer. So it was in 1523,

86 *Ralph Keen*

when Luther wrote his essay on this topic. For Luther, Jesus was the Incarnation and hence the turning point in the divine-human relationship, the inaugurator of the covenant of grace replacing the covenant of works. Luther saw in Diaspora Jewry a potential ally in the Evangelical cause; in his view, the Jews had resisted conversion to Romanism because its legalism was little more than the replacement of one system of ritual legalism with another one, with the Roman "Temple" being just as confining as the Jerusalem one. But as Luther believed, Jesus was also the redeemer whom the Jews of the Second Temple period sought, their error being their expectation of an earthly restoration rather than an otherworldly one. In other words, for Luther, Jesus was born a Jew but became the first Evangelical. And it was the task of latter-day Evangelicals, like the reformers, to continue Jesus's work among his people. This stance, occasionally called Christian philo-Judaism, is a strategic basis for proselytizing and, religiously at least, seeks the obliteration of autonomous Judaism (Kinzig 1994).

Twenty years later it had become clear to Luther that Jews would not convert *en masse* to the Evangelical faith. Construing this as evidence of Jewish stubbornness, the older Luther embarked on the virulent polemic against the Jews that ensured his notoriety ever since. In *On the Jews and Their Lies* (1543), an attack that is consistent only in its invective, Luther ranges from the ancestry of Japhet (whom he considers Noah's first-born son) to the identity of Shiloh, passing through such questions as the significance and uniqueness of circumcision (LW 47:147–8, 151–5, 186–8, 197). The work follows no discernible sequence and its underlying assumption, that the Jews are dishonest by nature, can only be substantiated by circular assertions. Toward the end, Luther claims that God had rendered the Jews insensible to the truth of the gospel (LW 47:67). The notion is found among the Church Fathers; the zeal with which it was expressed was Luther's own.

BEYOND WITTENBERG

All too often the first decades of the Reformation in Wittenberg (Saxony) are assumed to be the source from which all religious reform in the early modern period sprang, and the assumption is at least partially justified in many cases. However, a sense of common legacy comes apart when we turn to Geneva (Switzerland) in the middle decades of the sixteenth century, and to the Calvinist, or more correctly reformed, tradition that took shape there. For our topic the critical distinction occurs between evangelical and reformed attitudes to biblical law. Yet, as in Wittenberg, reformed perceptions of and policies toward Jews were products of the Christian community's self-understanding.

Usually grouped with Lutheranism in the category of magisterial reform movements—those imposed upon subjects by secular leadership, whether

Antisemitism in the Late Medieval and Early Modern Periods 87

monarchical or representative—the reformed tradition differs from its Wittenberg-based counterpart in one critical respect relevant to our subject: the role of divine law in the life of the believer. What is known as the Third Use of the Law is the explicit insistence among the reformed that divine law remains active, after grace, as a regulative norm in the Christian life. The Third Use means that, confounded by the inability to fulfill the demands of the law (the First Use) and directed to the divine forgiveness promised in the gospel (the Second), the Christian believer then applies his or her energy to revealed biblical law, embracing it gratefully, as a gift from God, rather than out of fear of divine wrath.

Calvin's undeniable importance in shaping the reformed tradition was mainly concentrated in writings of rigorous theology and exegesis; thus his attitudes to the Jews have not drawn as much attention as Luther's more topical interventions. Truth to tell, they are also less controversial than Luther's. On the other hand, Calvin's antipathy toward the Roman Church was trenchant and consistent, and his rhetoric drew some of the same parallels between Rome and the Jerusalem Temple found among his German counterparts (Baron 1969, 285–91). Accepting the dominant view that Jewish legalism could only bring anxiety to the conscience, Calvin accuses the Roman Church of inculcating a harmful scrupulosity in ritual (Calvin, *Inst.* iv.10.3; Calvin 1960, 1191).

Regarding relations between Christianity and Judaism, reformed and evangelical (Lutheran) doctrines are strictly distinct, and the defining boundary is the reformed doctrine of the use of biblical law. Like Luther, Calvin felt that the Easter event represented the end of Judaic legalism, and that the rituals and purity codes of the Old Law had been fulfilled and negated in Christ. But unlike Luther (although some interpreters see affinities between Calvin and Luther on this point), Calvin affirmed that biblical law continued to regulate the behavior of the faithful Christian, even after he or she had been released by the gospel of the fear of divine punishment. For Calvin and the reformed tradition that followed, Mosaic law is not set aside or superseded by the gospel; it continues as a norm for the conduct of the believing community. And observing it properly and rigorously is of paramount importance.

Thus in the eyes of the Swiss reformers, the Judaic remnant in the Diaspora was adhering to an improper legalism, one dominated by fear and expectation rather than observance motivated by freedom and gratitude. The effect of this difference was to locate the division between Jews and (reformed) Christians in the pious disposition as much as in external observance. That is to say, they were separate peoples in their intentions. To be sure, Mosaic law was not carried forward unaltered into the lived religion of the reformed; the defining practices were adaptations rather than adoptions. Most notable and durable was the importance of the Sabbath, strictly regulated and emphatically observed—on Sunday.

If Calvin imagined that his community would be the most perfect form of Christianity since the Apostles' own day, he was voicing an ideal in which the early Church was more continuous with the Old Covenant than his Saxon contemporaries seemed to believe. Specifically, Calvin held that the law is not superseded (*abrogated* is the theological term) in the Christian covenant, but rather holds a uniquely compelling regulatory power in the life of the believer. In brief, the Christian believer adheres faithfully to the law as a guide to what God desires from him or her. The Third Use of the Law ensured that reformed churches would be intentionally "Hebraic" in several ways, with a strict disciplinary system and enforced Sabbath observance, but without priestly sacrifices since the Christian Atonement was the final one. Ancient Judaism enjoyed unprecedented prestige among the spiritual followers of Calvin.

As for the flesh and blood Jews on the other side of the reformed covenant, the experience was far different. In their continued observance of the Old Law, they erred doubly: first, by failing to see that revealed law was meant to confound those attempting it (and hence sinfully persisting in trying to fulfill it), and second, by refusing the consolation of divine forgiveness offered by the gospel (and thus continuing to try to merit a grace that can only be freely given by God). Thus while the Third Use of the Law raised the Old Covenant to a new normative level, the first two uses had the effect of further marginalizing early modern Jewry.

As the reformed tradition expanded, however, policies toward Jews became slightly more elastic, whatever the religious attitudes may have been. In the Netherlands, for example, Calvinism secured a strong position in the commercial cities with substantial Jewish populations of long standing and even larger groups of Sephardic emigrants driven from the Iberian Peninsula at the end of the fifteenth century. Anti-Spanish (Habsburg) sentiment may have compounded the antagonism to Catholicism among the early Dutch Calvinists to render Jews the enemy's enemies, and hence friends to these Protestants under foreign domination, but such a convoluted explanation does not completely account for the more tolerant stance. The critical factor is simply that Calvinism was a minority confession in the Netherlands; that it was not a reformed commonwealth on the Geneva model; and that tolerance was as much needed by the minority church as it was by the Jews.

Lutheranism expanded primarily through the Germanic territories and northward, where Jewish communities were sparse and enjoyed the benevolent protection of their sovereigns. Calvinism, by contrast, quickly became an international movement that took root in various grades of political soil, including the newer constitutional states forming alongside the hereditary monarchies. Absolutist Christian rulers might have the power to decree that all their subjects be Christian, but democratic republics tended to set different conditions for citizenship. And as indicated earlier, the economic importance of the Jewish population of a territory often played a significant role in the shaping of policies of toleration.

ABSOLUTISM AND TOLERANCE

Constructions of national or regional identity in part fueled the territorial principle that has recently been absorbed under the rubric of confessionalization, that is, the historical approach that sees political identity shaped by the ruling power's adherence to a statement of faith, or confession. In the German lands the popularity of Tacitus's *Germania* (brought to new light in 1515 by the humanist Ulrich von Hutten) contributed to an ethnic consciousness that in earlier periods was only latent or altogether absent. Although a unified German state was still centuries away, more and more material appeared in the vernacular, and a writer like Luther could address the German people as compatriots. With such incipient cultural self-awareness came a sense of religious identity that identified authentic Germanness with Evangelical Christianity. And although there was still an impermeable boundary separating Christians and non-Christians, the shift of power in matters of religion from the Roman Church to the civil sovereign meant that each ruler now had the power to determine religious life in his territory.

Despite Luther's professed distrust of civil rulers, by the end of his life the territorial principle had taken hold sufficiently for him to imagine the confessional states that would constitute the political landscape in the following centuries. The secular sovereigns, in the interest of religion, would have been entirely within their rights to expel the Jews and (in some jurisdictions) confiscate their property: that is, to carry out exactly what Luther described in *On the Jews and Their Lies*. These measures could certainly have been taken but generally were not (Christians of opposing confessions were subjected to similarly harsh treatment more often); where moderation prevailed, expediency rather than religious toleration may have been the operative factor.

Religious history in the seventeenth century was dominated by the reformed tradition in its various manifestations, most notably in its sectarian forms. Calvin's confessional heirs took to new levels his ambitions to create an apostolic community, resorting at times to violent resistance against rulers they feared might threaten their piety. Reminiscent of Jewish resistance to Roman domination, revolutionary Calvinism was based on a strenuous identification with the covenantal people, a self-fashioning rigorously exclusive of the heirs of those early resisters against Rome. Sociological similarities aside, the religious conviction that God established only one covenant placed the radical Calvinists in antithetical opposition to their Jewish counterparts and forerunners. Because—and only because—of the closed nature of these reformed communities, there were few instances of actual anti-Jewish persecution.

Sectarianism was rife within Judaism itself at this time, especially among émigré Sephardic populations. Among the communities that found a home in northern Europe, the divisions among congregations in Amsterdam seem to have been especially sharp. Resettled in a tolerant mercantile setting after migrations that took them from the Iberian Peninsula to South America, these Sephardic families were converts, in their own way, to a stricter Judaism than their ancestors might have practiced. Lacking rabbinical leaders from within their own communities, these congregations called leaders from other regions who they thought were able to guide them in faith and practice. As a result a vigilant, even competitive, zeal for correctness began to show itself, with a notable casualty being one of the most creative minds among them: Baruch Spinoza. Condemned—in fact, banished from the community—for "heresies and abominations" that have never been clearly understood, Spinoza has been deemed a martyr to religious intolerance of intellectual independence. Less frequently acknowledged is the role that anti-Jewish intolerance, going back to 1490s Spain, played in setting off this sequence of events. The expulsion of Spinoza was not a case of anti-Jewish persecution turning inward as much as a product of the successive dislocations certain communities experienced during these centuries.

Spinoza himself was one of the eminent advocates of freedom of thought and expression, and in his own work held that restrictions on such freedom only exacerbated the ages old mutual hostility of Christians and Jews. Oppression and resentment, Spinoza felt, could be remedied by tolerance in the realm of ideas. But only in the next century would his proposals be taken up and help to usher in an era less dominated by religious controversy than his own.

The aftershocks of the Reformation reverberated well into the seventeenth century; it was only with the dawn of the Enlightenment that new terms, such as individual freedom and secular social order, began to change the civil status of Jews. Until then, political discourse was dominated, though not exclusively, with the question of how a Christian territory or state might best function as one. What ought the adjective in the political concept "Christian nation" really to signify?

The Protestant states underwent upheavals originating in part in the territorial principle. The Thirty Years War (1618–48) pitted Lutheran and reformed states against each other; devastated economies as well as the landscape; and signified the beginning of the end of Absolutism. In its place the discourse of tolerance, marginal in the sixteenth century, reappeared in new form. Whether from expediency or an enlightened attitude toward doctrinal differences, toleration entered mainstream political thought toward the end of the seventeenth century. In scope and application, however, this tended to be strictly limited to Christian confessions, and not even all of those: a Protestant ruler might still exclude Catholicism (often regarded as an alien sovereign power) in the interest of preserving social order. Judaism in its fragmented and fragile state posed no similar threat, but Jewish culture and language articulated an otherness that was difficult to reconcile.

This question of what defined a Christian nation was not so urgent in the Catholic lands where the division of jurisdictions between secular and

Antisemitism in the Late Medieval and Early Modern Periods 91

ecclesiastical powers remained largely stable. Early modern Catholicism strived for an intentional strengthening of the Catholic Church, amounting in some sectors to a new initiative to Christianize Europe (and beyond). As it was conceived, the task involved expanding the powers of the Inquisition. The agency that had been the enforcer of doctrinal orthodoxy in the later Middle Ages now became a missionary arm as well, in effect compelling non-Catholics to obedience to the Roman Church. The Inquisition gained its reputation for ruthlessness during this period, and tensions between the church and the Jewish communities in its midst were painfully intensified. With harsh sanctions aimed at eliminating the *converso* population for fear of subversive elements, the Spanish Inquisition became a shaper in the racialization of Jewish identity: Jewishness was in the blood and hence not nullified by conversion to Christianity.

While all generalizations are hazardous, this much can be said with some accuracy: the reforms of Christianity that shaped so much of the social history of the early modern period did little to relieve the plight of Jews in their western European Diaspora. On the contrary, the phenomenon of confessionalization may have worsened their condition, having consolidated ecclesiastical and political identities and, moreover, reinforcing religious obedience with the powers of the state. Confessionalization, as it is now understood, allowed an intensification of the exclusiveness that Jacob Katz describes as the defining quality of medieval Christendom (24–7). Whereas Jews had enjoyed civil protection from their monarchs, beneficiaries of a formalized marginality, the rulers' possession of religious power jeopardized the tenuous security of Catholic Christendom.

While tolerance continued to be practiced in those territories where it was expedient to do so, as a value in its own right it would not enter the realm of mainstream social thought until the Enlightenment. By that time confessional divisions and controversies had exhausted the populace both rhetorically and militarily. By the end of two centuries of conflict, it would be clear that medieval civilization had held more reliable guarantees of tolerance than Reformation era Christianity.

CONCLUDING REMARKS

By the end of the seventeenth century, the Jewish remnant had a role in intellectual life similar in importance to that which earlier generations had held in economic life. The early Enlightenment was a rebirth of learning along different lines from its humanist predecessor in at least one respect: critical study of the Bible demanded a level of knowledge of Hebrew that only Jewish authorities possessed. Also during these decades, when antiquity was being viewed in new ways, the proselytizing philosemitism of the early reformers continued to be found among Christian theologians.

Both medieval Catholicism and Reformation era Protestantism harbored forms of Christian anti-Judaism, yet each held to its own species of opposition. As soon as we look past the generalizations, we find it difficult to say whether the two forms are related or distinct. To the extent that they are grounded in a religious view of the relation of Judaism to Christianity, they are obviously related— and equally distinct from the racial antisemitism that would follow in the nineteenth and twentieth centuries. But the new ways in which the early modern period understood the defining properties of Christian culture point to a seismic shift separating medieval Christendom and the dawn of modernity. Henceforth Judaism indicated a cultural or ethnic tradition as well as the religion allegedly superseded by Christianity. Whether motivated by religious or political interests, or an unstable combination of both, the creation of the early modern state allowed for new mechanisms of exclusion.

CITED PRIMARY SOURCES

Calvin, John, *Institutes of the Christian Religion*, ed. John T. McNeill (Philadelphia: Westminster Press, 1960).

Luther, Martin, *Luther's Works, American Edition*, 55 vols, ed. J. Pelikan and H. Lehman (Philadelphia: Fortress Press, 1955–86).

Reuchlin, Johannes, *Recommendation Whether to Confiscate, Destroy and Burn All Jewish Books*, ed. and trans. Peter Wortsman (Mahwah, NJ: Paulist Press, 2000).

RECOMMENDED READINGS

Baron, Salo Wittmayer, *A Social and Religious History of the Jews*, vol. 13 (Philadelphia: Jewish Publication Society, 1969).

Bonfil, Robert, "Aliens Within: The Jews and Antijudaism," in Thomas A. Brady, Heiko A. Oberman, and James D. Tracy (eds), *Handbook of European History 1400– 1600*, 2 vols (Leiden: E. J. Brill, 1994), 1:263–96.

Edwards, John, *The Jews in Christian Europe 1400–1700* (London/New York: Routledge, 1988).

Edwards, Mark U., Jr., *Luther's Last Battles: Politics and Polemics, 1531–46* (Ithaca: Cornell University Press, 1983).

Foa, Anna, *The Jews of Europe after the Black Death* (Berkeley: University of California Press, 2000).

Friedman, Jerome, "Jewish Conversion, the Spanish Pure Blood Laws and Reformation: A Revisionist View of Racial and Religious Antisemitism," *Sixteenth Century Journal* 18 (1987): 3–30.

Katz, Jacob, *Exclusiveness and Tolerance: Studies in Jewish-Gentile Relations in Medieval and Modern Times* (New York: Schocken, 1962).

Kaufmann, Thomas, "Luther and the Jews," in Dean Phillip Bell and Stephen G. Burnett (eds), *Jews, Judaism, and the Reformation in Sixteenth-Century Germany* (Leiden: E. J. Brill, 2006), 69–104.

Kinzig, Wolfram, "Philosemitismus: Zur Geschichte des Begriffs," *Zeitschrift für Kirchengeschichte* 105 (1994): 202–28.

Kirn, Hans-Martin, *Das Bild vom Juden in Deutschland des frühen 16. Jahrhunderts dargestellt an den Schriften Johannes Pfefferkorns* (Tübingen: J. C. B. Mohr, 1989).

Langmuir, Gavin I., "The Faith of Christians and Hostility to Jews," in Diana Wood (ed.), *Christianity and Judaism* (Oxford: Blackwell, 1992), 77–92.

Lindberg, Carter, "Tainted Greatness: Luther's Attitudes Toward Judaism and Their Historical Reception," in Nancy Anne Harrowitz (ed.), *Tainted Greatness: Antisemitism and Cultural Heroes* (Philadelphia: Temple University Press, 1995).

Marius, Richard, *Martin Luther: The Christian between God and Death* (Cambridge, MA: Harvard University Press, 1999).

Oberman, Heiko A., *Luther: Man between God and the Devil*, trans. E. Walliser-Schwarzbart (New Haven: Yale University Press, 1989).

Overfield, James H., *Humanism and Scholasticism in Late Medieval Germany* (Princeton: Princeton University Press, 1984).

Parkes, James, *The Conflict of the Church and the Synagogue: A Study in the Origins of Antisemitism* (New York: Atheneum, 1979).

Rummel, Erika, "Humanists, Jews, and Judaism," in Dean Phillip Bell and Stephen G. Burnett (eds), *Jews, Judaism, and the Reformation in Sixteenth-Century Germany* (Leiden: E. J. Brill, 2006), 3–31.

Werblowsky, R. J. Zwi, "The Safed Revival and Its Aftermath," in Arthur Green (ed.), *Jewish Spirituality*, 2 vols (New York: Crossroad, 1997), 2:7–33.

Wilkin, Robert L., *John Chrysostom and the Jews: Rhetoric and Reality in the Late Fourth Century* (Berkeley: University of California Press, 1983).

Yerushalmi, Yosef Hayim, "The Inquisition and the Jews of France in the Time of Bernard Gui," *Harvard Theological Review* 63 (1970): 317–76.

6

Antisemitism in the Age of Mercantilism

Jonathan Karp

In recent decades the image of the early modern period in Jewish history—roughly from the Spanish expulsion to the Enlightenment—has undergone major revision. Once seen in terms of ceaseless wandering, spiritual stultification, and cultural insularity, the period now appears one of vital structural change and religious creativity. Research into Jewish mysticism and Kabbalah, into the inner world of New Christians and *conversos*, into Jewish economic life, and such phenomena as Christian Hebraism has lent the period a strong sense of its own distinctiveness, rather than being a mere afterthought to the Jewish Middle Ages. Yet despite fresh insights, no concomitant reevaluation of anti-Judaism and antisemitism during these centuries has emerged.

In fact, few of the most pronounced anti-Jewish motifs were entirely novel to this period. The blood libel, for instance, which persisted in central and eastern Europe well beyond the sixteenth century, was a medieval invention, as was the stereotype of the Jew as usurer, while the Christian phobia of Judaizing heresy went back to the earliest phases of Christianity. Still, originality is not everything. The reformulation and amplification of familiar themes within shifting historical settings can sometimes signal the most important new developments. Such is the case with attitudes toward Jews and Judaism in the age of mercantilism. Instead of offering a comprehensive portrait of antisemitism during this period, the present chapter argues that one familiar theme—the image of Jews as powerful and dangerous economic actors—provides the glue that fuses many other dimensions of contemporary antisemitism into a relatively coherent and meaningful whole.

In Jonathan Israel's classic interpretation, Jewish history in the age of mercantilism is characterized by profound shifts in population and a relative increase in residential and cultural separation from non-Jews, paradoxically combined with increased economic integration. This meant that attitudes toward Jews often developed without close contact or deep knowledge of them. Shakespeare's *Merchant of Venice* is a case in point. It has often been observed that when Shakespeare wrote this play there were no Jews living openly in England, although a handful of New Christians, some of whom may have observed Jewish practices in secret, resided in London. Yet even had the playwright visited Venice—as some scholars speculate—and acquired his knowledge of Jewish usurers there, he would have gotten the story wrong. There certainly were Jewish moneylenders in late sixteenth-century Venice, but none fit the description of Shylock very accurately. Most were lenders of limited means, many of them pawnbrokers, whose clientele were quite poor. Jews were needed in Venice to provide such services, since unlike many Italian cities Venice lacked a Franciscan *monte di pietà*, that is, a loan bank to the poor.

As for wealthy Jews, an observant visitor to Venice in Shakespeare's day would have noticed that Jews—particularly Sephardim—were increasingly prominent there as merchants rather than moneylenders. In fact, a Jew could have been the "merchant of Venice" (who borrows 3000 ducats) as easily as a Christian. Shylock, it seems, more closely resembles the medieval stereotypes upon which he is based than contemporary Jewish types. But that is precisely the point: while Shakespeare's rendering of the Jew displays vital psychological features in keeping with the sensibility of his times, the image of Shylock himself is a stock holdover from another time and place (Karp 2008, 12–13 and the references therein).

Christopher Marlowe's *Jew of Malta* is another hybrid creature possessing features that recall medieval motifs. But in contrast to Shylock, Marlowe invests the Jew Barabas with numerous contemporary resonances. He is, for instance, a caricature of the Machiavellian anti-hero: devious, ruthless and cynical ("Machevill" actually appears in the prologue to introduce the play). No compunction of morality or propriety can stand in the way of his monstrous pursuit of power. He is a cold-blooded murderer who openly boasts of his gratuitous killings of Christians and a cynical manipulator of anyone willing to abet his rise, including his daughter Abigail. While Barabas functions as a means of exposing the moral hypocrisy of many Christians (for whom religion and money have become the sinews of worldly power), his Jewish nature is composed of an almost superhuman if not supernatural evil.

Nevertheless, in contrast to Shakespeare's Shylock, a faint historicity animates Marlowe's depiction of Barabas. The character likely alludes to a famous Jew of the time, Don Joseph Nasi. Born to a wealthy family of Portuguese *converso* merchants, Don Joseph had been a banker to Charles V in Antwerp and later operated in Venice before emigrating to Turkey where, revealing himself openly to be a Jew, he rose to a high position in the court of Sultan Suleiman the Magnificent. Upon his accession to the throne, Suleiman's son Salim II made Don Joseph the Duke of Naxos and ruler of a number of neighboring Greek islands. Don Joseph remained an advisor to Salim, occasionally deploying his diplomatic skills to play Spanish, French, and Dutch interests against one another in the service of his patron and possibly himself. Marlowe would have known of him by reputation, heavily embellished with legend, as a nominal Christian, who revealed his underlying Jewishness in the sinister service of an expanding Muslim empire.

What was medieval cliché in Barabas' portrait was its depiction of the Jew as demonic infidel; what was current, in contrast, was its portrait of the Jew as a chameleon "whom we may rank with...Proteus for shapes," empowered by finance and driven to international mischief making by an insatiable yearning for revenge (Marlowe 1986, 344). Both Shylock and Barabas appear to harbor legitimate feelings of grievance at their harsh treatment as Jews, experiences that are seen to fuel a drive for vengeance so vehement that it crosses all legitimate bounds. This recognition that the Jew's crimes are ultimately rooted in Christian persecution would become a stock motif of the Enlightenment. Here it is still a kind of mad reflex of paranoia, but the point is that contemporaries could regard as plausible the notion that a Jew would be able to seize hold of considerable worldly power in pursuit of his vindictive and destructive ends.

Far more contemporary than the clichéd image of the Jew as avaricious usurer is the notion of an unholy alliance between Jewish money and worldly power—as epitomized by Barabas too. This was what Martin Luther had railed against in his 1543 *On the Jews and Their Lies*, namely, the use of Jewish moneylending by emperors and princes as an illicit means to extort revenue from humble, suffering Christians. But in Luther's case the notion was almost preposterous, since in his day Jewish finance in central Europe had reached its historical nadir. The charge was far more credible, however, in southern Europe, as we have just seen in the case of Joseph Nasi, and in Poland, as we shall discuss shortly.

The perception of Jewish power lingered even where Jews did not, in sixteenth-century England, for instance, from which Jews had been expelled in 1290, and still more so in contemporary Spain. In 1391, riots throughout Spain resulted in conversion of Jews on a mass scale. Successive decades saw the number of these New Christians grow steadily. The large number of converts came to constitute a new social category—ethnic Jews no longer constrained by anti-Jewish restrictions—whose increasing influence and prosperity provoked resentment and jealousy. Many of the converts and their descendants rose to high positions in Spanish economic, cultural, and even religious life. Mistrust over the real nature of their religious loyalties led to the creation of Purity of Blood (*limpieza de sangre*) Laws which, starting in the 1450s, barred New Christians from municipal offices, guilds, monastic orders, indeed, eventually much of the corporate framework of Spanish society. Although denounced by Church authorities as contrary to Christian doctrine, purity of blood laws continued to multiply during the sixteenth and seventeenth centuries. Long after Jews and Judaism were proscribed, then, Christian descendants of the former Jewish population of Spain remained stigmatized. As one statute declared, "all of them are as if born with polluted blood, and therefore they are denied all honors, offices, and titles" (in Kaplan 1988, 154).

During the seventeenth century, at a time of precipitous national decline, these laws came to satisfy a pressing psychic need. As Yosef Kaplan has argued, denunciations of *marranos* served to reassure Spanish Old Christians of their

Antisemitism in the Age of Mercantilism

own continued status as the divinely chosen *Verus Israel* (true Israel), the holy warriors who in 1492 had decisively vanquished the people rejected by God (154). Yet by the seventeenth century religious difference no longer served as a meaningful criterion for distinguishing New Christians, since crypto-Judaizing had been all but eradicated among Spanish New Christians. Consequently, novel indices of Jewish identification had to be created. These were typically "ethnic" characteristics: social and economic behaviors, such as concentration in mercantile occupations, as well as physical or racial attributes, some of a realistic and others of a fantastical nature. Old Christians came to fear not just moral corruption from exposure to crypto-Judaizing heresy but actual physical contamination from mere proximity to the New Christians' polluted blood (Yerushalmi 1982).

While the notion that contact with infidels leads to impurity is an ancient one (and one found in seventeenth-century Judaism), the association here is altogether more disturbing: the representation of Spanish Jewry's mass conversion to Christianity as a sinister plot to infiltrate and undermine Christendom. Another case of an early modern amplification of medieval precedents, this one too would later take on the character of a global conspiracy. Some Spanish texts from the late sixteenth and early seventeenth centuries already depict the far-flung New Christian and Sephardi Jewish trading Diaspora as part of an international plot to destroy Christian Spain. As Carsten Wilke has observed, Don Francisco de Quevedo's 1635 *La hora de todos* (*The Hour of All Men*) imagines a meeting in Ottoman Salonica of Spanish politicians and Sephardi merchants conniving to replace the Christian faith, not with the law of the Old Testament but with a distinctly Sephardi form of "Judaism"—the worship of money and credit.

An important element in the emergence of this new mythology was the success of Portuguese merchants from New Christian backgrounds in securing their prosperity in the very heart of Christendom, the Papal territories. Portuguese travelers and statesmen marveled at the Renaissance popes' readiness to settle within their own lands heretics, i.e. former converts, who had now openly reverted to Judaism. In port cities formally outside of the pope's direct rule, such as Venice and Livorno, nominal New Christians received tacit and sometimes overt permission to practice Judaism as part of the *quid pro quo* for engaging in useful trade. It infuriated pious Christians to learn that the papal port of Ancona had itself become a place of refuge to Portuguese New Christians who were practicing Judaism with the evident approbation of Pope Julius III himself. The ability of heretical New Christians to behave with impunity before the Vicar of Christ, as well as the emerging alliance between groups of wealthy Sephardi merchants and Ottoman sultans, exacerbated the siege mentality and betrayal many Christians had felt in the face of Ottoman expansion, of the venal behavior of the Renaissance papacy, and of the Reformation's outbreak in northern Europe. Yet this situation would not persist indefinitely. The critics at last found their champion in the successor to Julius III, Cardinal Giovanni Caraffa, who as Paul IV acceded to the papal throne in 1555. In addition to spearheading

98   *Jonathan Karp*

Counter-Reformation efforts at Trent, the new pope quickly arranged for an investigation of the Ancona New Christians, leading to their arrest *en masse* and the execution of the recalcitrant Judaizers in *autos-da-fé*.

The Counter-Reformation shift in papal Jewish policy exacted a harsh toll not just on former New Christians but on Italian Jews as a whole. Caraffa had been responsible for the confiscation and public burning of the Talmud in 1553, and with his bull *Cum nimis absurdum*, issued two years later, he sought to return Catholic Jewish policy to the medieval strictures of the Fourth Lateran Council of 1215. This entailed the effective segregation of the Jewish community through the imposition of special clothing, severe restrictions on Jewish livelihoods, and the proscription of the employment of Gentiles in Jewish homes and, at least in theory, of the exercise of any worldly, including economic, authority over Christians. The bull exceeded medieval precedents, however, in its call for the establishment of ghettos (only the ghetto in Venice served as a true precursor). These ghettos would become a hallmark of Jewish life in urban Italy right up through the nineteenth century.

Yet recent scholarship has persuasively demonstrated that the Counter-Reformation policies represented a compromise rather than a total negation of Judaism. For instance, in the aftermath of Paul IV, the Church's agreement to censor rather than proscribe the Talmud not only enabled continued study of this core work of Judaism but even transformed its interpretation by many Jews, subtly enabling accommodation and adaptation to larger forces of social and cultural change (Raz-Krakotzkin 2007). And while the ghetto imposed a dangerous and degrading existence on its residents, paradoxically it may also have provided refuge to Jewish communities. Jewish residential isolation helped appease Christian anxieties that might have otherwise found more violent expression. As Robert Bonfil notes, under the ghetto system, "Accusations of ritual murder disappeared almost completely and the frequency of attacks and pogroms declined markedly, as did the tendency to expel the Jews" (72). It has even been asserted that the ghetto enabled Italian Jews to maintain their facility with general Italian culture, albeit in the manner of a time lag, which lent Italian Jewry the eccentric and antiquated features of an ethnic subculture (Stowe 2001).

Scholars have also recently begun investigating the effects of the Counter-Reformation on Jewish life in eastern Europe. The Jewish community of early modern Poland evolved during the Middle Ages from the usual push-and-pull factors of migratory movements, in this case emanating from central Europe. Poland was a classic case, observed time and again in Jewish history, of a frontier region whose rulers wished to attract Jews and other colonists in the hope of developing urban commerce. The medieval Jewish community derived largely from German lands emigrating between the thirteenth and fifteenth centuries, a period of rising antagonism in central Europe between burghers and Jews. In this sense, Jewish migrants in Poland found themselves oddly at home, since they tended to live in the western and more urbanized portions of the country,

Antisemitism in the Age of Mercantilism

often alongside the very same type of German townsmen—fellow migrants and colonists—with whom they had previously sparred. Some of these "Polish" burghers succeeded in winning privileges of *de non tolerandis Judaeis*, a status precluding Jews from settling within the city walls. Thus although medieval Poland certainly represented a freer environment than Germany for Jews, its fundamental social structures and conflicts were not qualitatively different from the places they had left behind. Jews served the Polish king as they had German princes and emperor, as tax and toll collectors and moneylenders, although a handful rose to higher positions as minters and even royal administrators.

All this began to change during the sixteenth century when the Polish nobility (at about 10%, a relatively large stratum) won major concessions, including the right to elect the king and approve all laws, treaties, and taxes. While the Crown endured into the eighteenth century, Poland effectively became a Republic of the Nobles, though in actuality it was only the magnates, the wealthiest land-owners among the nobles, who ruled. By the second half of the sixteenth century, the upper nobility had wrested control of much of the Jewish population from the king. Especially after the 1569 Union of Lublin, which opened huge territories in Lithuania to the Polish magnates, Jews were encouraged to settle in the eastern hinterlands, occupying villages in the midst of noble estates, some encompassing vast territories.

This fresh wave of Jewish colonists in the East, comprising a majority of Polish Jews by the eighteenth century, continued to perform traditional economic roles, such as tax and toll collection. But they also participated directly in the management of the estates. Jews purchased on a renewable basis the rights to collect revenue on the use and sale of estate assets, including grain, livestock, fuel, and alcohol. By this means Jews often came to exert control (including the exercising of judicial and punitive powers) over the mostly peasant population living on or tied to the estate. There were cases in which Jews were even able to lease the revenue and monopoly rights to entire towns and villages. Here too only the wealthiest stratum of Jews held these leases directly; others might be sublessors or their employees. Yet despite this stratification, the Jewish economy of eastern Poland and Lithuania ultimately relied on the managerial services provided to nobles, with the Jewish population as a whole functioning as agents and allies of this most powerful group.

Once again, Jews now found themselves in the crosshairs of explosive social and religious resentments. In 1648, the Polish-controlled Ukraine was seized by a rebellion of Greek Orthodox Cossacks under the leadership of the hetman, Bogdan Chmielnicki, against their overlords in the Polish Catholic nobility. Orthodox peasants quickly joined the rebellion, meting out retribution to the Jews as much as to their noble protectors. In later assessing the sources of the uprising, which decimated Jewish communities throughout Ukraine, Volhynia, and Podolia, the Jewish chronicler Nathan Hanover acknowledged Jewish complicity in the terrible exploitation of the peasants: "For they [i.e., the Jews]

100   *Jonathan Karp*

ruled in every part of [Little] Russia, a condition which aroused the jealousy of the peasants, and which was the cause for the massacres" (36).

Remarkably, however, the Jewish community was able to recover relatively quickly from the devastation wrought by Chmielnicki and the succeeding invasions from Moscovy and Sweden. Not only did their numbers return to and then exceed pre-1648 figures, but Jews even strengthened their economic ties to the nobility in Lithuania and southeastern Poland. This powerful bond proved a bane to both peasants and Catholic Church officials. The Polish Church's criticisms of it echoed traditional doctrinal opposition to Jews' exercising authority over Christians. But its condemnations must also be understood in relation to Counter-Reformation politics.

Unlike contemporary Italy, Protestant dissent constituted a genuine threat to Polish Catholicism during the sixteenth century. Many nobles found Calvinism (and occasionally even Anti-Trinitarianism) appealing, in large part because it offered a mechanism for asserting noble independence from a Church that had long served as a bulwark of Crown authority. While this dissent was gradually reined in during the seventeenth century, it nevertheless prompted the Polish Church to heighten its anti-Jewish rhetoric in an effort to weaken noble opposition and identify Polish nationhood with the Catholic faith. The situation reached a climax during the eighteenth century, when the Church concluded that the Jewish-noble alliance threatened its authority among the laity as a whole. "For what can be worse than Jews ruling the manors in place of the lords of the manor, managing and governing according to their will, and subduing Christians by forcing them to obey their orders?" (Teter 2006, 89) Such accusations could stretch to absurd lengths of exaggeration, as in the case of cleric Stefan Zuchowski's insistence that nobles had made Jews more powerful than themselves. While the gentry fight wars and pay taxes, Zuchowski reasoned, while the clergy "serve human souls" and the serfs "work hard tilling the soil," the "Jews serve neither in war nor at the altar, nor do they till the soil, they only make money by swindling and deceit," giving oversized dowries to "their detestable kids," while bribing the nobles for protection. Meanwhile, he lamented, the nobles "defend the Jews but they attack the clergy!" (97).

Such hyperbole attests to the Church's frustration in its failure to drive a wedge between the magnates and the Jews. That relationship remained a basic fact of life in Poland right up to the end of the eighteenth century. Even the partial recovery of the Polish burghers and their successive attempts to subordinate their Jewish competitors through proposals for general civic reform fell by the wayside. It was only with the effective demise of the Polish kingdom through the partitions of 1772, 1793, and 1795 that east European Jews gradually lost the protection of their noble patrons and became subject to the rationalizing policies of the absolutist regimes of Prussia, Austria, and Russia by the nineteenth century.

While it is easy to comprehend the outrage of the Polish Church and burghers at Jews' evident economic clout, it is perplexing to find the same complaints reverberate in sixteenth-century Germany. When Luther penned his denunciatory *On the Jews and Their Lies* in 1543, the Jewish population there had ebbed to its lowest point since the early Middle Ages. Expulsions in the aftermath of the Black Death in 1348 were followed by a further series of attacks during the late fifteenth century, in this case catalyzed by accusations of Jewish ritual murder but also reflecting the effort of town councils to assert or reassert their independence against the encroachment of territorial lords. As in early modern Poland, the Jews of late medieval Germany had functioned as economic agents of the elite—in this case the emperor and, by extension, the territorial lords. The emperor's claims to imperial ownership of the Jews in his lands, the notion of chamber serfdom or *servi camerae*, allowed him to pawn or sell rights to Jewish taxes to princes, nobles, and even town patricians. In the eyes of the local burghers, Jews were thus not just infidels but unwholesome instruments of feudal exploitation.

What is curious is that by Luther's day the situation just described barely existed. The once wealthy and proud Jewish community had been effectively marginalized and despoiled through the continuous financial expropriations of their imperial and princely protectors. Luther appears to be speaking in a time warp when he accuses these lords of soaking their Christian subjects by taxing the Jews' usurious loans. According to Luther, this arrangement even encourages Jews to pose as nobles themselves by letting "us work in the sweat of our brow to earn money and property while they sit behind the stove, idle away the time, fart, and roast pears" (266). Yet however grotesque and anachronistic his charges, Luther succeeded in pressuring German Protestant rulers and even some Catholic ones into driving Jews out of their few remaining havens, so that by the 1580s the centuries-long process of curtailing the Jewish presence in Germany appeared nearly complete. In fact, the refugees did not always have to flee as far as Poland. Many retreated instead to the countryside, which would prove to be a development of no small consequence. The shift marked a major demographic and economic reorientation of German Jewry, albeit one with deep roots in the preceding century. Now Jews ceased to draw their principal livelihood from moneylending, as had been characteristic since the high Middle Ages, and relied instead on rural trade in livestock and grain, as well as the peddling of housewares and second-hand clothing.

In this way the anti-Jewish onslaught of the period 1470–1570 actually paved the way for the recovery of German Jewry. Jews' commercial endeavors in the countryside would be one leg of a three-legged stool making possible a partial repopulation of German territories after 1648. The others were, first, a transformation of European military strategy in the second half of the seventeenth century that necessitated substantially larger and more mobile armies than before, as well as the supplies necessary to feed and clothe them; and second, the diffusion of Roman law in the German lands from about 1500 on, the effect of which was to create conceptions of citizenship focused on the individual—rather

102 *Jonathan Karp*

than the corporate group—in relation to the state. As Adam Teller points out, Jews in Poland were almost always treated as a corporation, with privileges granted to them collectively. Jews in seventeenth-century Germany, in contrast, were distinguished on the basis of their individual contributions to the state and rewarded as individuals with letters of protection (*Shutzbriefe*), if they could demonstrate their usefulness for some indispensable service (109–41).

The coalescence of these three elements after 1650 gave rise to the phenomenon of the Court Jew. The Peace of Westphalia had made Germany more politically fragmented than ever, while at the same time establishing the principle of sovereignty as a veritable dogma of statecraft. The Baroque court life epitomized by Louis XIV's Versailles encouraged state expenditure on both military expansion and royal embellishment. Yet the preceding century's record of royal insolvency left Christian bankers wary of advancing the funds necessary for these outlays. This left the door open for enterprising Jews. They could fill the gap not just by mobilizing funds but by making use of their knowledge and connections in Poland, principally for grain, and in the German countryside, where local Jewish merchants and peddlers could help to get hold of horses, metals, clothing, and other essential materials. Although these networks were never exclusively Jewish, Jews generally enjoyed a comparative advantage in marshalling supplies faster and cheaper than their Christian competitors.

As a result, some Court Jews, the Oppenheimers and Wertheimers in Austria, Israel Aron and the Gomperz family in Prussia, Leffmann Behrens in Hanover, Joseph (Jud Süss) Oppenheimer in Württemberg, among many others, received residential privileges for their families and retinues, enabling the creation of beachheads for the gradual further settlement of Jews in German territories. These Court Jews, sometimes enjoying extensive latitude in the administration of state finances, naturally attracted the opprobrium of Church officials at court. Their vulnerability as Jews made them especially useful to various secular rulers, since when necessary they could always be thrown to the wolves.

It was not just the Jewish elite that attracted condemnation but the communities of Jewish merchants and small-scale traders that followed in their wake. The Cameralist economic doctrines of the time favored bureaucratic centralization in order to weaken the power of guilds and corporations. However, it was not a simple matter to run roughshod over the guilds' traditional monopoly rights to specific markets and goods. The reintroduction of Jewish populations to the town life of seventeenth-century Germany reignited old resentments at a moment when guilds faced unprecedented threats from the overweening state. Their petitions to rulers complained of the Jews' unfair business practices, of the cheap goods they hawked that undersold the market, and of their fundamental dishonesty that defrauded customers. After some fifty wealthy Jews, recently expelled from Vienna, were invited into Berlin in 1671 by the Great Elector Frederick William, the guild merchants of the city petitioned the ruler with the complaint that:

Antisemitism in the Age of Mercantilism 103

these infidels run from village to village, from town to town, offer this and take that, whereby they do not only dispose of their discarded and wretched goods and deceive the people with old rags, but they spoil all commerce and particularly the retail trade, especially in silver, brass, tea, and copper. (in Poliakov 1974–85, 3:14)

Even if the guilds usually failed to dislodge new settlements of Jews, their exhortations proved a constant drag on the livelihood and welfare of the Jewish communities. The impecunious majority of Jews was subjected to the harshest restrictions of residence, livelihood, and even permission to marry and bear children. Popular antisemitism—and personal distaste for Jews among many rulers and administrators themselves—led to a progressive narrowing of the range of permitted activities, even under enlightened kings, such as Frederick the Great. General improvement in these circumstances came only with the reforms of late Enlightenment and especially in the wake of the French Revolution, when debates over Jewish emancipation in Germany were in full swing.

Germany was remarkable for the intensity of its cultural ambivalence toward commerce. It was a land that had produced a rich town life during the Middle Ages. The colonizing efforts of its urbanites had created a diaspora of burghers (craftsmen, manufacturers, retail and wholesale traders) throughout eastern Europe, in many ways exceeding that of the Jews. Yet the burghers' fundamental conservatism made them suspicious of innovators and jealous of rivals. The proliferation of small towns, sometimes called "home towns," throughout the German countryside lent the German burgher mentality a broad influence on the national culture at large, especially when fused with similarly conservative religious values, particularly in Catholicism and Lutheranism (Walker 1971). All of this made Jewish commerce arguably more controversial in Germany than elsewhere because it symbolized the very antithesis of an idealized wholesome burgher life and social structure.

Yet it would be easy to overstate the point. Even the Atlantic trading cultures of Holland, France, and Britain exhibited many of the same hostile attitudes toward Jewish trade. In the French Atlantic colonies Jews initially benefited from the mercantilist policies of Colbert that favored population growth and state support of merchants. But these policies came under constant attack from Jesuit critics fearing that by means of colonial trade Jewish influence would spread to the New World and contaminate missionary efforts there. Jesuits caught the ear of Louis XIV in the 1680s when the king abruptly changed policy on religious toleration, more notoriously with regard to Huguenots than Jews, but nonetheless prohibited Jewish settlement in Martinique, Guadeloupe, the French Antilles, Cayenne, and other colonial possessions. Later dubbed the *code noir*, the royal decrees provided the legal basis for the Jews' expulsion from Louisiana in 1723. Thus France became perhaps the only seaborne power of the day to treat Jews in its colonies worse than in the metropole.

A similar opportunity presented itself to the Dutch administration in 1654 when the governor, Peter Stuyvesant, sought the backing of the directors of the

104   *Jonathan Karp*

West India Company to turn back recently arrived Jewish refugees from Recife, whence they had fled following the Portuguese reconquest of Brazil from the Dutch. Stuyvesant appealed to the directors that "the deceitful race—such hateful enemies and blasphemers of the name of Christ—not be allowed further to infect and trouble this new colony." While professing to share the governor's concern that "the new territories should no more be allowed to be infected by people of the Jewish nation," the directors nevertheless rejected Stuyvesant's petition, in part, they acknowledged, "because of the large amount of capital which [the Jews] still have invested in the shares of this company" (in Marcus 1996, 29–33).

It was in Protestant commercial empires like the Netherlands and Britain that attitudes to Jews appeared most variegated and contradictory. This should be understood not merely as attitudinal ambivalence but as a genuine conflict of motives and goals. Here strict Calvinist anti-Jewish theology vied with mercantilist prerogatives emphasizing the Jews' commercial utility. In Cromwell's England, the same opposing considerations were further complicated by such factors as economic objection to Jewish readmission, spearheaded by the Corporation of the City of London's guild-like fear of Jewish mercantile competition, and religious support of Jews by Puritan millenarians like Cromwell himself who saw in their repopulating of Britain a precondition for the Second Coming.

In seventeenth-century Britain and the Netherlands, moreover, the position of the Jews cannot be properly evaluated without considering their relationship to the *other* Others, specifically Catholics. In the eyes of many statesmen "papists" posed much more of an immediate political threat to Protestant regimes than did Jews. Thus the political philosopher James Harrington favored employing Jews as commercial and agricultural colonists in Ireland, where they would be useful in policing or even displacing native Catholics, while also opposing the settlement of Jews in England itself (Karp 2008, 12–68). Later in the century, John Locke would permit toleration of Jews in Britain while denying it to papists and atheists. There were further contradictions. For instance, despite all of the advances made by seventeenth-century Britain on behalf of religious toleration, medieval myths of demonic Jewish behaviors retained their potency, and not just among the general populace but within the educated elite as well. In his study of seventeenth-century Christian Hebraism, Jason Rosenblatt confesses he cannot be sure that even the most liberal-minded and latitudinarian of Hebraist scholars, such as John Selden, did not subscribe to barbaric notions about the practices of contemporary Jews. "What can be asserted," admits Rosenblatt, "is that no Christian can be found in early modern England who unequivocally rejected the blood libel" (160–1 n 10).

Even the most positive treatment of Jews in the mercantilist period, such as was found in Amsterdam and Livorno, or the Dutch and British colonies of Suriname and Guyana, favored them because of their purported economic utility and not out of a forthright recognition of their human rights. Of course, it would be anachronistic and unrealistic to expect otherwise. Yet the granting of privileges on the basis of commercial utility brought with it a host of accompanying dangers. The rationale of utility was easily challenged by groups that regarded themselves as the victims rather than the beneficiaries of Jewish economic activity. Indeed, granting them privileges on the basis of their purported commercial usefulness lent Jews an aura of influence in a culture still sufficiently Christian to regard Jewish power as a violation of the most sacred precepts of moral economy.

While no single motif encompasses all of the important antisemitic trends during the early modern period, the image of Jews as infidels granted power to rule Christians by means of economic privilege is among the most potent and pervasive. The observation made at the start of this chapter that there is little new in early modern antisemitism indeed holds true for this case as well. Yet the evident rise to new heights of a group that had appeared vanquished and humiliated following the Iberian expulsions breathed fresh life into old anxieties. The first traces of capitalist globalization rendered the medieval notion of Jewish conspiracies more palpable than ever, especially when reinforced by the emergence of real Jewish commercial networks across Europe, the Mediterranean, and the Atlantic. But by the early eighteenth century the cracks in this picture were also beginning to show. The actual poverty that plagued Jewish communities everywhere—in prosperous Amsterdam no less than rural Poland—generated new fears among Christians of Jewish deviance and criminality. For the Age of Enlightenment the question would be not how to segregate and demote them as Jews but whether they could be truly integrated and elevated as human beings.

CITED PRIMARY SOURCES

Hanover, Nathan, *Abyss of Despair*, trans. Abraham J. Mensch (New Brunswick, NJ: Transaction Publishers, 1983).

Luther, Martin, *On the Jews and Their Lies*, in Franklin Sherman (ed.), *Luther's Works: The Christian in Society IV* (Philadelphia: Fortress Press, 1971).

Marcus, Jacob Rader (ed.), *The Jew in the American World: A Source Reader* (Detroit: Wayne State University Press, 1996), 29–33.

Marlowe, Christopher, *The Complete Plays*, ed. J. B. Steane (Harmondsworth: Penguin, 1986).

RECOMMENDED READINGS

Bell, Dean Phillip, *Jews in the Early Modern World* (Lanham, MD: Rowman and Littlefield, 2008).

Bonfil, Robert, *Jewish Life in Renaissance Italy* (Berkeley: University of California Press, 1994).

Israel, Jonathan, *European Jewry in the Age of Mercantilism, 1550–1750* (Oxford: Clarendon Press, 1985).

Kaplan, Joseph (Yosef), "Jews and Judaism in the Social Thought of Spain in the Sixteenth and Seventeenth Centuries," in Shmuel Almog (ed.), *Antisemitism through the Ages* (Oxford: Pergamon Press, 1988).

Karp, Jonathan, *The Politics of Jewish Commerce: Economic Thought and Emancipation in Europe, 1638–1848* (New York: Cambridge University Press, 2008).

Poliakov, Leon, *The History of Anti-Semitism*, 4 vols (London: Routledge and Kegan Paul, 1974–85).

Raz-Krakotzkin, Ammon, *The Censor, the Editor, and the Text: The Catholic Church and the Shaping of the Jewish Canon in the Sixteenth Century* (Philadelphia: University of Pennsylvania Press, 2007).

Rosenblatt, Jason, *Renaissance England's Chief Rabbi, John Selden* (Oxford: Oxford University Press, 2006).

Rosman, M. J., *The Lord's Jews: Magnate–Jewish Relations in the Polish-Lithuanian Commonwealth during the 18th Century* (Cambridge, MA: Harvard University Press, 1990).

Roth, Cecil, *Doña Gracia of the House of Nasi* (Philadelphia: Jewish Publication Society of America, 1977).

Stowe, Kenneth, *Theater of Acculturation: The Roman Ghetto in the Sixteenth Century* (Seattle: University of Washington Press, 2001).

Teller, Adam, "Telling the Difference: Some Comparative Perspectives on the Jews' Legal Status in the Polish-Lithuanian Commonwealth and the Holy Roman Empire," *Polin* 22 (2009): 109–41.

Teter, Magda, *Jews and Heretics in Catholic Poland: A Beleaguered Church in the Post-Reformation Era* (New York: Cambridge University Press, 2006).

Walker, Mack, *German Home Towns: Community, State and General Estate, 1648–1871* (Ithaca: Cornell University Press, 1971).

Wilke, Carsten, Unpublished paper delivered to the seminar on "Jews, Commerce and Culture" at the Katz Center for Advanced Judaic Studies, Philadelphia. January 28, 2009.

Yerushalmi, Yosef Hayim, "Assimilation and Racial Anti-Semitism: The Iberian and the German Models," *Leo Baeck Memorial Lecture*, 1982.

7

The Enlightenment, French Revolution, Napoleon

Adam Sutcliffe

The Enlightenment was, on balance, good for the Jews. Critiques of religious intolerance gathered strength over the course of the eighteenth century, and by the 1780s reformist attention began to focus on the discriminatory laws that had long regulated Jewish life across Europe. In 1782, the Edict of Tolerance promulgated by the self-consciously enlightened Habsburg emperor, Joseph II, cautiously opened up new educational and economic opportunities to the Jews of Austria, while in 1790 and 1791, the revolutionaries of the French National Assembly decided after much debate to consider Jews eligible for full citizenship, initiating the process of Jewish emancipation that was then exported across Europe by Napoleon. The ensuing advance of Jewish civic rights, although faltering and uneven, enabled an extraordinarily dramatic enlargement of the economic and cultural horizons of the droves of Jews who joined the ranks of Europe's burgeoning urban bourgeoisie in the early nineteenth century.

The relationship between Judaism and the Enlightenment was, however, far from straightforward. Not only did few thinkers before the 1770s show much serious interest in promoting more tolerant attitudes to Jews, but the arguments of eighteenth-century reformists—to say nothing of their opponents—were often embedded within ambivalent or explicitly hostile attitudes toward both Judaism and contemporary Jewry. Crudely negative stereotypes of Jews, and lurid associations of Judaism with barbarism and primitivism, recur in the writing of several celebrated Enlightenment thinkers. This has led some scholars to deem the Enlightenment as fundamentally, indeed lethally, antisemitic. Far from challenging traditional prejudices, they have argued, intellectuals such as Voltaire—the most relentlessly anti-Jewish *philosophe*—merely drew on and recast medieval religious hatreds, imbuing them with renewed force in a modernized secular form (Hertzberg 1968, 6–11; Katz 1980, 27–33).

Eighteenth-century writers and thinkers certainly exhibited something of a preoccupation with Judaism. A search on the word *juif* and its variants in the leading database of eighteenth-century French literary texts (ARTFL) produces

108 *Adam Sutcliffe*

60% more hits than an equivalent search on the word *anglais*. These terms occur with almost equal frequency in the monumental *Encyclopédie* (1751–72), while Voltaire referred almost twice as often to Jews as to the English (Schechter 2003, 36, 56). How can we make sense of the fact that this small minority—fewer than 40,000 Jews resided in France in the late eighteenth century, out of a total population of approximately 20 million—inspired almost equal interest as France's most significant neighbor and commercial rival?

Debates invoking Jews were almost always about much more than Jews—in the context of late eighteenth-century France, as Ronald Schechter has argued, Jews figured as a key conceptual tool in debates on the nature of citizenship and the possibility of cultural transformation (35–7, 66–109). Judaism was also frequently at the center of eighteenth-century attempts to attack, defend, or reappraise the Bible. Jews thus bore a heavy associational freight, rooted in the historical and hermeneutical relationship between Judaism and Christianity, and overlaid by the complex realities of contemporary economic and cultural relations between Christians and Jews. In order to understand eighteenth-century attitudes toward Jews and Judaism we must patiently unpick these associations. There is very little value in considering antisemitism in this period in intellectual isolation, or as a psychic attribute of certain individuals. It can only be meaningfully understood when set in this wider context.

"To the early Jews religion was transmitted in the form of written law because at that time they were just like children" (Spinoza 2003, 504). Arguing thus in his *Theological-Political Treatise* (1670), the Dutch Sephardic renegade Baruch Spinoza asserted a connection between Judaism and cultural infancy that later became a key Enlightenment hallmark. The idea that religious truths were expressed in the Bible in a simplified form in order to be within the grasp of their intended human audience—the theological principle of "accommodation"—was widely assumed by both Jewish and Christian medieval exegetes. Spinoza, however, gave this concept a more historical and philosophical inflection. The supposed miracles recounted in the Jewish Bible, Spinoza argued, reflected nothing more than the ignorance and superstition of the ancient Jews, for whom the unfamiliar could only be apprised as miraculous, while the legalistic strictures of their religion similarly reflected their immature inability to recognize the morally innate basis of human ethics.

This infantilization of Judaism swiftly took on a more pointedly hostile resonance in the hands of the first wave of Enlightenment anti-religious polemicists, many of whom were strongly influenced by Spinoza. Several clandestine manuscripts circulating in the philosophical underground of early eighteenth-century France sought to discredit the Old Testament as nothing more than an insignificant and implausible account of the miserable wanderings of an obscure desert tribe. Denigrating statements by classical authors were marshaled as supporting evidence that the ancient Jews had been leprous, primitive, and widely despised because of their absurd customs, clannish attitudes, and extreme

The Enlightenment, French Revolution, Napoleon 109

credulity. The argumentative purpose of these sharply anti-Jewish attacks was almost invariably to undermine the authority of Christianity and its key tenets. The identification of Jesus as the Messiah by his first Jewish disciples, concluded one of the most polemically ferocious manuscripts, was implausibly based on little more than "the sentiments of a few members of the vilest rabble" (in Sutcliffe 2003, 187).

Spinoza's naturalistic interpretation of the Old Testament was also developed by several of the early eighteenth-century British Deists. John Toland, like Spinoza, sought to deprivilege the Bible by reading it in purely secular terms as an account of early Jewish history. Drawing on the earlier work of the Hebraist scholars John Marsham and John Spencer, who in the 1670s and 1680s argued that Judaism had been profoundly shaped by Egyptian influences, Toland presented Moses as a highly skilled civic lawgiver, formed by his induction into the esoteric Hermetic tradition of Egyptian priestly wisdom. Toland's approach to ancient Judaism was complex and fluid, incorporating a powerful strain of admiration for Moses as a supremely masterful legislator (an Enlightenment topos to which we will return). However, his Mosaic counter-history was also highly critical. In stark contrast to the arguments of his polemical adversary, the traditionalist French Bishop Pierre-Daniel Huet, who had attempted to demonstrate that all world religions were distorted derivations from an original Mosaic blueprint, Toland portrayed Jewish rituals as themselves highly derivative, and emphasized the ignorance and superstition of the ancient Jews. He thus fueled the anti-Judaic strain in eighteenth-century rationalist biblical criticism.

Several other Deists similarly relished using the critical interpretive strategies developed by Christian Hebraist scholars to undermine the theological orthodoxies that these scholars had sought to reinforce. Anthony Collins, for example, deftly juxtaposed allegorical and literalist readings of the Old Testament in order to destabilize all attempts to fix this text as a reliable basis for the truth of the New Testament. Only allegorical readings of the Old Testament prophecies, Collins argued, could lend support to Christianity; but such readings, characteristic of the Jews at the time of Jesus, were inherently fanciful, enigmatic, and uncertain. Collins' arguments were not directly anti-Jewish, although their impact was in part based on the negative associations of a Judaizing interpretation of Christianity. This implication was clearly perceived and amplified by many of Collins' readers. The avowed atheist Baron D'Holbach masked his own authorship of *The Spirit of Judaism* (1770)—one of the most vehemently anti-Jewish texts of the French Enlightenment—by presenting it as a translated work of Collins. Noting that Christianity was simply reformed Judaism, D'Holbach lambasted the unsociability and senseless superstition of this ancient religion, and concluded with an exhortation to Europeans to free themselves from its yoke: "Leave to the stupid Hebrews, those fanatic imbeciles, those cowardly, degraded Asiatics, these superstitions that are as degrading as they are senseless; they are not appropriate for inhabitants of your climate" (10, 170).

110 *Adam Sutcliffe*

Voltaire's frequent and highly polemical assaults on Judaism and the Jews were heavily influenced both by the British Deists and by the clandestine manuscripts of the French philosophical underground. "It is with regret that I discuss the Jews," he claimed in the article on "Tolerance" in his *Philosophical Dictionary* (1764): "This nation is, in many respects, the most detestable ever to have sullied the earth" (20:518–19). However, almost a third of the entries in this volume consisted of charged assaults on Jewish scripture, and an anti-Jewish animus preoccupied him from early texts written in the 1720s through to one of his last texts, a rejoinder to some Jewish critics mockingly titled *One Christian against Six Jews* (1776). These attacks are too constant to be plausibly ascribed to negative experiences involving Jews (such as the bankruptcy of Voltaire's Jewish London banker in 1726), or to the flamboyant excesses of his biting satirical style. Throughout his career Voltaire repeatedly returned to a core of stock themes: the historical irrelevance and unoriginality of the Jews; the absurdity of their religious texts; and their persistent arrogance, immorality, and barbarism. His compulsion to do so stems from the troublesome significance of Judaism for his wider intellectual project.

Among other things, Voltaire saw himself as a historian, and in his vast *Essay on Customs* (1756) he attempted to advance a new and commanding vision of global history, emphasizing the grandeur and antiquity of Chinese and other Asian civilizations. He wrote almost nothing in this history about the Jews: his aim, as he stated in the work's introduction, was to "adhere to the historical," of which, because of the absurdity and unreliability of the Bible, there was very little about Jews to be said (11:110). The argumentative purpose of the work, indeed, was less to illuminate early Chinese history than to destroy, through comparison, the historical and moral authority of the Hebrew sacred narrative. That narrative, however, could not be so easily displaced. Voltaire's repeated dismissal of the Jewish Bible as mere fairy tales and absurdities failed to engage with the nature of religious approaches to this text, or to provide any evidentially compelling alternative account of the Jews and their Bible. Judaism, because of its position at the foundation of Judaeo-Christian mythic history, represented in Voltaire's thought the kernel of myth that remained, despite all his efforts, ultimately impervious to his rationalist Enlightenment critique.

Voltaire has rightly been accorded a prominent role in the history of antisemitism (Hertzberg 1968, 280–313; Poliakov 1975, 3:86–107). It is, however, inadequate simply to condemn him as an antisemite. He was not utterly without compassion for Jews, advancing one of his most vigorous pleas for religious tolerance through the imagined voice of the second-century Rabbi Akiva (24:282 ff). More significantly, the harshness of his hostility to Judaism was not simply a detachable epiphenomenon of his philosophy. Voltaire's attempt to topple the traditional mythic basis of Judaeo-Christian historical self-understanding could never be conclusively achieved, and the resilient endurance of Judaism and its belief system constituted the most stubborn reminder of the limits of Enlightenment

The Enlightenment, French Revolution, Napoleon

explanation. Voltaire's animus toward Judaism should therefore be understood not simply as the product of his individual psychology or prejudice, but rather as a particularly vivid example of the hostility that could be generated by the indigestibility of Judaism for mainstream Enlightenment thought.

Voltaire was an extreme case. No other leading Enlightenment writer exhibited such a pronounced obsession with Jewish themes, although very few ignored them entirely. Denis Diderot, the leading editor of the *Encyclopédie*, broadly shared Voltaire's attitude toward Judaism, and several articles in that work take a generally denigrating approach to Jewish themes, emphasizing Jewish primitiveness and lack of originality and criticizing the mind-numbing legalisms of rabbinic literature. However, although he puts a stereotypically lascivious Jew into one of his fictional texts, Diderot elsewhere expresses admiration for the poetic power of the Jewish Bible and approval of the greater acceptance of Jews in Holland. His overall attitudes toward Jews and Judaism should therefore be seen as mobile and complex. A loosely similar ambivalence is manifested in the writings of Jean-Jacques Rousseau, although Jews figure only very marginally in his writings. While expressing scorn for the primitivism and fanaticism of Jewish culture and religion, Rousseau regarded Moses in reverential terms, following Toland and others in casting him as a model legislator (Schechter 2003, 54–65).

Jews were not only portrayed negatively by Enlightenment thinkers. A sharply contrary image also frequently recurred: the Jew not as inferior to others, but superior; not impervious to Enlightenment ideals, but rather the epitome of them. One of the most notable examples of this was the Marquis d'Argens' bestselling six-volume *Jewish Letters* (1735–8). Taking his cue from Montesquieu's enormously successful *Persian Letters* (1721), d'Argens similarly satirized the vanity and hypocrisy of elite European society though the deadpan observations of three culturally sophisticated and theologically deist Sephardic travelers. D'Argens here reverses the usual relationship between Christians and Jews: far from casting them as insular and narrow-minded, he uses these "philosophical Jews" to exemplify his own universalistic rationalism, and it is through them that he, in *faux-naïf* style, condemns Christian superstition and dogma (Sutcliffe 2003, 208–12).

A similarly idealized and universalist representation of Judaism appears in the dramas of Gotthold Ephraim Lessing, the most famous eighteenth-century German advocate for toleration. The eponymous hero of Lessing's *Nathan the Wise* (1779) was modeled on his friend the Jewish philosopher Moses Mendelssohn, and it is through Nathan that Lessing dramatically develops his view that all religions are identical in the one matter that we should regard as of any significance: their moral teachings. Lessing has generally been regarded by critics, with good reason, as a notable philosemite. However, his writings offer no real appreciation or acknowledgement of the actual distinctiveness of Judaism or of Jewish culture. Lessing and d'Argens' "philosophical Jews" are portrayed in pointed contrast not only to the prevalent hostile stereotypes of Jews, but also to any view of Judaism as legitimately distinct. Although expressed in very different terms from the polemics of Voltaire, these idealizations of Judaism as pure universalism also bear witness to the virtual impossibility for Enlightenment thinkers to recognize, in rationalist terms, an enduring and meaningful place for Jewish difference.

* * *

The closest eighteenth-century engagement with Judaism, however, was not by rationalists but by committed Christians. Traditional mainstream Christianity was under challenge from the Enlightenment, and many theologians, particularly in Protestant northern Europe, attempted to apply more sophisticated tools of critical erudition to Hebrew religious texts in order to inoculate their belief systems against the more radical strains of Enlightenment thought. This strand of Christian Hebraism reached its climax in England in the third quarter of the eighteenth century with Benjamin Kennicott's project to produce a definitive Hebrew text of the Old Testament. Kennicott sought to liberate the Bible from what he regarded as its Jewish distortions—in particular, he sustained a long-standing Hebraist hostility to the vowel points added by the early medieval Jewish Masoretes. In the process, however, he provided a context for notably learned and courteous theological debate between Jews and Christians (Sheehan 2005, 183–5).

In contrast, the tone and impact of the work of Johann Andreas Eisenmenger, a Hebraist at the University of Heidelberg, was vehemently anti-Judaic. A thorough and linguistically competent talmudic scholar, Eisenmenger was nonetheless driven by a firm belief that all Jews were ferociously and implacably anti-Christian. In his *Judaism Exposed* (1700) he produced a vast compendium of extracts from the Talmud and other rabbinic sources ostensibly demonstrating this. Eisenmenger's extracts were authentic and in the main accurately reproduced and translated, but misleadingly wrenched out of context and crudely misinterpreted. He also catalogued and endorsed old blood-libel allegations against Jews. *Judaism Exposed* was so incendiary that prominent Jews sought to and succeeded in securing the suppression of the first edition. When published in 1710 it made readily available for the first time apparently authoritative textual evidence of Jewish malevolence, and since the later nineteenth century this text has been the indispensable sourcebook for antisemites.

Another scholarly approach, which first came to the fore in mid-eighteenth-century England, was the aestheticization of the Hebrew Bible. The bishop and Oxford Professor of Poetry Robert Lowth in his *Lectures on the Sacred Poetry of the Hebrews* (1753) directed attention to the "Oriental" linguistic patterns of Hebrew scriptural poetry, in which he attempted to locate the essence of a divinely inspired sublime quality. Lowth's approach was extremely influential in Germany, where it fed into a critical discourse that both idealized and infantilized Hebrew literature and culture. Johann Gottfried Herder, in his *On the*

The Enlightenment, French Revolution, Napoleon 113

Spirit of Hebrew Poetry (1782), lauded the pure intensity of this "most simple, perhaps... most truly heartfelt poetry in the world." Herder valorized this poetry as a product of "the childhood of the human race," reflecting the earliest and most uncorrupted expressions of human thought (1:21, 46). Following Lowth, he also situated this poetry outside European culture, relating it to the simpler and emphatically foreign cadences of the Oriental or Asiatic world.

Language, for Herder, was crucially constitutive of the distinctive nature of individual cultures. The Hebrew Bible was for him a key piece of evidence in making this case, and his approach to this text was simultaneously both reverential and exclusionary. Herder regarded the Hebrew language, and the culture expressed through it, as superlatively sincere and resonant; however, in insisting on the enduringly incorruptible simplicity of this tradition he also froze Judaism as an exception to his general theory of the organic development of languages and cultures. Uniquely stuck at a developmental moment of near-originary infancy, and eternally shaped by its Oriental roots, Judaism in his contemporary European setting could only be understood as an inauthentic deviation from this admirable but profoundly alien cultural essence. It would do violence to the complexity of Herder's views simply to regard him as an antisemite. Not only was his aesthetic and linguistic theory profoundly admiring of the Jewish heritage, but he also was not opposed to the idea of Jewish emancipation. However, the exceptionality he freighted on Jews placed implicitly insuperable obstacles to their normalization. As Hannah Arendt shrewdly argued in one of her early essays, his vision of the Jewish entry into the modern world effectively required Jews to make a quasi-impossible transformative leap into the present, abandoning their history and culture, which for Herder inescapably belonged to a different era, region, and climate (15–16).

Johann David Michaelis, the leading Hebraist of late eighteenth-century Germany, shared many of Herder's core assumptions, and was, like him, also strongly influenced by the orientalizing aesthetic theory of Robert Lowth. Michaelis believed that the Hebrew Bible could most profitably be elucidated through the advancement of detailed geographical and ethnographic knowledge of the Near East. The customs of the contemporary nomads of Arabia were, he claimed, almost identical to those of the ancient Israelites—far more so than those of contemporary Jews, whose habits had been distorted by the geographically alien influences of Hellenic, rabbinic, and European culture. Michaelis' forceful marshalling of this argument was decisive in persuading the Danish crown to sponsor a major expedition to the Near East in the 1760s, under his scholarly direction (Hess 2002, 69–79). In his sprawling six-volume work, *Mosaic Law* (1770–5)—the most comprehensive eighteenth-century German study of this subject—Michaelis drew on the ethnographical observations of contemporary Arabian culture published by the sole survivor of that trip, Carsten Niebuhr, as corroborating evidence for some of his interpretations of Jewish law. This was germane to him because his overarching purpose in this work was to elucidate

114   *Adam Sutcliffe*

Jewish law as a particular product of a specific time and place, and thus decipherable only in those terms. Michaelis sought to defend the authority of the Bible by carefully demarcating its reach. Moses, he stressed, tailored his laws to suit the "hard-heartedness of the Jews"; his legislation was not, thus, perfect in an absolute sense, "but only the best suited to the then circumstances of the people; not the best for a Platonic, but for an Israelitish republic" (1:15, 18–19).

Michaelis saw the ancient world, and the Hebrew texts he studied, as constitutive of the true essence of Judaism. He therefore regarded it as utterly appropriate for him to intervene as an expert voice in the debate over the regeneration of the Jews that was unleashed by the Prussian scholar and government official Christian Wilhelm von Dohm's *On the Civic Improvement of the Jews* (1781). Against Dohm's argument that an extension of civic rights to Jews would lead to their integration, Michaelis insisted that this goal was unattainable, because the very purpose of the Mosaic law was to preserve the Jews as a separate people. In making his case for Jewish immutability, Michaelis melded biblical, cultural, and biological arguments, all of which, in his view, were aspects of a single, holistic Jewish nature. His most emphatic rejection of Jewish emancipation was on military grounds: the Jews could never serve modern states as loyal and ardent fighters, he claimed, because their religion forbade them from eating with other soldiers and from fighting on the Sabbath, and because they were in any case too short (Dohm 1781–3, 2:41–51).

Michaelis has been regarded by some commentators as a key figure in the emergence of modern racial antisemitism. He unabashedly viewed the Jews' inferiority as inscribed in their bodies, and, as Jonathan Hess has emphasized, fleetingly seemed to imagine their quasi-repatriation to more appropriate climes, as laborers on colonial "sugar islands" (42–3, 79–89). However, Michaelis' view of Jews was much more profoundly scriptural than physical. He shared with Lowth and Herder the prevalent concern among late Enlightenment Protestants to sustain the meaningfulness of the Bible by reasserting, on their own terms, the bonds between living Jews and that ancient text. The stakes riding on the issues raised by Dohm's essay were, for these thinkers, essentially theological rather than political. Michaelis' racialization of Jewish difference features only marginally in his writings, and was incidental to his broader rearticulation, in the semi-scientific rhetoric of late-eighteenth-century scholarship, of the long-standing Christian insistence that the truth of all aspects of Jewish being was to be sought in scripture.

Nonetheless, these scattered hints in Michaelis' argumentation ominously signal the fraught interrelation, from the outset, of two currents of thought that emerged almost simultaneously in the final quarter of the eighteenth century: the debate on Jewish emancipation and the classification and hierarchization of "race." At the fore of the racial discourse was Michaelis' colleague at the University of Göttingen, Johann Friedrich Blumenbach, who in his *On the Natural Varieties of Mankind* (1775) divided humanity into five races, coining the term

The Enlightenment, French Revolution, Napoleon   115

Caucasian to describe the original and "most beautiful" human type. The place of Jews in this schema—which rapidly established itself as highly influential in the emerging discipline of physical anthropology—was slippery. Blumenbach and other late-eighteenth-century medical thinkers were unsure whether to consider Jews a race. Jewish diasporic diversity problematized these scholars' general analytical drive to align geography with race and culture, and it was in large measure for this reason that the debate on Jewish emancipation immediately emerged as a key test case for theories of racial immutability. There was a clear consensus, however, that Jews fell within the Caucasian family, and were thus regarded as white and implicitly as at least relatively beautiful (Eze 1997, 79–90, 105). Throughout the Enlightenment era the precise racial status of Jews was far from clear, and the issue sparked controversy not so much because of straightforward anti-Jewish prejudice as because the Jewish case straddled delicate boundaries of politics, geography, biology, and theology.

Blumenbach's influential explanation for human racial diversity as the result of degeneration from the ideal Caucasian stock inspired more optimistic, reform-minded thinkers to explore the reversal of this process, and here again the case of the Jews was the focus of particularly widespread fascination. Christian Wilhelm von Dohm—the first outspoken advocate of Jewish regeneration—fully shared the consensus view that the Jews of his own era were a sorry band: unhealthy, dishonest, hostile to others, and theologically mired in legalistic pettiness. Unlike Michaelis, however, he regarded this not as their natural state, but as a result of a process of degeneration caused by the discriminatory and hostile treatment they have suffered at the hands of Christians. Once embraced by the broader political society, Dohm insisted, the Jews would rapidly regenerate themselves: their interests would before too long align with those of the states in which they lived, and they would return to the spirit of their noble "ancient Mosaic constitution," suitably altered to fit "changed times and circumstances" (1:144).

Dohm's negative view of his Jewish contemporaries has led him also to be identified as a notable forerunner of modern antisemitism. However, these assessments generally fail to acknowledge the theologico-political complexity of his view of Jews and Judaism. Dohm's cultural and economic critiques of the Jews of his day, pervasively shared by contemporary commentators, were offset by his extremely positive view of their productive and civic potential. His evocation of the grandeur of the Mosaic republic links him to a long tradition of civic republican support for greater openness to Jews: a perspective that had been highly influential in seventeenth-century Holland and was exemplified in England by James Harrington and John Toland. Despite the superficially apparent contrast between Dohm's bureaucratic pragmatism and Michaelis' theological rigidity, Dohm's vision of Jewish regeneration was also strongly based on a sense of the theological exceptionalism of the Jews. Although the impact of Dohm's arguments marked a key turning point in

Jewish history, his attitudes to Jews were both highly ambivalent and heavily indebted to long-standing Christian influences.

* * *

The late-eighteenth-century initiation of the process of Jewish emancipation was, however, by no means shaped purely by theological or theoretical concerns. The actual nature of Jewish economic activity was also the focus of keen concern, especially where this was related to significant tensions between local Jewish and Christian populations. This was particularly the case in Alsace, home to more than half of the 40,000 Jews living in France in this period, most of whom made their living from small-scale trading and moneylending in rural areas. In 1777 and 1778, thousands of debtors in Alsace refused to continue their repayments to Jewish moneylenders, producing payment receipts rejected as forgeries by both the moneylenders and the highest court of Alsace. The likely forger and insti-gator of this "affair of the false receipts" was François Hell, an Alsatian bailiff who, in an inflammatory pamphlet published in the midst of the affair, cast Jews as an alien "nation in the nation," inimical both to Christian morality and to national community (Schechter 2003, 67–73). Hell became a popular hero as a result of the affair, and consequently in 1789 secured a seat in the National Assembly, where he was an outspoken opponent of Jewish citizenship rights. Appealing to Christian and to patriotic values, and also to populist instincts of economic self-interest and hostility to otherness, Hell concocted the potent rhetorical brew that was to become the dominant form of antisemitism in the nineteenth century.

Despite the many pressing issues facing the post-revolutionary French regime, the National Assembly devoted many hours of impassioned debate to the status of the Jews, before deciding in January 1790 to recognize members of the small Sephardic community as French citizens and then, in September 1791, to extend similar recognition to Ashkenazic Jews. The issue of Jewish citizenship was considered significant not simply as an outer limit case of the extent of French democracy and nationhood, but also as a key testing ground for perhaps the most crucial point of contestation facing all programs of enlightened or revolu-tionary reform: whether human transformation was truly possible. François Hell and other opponents of Jewish emancipation regarded Jewish otherness as immutable. Proponents believed the opposite, eagerly anticipating that once the Jews no longer faced economic and political discrimination they would before too long lose their distinctiveness and melt into the unified mainstream of French society. This expectation is resonantly captured by the famous words of the Count of Clermont-Tonnere, one of the leading advocates of Jewish civil rights in the Assembly: "The Jews should be denied everything as a nation, but granted everything as individuals" (in Mendes-Flohr and Reinharz 1995, 115).

Both sides shared a broadly similar and predominantly negative view of contemporary Jewry. Even the Abbé Grégoire—a leading proponent of Jewish

The Enlightenment, French Revolution, Napoleon

rights before, during, and after the French Revolution, and much fêted by Jews as their great emancipator—was no exception to this. Grégoire expressed his admiration for Jewish family life, charitable institutions, and respect for elders and for education. However, he also regarded them as generally dirty, economically rapacious, and culturally, sexually, and physically degenerate. Like Michaelis, he believed the bodies of Jews to be weak and defective, but unlike Michaelis he insisted that their economic and political emancipation would herald their regeneration on both a physical and a spiritual plane. His vision of Jewish spiritual renewal was most explicitly dejudaizing, tinged with overtones of Christian conversionist millenarianism. The fully regenerated Jew envisaged by Grégoire—rather like the imagined philosophical Jew of Lessing and d'Argens—was a universalized figure of virtue, and no longer Jewish in any recognizable sense (Sepinwall 2005, 56–80).

It makes little sense to interpret the debate over Jewish civic rights as a battle between villains and heroes or antisemites versus philosemites. Both camps drew on a shared tradition of Christian European attitudes to Judaism that was steeped in complex ambivalence. There was a general consensus of disdain toward both the religious and the economic aspects of Jewish particularism. However, the exceptional prophetic and eschatological significance of Jews and Judaism for Christianity was enduringly significant in the late eighteenth century not only for theological traditionalists but also for reformers such as Dohm or Grégoire, who modulated into a semi-secular register the great promise of the final conversion of the Jews to the universal norms of practical economic productivity and political citizenship. The evaluative valence of this stance cannot be straightforwardly distilled. If antisemitism is equated with an enthusiasm for the extinguishing of Jewish religious orthodoxy and socio-cultural distinctiveness, then this description much more closely fits the reformers than it does theologians like Michaelis. However, the ultimate triumph of pro-emancipation arguments, enthusiastically supported by the large majority of west European Jews, was imaginable in this period only as a *quid pro quo*. The association of Judaism with the primitivism of the past was deeply baked into the Christian framing structures of the Enlightenment era. The entry of Jews into the modern era thus required a dramatic change in Jews themselves, most pithily summarized by Immanuel Kant in his *The Conflict of the Faculties* (1798) as "the euthanasia of Judaism" (Mack 2003, 23–41).

Jewish emancipation on the French revolutionary model was exported across much of Europe by Napoleon, who was celebrated as a great liberator by many Jewish communities in the Rhineland, Italy, and elsewhere (Schwarzfuchs 1979, 22–3). Napoleon attenuated the hostility of the revolutionary era toward religion, focusing his project of Jewish regeneration on political loyalty and economic productivization. It was, unsurprisingly, in Alsace that the tensions surrounding this project first came to the fore. Complaints over Jewish moneylending were

118 *Adam Sutcliffe*

drawn to Napoleon's attention in Strasbourg in 1806. In response, Napoleon attempted to cut to the core of the issue as he understood it, and to find a definitive resolution. Later that year he convoked in Paris an Assembly of Jewish Notables, charged with answering a battery of questions concerning whether the Jews were both willing and able to integrate into the French nation as patriotic and loyal citizens.

The members of the Assembly did their best to supply the emperor with the answers that it was clear he wanted, and in order to seal the authority of these pronouncements Napoleon had them ratified by a Great Sanhedrin, convened by him on the ancient model. In this gesture we see perhaps the most vivid example of the fractured historical consciousness that so frequently character- ized attitudes to Judaism in this era. Napoleon's summoning of the Parisian Sanhedrin signaled the belief that the true essence of Judaism remained in its ancient past. However, this was also an act of unprecedented theological intervention, with Napoleon casting himself as the key transformative force blasting the Jewish people into the modern era. The original purity of the Jewish law, he asserted, had been altered and confused by rabbinical inven- tion and disagreement, but would be reestablished by the Sanhedrin's enshrinement "near the Talmud" of the doctrinal clarifications he had elicited (Mendes-Flohr and Reinharz 1995, 134). In a sense echoing his self-crowning as emperor in 1804, Napoleon thus grandly inserted himself into Jewish history as the renewing agent of the time-honored authority structures of the past.

Napoleon's policy toward the Jews was heavy with symbolism. But it was also shaped by pragmatism, and particularly by a pressing desire to placate the wide- spread hostility toward Jews in eastern France. The normalization of the Jews, Napoleon decided, required exceptional measures. To this end he issued three decrees in March 1808. The first two of these dealt with organizational matters, imposing on French Jewry a consistorial structure modeled on French Protes- tantism, but charged with particular responsibilities of surveillance and civic education. The third decree imposed many discriminatory regulations on Ashkenazi Jewish moneylending, retroactively deeming many loans invalid, and also restricting the freedom of movement of the Ashkenazim and banning any new Jewish settlement in Alsace (Mendes-Flohr and Reinharz 1995, 139–41). This decree flagrantly undermined the civic equality of Jews granted after the Revolu- tion, and was soon dubbed by Jews as the "Infamous Decree." Although these exceptional measures were not renewed when the decree expired in 1818, Jewish economic distinctiveness, and the anti-Jewish hostility related to this, remained an enduring focus of tension in early-nineteenth-century France. The obligatory aim of Jewish emancipation, implicit since the serious emergence of the idea in the early 1780s, was the rapid disappearance of all significant differences between Jews and non-Jews. Napoleon explicitly placed the onus of change on the Jews themselves. In doing so, he effectively condoned all popular suspicion or anger

The Enlightenment, French Revolution, Napoleon 119

toward Jews as a legitimate response to their failure to attain the full economic normalization expected of them.

* * *

Attitudes to Judaism in the Enlightenment era were, above all, highly ambivalent. Although some prominent figures—most notably Voltaire—were particularly venomous toward Jews and Judaism, in general it makes little sense to attempt to identify a lineage of pure antisemitism running through this period. Hostility toward Jewish religious traditionalism was often combined with an idealization of the past glory and future potential of the Jews, while disdain for the cultural, economic, and physical condition of contemporary Jewry was a ubiquitous hallmark of the proponents of Jewish emancipation. It is also largely misleading to search in this period for the bridge between medieval religious antisemitism and modern secular antisemitism. Theological assumptions conditioned even the most apparently modern currents of Enlightenment thought in many ways, and perhaps nowhere is this more evident than with regard to Jews. Nonetheless, this was indeed a period of self-conscious transformation, and attitudes and policies toward Jews were deeply bound up with attitudes and understandings of the changes wrought by the Enlightenment. The sharpest divide in the eighteenth century was not between supposed friends and enemies of the Jews, but between those who sought to herald Jewish transformation and those who regarded this as impossible. In the closing phase of the Enlightenment the former camp triumphed. European Jewry was indeed transformed as a consequence, but not in the way that the early reformers had anticipated. It was only then that the Jewish Question emerged as a supposed problem and puzzle, and antisemitism intensified, on occasion amplifying certain strands of eighteenth-century thought and rhetoric, but largely shaped by the distinctively post-Enlightenment conditions of the nineteenth century.

CITED PRIMARY SOURCES

Dohm, Christian Wihelm von, *Über die bürgerliche Verbesserung der Juden* (Berlin and Stettin, 1781–3) [Repr., Hildesheim: Georg Olms, 1973] [Vol. 2 includes Johann David Michaelis, "Herr Ritter Michaelis Beurtheilung" (1782)].

Herder, Johann Gottfried, *On the Spirit of Hebrew Poetry* (London, 1833).

Holbach, Baron d', *L'Esprit du Judaisme, ou Examen raisonée de la loi de Moïse* ("London," 1770).

Mendes-Flohr, Paul, and Jehuda Reinharz (eds), *The Jew in the Modern World: A Documentary History* (New York: Oxford University Press, 1995).

Michaelis, Johann David, *Commentaries on the Laws of Moses*, 4 vols, trans. Alexander Smith (London, 1814).

Spinoza, Benedictus de, *Theological-Political Treatise* (1670), trans. Samuel Shirley, in Michael Morgan (ed.), *Spinoza: Complete Works* (Indianapolis: Hackett, 2003).

Voltaire, *Oeuvres completes*, 52 vols, ed. Louis Moland (Paris: Garnier, 1877–85).

RECOMMENDED READINGS

Arendt, Hannah, "The Enlightenment and the Jewish Question" (1932), in Jerome Kohn and Ron H. Feldman (eds), *Hannah Arendt: The Jewish Writings* (New York: Schocken, 2007), 3–18.

Eze, Emmanuel, *Race and the Enlightenment* (Oxford: Blackwell, 1997).

Hertzberg, Arthur, *The French Enlightenment and the Jews: The Origins of Modern Anti-Semitism* (New York: Columbia University Press, 1968).

Hess, Jonathan, *Germans, Jews, and the Claims of Modernity* (New Haven: Yale University Press, 2002).

Katz, Jacob, *From Prejudice to Destruction: Anti-Semitism 1700–1933* (Cambridge, MA: Harvard University Press, 1980).

Mack, Michael, *German Idealism and the Jew* (Chicago: University of Chicago Press, 2003).

Poliakov, Léon, *The History of Anti-Semitism*, vol. 3: *From Voltaire to Wagner* (London: Routledge and Kegan Paul, 1975).

Schechter, Ronald, *Obstinate Hebrews: Representations of Jews in France, 1715–1815* (Berkeley/Los Angeles: University of California Press, 2003).

Schwarzfuchs, Simon, *Napoleon, the Jews and the Sanhedrin* (London: Routledge and Kegan Paul, 1979).

Sepinwall, Alyssa Goldstein, *The Abbé Grégoire and the French Revolution* (Berkeley/Los Angeles: University of California Press, 2005).

Sheehan, Jonathan, *The Enlightenment Bible* (Princeton: Princeton University Press, 2005).

Sutcliffe, Adam, *Judaism and Enlightenment* (Cambridge: Cambridge University Press, 2003).

8

Political Antisemitism in Germany and Austria, 1848–1914

Richard S. Levy

Jew-hatred was already millennia old before the modern forms, terminology, and methods of political antisemitism emerged in German-speaking Europe in the second half of the nineteenth century. The explanations for why antisemitism developed when and where it did vary greatly. In his influential *A Word about Our Jews*, the leading German historian Heinrich von Treitschke explained:

When, with disdain, the English and French talk of German prejudice against Jews, we must answer: You don't know us. You live in fortunate circumstances that make the emergence of such "prejudices" impossible. The number of Jews in western Europe is so small that it cannot exert a palpable influence upon your national mores (in Levy 1991, 70).

Treitschke, defending what he considered a justified uprising of the German *Volk* against Jewish presumption, thought he had clinched his case by alluding to numbers and the threat that such concentrations of Jews posed to a young nation. When he wrote *A Word* in 1879–80, 560,000 Jews lived in the German Reich. In the Austrian capital of Vienna there were nearly 73,000 (10% of the city's inhabitants), almost twice as many as in Paris (40,000) and a great many more than in all of Britain (46,000). But, sizable though the concentration of Jews was in central Europe, especially in its large metropolises, mere numbers cannot account for the appearance of antisemitism there. Further east in Europe, millions of Jews lived out their often insecure and impoverished lives without provoking the new, more systematic and sustained, forms of hostility and persecution taking shape as Treitschke wrote.

It was the quality of the Jews rather than their quantity that helped engender antisemitism in central and western Europe. Albert Lindemann has linked the genesis of antisemitism to what he aptly calls the "rise of the Jews," their astonishing individual and group upward mobility during the course of the nineteenth century (20–3, *passim*). As contributors to the arts and sciences, consumers of higher education, accumulators of wealth, innovators in business, revolutionizers of the media, leaders of political parties and social movements, and holders

122 *Richard S. Levy*

of public offices, Jews manifestly flourished. Although Treitschke spoke of "the inexhaustible Polish cradle" from which "there streams over our eastern border a host of hustling, pants-peddling youths," what really filled him with dread was that their "children and children's children will someday command Germany's stock exchanges and newspapers." He had in his lifetime experienced enough of the rise of the Jews to prophesy this alarming future.

Well into the eighteenth century, Jews in German-speaking Europe were part of either a tiny very privileged group—the so-called Court Jews whose economic services were vital to some prince or other—or a much larger group of the severely unprivileged. At the end of the eighteenth century, an estimated 80% of German Jews lived in poverty, subject to limitations on their freedom of movement and right to earn a living. A century later, Jews in Frankfurt am Main were paying four times more taxes than Protestants and eight times more than Catholics, a sure sign of their appreciably greater income levels. In the 1880s, Jews made up over 9% of the university student population of Prussia, nearly ten times their proportion of the general population. Half of the female students in Vienna's high schools in 1900 and a third of the student body at the University of Vienna were Jewish. Finally, no matter how compiled, lists of the era's luminaries in philosophy, literature, music, and science are always heavily populated with Jews.

Of course, such success stories were not universal. The rise of the Jews was far from even. Poverty was still the condition of many, so too exclusion or denial of advancement in the civil service or academic work. Nevertheless, antisemitism, once it achieved a foothold, clung tenaciously to the perception of an empowered and virtually monolithic Jewry. It did so despite all objective evidence to the contrary, evidence that showed Jews to be more fractious and fragmented than at any previous moment in their history: Orthodox, Reformed, and apostate, Yiddish, Czech, Magyar, and German-speaking, liberal and socialist, assimilationist and Zionist—diversity, not uniformity, was the hallmark of central European Jews. To have acknowledged this reality, however, would have robbed antisemitism of its compelling attraction for believers—its capacity to explain all. They could not afford to make fine distinctions, allow meaningful exceptions, or accept human complexity. For them, there had to be a single Jewry with a single menacing agenda in the present and throughout the ages.

That the material and social advances of the Jews should be found objectionable by their neighbors was highly likely. A people long regarded as morally and physically corrupt was seen to be thriving while honest, hard-working natives struggled. This violated an established expectation at least as old as St. Augustine's doctrine of Jewish witness, which held that it was the earthly function of Jews to live dispersed, subjugated, and in misery, thereby demonstrating the superiority of God's new chosen people, the Christians. A secularized version of this notion, still very much alive in the nineteenth century, produced moral outrage that alien Jews rather than real Germans or Austrians should be doing so well.

Political Antisemitism in Germany and Austria 123

Not everyone felt this way, however. By the mid-nineteenth century, freeing Jews from age old restrictions on citizenship, habitation, and occupation had come to be seen as one of a number of self-evidently necessary reforms for a modern country. These reforms had been realized in the revolutions of 1848, but had, with a few exceptions, been withdrawn when the old regimes regained power. The Habsburg empire in 1867 and the North German Confederation in 1869 (extended to the unified Reich in 1871) finally abolished all remaining disabilities resulting from religious identity. Jews and their liberal allies regarded this as the culmination of a century-old struggle for Jewish emancipation, the long overdue achievement of legal equality. Emancipation had awakened localized popular opposition in 1848, but twenty years later it was not a matter of much interest to most non-Jewish Germans or Austrians. They had looked on passively as the governing elite and progressive political forces legislated the change. The reaction of those who would soon be calling themselves antisemites was far more passionate.

They saw emancipation as signaling a portentous reversal in the relations between Jews and non-Jews. Jews had not merely gained equality; they had been empowered, thanks to their liberal co-conspirators or dupes. Emancipation had enshrined in law the rise of the Jews, which was habitually explained as the result of ill-gotten gains rather than hard work. Karl von Vogelsang, the mentor of the Austrian Christian Social Party, declared, "Christians in Austria are being robbed, dominated, and reduced to pariahs by the Jews" (in Lindemann 1997, 199). Jews had been carelessly or traitorously given not just membership in the nation, but the means to dominate it. The continuing progress of the Jews, coupled with their legal emancipation, gave birth to organized antisemitism and thereafter continued to shape its outlook and ideology. From the late 1870s forward, the antisemitic movements in Germany and Austria hinged on fantasies of enormous Jewish power, acquired in illegitimate ways, and used with heartless efficiency to subvert all that was holy and good.

It is not coincidental that the neologism *antisemitism* dates from the last stages of the struggle for Jewish equality. A decade after emancipation became law, Wilhelm Marr named his infant political party the Antisemites' League, at least in part to distinguish it from more traditional sorts of anti-Jewish competitors. Treitschke employed the word in November 1879, and it then appeared in Vienna in January 1880 in the prestigious *Neue Freie Presse*. Over the next fifteen years, variants of *antisemitism, antisemite,* and *antisemitic* made their way out of the German-speaking world into nearly every European language.

Neologisms are rarely fortuitous. This word, and its rapid adoption, reflects a movement achieving self-awareness and then seeing its implicit claims of newness accepted by allies, enemies, and bystanders. Older forms of Jew-hatred might have been adequate to tell people what to *think* about Jewish empowerment, cultural presence, and material success; it could give voice to their rejection of Jewish celebrity and even explain how such a thing could have happened; those offended by the rise of the Jews had merely to reach for culturally embedded stereotypes, prejudices, and expectations to frame their anger or dismay. Anti-Jewish feelings were a part of the life experience of Europeans; it was the rare individual who remained unaware of this received wisdom and an even rarer one who overcame its legacy. In 1819 and again in 1848, that is, within living memory, anti-Jewish animus had produced waves of popular violence. Yet such outbreaks were not the norm. More often than not, as Hitler later lamented, the emotion-laden Jew-hatred of the mob, never led to permanent changes in relations (http://www.h-net.org/~german/gtext/kaiserreich/hitler2.html#point1). In contrast to traditional Jew-hatred, antisemitism was action-oriented from its inception. It went beyond mere feeling by demanding that the victims of the Jews *act*, in one way or another, to disempower the enemy. The new word—signifying a new approach to the so-called Jewish Question—was necessary because the Jews had managed to evade the time-honored boundaries and barriers that wise forebears had established to keep them at bay. Now, however, the enemy was no longer at the gates, he had crept within the citadel.

Just as the rise of the Jews produced a new conception of the Jewish problem, it also called forth new anti-Jewish activists. Antisemitism in Austria and Germany was the creation of intellectuals whose motives ranged from sincere fear of Jewish power to cynical calculation, from naked personal ambition to a selfless desire to serve the nation. Between 1848 and the turn of the twentieth century, they fashioned an ideology that has proven both durable and seductive, a body of simple ideas that can explain past, present, and future and which has at times guided men's rage and fear along singularly destructive paths. Few of them today would qualify as great thinkers, but in their own day they were able to articulate powerful myths, gain the attention of a broad public, and move at least a portion of it to action. While it is tempting to dismiss antisemitic ideologues as intellectual pygmies or envious losers, little is to be gained by such trivialization. For every Wilhelm Marr, whose life was a series of failures and disappointments, there was a Richard Wagner, Adolf Stoecker, Heinrich Class, or Karl Lueger, men of talent who knew worldly success. Antisemitism certainly attracted more than its share of cranks and rabble-rousers, but in Germany, Austria, and many other places it also appealed to university student elites, which could often be found in the vanguard of the political movement. Whether failures or successes or something in between, not all of those who became active in the movement answered to the same profile. The more prominent among them, however, shared some important characteristics that may explain what drew them to the ideology.

Antisemitism as a movement quickly found its home on the right side of the political spectrum, among ultranationalists, cultural pessimists, "life reformers," romantic reactionaries, and, especially, Christian conservatives. Well before an organizational structure emerged in the last quarter of the nineteenth century, embattled Christians, Catholic and Protestant alike, had come to classify most

Political Antisemitism in Germany and Austria 125

forms of progressive politics among those modern evils that undermined religion. They were certain democracy was pure folly and that the common people, whether they knew it or not, required hierarchy and authority to be truly happy. Jews, judging from their notable role in the Austrian and German revolutions of 1848 and their close identification with liberalism and socialism in the years that followed, seemed hell-bent on destroying the sacred bonds of the community. Antisemitism provided people who thought this way with a means of lashing out against the evils of modernity and their agents, the rootless, restless Jews. Protestant clergymen made their way into German antisemitic politics and often wielded significant influence. In Austria, Catholic priests played a highly public role in the spread of Christian Social antisemitism.

Hostility toward Jews was not a right-wing monopoly, however. Radical democrats and socialists might also harbor and give voice to many anti-Jewish sentiments. But there was a crucial difference. Rarely did these men make the leap from traditional anti-Jewish prejudice to antisemitism. They did not urge action against Jews or, with occasional exceptions, attempt to exploit generalized anti-Jewish feelings for political ends. The reason for this difference, however, is not to be found in any greater appreciation of Jews among people on the Left than among those on the Right. Both were schooled in the traditional anti-Jewish stereotypes, and both were probably equally angered by the rise of the Jews. The difference had to do not with Jews but with divergent views of the masses of humanity and their potential for democratic emancipation. The democratically inclined believed this possible and were only rarely persuaded that solving the Jewish Question would in any way hasten the arrival of human freedom. Notwithstanding their often negative feelings about Jews, they directed their efforts at other enemies. Antisemites, no matter their other differences, were adamantly united in their rejection of democracy. Although many important early proponents, including Wagner, Lueger, Marr, Bruno Bauer, Georg von Schönerer, and Otto Glagau, got their first political experience in liberal or radical ventures, none of them wedded his antisemitism to liberal or democratic values or agendas.

Before turning to antisemitism, they had, for a variety of reasons, experienced a prior loss of faith in the masses and even the possibility of achieving democracy in the immediate or remote future; the human material they had to work with simply could not support such utopian fantasies. At times, antisemites—Georg von Schönerer might serve as their exemplar in this regard—appeared in the guise of populists, as protectors of the little man, or as fearless exposers of corruption in high places. Nevertheless, their programs were, in fact, uniformly antidemocratic. Their solutions of the Jewish Question promised prosperity, national salvation, or moral regeneration but did not envision democracy as possible or desirable. The masses were too unreliable, too likely to fall victim to Jewish cunning, to be trusted with governing themselves or making the important decisions.

For those antisemites who had cut loose from progressive politics as well as those of their colleagues who had never understood its appeal, a stark problem remained: the German masses had been enfranchised (at the same time as the Jews had been emancipated). A political solution of the Jewish Question in Germany or in Austria, where enfranchisement came only gradually, would find it impossible to ignore this fact. Those who had little or no faith in the political intelligence of ordinary citizens would somehow have to win their votes, if they were to have the slightest hope of solving the welter of problems they attributed to an empowered Jewry. After the emancipation of the Jews and the enfranchisement of the *Volk*, the creation of a mass movement became an unavoidable necessity. A few individuals saw or soon came to see the politicalization of antisemitism as a veritable fool's errand. Ironically, the great majority of others were filled with optimism, having convinced themselves that antisemitism had a striking advantage when it came to harnessing the raw power of the masses.

A politicized Jew-hatred actually promised a new and improved way of moving the herd in desired directions. History, properly understood, had shown that the *Volk* could be better mobilized by hatred than by reason, that its passions were far easier to access than its good sense. One merely had to direct the people's already existing anti-Jewish prejudices toward the proper political ends. The fight against Jewry could therefore begin immediately, without making any great demands on the intelligence of the common man. There would be plenty of time later to take on the difficult task of educating merely prejudiced voters and thus transforming them into authentic, dedicated antisemites ready to engage in the long struggle. Although often accused of being manipulative demagogues, the founders saw no inherent contradictions in their view of the situation. It was a happy coincidence that the times called for exactly what the *Volk* was perfectly suited to accomplish. A properly led modern political movement could mobilize the people, foil the schemes of the Jews, and save the nation from destruction.

* * *

The path to this goal became clear only gradually. The years from 1848 to 1879 can be regarded as a time of false starts, cautious experimentation, and the beginning of a discourse on new ways of dealing with the Jewish Question. Even those who felt the Jewish peril had to be addressed sooner rather than later thought testing the waters to be the wisest course. Wilhelm Marr's experience argued in favor of caution. Once a man of the democratic Left, he had been disenchanted by the failures of his revolutionary efforts in 1848 and gone into voluntary exile. When he returned to his native Hamburg in 1859, he was a different man. No longer an advocate of egalitarian principle, he had sought and found a new understanding in white supremacy, eugenics, and racism. He made his political reorientation known in 1862 with *A Mirror to the Jews*, a bitter settling of scores with local political rivals, but also an argument for denying equal rights to Jews. The book repeated the familiar charges of Jewish mendacity,

Political Antisemitism in Germany and Austria 127

ethical inferiority, instinctive hatred for all non-Jews, and fanatical adherence to a hollow religion—all ideas that could be found in Voltaire or the Young Hegelians. But Marr gave his indictment a pointedly racist rationale, alluding to "tribal peculiarities" and "an alien essence." He advised his readers that "the Jews have to adapt to us, not we to the Jews," yet, he warned, only a very, very few of them could succeed in becoming real Germans. The book, printed at the author's expense because it could not find a publisher, stirred some local outrage and then dropped from view. The public, Marr learned, was simply not attuned to discussions of the Jewish Question.

Chastened by this reception, Marr waited seventeen years before he felt confident enough again to raise these issues in print. In 1879, posing once more as historian, literary critic, psychologist, philosophe, economist, and moralist, the "dispassionate chronicler" could no longer confine his story to the petty politics of Hamburg because now, as his title proclaimed, he had some truly dire news to impart: *The Victory of Jewry over Germandom.* He may have still been motivated by personal grudges against Jews, whom he blamed for the crumbling of his journalistic career, but now he saw larger forces at work that explained the awesome growth of Jewish power since last he wrote. He understood more clearly than in 1862 that it was race that had shaped world history from the Babylonian Captivity to the present moment. A Jewish conspiracy eighteen hundred years in the making, a "Thirty Years War" (since 1848) waged by a triumphant Jewry, were about to bear their deadly fruit. The book was a sensation. Published in February 1879, it went through twelve reprintings by the end of the year. Unlike all the twenty-two other books and countless journalistic pieces Marr had written since the 1840s, this one was taken note of by serious thinkers, the mainstream press, and a large public.

Victory was superior to Marr's other works, more systematic and passionate than his previous efforts; its attack was more sustained and rhetoric more incisive. Still, the enthusiastic reception cannot be explained solely by the quality of the writing or persuasiveness of the argument. It was really Marr's timing that had improved. Much had changed in Germany between 1862 and 1879. A dynamic capitalism, with its many social casualties, a militant socialist movement, a crisis in agricultural prices, rapid urbanization, and a host of other disruptive developments had readied large segments of the population for Marr's message and prepared the ground for organized antisemitism.

The organizing impulse gathered speed after *Victory* and soon supplied the necessary structure for those who sought to act against the Jews. The antisemitic political parties and associations that took root in the German empire in the early 1880s, and somewhat later in German Austria, bore many different names and conducted fierce debates with one another on questions of strategy and ideology, but this should not obscure their several similarities. All of them drew the bulk of their initial membership and broader electoral support from artisans, family farmers, low-level bureaucrats, school teachers, petty retailers, and small property holders. These were the people hit hardest by their nations' rocky transformation from an agricultural to an industrial market economy, a much swifter and more methodical process in Germany than in Austria, it is true, but producing similar turmoil in both places. Already battered, the fortunes of these "little people" fell precipitously after the Crash of 1873.

The *Krach* had begun, most suspiciously, in a Viennese banking house owned by the Rothschilds; the ensuing financial panic then spread to Germany and beyond, causing great hardship during the following two decades of economic dislocation. Measuring their own decline against what appeared to be the dramatic ascent of Jewry, and refusing to notice that Jews were also victimized by the crash, these desperate, confused, but angry people were ripe for the antisemitic explanations of their troubles supplied by Marr and many others. The charge that the Jews had caused the calamity was unfair, but the presence of several Jewish names among those who seemed to be cashing in on the crisis was all the proof many Germans and Austrians required. One publicist claimed, without citing any evidence, that 90% of the fraudulent bankruptcies—a prominent feature of the financial collapse—was the work of Jews. Another accused Jews of battening off the misery of honest people and saw this as "the excellent results of [Jewish] emancipation." Not to be outdone, Marr announced that 1873 represented nothing less than a shift in the total wealth of the nation in favor of the Jews.

In the sour atmosphere of economic downturn and dashed dreams, a revulsion against progressive and modern trends provided political antisemitism with its dynamism. Many felt themselves the innocent victims of anonymous forces possibly too great to resist. Marr unmasked the dark powers gathering over Germany, Austria, and the world. Jewry was the enemy, and it had to be combated "coldly and rationally," that is, politically. The pessimistic tone of his *Victory of Jewry over Germandom* could not conceal a call to action—but action of a new sort. Marr specifically rejected the old undisciplined anti-Jewish measures—religiously motivated persecution, expulsions, pogroms, haphazard discrimination. These had plainly failed to halt the march of the Jews. Now, after the *fait accompli* of emancipation, it was too late for such intermittent and half-hearted gestures. Naïve Germans had once thought that merely maintaining the status quo would suffice to keep the Jews in their place. No longer. The status quo had actually embraced Jewish equality and released the Jews' own brand of ruthless realism. This threatening new reality meant that traditional methods had to give way to a continuous political effort, institutionalized in parties, propaganda associations, and newspapers. What was implicit in *The Victory of Jewry* became explicit in Marr's next pamphlet, tossed off in July 1879, *Elect No Jews!* It bore the heartening subtitle, "the way to victory of Germandom over Jewry," and it launched antisemitism into the political culture of Germany.

Marr was but one among a group of disparate individuals who, while divided on too many key issues to form a unified political organization, were nevertheless

Political Antisemitism in Germany and Austria

in basic agreement on the kind of action necessary to defeat the common enemy. The way to the victory over Jewry lay in the Reichstag, not in the streets. Although a political party specifically devoted to antisemitism was unprecedented, the strategy adopted by the several antisemitic parties in Germany in the decade of the 1880s was essentially conventional. Organizing at the grassroots level, writing, speaking, electioneering, winning a majority (or sizable minority) of mandates in municipal, state, and national parliaments, presenting and passing legislation in these bodies—this was the agenda that would beat back the Jews.

A dramatic first step toward this goal was the Antisemites' Petition, circulated during the summer and autumn of 1880 by activists in the new parties and university student sympathizers and intended to act as a national plebiscite on the Jewish Question. More than a quarter million signatures were gathered on a document asking the government to prohibit or at least limit Jewish immigration, exclude Jews from positions of authority over Germans, end the employment of Jews as teachers in the public elementary schools, and conduct a special census to determine exactly how many Jews there were in Germany. Enactment of these measures would have overturned Jewish emancipation, something Chancellor Otto von Bismarck's government, several months before receiving formal delivery of the petition, announced it would not consider. The antisemites, however, persevered. Undoing emancipation became the basic goal of all their parties.

Enthusiasm at the start of the movement encouraged the eventual formation of nearly 140 local reform clubs, reservoirs of the funds and the people with which to conduct vigorous election campaigns and carry on the work of enlightenment regarding the Jewish Question. The founding of antisemitic newspapers proceeded at a rapid pace, holding out the hope of ending the Jews' alleged stranglehold over public opinion. On occasion, one or more of the parties was able to capture the headlines, putting the Jewish Question before the public in arresting ways. Further, as the antisemites demonstrated their ability to mobilize elements of the population, particularly the Protestant lower middle class in the towns and countryside, they gained the attention of powerful conservatives and agrarians. Even Bismarck showed interest in using the antisemitic parties to undermine his left-liberal enemies in the national capital.

Despite these indicators of potential effectiveness, the parliamentary solution of the Jewish Question in Germany was a failure in its own terms and in the eyes of its contemporaries. Hopes of conquering an electoral majority evaporated quickly. Unable to penetrate the Catholic or working-class masses, the antisemites of the imperial era were left with the lower middle class upon which to build. They never succeeded in overcoming the deep divisions that characterized these social strata or in recruiting any but a small minority of them. Moreover, funding from this base proved insufficient to run increasingly expensive election campaigns. Yet financial dependence on the German Conservative Party and the successful lobbyists of the Agrarian League, when it could be prised free, raised doubts about the antisemites' independence. These power brokers doled out support to chosen antisemitic candidates at election time but kept their distance from rowdier and less politically reliable elements. To "sincere" antisemites the leaders of these rich organizations seemed only interested in exploiting the Jewish Question rather than solving it. Neither could it be said that the movement was well served by its own leaders. Personal rivalries, endless lawsuits, and embarrassing scandals preoccupied them. "Generals without troops," they could not stifle the ambition to be solely in charge of even small armies, one of the reasons that the parties could not sustain their brief moment of (relative) unity between 1894 and 1900.

The antisemites' best showing came in the Reichstag elections of 1893 with 16 deputies out of a total of 397. This was a marked improvement over the single seat won in 1887 and the 5 in 1890, but the winners, representing mostly Hessian and Saxon districts, sat for three distinct parties, thereby diminishing the effect of the victory. Perhaps 350,000 votes (4.4%) were cast for identifiable antisemites, some of whom joined other parties in the Reichstag. From this point, however, their percentage of the vote declined steadily. In the last Reichstag elections before World War I, they scratched together only 131,000 votes, and during the course of the war the 6 remaining antisemitic deputies, still in two different parties, disappeared into various right-wing formations, bringing an end to their autonomous existence. State parliament and city council elections sometimes showed better results, but even here the prospects for passage of antisemitic legislation were diminishing rather than improving by 1914 (Levy 1975, 85–90, 251–6).

Not a single piece of anti-Jewish legislation passed the national parliament, even though several bills were presented, a few of them repeatedly. Although the thundering oratory of Court Chaplain Stoecker could command parliament's attention, the other antisemitic deputies, unable to meet the high standards of that body or contribute anything substantial to the legislative process, were frequently objects of ridicule. The strength of the Catholic Center and the Social Democratic parties, whose leaders rejected parliamentary antisemitism, and the opposition of the small but articulate liberal parties, doomed attempts to use the Reichstag for solving the Jewish Question.

Challenging the "Jewish press" with their own powerful journalistic establishment also proved a pipedream for the antisemites. From its emergence in the late 1870s until the Nazi takeover of 1933, the antisemitic political movement never managed to organize an effective press effort. Every individual with leadership ambitions had to have his own journal; several Reichstag deputies earned (perilous) livelihoods by starting up a paper. Instead of pooling resources and centralizing efforts, ruthless and debilitating competition prevailed. Between 1890 and 1897, the period of political antisemitism's greatest popularity, thirty-six newspapers were in print; by 1898, supply had adjusted to demand, leaving only

Political Antisemitism in Germany and Austria 131

seven still in operation. Their political enemies delighted in pointing out that these publications exhibited exactly the traits the antisemites attributed to the "Jew-press": poor production values, devotion to automobile crashes and celebrity sex scandals, biased and inaccurate reporting, coarseness of tone, and an often fatal vulnerability to libel suits. These were papers that only the committed bothered to read.

This bankruptcy of conventional, parliamentary antisemitism led to a gradual radicalization of outlook. The belief could no longer be sustained that, once the people had been recruited to antisemitism, only minor tampering with the constitution of the Reich would be necessary in order to drive the Jews from power. By the turn of the century, antisemitic politicians inside and outside of the parliament began casting about for more effective methods in a struggle against the Jews that many of them now feared they were losing. Universal suffrage, the loyalty of non-Jewish government officials and public figures, the legal, educational, and economic systems—all came under attack. With the death or withdrawal of the founder generation of leaders the way was gradually cleared for those who had never accepted the feasibility of solving the Jewish Question through party politics. For deeply undemocratic men like the successful publisher Theodor Fritsch, parliaments and parties were symptoms of the Judaic disease afflicting Germany. According to him and the group that gathered around his journal *Hammer*, all levels of German society would have to be infused with antisemitism before sweeping measures to cleanse German life of false values could be undertaken. Normal politics were futile in this struggle for survival. On the eve of World War I, Fritsch called for an organization whose job it would be to mete out revolutionary justice to "left-wing criminals and Jews," destroy the Reichstag, and establish "a constitutional dictatorship" (in Levy 1975, 260).

* * *

The history of political antisemitism in Austria, although it resembled the German phenomenon in many ways, followed a different course. It, too, offered a variety of options for those who wished to act against Jews. Georg von Schönerer, another former leftist, grew contemptuous of a temporizing liberalism that could not recognize the mounting threat against German dominance in the Habsburg empire and whose tolerance of corruption had produced the *Krach* of 1873. A populist champion of the lower middle-class victims of the crash, Schönerer first cooperated with like-minded Jews, socialists, and other nationalists in issuing the Linz Program of 1882, one of the points of which called for German Austria's closer connection to Germany. But by 1885, Schönerer decided that Jews were inappropriate allies in the defense of German hegemony and added a twelfth point to the Linz Program calling for their complete exclusion. From then on, his rhetoric grew ever more extreme, attacking not just Jews but the Habsburg dynasty and Catholic religion. In the process he made certain that he would never achieve a mass following. His movement remains important,

132 *Richard S. Levy*

however, because of what Adolf Hitler, one of its outspoken admirers, said it taught him about combining "correct [antisemitic] theory" with radical politics (*Mein Kampf*, 1943, trans. R. Manheim, 98–101; on Lueger, 55, 69).

Hitler also admired the other major proponent of Austrian antisemitism, Karl Lueger, who began his political life as a liberal but by the 1880s had moved into the anti-liberal, nationalist circles where he came into contact with the pan-German Schönerer. Their collaboration soon ended, however, when Lueger found a more attractive set of principles in the Christian Social movement forming under the tutelage of the Catholic ideologue Karl von Vogelsang. Austro-liberalism, closely identified with the rise of the Jews, was still the enemy, but Catholicism and loyalty to the Habsburgs distinguished the Christian Social Party (founded in 1891) from Schönerer's Pan-Germans. These stances, more in keeping with the views of its core constituency, allowed the Christian Socials to build an impressive mass movement from among the same social groups that supported the antisemitic parties in Germany and elsewhere. A gifted leader, Lueger rode the movement to great personal power and enduring popularity. He was chosen mayor of Vienna three times before Kaiser Franz Joseph, who disapproved of his demagoguery and antisemitism, finally sanctioned his election in 1897. He held the office until his death in 1910, and his party remained a major power in national politics into the 1930s. Even today, traces of its style can still be found in Austrian politics.

Austrian Christian Social antisemitism began its exercise of power just as parliamentary antisemitism in Germany began its downward slide. It is natural to ask why these trajectories were so different. Both were born as movements protesting the economic and social consequences of modernization. However, by any objective standard, there was much more to protest in the Habsburg empire than in the relatively vibrant, ascendant German Reich. By the mid-1890s, Germany had emerged from twenty years of economic uncertainty and was embarking on a period of steady and extraordinary growth. Austria, and particularly the small peasants and lower middle-class town dwellers that backed the Christian Socials, experienced no such upward surge. Thus, the problems that triggered antisemitism remained pressing, making Lueger's constituents more dependably responsive to his promises of help and hope.

Further, the Habsburgs ruled over an empire being torn apart by ethnically based nationalism. Ethnic conflict and its reckless excesses in the public sphere were a more familiar, more acceptable part of the Austrian than German life, and this fact benefited Lueger's movement. German antisemites found it constantly necessary to reassure their contemporaries that antisemitism was respectable, vitally important, and not the least bit unsavory. Austrian political culture, riven by ethnic hatreds, made few such demands on Lueger and his followers. The mayor's own raucous style spurred his followers to go further. When Councilor Bielohlawek, for example, said in a speech "yes, we want to annihilate the Jews," he could be fairly certain that neither Lueger nor an

Political Antisemitism in Germany and Austria 133

outraged public would censure him. In such a climate, singling Jews out for political attack was unlikely to seem anything but normal and suitable. Austrian antisemites contributed to this atmosphere and then exploited it adroitly.

Another factor favoring Austrian antisemitism's greater success was the political constellation in which it operated. In both Germany and Austria, liberalism had come under a broad-based attack, not just as the party responsible for Jewish emancipation and as the champion of the laissez-faire economics that produced the miseries of the *Krach*, but also as a system of values. Hallowed liberal beliefs in human equality, the rights of man, and the efficacy of reason in public discourse were subject to assault. Although liberalism had lost some of its moral authority during the last decades of the century, it remained a force in Germany, and its most principled elements could reliably be expected to oppose antisemitism. Influential left-liberal intellectuals and politicians publicly defended the rights of Jews in newspapers, universities, antidefamation leagues, and on the floor of the Reichstag. Austro-liberalism, by contrast, had been so utterly defeated and thoroughly discredited by its enemies, the Christian Socials chief among them, that even the occasional symbolic gesture was without much consequence.

Liberals, when effective, made their influence felt among the well-educated. Antisemites, however, had also to be confronted in the streets, which meant that the attitudes and behaviors of the mass parties were a crucial part of the contest. In Germany, socialists and Catholics had experienced the full repressive power of Bismarck's government, convincing at least the leaders of their respective parties that it was folly to let themselves be distracted by the Jewish Question. No matter their opinions about Jews, the real threat to their existence emanated from a state they saw dominated by capitalists and Protestants. They refused to engage in antisemitic politics and at least occasionally spoke out forcefully against its goals, greatly helping to cut the antisemites off from masses of potential followers. Austrian Catholics never experienced this kind of state persecution, and the hounding of the Social Democrats in Austria never reached the German level in this era. Austrian Catholics, including the lower clergy, were Lueger's chief backers. The Austrian socialists were at best ambivalent about antisemitism, not above occasionally dabbling in its exploitation, and therefore less an obstacle to Christian Social growth.

Thus, on the eve of World War I Austrian political antisemitism was much more successful, much more menacing, than its German counterpart. It commanded great, relatively stable public support, had crushed its liberal competitors, and represented the only instance of antisemites actually wielding power in a great city. Yet how ought that success be interpreted? And should it be regarded as success at all?

As far as legislative achievements against Jewish power went, the Austrian record was every bit as dismal as the German. The constitutional arrangements of the Habsburg empire offered only limited opportunities to proceed against Jewish citizens. But even allowing for this constraint, the Christian Socials were still markedly less active in the sponsoring of antisemitic bills than their German counterparts. Such lack of parliamentary initiative fed the widely held suspicion that Lueger was really no more than a cynical opportunist when it came to the Jewish Question and that his antisemitism was all talk and no action. Whether true or not, Austrian legislatures passed no antisemitic laws before the *Anschluss* of 1938, whereupon the Germans introduced them by decree.

Measuring either movement in terms of its primary objective—the disenfranchisement and disempowerment of the Jews—would have to call into question any application of the term *success*. True, Jews in both countries had been psychologically wounded by three decades of rejection. That so many of their countrymen from all levels of society impugned their patriotism, ethical values, German cultural identity, and material well being was unsettling. That a smaller portion of them actually strove to overturn Jewish emancipation, while the others looked on with apparent indifference, produced a gnawing anxiety. Meanwhile, in the real world and despite the unpleasantness, the rise of the Jews continued, even accelerated. Many told themselves that antisemitism would inevitably fall to the forces of progress. Until then they could depend upon governments committed to the protection of their physical existence, as well as their rights and property. Through the 1920s both Austria and Germany were viewed as safe havens and desirable destinations for Jews who lived in countries far more inhospitable to their presence.

Given the parliamentary failures of the movement to stem the growth of Jewish power, probably no German antisemites and only a few Austrians would have professed satisfaction about progress toward their goal. Some might have taken heart in the spread of antisemitism into extraparliamentary voluntary associations, a few of which had middle- and upper middle-class members. But most of these were quite small and pursued a diversity of goals that had little direct bearing on the Jewish Question; their records in combating Jewish power over the long haul were at best questionable. There was also little hard evidence to suggest that antisemites had succeeded in expanding the number of true believers from the general population who were prepared for long-term, disciplined struggle.

As World War I approached, Theodor Fritsch, one of the more thoughtful activists and a deeply pessimistic man, was convinced that party-political antisemitism had squandered the movement's energy, that the winning of the people over to antisemitism was a battle that had made no progress and had to be begun anew. He lived long enough to see antisemitism transformed by war and revolution. Still, even after the rise of the Nazis, Fritsch wondered aloud whether he had wasted his life. He was not sure that the world was any closer to solving the Jewish Question, despite his half-century of work. But, as we know, his gloom was not fully warranted. Even though the movement he fostered did not succeed by its own ambitious standards, its endlessly repeated and widely disseminated libels, threats, and accusations were about to show results. In the 1920s, as Jews

Political Antisemitism in Germany and Austria 135

came under increasing pressure, as their persons, businesses, synagogues, and cemeteries became targets for violence, and as their rights were being challenged more doggedly than ever before, they found fewer and fewer of their countrymen willing to come to their defense. Organized antisemitism, despite its record of failure, might be credited with having contributed to this one success. It helped isolate Jews from non-Jews, psychologically and emotionally, well before the Nazis did so physically and finally.

RECOMMENDED READINGS

Boyer, John W., *Political Radicalism in Late Imperial Vienna: The Origins of the Christian Social Movement, 1848–1897* (Chicago: University of Chicago Press, 1981).

Geehr, Richard S., *Karl Lueger, Mayor of Fin de siècle Vienna* (Detroit: Wayne State University Press, 1990).

H-German: G-Text Primary Source Archives. Available at: http://www.h-net.org/~german/gtext/

Hoffmann, Christhard, Werner Bergmann, and Helmut Walser Smith (eds), *Exclusionary Violence: Antisemitic Riots in Modern German History* (Ann Arbor: University of Michigan Press, 2002).

Levy, Richard S., *The Downfall of the Anti-Semitic Political Parties in Imperial Germany* (New Haven: Yale University Press, 1975).

—— (ed.), *Antisemitism in the Modern World: An Anthology of Texts* (Lexington, MA: D. C. Heath, 1991).

Lindemann, Albert S., *Esau's Tears: Modern Anti-Semitism and the Rise of the Jews* (Cambridge: Cambridge University Press, 1997).

Niewyk, Donald L., "Solving the 'Jewish Problem': Continuity and Change in German Antisemitism, 1871–1945," *Leo Baeck Year Book* 35 (1990): 335–70.

Pauley, Bruce F., *From Prejudice to Persecution: a History of Austrian Anti-Semitism* (Chapel Hill: University of North Carolina Press, 1992).

Pulzer, Peter J., *The Rise of Political Antisemitism in Germany and Austria* (New York: Wiley, 1964).

Rürup, Reinhard, "Emancipation and Crisis. The 'Jewish Question' in Germany 1850–1890," *Leo Baeck Year Book* 20 (1975): 13–25.

9

Antisemitism in Modern France: Dreyfus, Vichy, and Beyond

Richard J. Golsan

INTRODUCTION: TWO FRANCES?

Perhaps more than any other European nation in the modern era, France has had, and continues to have, an extraordinarily complex and often paradoxical relationship with Jews and with the problem of antisemitism. On the one hand, earlier than other European nations France recognized the rights of Jews to live as equals with other citizens and to enjoy lives devoid of persecution. At the time of the French Revolution, Republican France, in its self-proclaimed role as champion of human rights, emancipated French Jews from their earlier bondage and guaranteed their rights under the law. During the upheaval of 1789, an initial step was taken in this direction with the adoption of the Declaration of the Rights of Man. Article Ten of that declaration, which essentially guaranteed religious freedom, stated: "No one should be troubled for his opinions, *even religious ones* [emphasis mine], provided that the manifestation of these opinions does not disturb public order established by law." On September 27, 1791, Jews were emancipated by the National Assembly under the new constitution. They were given the full rights of citizens provided that they swore an oath of loyalty to the Republic. According to Paula Hyman, as a result of these and other measures, throughout most of the nineteenth century French Jews generally felt secure in their rights and in their citizenship (8) and even considered antisemitism to be un-French, a "German import." Such was their level of integration into French society and into the French Republic in particular that the most fervently committed became known as *fous de la République*—"fanatics of the Republic." During the Third, Fourth, and Fifth Republics, Jews have thrived and achieved great stature as public servants, artists, educators, and intellectuals.

On the other hand, France as a nation has also experienced, and continues to experience, remarkable levels of antisemitism, as well as episodes of murderous xenophobia directed primarily, if not always exclusively, at Jews. The Dreyfus Affair is certainly the most spectacular manifestation of Jew-hatred in modern

French history, and some consider it to have prepared the ground for the Nazi genocide of the Jews a half-century later. But there have been—and continue to be—many other outbursts of extreme hatred of and violence directed at Jews in France since their emancipation in 1791. The naturalization of Algerian Jews accomplished by the Crémieux Decree of 1870 prompted riots in mainland France and in Algeria, as did periods of increasing Jewish immigration. Moreover, extreme nationalism—and times of national instability and insecurity—have also produced high levels of antisemitism often bordering on the murderous, in language if not in deed. For example, Edouard Drumont's 1886 bestseller, *La France juive*, vented its hatred in hyperbolic and often obscene language against the Jews, their "decadence" and their destructive presence in France. During the 1930s and into the Occupation, writers and intellectuals on the far Right voiced the crudest of sentiments in sometimes wildly excessive prose. The novelist Louis-Ferdinand Céline, author of the masterpiece *Journey to the End of the Night*, permanently sullied his reputation with many admirers by writing antisemitic pamphlets that viciously denounced Jews and praised Hitler. Fascist journalists regularly attacked Jews and called for their elimination from France in reactionary and later collaborationist newspapers and weeklies like *Je suis partout* and *La gerbe*. During the so-called Dark Years between 1940 and 1944—certainly the darkest years for Jews in French history—the Vichy regime under war hero Marshall Philippe Pétain not only willingly participated in the Nazi Final Solution, it imposed a draconian state antisemitism of its own, with little or no encouragement from the Nazis. We will return to Vichy's antisemitism shortly.

In the post-World War II period and in the wake of the Holocaust, overt antisemitism in writings by intellectuals have typically been replaced by more subtle strategies for conveying contempt and denunciation. What the French call "negationism," or the denial of the Holocaust, has proponents on both the extreme Right *and* extreme Left. It also occasionally and surprisingly recruits respected religious figures like *l'abbé* Pierre, champion of France's homeless. The leader of the right-wing and xenophobic National Front, Jean-Marie Le Pen, characterized the Holocaust as a "detail of history" in 1987 (for which he was later prosecuted under French law), and repeated the assertion as recently as April 2008.

In 2000, the writer Renaud Camus a self-styled defender of a "certain idea of France" and of French tradition lamented the number of "foreign"—read Jewish—names on the radio and in the media while expressing a nostalgia for a purer *vieille France* (Old France) apparently devoid of Jews, or at least a France where Jewish influence is minimized. For those familiar with the history of antisemitism in France, Camus's comments call to mind the dubious distinction made by the fascist writer and intellectual Maurice Bardèche in a 1982 interview with Alice Kaplan, in which he distinguished between two kinds of French antisemitism: an antisemitism "under the skin" characterized by a visceral and

138   *Richard J. Golsan*

hysterical hatred of Jews, and a more *civilized* "antisemitism of reason" that aspires to "limit Jewish influence in France." The latter, shared by most Frenchman before World War II according to Bardèche, is the result of a disproportionate presence of Jews "in [French] intellectual and political life." As a result of their presence in these areas, he argues—in an eerie prefiguring of Renaud Camus's comments almost twenty years later—that one simply *hears* Jews too much (Kaplan 1986, 172–3). Whether or not one accepts Bardèche's distinction between an antisemitism under the skin and an antisemitism of reason, *both* antisemitisms played their part in the coming of Vichy and its murderous complicity in the Nazi Final Solution.

Verbal manifestations of antisemitism in modern and contemporary France have unfortunately been accompanied by violent acts against Jews right up to the present. During the past two to three decades, episodes of violence include the October 1980 bombing of the synagogue on the Rue Copernic in Paris by right-wing extremists, which killed four and wounded twenty, and the May 1990 desecration of the Jewish cemetery in Carpentras, which prompted large-scale national protests. More recently, what some consider to be a new form of French antisemitism has emerged, especially among many poorer North Africans and Africans living primarily in the blighted suburbs of France's larger cities. With the spread of Islam in France—the Muslim population today is estimated to be more than five million—and the seemingly endless tensions and strife between Israel and the Palestinians, Jews have become the targets not only of Jew-hatred but of hatred of the state of Israel itself. The result has been instances of the defacing and burning of synagogues, attacks on Jewish school children, and, most shockingly, the 2006 torture and murder of a young Jewish salesman by a youth gang in the suburbs of Paris. While this "new" French antisemitism does have new sources, the sociologist Michel Wieviorka has concluded that, in the end, it still derives principally from more traditional sources of antisemitism: envy of Jewish wealth and influence, paranoia, and so forth (58).

As this brief and fragmentary look at both French efforts on behalf of Jews since 1789 and French antisemitic practices during much the same period might suggest, there is—at least superficially—an almost schizophrenic quality to France's relations to Jews in modern times. To a significant extent, this characteristic has historically been attributed to two sharply divergent and often clashing visions of what constitutes the real, or "true France." For some, true France was and still is first and foremost a Catholic France (although many who embrace this vision are not Catholics themselves), historically the "favorite daughter of the Church," a nation of traditions where the notion of Frenchness and the term *French* are reserved for *Français de souche*, that is, French men and women whose stock goes back hundreds of years. In this mythical *patrie*, outsiders and foreigners are largely marginalized, and certainly should not be in positions of power and influence in French society. This vision of France is generally both reactionary and antisemitic.

Antisemitism in Modern France 139

For others, France is the global proponent of the Republican model, the universal defender of the rights of man. According to this vision of the *patrie*, whose motto is "Liberty, Equality, Fraternity," all citizens are equal under the law. Each benefits directly and individually from the protection and benevolence of the state. This vision of France is, of course, fundamentally left-leaning and opposed to antisemitism and other forms of religious, ethnic, and racial intolerance.

As one might expect, there are a number of serious difficulties with the "two Frances" thesis as an explanatory model for both French "schizophrenia" and French antisemitism *in toto*. First, the model presupposes that historically French antisemitism is exclusively a right-wing and, to a significant extent, a Christian and Catholic phenomenon. But this is a misleading assumption in significant ways, especially for nineteenth-century France. In his classic study *Anti-Semitism in Modern France*, Robert Byrnes notes that before the mid-1880s most antisemitism in France came not from the Right, but from the Left. The culprits, Byrnes continues, were the French Socialists, who despised Jews for essentially two misguided reasons. First, some hated Christianity on the assumption that it profited from and defended bourgeois society. Since these French Socialists saw Judaism as "the forerunner, parent religion and spiritual source of Christianity," they hated Judaism and Jews as well (115). Second, many hated Jews directly as the putative financiers of, and real power behind, international capitalism. According to Byrnes, this form of antisemitism figured in the writings of Karl Marx, and was personified in the invective directed by socialists (and others) against the Rothschild banking family. Finally, antisemitism figured in rivalries among nineteenth-century French socialists. Charles Fourier and his followers were antisemitic in part out of jealousy over the success of their fellow socialists, the Saint-Simonians, a group they viewed as dominated by Jews.

The two-France model also fails to take into account fluctuations in antisemitic hatred attributable to periods of either intensified nationalism or extreme national crisis brought on, most directly, by external events and influences. The Dreyfus Affair occurred, as we shall see, in an environment of passionate nationalism, whereas the extreme antisemitism of the 1930s was attributable in part to the growth of fascist leagues—which themselves were influenced or inspired by the success of fascism in other European countries, Germany and Italy in particular—and a growing sense of national insecurity, decline and decadence, and impending catastrophe. Finally, the Vichy regime itself is inconceivable without the disastrous French military defeat at the hands of Hitler's Wehrmacht in May–June 1940, the chaotic exodus of the French in the north of France in the face of the advancing German army, and the "suicide" of the Third Republic, which, in effect, voted itself out of existence and created the Vichy dictatorship in summer 1940.

It should be apparent from the previous discussion that any effort to offer a comprehensive definition of French antisemitism in the modern era and to

140 *Richard J. Golsan*

explore all of its manifestations and metamorphoses over time is an extremely difficult and complex task, and well beyond the scope of the present chapter. What I propose to do in the remaining pages, therefore, is first to examine the psychology or mentality of the antisemite in the French context in order not only to identify certain continuities in the phenomenon itself, but to understand why antisemitism for its proponents is not only a deep-seated psychological need but a *metaphysical* need as well. I will base this discussion on Jean-Paul Sartre's classic 1944 essay, *Anti-Semite and Jew,* an indispensable work for understanding French antisemitism and perhaps other forms of racial hatred in France as well. I will then look more closely at two crucial and *defining* moments in modern French history when antisemitism became the major symptom of a crisis of national identity and, in the latter of the two cases, of national hegemony. These are the Dreyfus Affair and the crisis of the 1930s, culminating in Vichy. I will conclude with a very brief look at the legacy of this historical antisemitism in France today.

SARTRE'S *ANTI-SEMITE AND JEW*

Shortly after the Liberation of France by the Allies in the fall of 1944, Jean-Paul Sartre published a short book entitled *Réflexions sur la question juive,* translated into English as *Anti-Semite and Jew.* Consisting of both an incisive psychological portrait of the antisemite and a biting analysis of a French society and culture that breeds and harbors him, *Anti-Semite and Jew* was written in response to the disturbing reality that, despite the horrors of recent Nazi deportations of the Jews and the Vichy regime's official antisemitism and complicity with the Nazis, antisemitism persisted, and indeed thrived in a variety of contexts in the postwar period. Equally disturbing, the resurgence of antisemitism in France was largely downplayed and even ignored by many, and for a variety of reasons. Members of the victorious Resistance were intent upon stressing their own martyrdom exclusively. The followers of Charles de Gaulle preferred to emphasize the sufferings and courage of *all* the French, rather than dwell on the fate of any particular minority. This they did in the name of national unity. Finally, the French Jewish community itself thought largely in terms of reintegration and therefore tended to downplay its own victimization which, after all, distinguished it as a group distinct from other French. While this was very much in line with the prewar ethos of assimilated French Jews, it also reflected a more current—and sinister—reality: many of the French police who had arrested and deported Jews under Vichy and the Nazis were still exercising power. In these circumstances, it seemed unwise to many French Jews to call undue attention to themselves. Given all these considerations, it is not surprising that a general state of amnesia prevailed where Vichy and Nazi crimes against the Jews were concerned, and it was this willful forgetting that Sartre reacted against in his essay.

Antisemitism in Modern France 141

Sartre begins *Anti-Semite and Jew* by challenging a number of misapprehensions and falsehoods associated with antisemitism in France. First, he sharply attacks the notion that antisemitism is an opinion like any other opinion. He characterizes it instead as a "doctrine that is aimed directly at particular persons and that seeks to suppress their rights and to exterminate them" (9). It is, moreover, a "free and total choice" that consumes the individual; it is a "comprehensive attitude that one adopts not only toward Jews but toward men in general, toward history and society; it is at one and the same time a passion and a conception of the world" (17).

As a passion antisemitism manifests itself primarily in terms of a deep-seated hatred, a hatred that, Sartre notes, frees the antisemite from having to rationally justify his outlook or recognize the rights of others that he loathes. Such a "strong emotional bias," Sartre continues, can give the "lightning-like certainty" that "alone can hold reason in leash" and "remain impervious to experience" (19). In other words, antisemitism is a profoundly *irrational* passion.

What are the ontological and psychological, as well as the moral implications of the passion? For Sartre, first of all, to embrace such a passion constitutes an escape from the freedom and responsibility that define the human condition. Antisemitism, in fact, expresses a deep-seated fear of the latter. As Sartre puts it, "[t]he antisemite is a man who wishes to be pitiless stone, a furious torrent, a devastating thunderbolt—anything except a man" (54). So essential, then, is the object of the antisemite's hatred to his or her self-definition, to his or her very *being*, that, as Sartre asserts in a famous phrase: "If the Jew did not exist, the antisemite would invent him" (13).

Unable—or unwilling—to understand the complexities of modern society, the antisemite also sees the world in morally archaic, Manichaean terms. From the antisemite's perspective, the Jew is free like other men, but free *only* to commit evil. Therefore, any and all actions that the antisemite takes against the Jew are unequivocally for the good. Indeed, the antisemite's life is completely consumed in irrationally and compulsively unmasking and denouncing "Jewish Evil," and mapping out its menacing presence.

In cultural and historical terms, how does the antisemite define himself? Sartre asserts that he not only claims for himself the role of defender of the "true France," of authentic French culture and society, he is also the nation's real proprietor. He "possesses" France's great writers, for example, the cultural heritage they embody, and the beautiful language they use. Indeed, the Jew may speak a purer French, he may know grammar and syntax better than the antisemite, but he has only been speaking the language for a very short time, whereas the antisemite, the "authentic Frenchman," has been speaking the language for a thousand years (24). In political and even legal terms, this attitude places the antisemite outside or above the law. He alone knows what is best for the country, and feels absolutely free to act upon that knowledge. "The *real* France," the antisemite believes, "has delegated to him the powers of her High Court of

142   *Richard J. Golsan*

Justice" (50). Needless to say, while he may see himself as a "criminal in a good cause," he becomes a threat to society. And it is French democracy's tolerance of, and indeed *complicity* with him, that for Sartre ultimately constitute the greatest danger.

In *Anti-Semite and Jew* Sartre provocatively asserts that there may be little real difference between the antisemite and the French "democrat" insofar as the Jew is concerned, because "whereas the former wishes to destroy him as a man and leave nothing but the Jew, the pariah, the untouchable...the latter wishes to destroy him as a Jew and leave nothing in him but the man, the abstract and universal subject of the rights of man and the rights of the citizen." In fact, the democrat is himself "tinged with antisemitism" because he is "hostile to the Jew to the extent that the latter thinks of himself as a Jew" (57).

Historically antisemitism in France and elsewhere is most pronounced in periods of crisis and, Sartre argues, in Republican France it is the democrat who in these times of crisis makes all the concessions to the antisemite, not only out of a misguided loyalty to the "myth of national unity" but because the antisemite *intimidates* through his anger, his passion.

In 1940 and during the German Occupation, the tragic consequences of this mindset were all too evident. "If France could be saved at the cost of a few sacrifices," the French wondered, "was it not better to close one's eyes?" The result of this willful blindness was Vichy's anti-Jewish statutes, French complicity in the Final Solution, and other crimes. And of these crimes, Sartre is adamant that *all the French were guilty*. Complicit in antisemitism, the French were also complicit in Nazism because "antisemitism leads straight to National Socialism." As a result, France's antisemites "have made hangmen of us all" (151). The tendency of the French in the postwar period to tolerate, to accommodate the antisemite for the same reasons as before, and to remain silent about the recent genocide of the Jews means that the same crimes might repeat themselves in the future, for nothing has truly been learned.

Sartre's *Anti-Semite and Jew* is an extraordinarily astute work in psychological as well as historical terms. It debunks, among other fallacies, Maurice Bardèche's distinction mentioned earlier between two kinds of antisemitism that characterize modern France: one under the skin and one of reason. As Sartre demonstrates, antisemitism is by its very nature an *irrational passion*, and one that excuses the antisemite from thinking, from *reasoning* at all. If there are two kinds of antisemitism according to Sartre's analysis, one is indeed that of the passionate Jew-hater, but the other antisemitism is essentially one of accommodation, of complicity, belonging to the "democrat," that is, the French citizen of *Republican* France. The latter accommodates the hardcore antisemite out of fear and intimidation, as Sartre notes, but also as a result of the French Republican values he or she espouses. These values insist on the universal rights of *all men*, but they are in Sartre's view fundamentally intolerant of *difference*, of ethnic and religious distinctions, freely chosen or otherwise.

Antisemitism in Modern France 143

This is why the French Republican—Sartre's democrat—is tinged with antisemitism himself. He is intolerant of and even hostile to the Jew who thinks of himself as a Jew.

In significant ways, Sartre's observations help to explain why antisemitism flourished, and flourished widely, during the two *Republican* moments we are about to examine, the Dreyfus Affair and the 1930s. They also help explain why, in specific instances, even the proponents and institutions of the Republic were themselves tinged, to use Sartre's phrase, with the very antisemitism to which they were in principle fundamentally opposed. In his excellent recent study, *Jewish Destinies*, Pierre Birnbaum cites several instances of this phenomenon, of which two are particularly noteworthy. At the time of the Revolution, the great champion of Jewish emancipation, the Abbé Grégoire, fought fiercely to emancipate and integrate Jews into the national community. But his sincerest hope was that they would become good Republican Christians, that is, that they would convert to Catholicism. Granting complete freedom to Jews, Grégoire argued, "will mark a major step toward their reform, regeneration, and I daresay, conversion" (18). In other words, emancipating Jews was never intended to grant them freedom as a Nation, as a constituted body but only as *individuals* who would soon cease being Jews.

During the Dreyfus Affair, the racist passions raging in the public sphere also made that presence felt *within* institutions of the Third Republic itself, where many so-called state Jews served loyally. Nonetheless, Jews in the prefectural corps saw their careers derailed (149). Promotions were denied, and many were hounded in their professional capacities by antisemites in the press and elsewhere, with little or no protection from the Republic. As Birnbaum notes, even the most prestigious departments in the bureaucracy were affected, along, of course, with the Army, from which Dreyfus had come. In at least some of these persecutions within the Third Republic, the kind of "democratic" accommodation and complicity in the face of racist hatred to which Sartre alludes is difficult to miss.

FROM DREYFUS TO VICHY

In important ways, the Dreyfus Affair exemplifies many of the key features of French antisemitism as diagnosed by Sartre. Moreover, the explosion of antisemitism that characterized it and divided the nation occurred under conditions in which racism, xenophobia, and antisemitism traditionally thrive. First, France was experiencing a powerful surge of nationalist sentiment, exemplified politically in the failed Boulangist movement and characterized culturally in the integral nationalism of writers like Maurice Barrès, who celebrated a kind of mystical French rootedness very much in keeping with the reactionary Christian vision of the "true France." This nationalist zeal fed upon the unhealed wounds

144 *Richard J. Golsan*

suffered in the disastrous and humiliating French defeat by the Germans in 1871. The Franco-Prussian War resulted in the loss of Alsace and Lorraine, an influx of Jews from Alsace into Paris and other parts of the country, and a sense among some that France was in decline, in the grip of decadence.

Antisemitism was already on the rise when the Dreyfus Affair erupted in the mid-1890s. A deepening cultural and social malaise led to the formation of many sorts of protest organizations, among them antisemitic leagues and associations, often tied to the Catholic Church. Moreover, antisemitic firebrands spewed anti-Jewish hatred in the press and in books. By far the most important of these was Edouard Drumont.

It is worth dwelling on the case of Drumont for several reasons. First, he shared with other antisemites of the time the paranoid and conspiratorial view that the Third Republic was infested with Jews, whose aim was to take over the entire country. Moreover, conforming to Sartre's portrait, Drumont perceived the Jew not simply as a corrupting presence, but as Evil incarnate. The struggle against the Jew therefore constituted the absolute expression of the Good in his Manichaean universe.

As Pierre Birnbaum points out, Drumont also came to see and to characterize the Jew in pseudo-medical terms, as a carrier of mental illness. The Jew was riddled with neuroses and "epilepsy," and he contaminated and infected everything he touched. He was literally killing France, whose decadent corpse now released "a stream of rotten flesh, pus, foul gases, and crawling everywhere are worms named Dreyfus" (102). Drumont was also fond of terms like *putrefaction*, *dissolution*, *degradation*, and *degeneration* to describe the Jews and their effect, precisely the kind of hyperbolic language that, according to Sartre, characterizes the way in which the antisemite describes his obsessive and zealous struggle against Jewish evil.

The Dreyfus Affair was heaven-sent for a man like Drumont. It corroborated his most fevered fantasies of Jewish evil. The full details of the Affair are, of course, well beyond the scope of this essay, but the essentials are instructive. In 1894, Captain Alfred Dreyfus, an Alsatian Jew, was accused, court-martialed, and sentenced to imprisonment on Devil's Island for allegedly providing military secrets to the Germans. The documents used against him were forged. The real spy was in fact a Major Esterhazy. When Colonel Georges Picquart, and later Dreyfus's brother Mathieu discovered Esterhazy's guilt and denounced him, the latter was hastily tried in January 1898 and found innocent. It was at this point that Emile Zola published "J'accuse," his famous attack on the Esterhazy verdict. Later in 1898, it was discovered that a Colonel Henry had forged another document implicating Dreyfus, and when this forgery was revealed Henry committed suicide. Drumont organized a fund-raising drive to support Henry's widow, which became the occasion for widespread anti-Jewish rioting. In 1899, Dreyfus was tried again, and despite all the evidence of his innocence, he was found guilty again. However he requested, and received, a pardon. It was only later, in 1906, that his innocence was finally acknowledged and he was readmitted to the army.

In very general terms one can argue that what the Dreyfus Affair revealed in the first instance was a clash between the "two Frances" described earlier. Arrayed against each other were the defenders and institutions of a hierarchical, traditional and conservative and fundamentally antidemocratic France, the Catholic Church and the Army. On the other side were the defenders of the ideals of the Republic, such as equality, and therefore justice for all. Of course, these hard and fast categories dissolve when one considers the role of heroes like Colonel Picquart, who was himself unsympathetic to Jews, but who nevertheless defied military hierarchy and the military's institutions of justice by insisting on Dreyfus's innocence. Also resisting easy categorization were fervent Catholics and French patriots like the writer Charles Péguy, among Dreyfus's most committed supporters. Conversely, among right-wing delegates elected to the National Assembly and their supporters, including some who thought of themselves as defenders of the Republic rather than its enemies, there were many who were hostile to Dreyfus and staunchly antisemitic.

The Dreyfus Affair reveals many aspects of French antisemitism for which Sartre's analysis in *Anti-Semite and Jew* acts as a better guide than the two-France theory. Among these is the sheer *irrationality* of the French antisemite's hatred of the Jew. No matter what solid evidence was produced to confirm, *reasonably* and *logically*, that Dreyfus was innocent and that others were guilty, anti-Dreyfusards remained impervious to that evidence. Moreover, even after Colonel Henry admitted his guilt and committed suicide, common sense was again disregarded when he was transformed by Drumont and others into a victim and a martyr. Dreyfus was guilty of treason, no matter what, because he was a Jew. And his fellow-Jews shared in his guilt. As noted earlier, some state Jews serving the Republic were treated prejudicially, ostensibly by men who were not necessarily antisemitic themselves but who chose to accommodate the hatred of others.

Finally, in political terms, the Dreyfus Affair served for the first time to galvanize the major elements of the French radical Right around the issue of Jew-hatred. Antisemitism was the common denominator of this unholy alliance that would last through the 1930s and into the Occupation, and to a certain degree, beyond. Yet in the immediate aftermath of Dreyfus's rehabilitation in 1906, the Republic seemed to have been vindicated and antisemitism disgraced—or so the Dreyfusards hoped. Their optimism did not survive for long. Crises and conflicts emerged during the interwar years that dashed all hopes of harmony, issuing finally in the terrible state antisemitism of Vichy.

Among the most unsettling events of these years were new waves of immigration, which heightened French xenophobia. The immigrants were by no means exclusively Jewish. There were, among many others, Poles, Italians, Russians, and Germans. In the late 1930s, there were also Spanish Republican refugees

146 *Richard J. Golsan*

fleeing Franco. Eugen Weber notes that in the wake of World War I, France became "the world's leading host of immigrants." In Paris alone, between 1921 and 1931 the percentage of foreign residents increased from 5.3 to 9.2% (87). The simplification of the naturalization process in 1927 allowed some 70% of those who arrived between 1927 and 1936 to become naturalized. All this eventually strained French hospitality, and by the early 1930s a powerful wave of xenophobia swept the nation. Eventually, and especially after Hitler's coming to power in 1933, the Jews were once again singled out as the primary target of anti-immigrant sentiment. "*Jewish* and *refugee* became synonymous" (105). Moreover, as opposed to earlier immigrations, the newly arrived Jews from eastern Europe were not inclined to assimilate, preferring to maintain their own cultural and religious practices. Therefore, the French Jewish community that confronted the crises of the 1930s was not coherent and, as Paula Hyman asserts "far more complex than the community that faced the Dreyfus Affair" (31). Among assimilated French Jews well ensconced in French culture and society, there was concern and even animosity directed toward the newly arrived, as the latter were seen as outsiders who would bring down persecution on *all* Jews.

In discussing French antisemitism in the 1930s, it is important to consider a number of related factors and developments that served to intensify French anxieties bearing on national security vis-à-vis neighboring countries and in terms of the health and stability of French society itself. The greatest perceived threat to the security of the Third Republic was the rise of dictatorships, first in Italy, then in Germany, and then in the latter part of the decade, in nationalist Spain. By 1939, Republican France was surrounded on all sides by fascist or quasi-fascist dictatorships.

The rise of fascism was, moreover, not merely an external threat. For many inside France, including World War I veterans, disgruntled *petits bourgeois*, and writers and intellectuals, the appeal of fascism, with its cult of youth, militarism, and racism was that it offered a "new" path, a way to overcome and do away with a tired and corrupt Republic, pilloried as decadent and lacking in vitality and virility. The result was a new flurry of fascist or quasi-fascist movements. Among these were the Croix de Feu, the Francistes, and the Parti Populaire Français. Also, the expansion of the right-wing press included pro-fascist and pro-Nazi, xenophobic, and overtly antisemitic publications to which reactionary and fascist writers eagerly contributed.

The internal fascist threat to the Republic came to a head early in the decade when, on the night of February 6, 1934, the fascist leagues and other anti-Republican elements attempted to storm and take over the National Assembly. The pretext was the mysterious death of a Jewish swindler and immigrant named Sacha Stavisky, who was apparently murdered by the police to cover up his corrupt dealings with government officials. Stavisky was, as Eugen Weber points out, the perfect "metic" or dubious foreigner or outsider—a Jew—who, for the Right, summed up all the ills besetting the true France they loved.

The attempted coup d'état of February 6, 1934, failed. As a result, two years later the Popular Front of Léon Blum, committed to the struggle against fascism, came to power. But the initial optimism generated by the Popular Front soon ebbed. The French economy had taken a devastating blow in the global financial crisis of the early 1930s. Moreover, the country was still feeling the effects of the Great War. The huge loss of men had not been replenished: France continued to suffer from a low birth rate, which the Republic's enemies ascribed to its supposed decadence. How could such an enfeebled nation defend itself? For many, the culprit was the Jew, and Blum himself provided a convenient target, putting a Jewish face on the Republic itself. The slogan of "Better Hitler than Blum" was shockingly common on the far Right and among antisemites. That the slogan was explicitly treasonous only underscores Sartre's point that French antisemites historically considered the "Jewish Republic" a betrayal of the true France, and they therefore owed no loyalty to it.

In *Anti-Semite and Jew* Sartre notes that it was the complacency and accommodation of the so-called democrat, tinged with antisemitism himself, that paved the way for the horrors of Vichy. And it was in the 1930s, especially, that this accommodation tainted by antisemitism manifested itself even among Republican writers and intellectuals not generally inclined to racism. André Gide and Jean Giraudoux, among many others, voiced anti-immigrant (transparently antisemitic) sentiments. Giraudoux even went so far as to state that naturalized or not, the new arrivals would never be truly French. As the apparently inevitable war with Nazi Germany approached and increasing despair gripped the French, the Jew became the target of another group not normally prone to antisemitism. After the Munich agreements of September 1938, the pacifist Jean Giono wrote that it was the Jews who wished war with Hitler, and that the true French—and for Giono these were the peasants he idolized— should resist Jewish warmongering at all costs.

While the resurgence of antisemitism in the 1930s, accompanied by a disturbing willingness to accommodate, certainly prepared the terrain for the advent of Vichy, the horrors perpetrated against the Jews as well as other so-called foreigners by Pétain's regime cannot be fully comprehended unless one takes into account the catastrophic implications of the French defeat of May–June 1940. Politically, socially, and culturally, France was literally turned upside down. Once in power, the Pétainist regime's purpose was not simply to reestablish the nation along very traditional and reactionary lines, but to *punish* and indeed *eradicate* from the national community those responsible for the nation's defeat and humiliation at the hands of Germany. The traitor was the Third Republic itself, and as it soon became clear, the *Jewish* Republic personified in the figure of Léon Blum. In its zeal the Vichy regime not only eliminated democratic institutions in establishing itself as the dictatorial "French State," it set out to rebuke the leaders of the Third Republic by, among other measures, imprisoning them and trying some for treason.

148 *Richard J. Golsan*

The ultimate target of Vichy's vengeance was the Jews. Within two weeks of coming to power, the regime altered the naturalization policies of the 1920s that had been favorable to Jewish and other immigrants. It annulled the Marchandeau Law, which prohibited expressions of antisemitism in the press, and, in October 1940, promulgated the first of two Jewish statutes, which greatly restricted Jewish participation in French public life and in the media. In complete rejection of the French Republican tradition, the Jewish statutes were modeled on Nazi Germany's Nuremberg laws. Also, for the first time in French history, the state proposed a definition of the Jew.

In the spring of 1942, French officials negotiated with Nazi functionaries to help implement the Final Solution in France—with the participation of the French police and other security forces. The result was the arrest and deportations of Jews in the Occupied and Unoccupied zones. By late 1944, approximately 76,000 Jews were deported to the East. Only about 3% returned. As the war continued and the possibility of a Nazi defeat became likely, resistance in Europe and especially in France intensified. This only radicalized the Pétain regime, which became increasingly murderous and more openly fascistic. In late 1942, Vichy created a paramilitary police force, the Milice, or Militia, whose charter called for the absolute destruction of France's enemies: the Resistance and the Jews. By the end of the war, before its leaders fled with Pétain to Germany, the Militia was openly murdering Jews in the name of *la patrie*.

CONCLUSION: THE DUTY TO MEMORY

As Jean-Paul Sartre's analysis in *Anti-Semite and Jew* clearly demonstrates, already in 1944 many of the French understood that the horrendous persecutions of the Jews were not simply the excesses of a few fanatics, as was frequently claimed in the postwar years. Rather these crimes were the responsibility of *all* the French, whose politics of accommodation and complicity had paved the way to a disaster that, before the war, would have seemed inconceivable to most French.

As *Anti-Semite and Jew* also emphasizes, a great many of the French in the postwar period were intent on forgetting Vichy's murderous antisemitism for reasons that were in some instances laudable, but in others, cowardly and dangerous. As Sartre stressed repeatedly, such amnesia allowed the blight of antisemitism to once again creep into French public life.

Gradually, this situation began to change. In the early 1970s and continuing into the 1980s and 1990s, the veil—to use President George Pompidou's famous image—that covered the Vichy past began to slip away. Films and novels of the 1970s—most famously, Marcel Ophuls's documentary *The Sorrow and the Pity* and Louis Malle's fictional cinematic portrait of a collaborator in *Lacombe Lucien*—began to expose everyday individual complicity in state-sponsored

Antisemitism in Modern France

antisemitism, and even voluntary participation in Nazi crimes. By the 1980s, the notion of a *devoir de mémoire*, a duty to the memory of Vichy's—and France's—Jewish victims, began to take hold. The result was a kind of national soul-searching in the 1990s that resulted, most notably, in the trials on charges of crimes against humanity of former collaborators Paul Touvier, a former Militia member, and Maurice Papon, a Vichy civil servant who had ordered the deportation of Jews from Bordeaux during the war and then went on to have an illustrious postwar political career.

In a sense, these brief remarks concerning France's recent efforts to fulfill a duty to the memory of Jews persecuted and murdered under Vichy bring us full circle. As noted earlier in this chapter, antisemitism is alive and well in certain quarters in France today, even if it is perhaps due to changed reasons and circumstances. Nevertheless, this new antisemitism, running parallel to a duty to the memory of the victims of an earlier French antisemitism, points to a new "schizophrenia" in France where Jews and antisemitism are concerned. Whether and how this schizophrenia resolves itself remains to be seen.

CITED PRIMARY SOURCES

Sartre, Jean-Paul, *Anti-Semite and Jew: An Exploration of the Etiology of Hate* (New York: Schocken, 1976).

RECOMMENDED READINGS

Birnbaum, Pierre, *Jewish Destinies* (New York: Hill and Wang, 2000).

Byrnes, Robert, *Antisemitism in Modern France* (New Brunswick, NJ: Rutgers University Press, 1950).

Hyman, Paula, *From Dreyfus to Vichy* (New York: Columbia University Press, 1979).

Judaken, Jonathan, *Jean-Paul Sartre and the Jewish Question* (Lincoln, NE: University of Nebraska Press, 2006).

Kaplan, Alice, *Reproductions of Banality: Fascism, Literature, and French Intellectual Life* (Minneapolis: University of Minnesota Press, 1986).

Rousso, Henry, *The Vichy Syndrome: History and Memory in France since 1944* (Cambridge, MA: Harvard University Press, 1991).

Soucy, Robert, *French Fascism: The Second Wave* (New Haven: Yale University Press, 1995).

Weber, Eugen, *The Hollow Years* (New York and London: Norton, 1994).

Wieviorka, Michel, *The Renewal of Anti-Semitism in France Today*, vol. 1: *Occasional Papers, Department of European and Classical Languages and Cultures* (College Station: Texas A&M University, 2005).

10

Antisemitism in the English-Speaking World

William D. Rubinstein

Antisemitism in the English-speaking world has had a number of distinctive features. In modern times it has always been a minor issue, confined to the fringes of political life, and never the primary motivating force behind a major political movement. While antisemitism has obviously always existed throughout the English-speaking world, the forces of liberalism and constitutional rule inherent in the political, ideological, and institutional fabrics of these societies have been sufficiently strong to marginalize hatred of the Jewish people and limit the violent expression of it.

That there was nothing preordained about this relatively fortunate state of affairs is shown by the situation in medieval England. The history of the Jews in that period has been depicted as an extended tragedy, despite the efforts of recent historians to present a more balanced view. Medieval England saw the first ritual-murder charge since antiquity, following the discovery of the murdered body of a twelve-year-old boy, William of Norwich, in March 1144 in woods near the important East Anglian town of Norwich. Similarly, among the most notorious of all medieval ritual-murder accusations was that of Hugh of Lincoln, whose dead body was found near a Jew's house in August 1255. Under torture, the householder confessed to ritual murder. He and eighteen other Jews were executed. Hugh was declared a saint and his body buried in Lincoln Cathedral. The episode forms part of Geoffrey Chaucer's *Prioress's Tale* of 1387. In the previous century there occurred the equally notorious massacre at York of March 1190, when, in response to rioting against Jews elsewhere in England, the local Jewish community took refuge in Clifford's Tower, York. Besieged and terrified, about 150 Jews either committed suicide or were murdered. All Jews were expelled from England in 1290, the first time Jews had been expelled *en masse* from any European country.

For the next 366 years there were no legally established Jewish communities in England, although no doubt small groups of *marranos* and individual Jews lived there. Jews were absent, as direct participants, from any of the major political events of this long period (with the famous exception of Dr. Roderigo Lopez, Queen Elizabeth I's personal physician, who was executed in 1594 as a Spanish

Antisemitism in the English-Speaking World 151

spy). English history during these centuries was thus rarely if ever *about* Jews, although Jews certainly were to benefit from the fundamental changes that occurred in English society. In particular, three enormously significant changes during this period were to alter fundamentally the status and perception of Jews when they were allowed again to settle openly in England in 1656.

First, between 1534 and 1540 England became a Protestant nation, a process that continued and radicalized during the seventeenth century. The Reformation in England brought about a series of important changes of benefit to Jews in the long term. Most of the doctrines and rituals of the Catholic Church particularly injurious to the Jews were eliminated from Anglican practice, among them the centrality of the Crucifixion, the veneration of the Virgin Mary, and the emphasis on the role of the Jews in the death of Jesus. Even more radical variants of Protestantism emerged, as the established Presbyterian church in Scotland and the many Nonconformist sects (Baptists, Congregationalists, Quakers) in England. Most of these were predisposed to be sympathetic to the Jews, often viewing themselves, like the biblical Hebrews, as a chosen group that had entered into a direct covenant with God. Many emphasized the Old Testament over the New. All of these groups were profoundly hostile to Catholicism. Anti-Catholicism, at both elite and mass levels, became a key theme in Britain, tending to push antisemitism aside.

The second fundamental change was the establishment of capitalism. In Britain, this meant the removal of bans on usury and moneylending. It also involved the development of a worldwide trading and commercial empire based in the City of London and in British ports such as Liverpool. From the late eighteenth century, Britain experienced the "take off" into self-sustained economic growth in the formative stages of the world's first industrial revolution. English merchants, bankers, contractors, and, later, industrialists amassed enormous fortunes, some moving into the landed aristocracy, their property protected by strong laws and customs. Since very few Jews openly lived in England, Britain's economic development during the post-Napoleonic period was achieved virtually without Jews. Protestant Nonconformist groups such as Quakers and Congregationalists, as well as Scotsmen, fulfilled the entrepreneurial function that did Jews on the Continent, although the majority of prosperous businessmen were probably Anglicans. A successful Jewish financial and commercial elite, generally Sephardim, did emerge in the City of London in the eighteenth century, while, during the Napoleonic period, the legendary Rothschild family established a major presence in Britain. However, Jews never even remotely dominated British economic life. They were virtually absent during the nineteenth century from the economic elite of many British cities (Rubinstein 2000).

The third change was the beginning of constitutional government, with Parliament solely responsible for formulating laws, and with the rights of citizens protected by fundamental laws in a "Bill of Rights." The establishment of

152 *William D. Rubinstein*

constitutional government was, of course, a drawn-out process, but by the time of the English Civil War and Protectorate (1640–60) and the Glorious Revolution of 1688–9, the fundamentals of this process were set in place. By the eighteenth century it became impossible for a British government to continue in office without enjoying the confidence of the House of Commons. These principles underlay the basis of the government of the United States, established between 1775 and 1791. America went much further than Britain, establishing a republican form of government with powers sharply divided between the branches of government and between the national and state governments, and, in particular, forbidding the establishment of any religion or any official religious test for office holding. Britain's white-ruled colonies overseas—Canada, Australia, New Zealand, South Africa—enacted these liberal principles as a matter of course.

There were a number of other important factors in accounting for the relatively low levels of antisemitism in Britain and the English-speaking world. Jewish numbers in Britain were always low, totalling only about 6,000 (of a British population of perhaps 6 million) in 1730, and only 30,000 (of 15.5 million) in 1830. Jews adapted to the standards of dress, language, and appearance of the majority. There were few if any strictly Orthodox Jews with distinctive dress, living in closed communities prior to World War II. Nor were there large groups of distinctively dressed strictly Orthodox Jews anywhere else in the English-speaking world prior to the 1930s. Until recently, Jews tended not to separate themselves from the Gentile majority but rather sought to join it. Indeed, in America it was their over-rapid rise into middle-class numbers and aspirations that produced most of whatever hostility to the Jews there was in the period 1880–1945, not any desire to stress their nature as a separate and distinctive community.

Jews in Britain were seldom associated with the Left or with radical reformist movements prior to 1900. While this changed during the twentieth century, Jews never comprised more than an insignificant component of the British Left, which itself tended to be less extreme, adversarial, and ideological than elsewhere in Europe. There were only a handful of influential Jewish leftists in modern Britain, such as the professor of politics at the London School of Economics Harold Laski. Only a small minority of the early leaders of the British Labour Party were Jews, with no Jews at all sitting in the first two Labour Cabinets (1924 and 1929–31), and only one (Emanuel Shinwell) in Clement Attlee's cabinet of 1945–51. Jews were almost never found among leading cultural modernists in Britain, particularly among the deliberately provocative iconoclasts; Jewish cultural radicals before World War II were similarly rare, the American-born sculptor Sir Jacob Epstein being the most notable.

In short, in England, liberal gains or causes almost always occurred without reference to the Jews or any Jewish Question. Indeed, in the period immediately after the readmission of the Jews, a number of decisions and precedents were set

Antisemitism in the English-Speaking World

that were greatly to the advantage of Jews. Charles II, restored to the British throne in 1660, confirmed that Jews could remain in Britain after the overthrow of the Cromwellian Protectorate. He even gave evidence of philosemitism. He ignored a proposal made in 1679 by the Bishop of London that Jews be legally confined to ghettos. In 1689, the House of Commons passed a resolution ordering the Jewish community to pay a fine of £100,000. It was thrown out by the House of Lords, and thereafter there was never a question of Jews being subject to a special tax. As early as 1667, the Court of King's Bench declared that Jews could be sworn in using the Old Testament. Perhaps most remarkable was the *Rex vs. Osborne* judgment of 1732, in which publishers of a newspaper that made a blood-libel accusation against Portuguese Jewish migrants were convicted of seditious libel as "likely to inflame" the people "with a spirit of universal barbarity against a whole body of men, as if guilty of crimes scarce practicable and totally incredible" (Rubinstein 1996, 47).

To be sure, there remained a range of measures that discriminated against Jews. Most importantly, Jews were excluded from any public office by the necessity to swear an Anglican, or, occasionally, Christian oath. This excluded practicing Jews from serving in the House of Commons until 1858. The Anglican oath also excluded Protestant Nonconformists from Parliament until 1828 and Roman Catholics until 1829. By the last quarter of the nineteenth century, however, liberalism had apparently triumphed in Britain's treatment of the Jews. Many Jewish MPs served in Parliament and the first practicing Jew (Lord Rothschild) in the House of Lords in 1885. Benjamin Disraeli became prime minister for the first time in 1868, the first Jewish Lord Mayor of London, Sir David Salomons, was elected in 1855, and a range of firsts were achieved, often quietly and with little or no publicity.

During the whole of the period between the readmission of the Jews to England in 1656 and the late nineteenth century there were few overt and well-known examples of antisemitism in Britain. Perhaps the best known was the agitation over the so-called Jew Bill (The Jewish Naturalisation Bill) of 1753. Any foreign-born person wishing to be naturalized in Britain at the time had, as part of the process, to take Anglican Holy Communion, the ceremonial being included largely as an anti-Catholic measure. In 1753, because the Whig government of the day was friendly to the Sephardic financial community in London, the Jew Bill was passed, exempting Jews from the necessity to participate in an Anglican service. This measure, it should be noted, passed through Parliament. Almost immediately, however, an enormous antisemitic agitation against the Bill arose, fanned by the Tory opposition just before a general election. Propaganda depicting Jews as pigs and suggesting that St. Paul's Cathedral would be turned into a synagogue, swept the country. Although no actual violence occurred, well-known Jews became the objects of public odium. Parliament was forced to repeal the act. No further antisemitic agitation occurred in relation to it, and Jews were never again the objects of a comparable agitation. Historians

154   *William D. Rubinstein*

have been puzzled by this incident, which reveals both the latency of some popular antisemitism and the distinct limits to its appeal.

From 1881, large numbers of impoverished Yiddish-speaking east European Jews entered Britain, increasing its Jewish population from an estimated 65,000 in 1880 to 300,000 in 1930. Most settled in the East End of London, although many provincial cities, especially Manchester, Leeds, and Bradford, saw major increases in the number and visibility of their Jewish populations. At the time, Britain had *no* immigration barriers, and anyone could freely settle in the United Kingdom. This state of affairs was likely to heighten both antisemitism and demands for the restriction of immigration, particularly Jewish immigration from eastern Europe. In 1905, after a good deal of populist agitation, Parliament passed the so-called Aliens Act. It did not impose a quota system on immigrants but restricted their entry to a number of ports, and gave officials the right to turn away any would-be immigrants with no means of support. Historians have estimated that the number of Jewish immigrants dropped by about one-third in the period 1905–14, while immigrants from other European sources also declined.

The late Victorian and Edwardian periods are seen as something of a paradox in relations between the British majority and the Jews. There had been a good deal of hostility, tinged with antisemitism, toward Prime Minister Benjamin Disraeli (1868 and 1874–80), especially in regard to his skepticism, in 1878–80, about the so-called Bulgarian Atrocities inflicted by the Turks against the Christians of the Balkans. But this hostility emerged primarily from left-liberal Evangelical sources around Disraeli's arch-rival, William E. Gladstone, not from the extreme Right. Similarly, Disraeli's anti-Russian policies enjoyed strong support from Queen Victoria and the traditional Establishment. During the Boer War, so-called Rich Jew antisemitism was evident, aimed at the "Randlords"—wealthy South African gold and diamond magnates and financiers—and their supporters in the City of London. Many Randlords were Jews, of English or German birth, such as "Barney" Barnato and Alfred Beit, and much was made of their origins by antisemites. However, the most powerful of them all, Cecil Rhodes, was the son of an Anglican vicar.

Most of this anti-Jewish sentiment again came from the political Left in Britain, from radical commentators such as J. A. Hobson, who claimed that the Boer War had been engineered "by a small group of international financiers, chiefly German in origin and Jewish in race." He also claimed that "the Jews are *par excellence* the international financiers... [who] fastened on the Rand... as they are prepared to fasten upon any other spot upon the globe" (Rubinstein 1996, 111), but he later appears to have been embarrassed by these statements. Many socialists of the time, such as H. M. Hyndman, linked international Jewry, the City of London, and the British aristocracy in a scheme to expand the British empire and finance capital. This linking together of the landed aristocracy and financiers, especially Jews, has a long lineage on the British Left. It was made in almost identical form a century earlier by the celebrated radical writer

Antisemitism in the English-Speaking World

William Cobbett, who attacked Jews, Quakers, and Scotsmen as urban parasites, along with the British aristocracy. A similar critique is found in American radicalism of the populist era, which attacked urban finance capital, especially (although not exclusively) international Jewish finance.

The Edwardian period witnessed one well-known incident of violent antisemitism, which occurred in the unlikely venue of Tredegar and other mining towns in south Wales. In August 1911, a time of serious economic and political unrest in the Welsh mining communities, a gang of about two hundred young Welshmen attacked Jewish shops in Tredegar. Property was damaged but no Jews were injured and within a week the rioting ceased. No adequate explanation has been offered for these riots, which were apparently aimed at specific shopkeepers who were disliked by some of the local Welsh. Christian shopkeepers were also targeted, in what appeared to be an economically based disturbance, one that was not replicated elsewhere in Britain. The following year there occurred the Marconi Scandal, involving contracts awarded to the Marconi Telegraph Company. It had a strong Jewish component, since two Jewish cabinet ministers were involved, Herbert Samuel and Sir Rufus Isaacs (as well as David Lloyd George and other non-Jews). During the Edwardian period, many popular works of fiction contained antisemitic imagery, and there was a sense that an element of antisemitism, although clearly not on the continental scale, was on the rise, paradoxically when British Jews found it easier than ever to attain wealth and high status.

The unrest created by World War I, and especially the Bolshevik Revolution, began a period of much heightened antisemitism in Britain. In early 1920, the *Protocols of the Elders of Zion*, the notorious tsarist forgery outlining a vast Jewish conspiracy to control the world, was published for the first time in Britain under the title *The Jewish Peril*. England's best known serious newspaper, *The Times* of London, at first treated it as a valid work, although in August the paper recanted, publishing three articles exposing it as a fake. Other antisemitic conspiracy theory publications appeared in England at the time. A major component in the antisemitism of this period was postwar right-wing hostility to the government (1912–22) of David Lloyd George, a government that had included a number of Jews in senior positions and which, in 1917, had issued the Balfour Declaration, supporting the establishment of a Jewish homeland in Palestine. By the mid-1920s, most of this antisemitic mood vanished.

That antisemitism remained marginal to British popular consciousness was illustrated during the period after 1933 when Hitler came to power. The British Union of Fascists, sympathetic to both Fascist Italy and Nazi Germany, was founded in the early 1930s by the aristocratic former Labour politician Sir Oswald Mosley, who had become disillusioned with liberal democracy. His party attracted enormous publicity but few members—it temporarily peaked at about 50,000 members in 1934, but declined to only 5,000 a year later—and elected no MPs. Far from being sympathetic to British Fascism, the British Establishment

156   *William D. Rubinstein*

appeared to do everything possible to marginalize it. After 1934, Mosley was not allowed to speak or appear on the BBC, the sole British broadcaster, and he was imprisoned during most of World War II as a threat to national security. As news of ever more extreme Nazi atrocities against Germany's Jews became widely known, and as Hitler's ranting speeches, widely shown in newsreels, became ever more threatening, sympathy in Britain for Germany's persecuted Jews also grew, although it must be kept in mind that no one knew the fate that awaited Europe's Jews trapped in Nazi-occupied Europe. About 65,000–75,000 Jewish refugees from the Nazi Reich were allowed to settle in Britain, with tens of thousands more migrating to Palestine (despite limitations imposed in 1939) and the Commonwealth. Few if any flagrant expressions of antisemitism or antisemitic violence occurred in Britain during this period. However, in 1940, when it appeared likely that Britain would be invaded by Germany, tens of thousands of "enemy aliens"—citizens or former citizens of Germany or Italy, many of whom were Jews—were interned in prison camps. This example of wartime panic ranks as the low point of Britain's treatment of the Jews during this period.

After the end of World War II, a more substantial flare up of anti-Jewish hostility occurred in Britain, as a result of acts of terror by Zionist extremists in Palestine. The British public was particularly aroused in July 1947, when Irgun terrorists kidnapped two young British sergeants in Palestine (still a British Mandate), and then hanged them in retaliation for Britain's execution of Irgun members involved in an attack on Acre Prison. A wave of antisemitic violence spread to many British cities, including attacks on synagogues and Jewish shops. However, as in the past, this incident had no real sequel, although it may well have created a lasting sense of hostility to Zionism in some quarters.

After the establishment of the state of Israel in 1948, right-wing antisemitism plainly diminished. From the 1960s, right-wing antisemitism was replaced, as the major locus of hostility to the Jews, by an anti-Zionism emanating from extreme Left and pro-Arab sources. By the 1990s, anti-Zionism became widespread in Britain, especially, at least as many Jews in Britain saw it, in media outlets controlled by the British Left, such as the *Guardian* newspaper and the BBC, while the ever-growing Muslim community in Britain, numbering 1.8 million by the early twenty-first century, contained many extremists who preached a diet of hatred and violence against Israel, America, and Western democracy.

A number of conclusions can clearly be drawn from this survey. The Protestant Reformation and other key events of the early modern period had profound long-term benefits for the Jews in Britain, not least of all because they benefited indirectly from these changes, whose battlegrounds and warring factions seldom included Jews or Jewish issues. In the modern period British politics never veered to the extreme Left or Right but rather revolved around a center-right Conservative Party and a center-left Liberal and later Labour Party, both of which fully accepted democracy and the parliamentary process. Fringe extremist parties never gained significant followings, even in times of crisis.

Antisemitism in the English-Speaking World 157

One overall reason for this history of political moderation was the relative success and prosperity of the British middle classes and of the so-called British Establishment, its upper classes largely educated in modern times at fee-paying public schools and Oxford and Cambridge universities, and revolving around such focal points as the City of London and the Whitehall bureaucracy. Unlike every continental country, Britain never lost a war (the war with the American colonies excepted), while its traditional institutions and symbols of governance, especially the monarchy, remained intact. Even during the 1930s, Britain's middle classes enjoyed at least relative prosperity, while Britain's empire, until its gradual dissolution, made the country unquestionably one of the world's great powers. Britain thus never experienced the sense of extreme deprivation, of total military defeat, complete institutional breakdown, and economic collapse, that characterized Russia by 1917 or Germany after World War I.

British antisemitism was thus chiefly confined to discrete and disconnected events, which appear so anomalous that they continue to puzzle historians. There was probably less in the way of elite closure against the over-rapid and over-numerous upward mobility of Jews, especially those of east European origin, than in the United States. There is no evidence that Britain's universities closed their doors to Jewish students, for example, while Jews in considerable numbers became members of Parliament, knights, and peers after the mid-nineteenth century. Perhaps twenty Jews have sat in British cabinets since the first practicing Jew to hold cabinet rank, Herbert Samuel, did so in 1909. In recent years, two Jews have served as Foreign Secretary and one as Chancellor of the Exchequer, while Michael Howard, the son of a Romanian Jewish refugee, served as leader of the Conservative Party in 2003–5.

While there are obvious differences between Britain and the United States, there are also underlying similarities in the evolution of antisemitism. In contrast to the situation in Britain, the American Constitution forbade the establishment of any religion or the imposition of any religious test as qualifications for public office (although some individual states imposed religious tests for office-holding until the early nineteenth century). This placed Jews, as well as all other religious groups, on a legal footing of absolute equality for national office. American elites and national leaders almost without exception asserted their belief in the complete equality of Jews and other Americans. America's founding father, George Washington, movingly affirmed that the United States "gives to bigotry no sanction, to persecution no assistance," and that for "the children of the stock of Abraham . . . there shall be none to make him afraid" (Sachar 1992, 26). Whenever antisemitism became an issue, all subsequent American presidents went out of their way to assert publicly their respect for the Jewish community.

As in Britain, Jews were never the subject of specific, organized hostility by a political party. There was a major American party organized around religious hostility, the so-called Know-Nothing Party, which existed between 1849 and 1857, but it was anti-Catholic and opposed to the massive Irish immigration of the 1840s. At the 1856 presidential election, the Know Nothings nominated former President Millard Fillmore and secured 22% of the popular vote. No other example of a major political party with hostility to any religious group has ever been active in American history, and never against the Jews. To be sure, it can be argued that virtually the whole of American history was organized around ethnic and social division, the conflict over slavery and the endemic divisions over the status of blacks in the United States. This conflict led to the Civil War in which 600,000 men died and to struggles for equality that continued until the 1960s and beyond. But Jews were marginal to America's racial question, although some Jewish activists became prominent in the civil rights struggles of the post-1945 period.

There were, of course, some substantial differences between the two countries. America contained only a comparatively small Jewish community until around 1881, but after that, and rather suddenly, the American Jewish population became the largest in the world, growing from around 250,000 (of a total population of 39 million) in 1870 to around 4.5 million (of 142 million) in 1940. Jews coming to America encountered substantially different conditions than those coming to Britain, and it might also be argued that Jews generally have met less prejudice in frontier societies, where social hierarchies are relatively new and fluid, than in long-established countries.

In other respects, broad similarities worked to diminish antisemitism. Jews comprised a surprisingly small percentage of the economic elite of Gilded Age America from 1865 to 1929; until World War I or even the 1930s, Jews were not prominent as American radicals and were only rarely present in most radical movements in America before World War I. There were no prominent Jews among America's anti-slavery abolitionists, for example. Nor were Jews a part of modernist or bohemian movements in American culture, which in any case were, until the 1920s, less significant than elsewhere.

As in Britain, examples of American antisemitism often consisted of individual incidents rather than broad patterns of prejudice, although these have certainly existed in America, and are more notable and distinctive than in Britain. In general, American antisemitism, while always present, was not significant until the 1870s, when it became distinctly more visible and direct. By and large, this change coincided with the great migration of east European Jews to America and centered around efforts by America's WASP elite to close or restrict Jewish entry into America's elite. In addition, populist antisemitism among America's poor whites, especially in the Deep South, certainly existed, although Jews were never central to the worldview of southern populists. These trends were firmly in place before World War I but probably reached their zenith in the interwar period. There were, however, always countervailing tendencies, for instance the political ascendancy of Franklin D. Roosevelt and New Deal liberalism after 1932, and by the general strength of American democracy. After World War II, many of these kinds of antisemitism diminished significantly.

Antisemitism in the English-Speaking World 159

Probably the most serious example of antisemitism at its most murderous in American history was the case of Leo Frank. Frank, a graduate of Cornell University, moved to Atlanta, Georgia, in 1908 to superintend a pencil factory owned by his uncle. He was held in high esteem in the local community and was head of the local branch of the B'nai B'rith, the Jewish fraternal order. In April 1913, a fourteen-year-old girl employed by Frank, Mary Phagan, was found murdered in his factory. Frank was a suspect, in part, because he was ostensibly in the factory at the time of the murder but also because of his alleged sexual harassment of female employees (Lindemann 1991, 242). Local newspapers, including one with a Jewish editor, were generally injudicious in assuming Frank's guilt and prone to sensationalism in covering the trial. The state's solicitor-general, who prosecuted Frank, was an ambitious politician who seems to have misused the evidence to secure a guilty verdict. Frank was found guilty and sentenced to death, in part because Tom Watson, a well-known fire-breathing local populist politician, stirred up antisemitic hostility (Sorin 1992, 164). Frank's death sentence was commuted to life imprisonment by the state governor. In 1915, he was abducted from the Atlanta penitentiary to Marietta, the home town of the murdered girl, where he was hanged by a well-organized group consisting of many prominent citizens—not a typical lynch mob.

This was apparently the only time that a Jew was lynched in America because of antisemitic motives, a case that shocked and shamed the United States. Lynching at the hands of mobs in the United States was all too common, though not of Jews. In 1908 alone, 89 blacks and 8 whites were lynched in the United States, while between 1882 and 1968 no fewer than 4743 persons were lynched, of whom 1297 were white (Foner and Garraty 1991, 685). Nineteen Italians were lynched in Louisiana in the 1890s, apparently because they were friendly with blacks. The Leo Frank case did not lead to further violence against Jews (although that was feared for some time) and was apparently motivated also by anti-northern and anti-capitalist feeling, fueled by the brutal circumstances of the case (Lindemann 1991, 218, 271–2).

In the 1920s, the *Dearborn Independent* famously spread antisemitic charges. The newspaper was owned by Henry Ford, the great automobile manufacturer. A cranky, self-educated man, Ford had, during World War I, organized a "peace ship" to stop the conflict in Europe, a war Ford blamed on "German-Jewish bankers" (Baldwin 2001, 50–61). Like many others, he also charged that the Bolshevik Revolution was led by Jews. In 1919, he purchased the then-bankrupt *Dearborn Independent* and appointed as editor William John Cameron, an eccentric believer in the British-Israelite movement (which argued that the British were descended from the Ten Lost Tribes, and were actually the Chosen People). For the next two years Cameron ran a scurrilous antisemitic campaign in Ford's newspaper, publishing many of the newspaper's articles in booklet form as *The International Jew.* Heavily influenced by the *Protocols of the Elders of*

160 *William D. Rubinstein*

Zion, the newspaper's main aim was to convince readers that "the international Jew" was engaged in a conspiracy to take over the world.

Jewish leaders, led by Louis Marshall, the head of the American Jewish Committee, organized a campaign aimed at stopping the *Independent*. His efforts included effective liaison with President Warren G. Harding, a friend of Ford's, and threats of a boycott of Ford's automobiles. A personal attack in the newspaper in April 1924 on Aaron Sapiro, a lawyer for the Farmers' Cooperative Marketing Association, led to a suit by Sapiro against both Ford and Cameron for libel. Under pressure from many quarters, Ford backed down and issued a public apology in June 1927. Ford gained worldwide publicity for his campaign—he was, for instance, praised by Hitler in *Mein Kampf*—and ostensibly did harm to the image of Jews in America. Nevertheless, the whole episode also showed that, even during the racist and xenophobic 1920s, explicit antisemitism was considered by most prominent Americans to be unacceptable. Marshall was able to obtain the signatures of 121 prominent Americans, including all living former presidents, to a public declaration attacking Ford (Feingold 1992, 11–13). It was Henry Ford and the *Dearborn Independent* that appeared to be un-American, not America's Jews. (Leo Frank's trial and lynching, too, were widely condemned by American elites.)

Apart from such individual incidents there was the previously mentioned and seemingly contradictory pattern of WASP elite's attempts to limit the upward mobility of Jews. This pattern took many forms, especially the barring of employment in many elite firms to Jews, the so-called gentleman's agreements preventing Jews from purchasing or renting prestigious real estate, and the blackballing of Jews as members of prestigious social clubs and associations. One of the earliest and best known of such incidents occurred in 1877, when Joseph Seligman, a leading Jewish banker and friend of President Ulysses S. Grant, was refused permission to stay at the Saratoga Springs Hotel in upstate New York, purely on the basis of his Jewish origin.

To many American Jews, the most galling aspect of the pattern of elite antisemitism was the quota system in the admission of Jewish students to the best private universities. During the 1920s, unofficial quotas on the admission of Jews were imposed by Harvard and Yale, among others, generally limiting the number of Jews admitted in any freshman class to 10% of that class. The quota system at Harvard in 1922 under President A. Laurence Lowell became a national *cause célèbre*. Defenders of the quota argued that the old universities served principally to produce Protestant gentlemen, well-rounded men of the world, generally former athletes, who would eventually run America's government and leading businesses; the sons of recent Jewish immigrants simply did not fit in with that model. At Yale University, where this process has been studied in detail, Jews comprised between 8 and 13% of *every* freshman class admitted between 1919 and 1945. These percentages were higher than the Jewish percentage (around 3% at the time) in America's overall population, although lower than

Antisemitism in the English-Speaking World   161

the percentage of all applicants who were Jewish. Discrimination against Jewish faculty members at Yale was even more overt. In 1930, Yale's 158 full professors included only 4 Jews; in 1940, only 7 of 167 (Oren 1985, 320–1, 326).

As with many other aspects of American antisemitism, discrimination against Jews in higher education declined perceptibly after World War II, and largely vanished by the late 1960s. The Holocaust and the war against fascism had produced lessons that were widely learned and internalized. Universities increasingly assumed a role as centers of original research rather than nurseries of gentlemen imparting a traditional curriculum. By 1970, 103 of 468 full professors at Yale were Jews (Oren 1985, 326), together with nearly one-third of undergraduates. Indeed, "reverse discrimination," in which Jews were classified with the white majority, whose places were deliberately given to formally less-qualified blacks, Hispanics, and other non-whites, became a matter of increasing concern to the American Jewish community.

During the interwar period, Jews reacted to restrictions in various ways. Many Jews continued to work for small, Jewish-owned firms, and founded distinctively Jewish businesses. In Hollywood, Jews formed what has been termed "an empire of their own" in the great film studios, nearly all Jewish-owned. After 1945, many varieties of antisemitic barriers rapidly declined. Increasingly, Jews were fully accepted as part of the American mainstream. The McCarthy era did not produce an upsurge of right-wing antisemitism, as might have been expected. By the 1970s, hostility to a key Jewish interest emerged from the other extreme of the political spectrum, from left-wing anti-Zionism, which tended to demonize the state of Israel. Anti-Zionism became an increasingly significant part of the ideological far Left, as well as from some sources in the African-American community and from America's growing Muslim minority. Similar trends developed throughout the Western world.

Antisemitism in Canada was also historically low. For Canada, Britain remained the Mother Country, responsible until the 1920s for its foreign policy and the focus of much of its economy. Canada has notably lacked the world-conquering optimism that has been so much a part of the American psyche. It did not have to fight for its independence and has not had a pronounced national identity. The role of the state in Canada's development was greater than in the United States (Lipset 1996, 23–8, and *passim*). Perhaps more importantly, Canada contains two distinctive linguistic-ethnic groups, with Quebec entirely dominated by French-speaking Catholics whose history was largely shaped apart from models elsewhere in the English-speaking world. In French Canada, and in the South Africa of the Boers, it appears that the position of the Jews was generally worse than in the rest of the English-speaking world.

Quebec has a long history of blatant antisemitism, enunciated by French-speaking nationalists steeped in the most extreme forms of Catholic hostility to Judaism. This manifested itself in 1910, with the ritual-murder allegations by Jacques-Edouard Plamondon, a Quebec City notary, which "deeply shocked

162 *William D. Rubinstein*

the whole of Canadian Jewry" (Tulchinksy 1993, 9). Many other examples of Quebec-based antisemitism could be listed. In 1934, interns at Notre Dame Hospital in Montreal threatened to go on strike unless a Jewish intern, Dr. Samuel Rabinovitch, was dismissed, specifically because of his *nationalité*. Rabinovitch was a graduate of the University of Montreal, finishing first in his class (Abella 1987, 235–6).

While English-speaking Canada had a better record, in 1939, Joseph Rosenberg, the first sociologist of Jewish Canada, found that "anti-Jewish discrimination in social life is frequent in [British] Canada," with a range of exclusions similar to that in the United States (303). Even in English-speaking Canada, Jews found it at times difficult to become interns at hospitals or state schoolteachers (304). Canada's record in taking Jewish refugees from Nazi Germany in the 1930s was especially poor, and much worse than that of Britain or the United States. As in the United States, antisemitism radically declined after 1945. In a study of Canadian attitudes in 1984, 86% of Canadians held positive views of Jews, while only 14% held negative views (Weimann and Winn 1993, 97–111; Brym and Lenton 1993, 112).

The situation for Jews in Australia historically has been altogether brighter. Between eight and fourteen Jews arrived as convicts on the First Fleet of 1788, which established the earliest European settlement on the Continent, giving them a kind of legitimacy in Australia's historical consciousness. There appears to have been remarkably little overt antisemitism at any point in Australian history. Jews have consistently over the years comprised about 0.5% of Australia's population, with significant Jewish communities in Australia's two largest cities, Sydney and Melbourne. Australia's Jews have risen to the highest places; most remarkably a Jew, Sir John Monash was Australia's commander-in-chief during World War I, and its most celebrated soldier. When he died, one-third of Melbourne's population lined the route of his funeral to Melbourne's leading synagogue (H. Rubinstein 1991, 365–7).

Sir Isaac Isaacs was Australia's head of state, its governor-general (the representative of the British monarch in Australia). Jews also attained a wide range of other senior positions. The most notable ethnic conflict in Australia centered on hostility between Protestants from Britain, especially Orangemen from Ulster, and the large Irish Catholic population. Jews were entirely marginal to that conflict. Antisemitism did exist in Australia, consisting of discrimination by social clubs and populist articles in tabloid magazines, but it was of very little importance. After World War II, Australian Jewry developed a surprisingly vigorous community, with a wide range of day schools and other institutions.

The situation in New Zealand, Britain's other English-speaking outpost in the Antipodes, was similar, although the country's Jewish population has always been minute; by the early twenty-first century it numbered approximately 6,000 out of 4 million. A Jew, Sir Julius Vogel, and a man of Jewish descent, Sir Francis Bell, served as prime ministers in the late nineteenth and early twentieth centuries

Antisemitism in the English-Speaking World 163

(Levine 1999). On the other hand, New Zealand's record in taking Jewish refugees from Hitler was poor (Beaglehole 1988). As in Australia and North America, the frontier nature of New Zealand society with its unsettled social structure probably enhanced Jewish success.

As in Canada, the Jewish minority in South Africa found itself marginal to two white groups, the English and the Boers. There was a long history of hostility to South Africa's Jews by both the Boers and the English. Many Boers regarded South Africa's Jews as among the worst of the economic exploiters who had invaded their country, while many of the English settlers regarded Jews as parvenus, depicted in cartoons as "Max Hoggenheimer," a loud-mouthed multi-millionaire (Shain 1994, 62–3). During the interwar years, overt antisemitism, influenced by Nazism but also bitterly anti-British, grew among Boer nationalists. There were, however, also countervailing trends. Jews always enjoyed full civil rights as whites. Jews were prominent among the prosperous "Randlords" who developed South Africa's gold and diamond industries, and Jews remained very significant as entrepreneurs and professionals in twentieth-century South Africa. Many Dutch Protestant Boers were inclined toward philosemitism and favorable to Zionism. Boer leader Jan Smuts was regarded as one of the most committed Gentile Zionists in the world.

The election of the right-wing Boer party, the Nationalists, to power in 1948 gave rise to considerable Jewish apprehension. Successive Nationalist governments enacted the infamous system of Apartheid, increasingly isolating the country from world opinion. South Africa's Jewish community of 130,000 was, however, left alone. Many Jews tended to regard the Nationalists as less ominous than the prospect of a black Marxist government. South Africa also developed growing, but clandestine, military links with Israel. On the other hand, a number of Jews—probably greater than any other white group—were active in the struggle against Apartheid. The end of Apartheid in 1990 and the formation of a black majority government prompted the emigration of about one-third of South African Jews.

In 1922, most of Ireland, with its heavily Catholic population, became independent as the Irish Free State, while Protestant Ulster remained in the United Kingdom. The very small Jewish population—1500 in 1891, 4000 in 1946 (Keogh 1998, 9)—grew after 1881 mostly by immigration from eastern Europe. Many conservative Catholics were hostile to Jews, overtly or covertly. In 1904, a so-called pogrom occurred in Limerick, where Father John Creagh denounced Jews as leeches, guilty of having kidnapped and killed Christian children. He contrasted the wealth of local Jews with the poverty of the Catholics and organized a boycott of local Jewish traders (Keogh 1998, 26–53). Independent Ireland under Eamon De Valera was probably the closest approach to a narrow European clericalist dictatorship ever seen in an English-speaking country. Although De Valera was personally friendly to Jews, Ireland closed its doors to Jewish refugees and remained steadfastly neutral during World War II. In April 1945, De Valera

164 *William D. Rubinstein*

notoriously signed a book of condolence for Adolf Hitler when the dictator committed suicide. Nonetheless, the Irish Free State was never antisemitic and Judaism was officially included as a permitted religion in the Irish Constitution.

Throughout the English-speaking world, the forces of liberalism were sufficiently strong to marginalize and minimize serious or violent antisemitism. Neither ideological antisemitism nor visceral folk hatred of the Jews became significant in the English-speaking world, the partial exceptions occurring among Catholics who inherited a centuries-old tradition of clericalist antisemitism. The forces of liberalism in the English-speaking world resisted Nazism and ultimately, allied with Soviet Russia, destroyed the Nazi regime. The English-speaking world generally offered unparalleled opportunities for Jewish success and achievement, and rarely if ever ranked among those actively persecuting Jews—indeed, have mostly ranked as a place of refuge and protection for them.

RECOMMENDED READINGS

Abella, Irving, "Anti-Semitism in Canada in the Interwar Years," in Moses Rischin (ed.), *The Jews of North America* (Detroit: Wayne State University Press, 1987), 235–46.

Baldwin, Neil, *Henry Ford and the Jews: The Mass Production of Hate* (New York: Public Affairs, 2001).

Beaglehole, Ann, *A Small Price to Pay: Refugees from Hitler in New Zealand, 1936–46* (Wellington, NZ: Allen and Unwin, 1988).

Brym, Robert J., and Rhonda Lenton, "The Distribution of Anti-Semitisms in Canada in 1984," in Robert J. Brym, William Shaffir, and Morton Weinfeld (eds), *The Jews in Canada* (Toronto: Oxford University Press, 1993), 112–20.

Feingold, Henry L., *A Time for Searching: Entering the Mainstream, 1920–1945* (Baltimore: Johns Hopkins University Press, 1992).

Foner, Eric, and John A. Garraty (eds), *The Readers' Companion to American History* (Boston: Houghton, Mifflin, 1991).

Keogh, Dermot, *Jews in Twentieth-Century Ireland: Refugees, Anti-Semitism and the Holocaust* (Cork: Cork University Press, 1998).

Levine, Stephen, *The New Zealand Jewish Community* (Lanham, MD: Lexington Books, 1999).

Lindemann, Albert S., *The Jew Accused: Three Anti-Semitic Affairs—Dreyfus, Beilis, Frank, 1894–1915* (Cambridge: Cambridge University Press, 1991).

Lipset, Seymour Martin, *American Exceptionalism: A Double-Edged Sword* (New York: W.W. Norton, 1996).

Oren, Dan A., *Joining the Club: A History of Jews and Yale* (New Haven: Yale University Press, 1985).

Rosenberg, Louis, *Canada's Jews: A Social and Economic Study of Jews in Canada in the 1930s* (originally 1939; republished Montreal: McGill-Queen's University Press, 1993, ed. Morton Weinfeld).

Rubinstein, Hilary L., *The Jews in Australia—A Thematic History*, vol. 1: 1788–1945 (Melbourne: Heinemann, 1991).

Rubinstein, W. D., *A History of the Jews in the English-Speaking World: Great Britain* (Basingstoke: Macmillan, 1996).

—— "Jews in the Economic Elites of Western Nations and Antisemitism," *Jewish Journal of Sociology* 42(1–2) (2000): 5–35.

Sachar, Howard, M., *A History of the Jews in America* (New York: Alfred A. Knopf, 1992).

Shain, Milton, *The Roots of Antisemitism in South Africa* (Charlottesville: University Press of Virginia, 1994).

Sorin, Gerald, *A Time for Building: The Third Migration, 1880–1920* (Baltimore: Johns Hopkins University Press, 1992).

Tulchinsky, Gerald, "The Contours of Canadian Jewish History," in Robert J. Brym, William Shaffir, and Morton Weinfeld (eds), *The Jews in Canada* (Toronto: Oxford University Press, 1993), 5–21.

Weimann, Gabriel, and Conrad Winn, "Hate on Trial: The Zundel Affair, The Media, Public Opinion in Canada," in Robert J. Brym, William Shaffir, and Morton Weinfeld (eds), *The Jews in Canada* (Toronto: Oxford University Press, 1993), 97–111.

11

Antisemitism in Russia and the Soviet Union

Heinz-Dietrich Löwe

Russia, like many European countries, had expelled its Jews in the late Middle Ages, and afterwards contacts remained rare. Jews who converted to Christianity escaped any legal restrictions, a situation that held for the most part until the downfall of tsarism in 1917.

Russia and the Soviet empire looked to the West for ideas to reform government, society, economy, and in particular Jewish culture and character traits. France had emancipated its Jews in a revolutionary way, giving equal rights to all by 1791. Central European states through most of the nineteenth century labored to reconstruct the social, economic, and religious characteristics of the Jews they deemed unacceptable, and gradually granted them greater rights; these were understood to be the reward for the improvements made in Jewish behavior.

Within this framework Russia and the Soviet Union stood at the extreme of a policy of active intervention into internal Jewish affairs. Russia borrowed the aim of reconstruction from enlightened absolutism and the writings of Christian Wilhelm von Dohm, a Prussian bureaucratic reformer. Reconstruction meant the integration of the Jews into the state's administrative structure by a variety of means, for example, abolition of special Jewish corporatist institutions, and "productivization" of their economic activities (that is, removing them from "exploitative" activities, such as moneylending and inn-keeping, and moving them toward "productive" manual labor). Efforts were also made to introduce them to modern education, weaning them away from their traditional learning. However, the Russian state, deviating from the central European pattern, tended to dictate policies without immediately offering meaningful incentives.

Tsarist and Soviet systems both seemed to accept uncritically the panaceas of enlightened absolutism, at least during the earlier years of direct contact with Jews. The Bolsheviks, of course, applied this model in a socialist context. But it would be wrong to say, just by way of contrast, that tsarism did this in a capitalist way. Rather, it pursued its policies within a precapitalist corporatist

Antisemitism in Russia and the Soviet Union 167

framework. These two styles of interventionism shared an important common trait, however. Both helped create or reinforce popular antisemitic stereotypes.

TSARIST RUSSIA: FROM RECONSTRUCTION TO ANTISEMITISM AS REACTIONARY UTOPIA

Russia Meets her Jews: From Enlightened Neglect to Massive Intervention

Only with the Polish partitions of 1772, 1793, and 1795 did Russia acquire a sizable Jewish population. Polish ideas influenced tsarist concepts of Jewish reform, and Polish-Lithuanian popular attitudes of competition and rejection continued to bear on further policy developments. In the beginning, Catherine II, in accordance with the recipes of enlightened absolutism, integrated Jews into the local administrative and court system on an equal basis, but she left untouched the *kahal*, the self-governing body of Jewish communities. The regional and local *kahali* even gained in importance during her reign. Catherine was not inspired by religious or ethnic considerations, and in general she left the Jews to their own devices. But equal participation of Jews in local affairs met with strong popular resistance. In 1783, the empress found it necessary to reaffirm her ruling and to protect the economic rights of the Jews, for example, their renting of distilleries or breweries, a field of economic activity in which they remained prominent to the end of the tsarist regime.

Almost all Jews were engaged in urban occupations and therefore registered as burghers and required to reside in their city, even though a very large number actually lived in the countryside. Catherine waived this requirement, but her successors at times thought differently. Under Catherine the Pale of Settlement, which ultimately comprised fifteen western and southwestern provinces along with all of Congress Poland, arose by accident rather than by design. At first, the Senate, the highest administrative and judicial body of the empire, prohibited Jews from settling outside the two *gubernii* (provinces) of Belarus. This was not per se an anti-Jewish measure—none of the tsar's subjects were allowed to settle outside the *gubernia* they lived in—but it followed a protest by Moscow merchants, accusing Jews of huckstering and selling more than one kind of merchandise, thus breaking the rules of the moral economy as defined by corporatist medieval or early modern market regulations. This complaint also repeated ancient accusations and anticipated Jewish wrong-doing: "as it is known the Jews depreciate the currency; perhaps they will do this here, too." Obviously, anti-Jewish stereotypes reached Moscow before the city had had any meaningful contact with real Jews.

Russian officials saw Jews, Poles, and the Tatars as religious fanatics, similar in outlook, whose fanaticism had to be broken and their religious beliefs civilized.

168   *Heinz-Dietrich Löwe*

For these officials the corporatist structure introduced by Catherine and her policies toward Poles and Tartars provided tools with which to reconstruct the Jews. Open-minded reformers recommended integration as a first step. However, Gavriil Derzhavin, the first fact-finder in the region and minister of justice in 1802, was inclined to keep the Jews separate until they had been successfully reconstructed. He suggested creation of a chief rabbi to discipline the rest, the introduction of modern education, a ban on Jews from the alcohol trade, the abolition of the *kahal*, a reduction in the numbers of synagogues, and the weaning of Jews from the Talmud (which, he believed, promised them dominion over all other peoples). He also advocated strict separation of religious and secular spheres in Jewish society. Special Jewish garb had to be prohibited. Massive relocation into agriculture, forced labor on road and canal construction, and employment in government workshops were additional measures designed to convert the Jews into productive subjects.

The actual Law for the Jews of 1804 (*polozhenie dlia evreev*) was milder, although it was still based on the assumption that they had to be rendered less harmful. It did not aim for russification or assimilation. Only rabbis and people in authority in the Jewish community had to be able to read and write Russian, Polish, or German, after the passage of a certain period of time. Bowing to local resistance, the law did not dare to enforce Jewish participation in city government, and therefore the *kahal* was left intact for the time being. Still, rabbis lost the right to pronounce the *herem* (excommunication from the Jewish community). In light of the fierce conflicts between the Orthodox and the Hasidim in Lithuania this made sense, but the measure had another aim: the undermining of the *kahal* from within.

The Law expanded the boundaries of the Pale of Jewish Settlement, and, for the first time, gave it a clear legal definition. Traditionally, tsarism had integrated non-Russian peoples by co-opting their aristocracy. To make up for the lack of one among the Jews, the government used its economic powers to foster the development of a Jewish plutocracy. A few decades later, Tsar Nicholas I's officials, for example, intervened in the liquor monopoly to help the Gintsburgs, among other prosperous Jewish families, to become a new financial elite. Inviting Jews to enter government schools and universities was another way of encouraging class differentiation in the Jewish population.

Productivization in the 1804 law meant offering incentives for Jews to move from trade to crafts (with registration in the respective guilds). Rural Jews not active in working the land were seen as exploiters, and were to be driven from the countryside, but when that was attempted, it had catastrophic results and was soon abandoned (although this ill thought-out measure set a pattern that would be repeated). The often-raised notion of driving the Jews from the alcohol business had mixed or confused motives. Some feared that productivization might succeed too well and that wealthy Jews might transform the existing social system, defined in law by traditional estates, into informal, more modern,

Antisemitism in Russia and the Soviet Union

relationships defined by economic power. But in fact this and other elements of the 1804 law remained a dead letter.

Nicholas I, who succeeded to the throne in 1825, was more determined than his older brother to end Jewish separateness by productivization, education, religious reform, and integration into the state and social system of the empire. In one of his first acts he imposed the recruitment levy on the Jews without granting any rights in return, in contrast to other European states, where service in the military was part of general civil emancipation. The cantonist system, as this levy was termed, encountered massive evasion by the Jews. Boys who could not escape it were subjected from age twelve—often younger, though illegally—to a brutal life in the barracks until age eighteen, when they started their twenty-five year service. Petersburg policymakers did not themselves aim to convert Jews, but harsh officers and intolerant fellow-soldiers brought many to adopt Christianity. Imposing the actual selection of recruits on the Jewish communities had the additional effect of undermining traditional Jewish structures from within, and, in fact, brought them to the verge of collapse.

In 1844, the *kahal* was abolished, its place taken by a synagogue-board "of people of wealth and fixed abode," which could levy its own taxes. On the other hand, a new law allowed Jews to hold elected office, except in Vilna, and to take up to a third of the seats in urban governing bodies.

Productivization under Nicholas I involved enrolling the Jews into the appropriate estates or guilds, as envisaged in the 1804 law. Those not registered faced severe punishment, and their communities had to provide five times the normal recruitment levy. But these measures also failed; non-Jewish inhabitants resisted vehemently, and local bureaucrats were loath to force implementation.

Productivization again included attempts to involve Jews in agricultural production. By Nicholas' death in 1855, roughly 40,000 Jews had been settled in agricultural colonies. This was at least a moderate success. But periodic expulsions from the countryside of those not engaged in agriculture resumed. Certain areas of the Pale remained closed to Jews, as for instance the city of Kiev, and all border regions.

In 1840, special state schools teaching secular subjects and the Russian language were set up, financed by the Jews themselves. Religious instruction followed a government-inspired "Catechism of Judaism," which reduced the importance of the Talmud and the messianic elements of Judaism. Jewish resistance to these innovations proved strong, despite the fact that the schools exempted their pupils from military service. Three special state rabbinical seminaries taught a Judaism acceptable to Russian bureaucrats. Only graduates of these seminaries were to be rabbis—a measure, like so many others, that soon had to be abandoned.

Not all Jews resisted the government's interventions. A small but vocal Jewish secular intelligentsia shared many of the reconstructionist aims. However, the government usually chose not to employ them, as overseers of Jewish schools, as

170 *Heinz-Dietrich Löwe*

school directors, or as censors of Jewish books. Only a small number found places as teachers in Jewish schools. Officials, especially the locally based, distrusted these "rationalistic, rootless Jewish cosmopolites." To bring more secular schooling to Jews stood in stark contrast to official policy with regard to the Russian peasant majority, which the government was reluctant to educate. Jews who received a secular education thus found themselves in limbo, torn from their communities yet separated from Russian life. Russian society, unlike that of the West, had not yet developed the social milieus into which educated Jews might integrate, and the government seemed reticent or unwilling to create spaces for them.

Reforms, Hesitant Liberalization, and the Development of New Anti-Jewish Stereotypes

The Great Reforms of the 1860s under Alexander II abolished serfdom and freed the urban estates from premodern restrictions on their economic activities and movement. This made the remaining special regulations for Jews now plainly discriminatory. Status and power in principle would now be conferred by market forces or public opinion. But the government did not go far enough in dismantling its corporatism to give room for development of a modern political, social, and civic system that could have integrated the Jews. At the same time that Russian society began to demand more of its Jewish subjects, they became progressively less willing to surrender their cultural and national identity.

A government commission developed the policy of "rapprochement (*sliianie*) of the Jews to the indigenous population, as far as their moral status allows." The state strove to exercise strict control over whom to accept into Russian society and when. In practice this resulted in selective integration characterized by partial equality. Nonetheless, the new climate under Alexander II brought many positive measures and developments. Efforts to convert the Jews to Christianity were given up, and Jewish children flocked to public schools. The government rewarded some categories of Jews for achieving a degree of adaptation to the dominant culture. Merchants of the First Guild were freed from almost all restrictions on their economic activities, and they were allowed freedom of movement; similar liberties were soon granted to graduates of Russian universities. Pharmacists, medical practitioners, and midwives, as well as beer brewers, could now leave the Pale. Guild artisans with a master's certificate, a relatively small group, also gained these liberties. Other Jews enjoyed the right of residence only as long as they pursued the trade for which they held the requisite certificate, and only for themselves; children had to acquire their own title.

Alexander II quickly abolished the cantonist system, but it took some time before he could be persuaded to admit former Jewish soldiers to all regions of the

Antisemitism in Russia and the Soviet Union 171

empire. In urban self-government Nicholas I's one-third rule remained the limit for Jewish participation. Bodies of rural self-government (the *zemstva*) as well as the newly created courts and bar associations functioned without restrictions against Jewish subjects. Jews could go to the university and become employees of the government or of the *zemstva*, serving as doctors, judges, and lawyers.

Still, some discriminatory regulations remained in place or were revived. The right to buy agricultural land from landlords, granted in 1862, was revoked in 1864, based on the reasoning that "the peasant...just liberated from the burdening influence of the [largely Polish] landlords...would fall into a new dependence on the Jewish landlords, who command large sums, but are unreliable politically." Minister of War Dmitry Miliutin, otherwise a staunch reformer, justified the exclusion of the Jews from the Don Cossack region, arguing that they would introduce capitalism, making a small part of the population rich and the larger part poor. This would destroy traditional Cossack society and thereby an important base of loyal support for the tsar. Such pronouncements spoke clearly to the limits of concessions to Jews.

Institutional integration did not proceed very far either. The government proved unable, though encouraged by the reform-minded Jewish intelligentsia, to supervise the separate Jewish welfare system. The notorious convert to Christianity, Jakob Brafman, had urged this step in his book *On the Kahal* (1869). He also suggested that rural Jews be integrated into the peasant estate so as to give peasants the possibility of controlling the Jews and turning them into productive members of society. This suggestion did not sit well with either peasants or Jews, and, as so often, the government finally did not act on the notion.

After the Polish uprising of 1863, government officials in the Vilna school district, where there were large numbers of Jews, introduced new, strongly russifying schools. The government schools for Jews established after 1840 had been attacked for exposing Jews to a secular German influence; the language of instruction in the Vilna district was thus changed to Russian. But soon Vilna officials decided to discontinue these schools altogether, if alternatives were available. With respect to religious education, local officials had become convinced that the government gave too much honor to Judaism, in their eyes an outdated religion. If left in its unreformed state, Judaism could not support the development of a modern Jewish identity in Russia—but this perhaps would be for the best. The central government, too, gave up its efforts at reeducating the Jews and refrained from regulating schools run by Jews. The tsar's officials thus arrived at a policy best described as "malevolent neglect," because they feared the emergence of a modern Jewish identity. This policy revealed a striking loss of faith by the political establishment in its powers of amalgamation and assimilation.

During this time the stereotypes characteristic of a more modern antisemitism began to surface. While some officials advocated Jewish emancipation as good for Russian industrialization and thus enhanced national power, others feared

172   *Heinz-Dietrich Löwe*

the consequences of industrialization and the rise of new classes; Jews would develop industry to the detriment of agriculture. Only if industry and agriculture moved forward in equal measure could peasants be protected from "the subjugation of their lands and labor by Jewish capital" leading to "their early material and moral destruction." Before long the ministry of the interior declared its distrust toward exactly those modernizing Jews who until recently it had regarded most favorably: "into the worldwide Jewish *kahal*... with aims inimical to the Christian population, apparently also the Jewish capitalists have entered."

In this view clannishness and separation, enforced by the clandestine *kahal* under the leadership of Jewish capitalists and the cosmopolitan Jewish intelligentsia, would enable the Jews to exploit the masses and to enslave the peasants. The goal of these Jews was to change the existing order and to achieve power by means of liberal agitation for constitutional government. *Kosmopolit* (cosmopolitan) became nearly synonymous with Jew. A long list of accusations emerged, partly borrowed from the German antisemitic movement, but also from such sources as the famous novelist Fyodor Dostoevsky, Konstantin Pobedonostsev (the secular head of the Russian Orthodox Church), and the Slavophiles Ivan Aksakov and Yuri Samarin.

For Slavophiles, religion was of central importance, and they viewed educated Jews as the worst kind of atheists; Aksakov asserted that even "a believing Jew continues in his consciousness to crucify Christ." Aksakov, however, did not rely on religious prejudice; he was among the first to justify his antisemitism with anti-capitalist sentiments. The Slavophile idea of wholeness, and the concept of a Christian state contained within it, made it difficult to accommodate believing Jews. The social harmony it idealized was also impossible in modern class societies, condemned as Jewish inventions. The idea that only traditional estates could save society from modern capitalism made Slavophilism especially susceptible to antisemitism. Glorification of the peasant, coupled with the accusations of Jewish exploitation, gained ground especially among right-wing thinkers. In his *Diary of a Writer*, Dostoevsky feared for the peasants and for a Europeanized Russia: "A little, mean, depraved bourgeoisie will emerge, as will innumerable enslaved beggars... The Jews will drink the blood of the people and live by the depravity, humbling the people" (in Steven Cassedy, *Dostoevsky's Religion*, Palo Alto, CA: Stanford University Press, 2005, 66).

Counter-Reforms, Governmental Antisemitism, and Industrialization

In 1881, a sustained terrorist campaign finally claimed the life of Tsar Alexander II and shattered the confidence of court and bureaucrats. Six weeks later a major wave of pogroms erupted. When bewildered officials finally realized that this was not the much-feared social revolution, they searched for the

Antisemitism in Russia and the Soviet Union   173

causes of revolutionary unrest and pogroms alike. Conservative elements found the answers they were looking for in the unsettlingly swift social changes brought about by the reforms of the preceding reign. The policy consequences of this explanation fell heavily upon the Jews. In particular, their social mobility was now restricted, as the government took steps to shore up the corporatist structure, from which Jews were now excluded. They were also forbidden to vote or sit in the *zemstva*. Their numbers were drastically reduced in city self-government. Jews were excluded from juries and no longer accepted into bar associations.

The new deputy minister of the interior, arguing for yet more restrictive regulations, gave the following interpretation of the pogroms: "The last twenty years the Jews...have taken over not only trade and production, but...significant amounts of landed property...all but a few of them have bent every rule, not to increase the productive forces of the country, but to exploit the native inhabitants." Antisemitic and anti-capitalist policies now aimed to drive the Jews from the countryside by means of a curious mix of medieval market regulations and a return to the productivization myth. Once again, any form of the alcohol trade was forbidden to Jews. They were to be banned from trade in rural areas, except with wares produced by themselves. But yet again, many of the proposed measures were thrown out or watered down. Still, new discriminatory regulations hit many Jews hard, especially the Temporary Regulations of May 3, 1882. These forbade the Jews from settling anew in the countryside within the Pale of Settlement. Although officially "temporary," these regulations lasted until the end of the empire, providing the basis in following years for the expulsion of thousands of Jews from the countryside. The arch-reactionary Pobedonostsev provided the rationale: the state, he proclaimed, had to control and direct the economic forces; otherwise they would undermine the existing order. Thus, Jews, merchants, innkeepers, and moneylenders—"a great evil for the state and the local population"—had to be prevented from acquiring agricultural land and influence.

The government also retreated from its reliance on education as a tool for integrating Jews. Complaints had emerged by the late 1870s that schools, overcrowded by Jews, could no longer effect assimilation, but at first ministers were relatively unconcerned. They sought stabilization by restricting the entry of the lower classes into the elite high schools (*gymnazii*) and universities, because they would learn "to despise their parents, to be discontented, and...to hate the existing material inequality which is, in the nature of things, inevitable." A different motive led in 1887 to the setting of percentage norms for Jews in secondary and higher education: 10% for Jewish students within the Pale of Settlement, 5% outside, and 3% in Moscow and St. Petersburg. The reason given was that Jews were aligning themselves with the revolutionary cause and were exerting a corrupting influence on non-Jewish pupils. The new quota, or *numerus clausus*, for Jews in secondary and higher education increasingly alienated many Jews from the tsarist system.

174   *Heinz-Dietrich Löwe*

This policy of slowing down social change soon clashed with new measures
to accelerate industrialization. Because Jews were believed to be influential in
world trade and especially in international banking, Russian finance ministers
argued against restrictive laws aimed at them and circumvented anti-Jewish
legislation when possible. They favored more secure economic and property
rights for Jews, even for the much maligned small trader and artisan. But this
favorable attitude was not well received in other quarters. The policy of rapid
industrialization undertaken by Finance Minister Sergei Witte during the last
decade of the nineteenth century provoked an ideological response by right-
wing ideologues, many of them Slavophiles, deeply convinced that capitalism
would destroy everything that was dear to them in old Russia. They fought for
traditional estate structures, especially the preservation of the nobility and a
precapitalist peasantry.

When Russia adopted the gold standard in 1897, the Right in Russia reacted
angrily. This victory of the "Jewish stock exchange" and "Jewish money" over
agriculture and the producing classes stirred public debate and mobilized opposition against Witte. Right-wing economist Sergei Sharapov, the most influential antisemite of the 1890s, wrote:

gold meets...the approval of the capitalists,...economic science, and the political
press....The closely woven web of international Jewry, unconditional in its solidarity,
which can draw on vast reserves..., is concerned that the present situation should be
maintained at all costs, whereby international Jewries increase their wealth, the productive classes are destroyed and the old Christian structure of Europe collapses.

(in Löwe 1993, 108)

A broad spectrum of political opinion supported such views, from the antisemitic paper *Novoe Vremia* and its editor, Aleksei Suvorin, to, surprisingly, even
the right wing of the nascent *zemstva*, which were at this time turning into a
strong constitutional reform movement.

The regime, however, never consistently adapted its Jewish policy to this new
rhetoric. Only in 1903 did the new minister of the interior, V. K. Plehve, try to,
operating under the assumption that Russia's old corporatist structures could
prevent the triumph of capitalism and the exploitation of the masses by the
bourgeoisie. Consistent with these views, he actually made concessions to lower
class Jews, while placing limitations on Jewish big business. Merchants of the
First Guild now were forbidden to buy land outside the cities, but nearly two
hundred villages within the Pale of Settlement, so far closed to poorer Jews, were
opened up. Responding to defeat in the Russo-Japanese War (1904–5) and the
rising unrest in the country, Plehve moved to admit a number of Jews to the bar
association, hoping that they would calm their impatient fellow Jews. In keeping
with his suspicion of any non-Russian nationalist movements, however, he
banned the Zionist movement.

From Constitutional Reform to the Fall of Tsarism

At the height of the revolution of 1905, Prime Minister Sergei Witte promised equal rights for Jews, as well as for others. The first and second Duma would have acted favorably on this promise, but they were unable to prevent their own dissolution and the virtual coup d'état that changed the electoral law. With the Duma right wing thus strengthened, Tsar Nicholas II refused any concessions to the Jews, a decision his newly appointed prime minister Pyotr Stolypin learned about, ironically, after suggesting some measures to "placate the Jews." Still, Stolypin was influential enough with the tsar to prevent the government's propaganda use of the *Protocols of the Elders of Zion*. Later to be exposed as a hoax, the *Protocols* nonetheless voiced many of the fears of Russian conservatives; it laid out a Jewish-Masonic plot to install a merciless Jewish despot to rule over the old Christian states, destroy the nobility, sow class conflict, and foment revolution. Some twenty editions of the *Protocols* were published in Russia by various individuals before 1917.

After Stolypin's electoral law of June 3, 1907, further reduced the influence of the lower classes and the non-Russian nationalities, while increasing that of the Russians, a nationalistic atmosphere prevailed in the Duma. Almost all the new laws that expanded individual rights excluded the Jews (as for example those laws that adopted a new basis for discriminating against Jews by excluding even baptized Jews from service as officers or military doctors in the Russian army). Antisemitic actions took a radical turn. From the end of 1905 onward antisemitism developed a mass basis in the Union of the Russian People (URP) and other so-called Black Hundred organizations, local elements of which had played some role in the pogroms of October 1905 and more clearly in 1906.

In Odessa right-wing terrorists hunted down and killed left-wing agitators, politicians, and Jews. Elsewhere, the URP trained terrorists who killed prominent revolutionaries and Duma politicians. They also tried to assassinate former Prime Minister Witte and the leader of the liberals, Pavel Miliukov. Ideologically, the URP and other branches of the Black Hundreds, like their predecessors in the 1890s, made anti-capitalism the centerpiece of their antisemitism. They found their social basis mainly among the urban lower classes, especially in the still functioning artisan guilds or other corporatist structures of the petty bourgeoisie (*meshchan'e*). Many opposed constitutionalism as one of the weapons of the Jews; along with liberalism, capitalism, and stockholding companies, it was believed by many on the Right to be designed to destroy the existing social order. Liberals, in their eyes, were either dupes or co-conspirators, paving the way for socialists and revolutionaries. The Freemasons, seen as allies of the Jews, figured prominently in the writings of some of the more eccentric right-wingers, such as N. A. and G. V. Butmi (who also published a version of the *Protocols* in 1905 and 1906). The URP found considerable support among the clergy of the

176   *Heinz-Dietrich Löwe*

Russian Orthodox Church. Traditional Christian anti-Jewish stereotypes continued to provide fertile ground for antisemitism, and the Russian radical Right made ample use of Christian imagery and symbolism. But even the clergy and the episcopal press espoused an antisemitism that looked to modern political devices, owing less to tradition and more to that propagated by the Black Hundreds.

Paradoxically, political goals, not theology, were the driving force behind a revival of the Jewish blood libel in 1911. Right-wing leaders, supported by the ministers of justice and interior, turned a murder in the red-light district of Kiev into a sensational ritual-murder trial, designed not only to intimidate Jews but to accomplish other reactionary political purposes, including putting a halt to the growth of representative government. The public prosecutor made the broader political purposes of the trial starkly obvious:

The Jews are so convinced that they have captured the principal tool of society—the press—that they think no one would still dare bring such a charge against them...to some extent they are right. Capital largely is in their hands and, even if they lack legal rights, in reality they control all the world...and this is why they were astounded, when Beilis [the Jew accused of ritual murder] was brought to book: How could they dare when the state-Duma exists?...However, the government did dare it.

(in Löwe 1993, 289)

During the trial the minister of the interior took the opportunity to expel thousands of Jews dwelling outside the Pale of Settlement and excluded even more from voting for the Fourth Duma in 1912. Right-wing members introduced a legislative proposal in the Fourth Duma to outlaw *shekhita* (ritual slaughter), ostensibly to prevent cruelty to animals, in reality in order to undermine Jewish religious institutions, which financed themselves largely by the tax on kosher meat. But this measure failed to pass the Duma. Similarly, Beilis was acquitted, although the jury, composed largely of illiterate peasants, implicitly accepted that a ritual murder had indeed taken place.

The mounting pressure on Jews and the overt hostility toward them turned catastrophic during World War I. The government and Duma proved powerless to prevent the military from expelling all Jews from vast regions behind the front. As a consequence the Council of Ministers in 1915 had to expand the Pale of Settlement to include all cities of the empire. The Duma's Progressive Bloc proved incapable of doing anything to extend Jewish rights, although it had vaguely promised "to enter on the road to the emancipation of the Jews." The Bloc's conservative wing failed to honor even that moderate concession. A further betrayal came when the Duma refused to make use of its right to interpellate the government about a police hunt for Jews on the Moscow stock exchange and a circular from the ministry of the interior accusing the Jews of various misdeeds, including hoarding coins, furthering inflation, and of trying to destroy the harvest. These acts and accusations had all the appearance of official sanction,

Antisemitism in Russia and the Soviet Union 177

and set off violent attacks on Jews. Still, once the tsar had abdicated, the Provisional Government took only weeks to emancipate the Jews fully.

POGROMS

Writing the history of antisemitism under the tsars has often hinged on the role of violence, with a notable place in that history reserved for the pogrom. Therefore, this part of the chapter will close with a consideration of that phenomenon, which is by no means a simple one.

Contrary to widespread opinion, pogroms were not an everyday occurrence in Russia. Rather they appeared in three great waves, 1881–4, 1905–6, and 1917–21. Excluding the civil war period following the revolution of 1917, more than 95% of all pogroms took place in four years: 1881, 1882, 1905, and 1906. Again, contrary to widespread opinion, the pogroms were not government-organized or the work of any mysterious hidden hand. True, the police often were slow to respond, unwilling to protect Jewish victims, or even openly sympathetic to the rioters or *pogromshchiki*. But in many places the police acted swiftly, tried to repress rioters, and often, particularly in the wave of 1881 and 1882, succeeded.

The pogroms turned bloodier over time. Whereas in the 1880s, destruction of property was the prevalent result of pogrom activity, in 1905, violence escalated into street fighting and physical attacks against Jews. The police largely remained inactive, very often directed the rioters, and often intervened in their favor. Individual cases of the police actually inciting pogroms and even printing leaflets calling for them have been reported. Active participation by the so-called forces of order on the side of the *pogromshchiki* was especially common whenever Jewish self-defense groups got involved. In Odessa in October 1905, the police and the military frequently turned their weapons against students, Jews, and Jewish self-defense units. Barricades were erected and the intense street fighting suggested more than just a hint of civil war. The overall violence in 1905 seriously wounded thousands and claimed perhaps as many as 3,000 lives. For the far bloodier Civil War, the most recent estimate sets the number of Jews killed at up to 150,000.

In all three pogrom waves the political order appeared unstable and ripe for radical change. In the aftermath of Alexander II's assassination in 1881, the population at large realized that a power struggle was raging in St. Petersburg over whether to continue the reforms or to reassert autocracy and to slow down social change. On the eve of the revolutionary disturbances of 1905, the government, through its conduct of the trial after the pogrom in Gomel (1904), itself put the question: who shall rule? In October 1905, agitators roused the crowds with the slogan "the Jews want to rule over us." During the Civil War this slogan reappeared in many forms, as for instance in the *Protocols of the Elders of Zion*, which flooded the former Pale of Settlement. The widespread sense of instability present during all three waves of pogrom violence may have emboldened the rioters.

In seeking to understand the wave of 1881–2 and the isolated incidents of 1883–4, one may learn a few things from the very few pogroms that occurred both before and after those years. Prior to the first wave there had been three outbreaks in the city of Odessa in 1821, 1859, and 1871. Strikingly, they took place in that Russian city where Jews were the most modernized and integrated. Some Jews, both Russian subjects and foreigners, had achieved considerable economic and social success. This suggests that acculturated, integrated, and economically successful Jews may have been more intolerable to the broader masses than the orthodox poor and less assertive Jews. This hypothesis wins additional support when the few pogroms of 1884 and the infamous pogrom at Kishinev in 1903 are taken into consideration.

Outside Russia, pogroms also took place in situations when legal emancipation seemed imminent, as in central Europe in 1819 and 1848. Shortly before 1881, when Alexander II seemed ready to resume the reformist impetus of his early years, and before and during the revolution of 1905, equal rights were debated in Russia, too; before the Civil War of 1918–21 Jews had actually been fully emancipated.

Several of these underlying assumptions are supported by the fact that in 1881 and 1882 pogroms took place in the Ukraine almost exclusively. The new Ukraine had been opened for Jews in 1791. Freshly established Jewish communities were not as firmly under the control of their members as was the case elsewhere. Non-orthodox or economically successful Jews—those who were more likely to provoke resentment—became more visible outside the Jewish quarters and may have helped trigger pogrom violence. In the old Ukraine, by contrast, historical memory seems to have played a more important role. There, Jews had for centuries been agents of the nobility, especially after that nobility had enserfed the once-free peasantry. The ensuing social tension exploded during and after the uprising (1648) of Ukrainian Hetman Bogdan Chmielnicki. An estimated 50,000 Jews were killed. This massacre remained present in peasant memory and folklore far into the twentieth century.

Finally, economic dislocation was another likely underlying cause of anti-Jewish violence. In 1881, in the midst of a worldwide agrarian depression, small-scale traders and craftsmen in the Ukraine frequently served as ringleaders of pogroms, having put themselves at the head of thousands of seasonal workers from the north, who had been unable to find employment on the large estates.

Local commissions, established in 1881 to examine the causes of the pogroms, demanded the reinstatement of early-modern market regulations, insisting that under the conditions of free trade, ordinary people could not compete with the Jews. Local traders and craftsmen supported this view, seeing Jewish business practices as a breach of the moral economy that kept competition and rising prices in check. The participants in the pogroms of 1881 were driven by these and similar resentments against capitalist economic forms and the forces of modernity embodied in the Jews.

In October 1905, marches by revolutionaries and processions of loyalists clashed and the result was often anti-Jewish violence. It did not need much for a pogrom to get under way. Firing shots or defacing a portrait of Tsar Nicholas II was enough to inspire ordinary people to take their wrath out on the Jews. Often the local priest, or *pop*, took part in processions that boiled over into pogroms. But even when *popy* admonished crowds to abstain from violence against Jews, more often than not they were disobeyed. With the exception of the great majority of the intelligentsia and most of the workers of St. Petersburg and Moscow, all layers of society proved susceptible to pogrom agitation, with petty bourgeois elements most active.

Least researched are the pogroms of the Civil War. Throughout 1917 small incidents occurred when hungry people searched for food. The demoralization of the army after the October Revolution led to innumerable military forays victimizing Jews. Pogroms took many shapes, and many different groups were involved. They were organized by the military forces of those in power or aspiring to power. The waves of violence, however, turned most bloody in 1919, when the White Volunteer Army under General A. Denikin started to disintegrate. Antisemitic propaganda was used on a grand scale with thousands of copies of the *Protocols of the Elders of Zion* put into circulation. Wholesale expulsions of Jews during the war and the general hatred of them within the tsarist army were nurtured by an officer corps convinced by its own frantic accusations of espionage, sabotage, and profiteering. In this fertile soil, pogroms escalated in their murderousness. Often Jews were rounded up in the marketplace and massacred by machine gun fire. Out-of-control soldiers rampaged through the streets, and acts of individual cruelty abounded.

Pogroms were also perpetrated by the military units of the Ukrainian nationalist Symon Petliura, the anarchist movement under Nestor Makhno, and occasionally the Red Army, especially the famous Red Cavalry under S. Budennyi on its retreat from Poland in 1920. Although Lenin refused to investigate these atrocities and no energetic Bolshevik campaign against antisemitism resulted from these events, four hundred Red Army men were executed for taking part in the anti-Jewish violence.

THE SOVIET UNION AND ITS AFTERMATH

Recasting Jews in the Image of Soviet Man: Bolshevik Policy up to World War II

According to Lenin and Stalin, Jews lacked the most important constituent element of a nationality, territory, and were therefore simply a caste defined by religion and economic occupation, bound to disappear with the development toward socialism. However, if Jews had ever seen themselves in this light, they

180   *Heinz-Dietrich Löwe*

no longer did so in the twentieth century. These ideological assumptions proved to be sadly inadequate for a people that had only recently (re)discovered itself as a nationality.

The policies of the Bolsheviks contributed to the strengthening of antisemitism in Soviet society. In this respect, they were similar to the tsarist policies: both political systems pursued the three reconstructionist principles of enlightened absolutism—integration, productivization, and education.

Integration after 1917 came to mean sovietization. As in the tsarist era, it remained for a fairly long time socially conditioned. The Bolsheviks did not grant equal rights to all Jews but only to the toiling Jewish masses. Under both systems the groups deemed worthy of being integrated proved relatively small. This was true even of the proletarian element (the "masses"), at least until the industrialization of the 1930s. Also, both systems had to create and form those elements of Jewish society they preferred to rely on.

Aiming for productivization, both systems attacked the large number of Jews involved in trade, in one case regarded as unproductive, in the other as not merely unproductive but also hostile to socialism. In both systems productivization translated into agrarianizing Jews. For the Bolsheviks this was a temporary expedient. Their ideal would have been to proletarianize Soviet Jews, but there were simply not enough factory jobs to accomplish this goal prior to the rapid industrialization of the 1930s. In contrast to the Bolsheviks, the tsars had attempted to increase the number of Jewish craftsmen, supposedly the only major productive element in Jewish society. When it became possible, the Soviet system sought outright proletarianization because it regarded artisans as a historically doomed and socially retrograde force, to be tolerated only as long as they did not employ hired labor.

Both systems established special state schools to draw broader segments of Jewish society into the wider social and political system. Convinced that historical development was on their side, the Bolsheviks developed a broad Yiddish-language school system. Jews, yearning for new ways of life, soon responded favorably to the regime's clear advocacy of modernization, finding it far more attractive than the tsarist era's always ambiguous relationship to change. Co-optation of certain Jewish elements progressed quite far. State and party organizations were wide open to Jews who were willing to cooperate with the system individually on the latter's terms. Their ethnicity proved no grounds for exclusion.

Whereas the policies of tsarism with respect to religious reform were half-hearted, the Bolsheviks never seriously attempted it at all. Their few local experiments with the "living synagogue," parallel to the "living church" for Orthodox believers, were never consistently pursued and soon failed. The regime's attitude toward Judaism was unpredictable. Modern forms were an object of particular harassment while traditional forms, such as the Chabad movement of the Hasidim, experienced a few years of unexpected relative tolerance. Toward religion in general, the Bolsheviks were much more interventionist than the tsarist or, for that matter, any other regime in modern times. Openly hostile propaganda against the religiously oriented of Jewish society, interference in community affairs, harassment, and overt repression were to speed up the ultimate aim of integration. The belief that formidable enemies within Jewish society were resisting the new regime justified heavy-handed interference. In fact, the Bolsheviks were not mistaken about the resistance to their aims in various sectors of the Jewish population. The Zionists, the Bund (the All-Russian Jewish Workers' Party in Poland, Lithuania, and Russia), and even the old upper-middle classes proved able to mobilize the Jewish population to a remarkable degree. Later on, traditional Judaism also showed considerable tenacity.

In the field of Yiddish-language education and cultural politics the results of Bolshevik intervention yielded impressive results, although it must be borne in mind that the objective was sovietization rather than the formation of a national Soviet Jewish culture. As evidence of the official reluctance to foster a Jewish identity, the Soviet republics where most Jews lived, Ukraine and Belarus, decided not to offer higher education in Yiddish. This rendered Yiddish secondary schools much less attractive to those acculturated urban Jews who intended to pursue advanced studies. Even for the traditional, largely non-Russian-speaking Jews, education in Yiddish-language schools was strongly Soviet in content, and anti-religious propaganda stronger there than in the general schools. The aim was to break up the compactness and isolation of the Jews, ostensibly in the name of modernity, but in reality in order to sovietize them. In the 1930s, the Yiddish school system went into decline, in part because the authorities discontinued their support, for reasons never made clear.

For some time during the interwar period the regime treated the Jewish religion and its institutions relatively mildly. But these stretches of relative calm were interspersed with episodes of intense discrimination or direct repressions. The property of synagogues and other Jewish institutions was often made the target of allegedly spontaneous workers' campaigns for their conversion to more useful purposes, such as workers' clubs or public libraries. The authorities kept the numbers of synagogues down by forcing them to re-register, which became increasingly difficult. Repressive measures intentionally undermined the network of religious charitable institutions, historically vital to holding Jewish communities together. The state and other Communist organizations sometimes simply took over their property and assets. Show trials against circumcision, kosher slaughtering, and the *heder* (traditional schools for boys), as well as trials of rabbis and community activists, came in waves, although, at an early stage, they met with serious resistance. From the late 1920s onward, determined anti-religious campaigns, closing almost all synagogues, accompanied collectivization and forced industrialization. The terror of 1937 and 1938 did not bypass religious communities. Many rabbis and activists were judicially murdered. This program of sustained bouts of repression, alternating with phases of neglect and more

182   *Heinz-Dietrich Löwe*

haphazard persecution, seems to have been successful. In 1937, only 13–15% of all Jews declared themselves believers, compared to 47% among the rest of the population.

As in the cases of education and productivization, the Soviet Union pursued integration also with a high level of repressive force. "Bourgeois" Zionists were persecuted, although the Zionist sports organization, Maccabi, enjoyed some brief moments of semi-legality. The Marxist Bund and almost all Zionist socialist parties were outlawed early on. The only important special institution for Jews inside the Soviet system, the Yevsektsiya (the wholly subordinate Jewish section of the Communist Party of the Soviet Union), was abolished in 1930. Created to combat the overwhelming influence of non-Communist groups within the Jewish population, it was obviously never intended as a means of pursuing Jewish national aims. When industrialization and social change were about to destroy traditional Jewish milieus, the Yevsektsiya no longer had a function to perform and was duly denounced for nationalist deviation and disbanded.

The Communists also squeezed out secular self-help organizations, such as the credit-cooperatives, which before World War I had served nearly 50% of the Jewish population. By the mid-1920s, they had ceased to exist. The same fate pursued the surviving *arteli*, traditional cooperative workshops formed by poor Jewish artisans. By the early 1930s, they had been disbanded or integrated into general cooperatives.

Because most Jews belonged to the bourgeoisie or petty bourgeoisie, social strata the Communists regarded to be naturally hostile, the state's aggressive policies toward them came dangerously close to an undeclared form of antisemitism. For example, the Ukrainian GPU, the predecessor organization of the KGB, declared in an official document in 1925:

The Jewish population of the *shtetl*, numbering 2 million, must inevitably...become the victim of our economic policy. Our struggle against the petty bourgeoisie for the markets in the *shtetl*..., for a direct link with the peasants with a view to satisfying their needs with the products of our large- and small-scale industry...is the struggle against the Jewish masses which serve, in fact, as an almost pure embodiment of this petty bourgeoisie.

Because Jews as a whole were seen as an exploitative class, the struggle against the Jewish bourgeoisie could not be pursued by purely economic measures. That in 1925–6, 72.3% of all urban and 29.7% of all rural Jews of the Ukraine were qualified as *lishentsy* (non-working class) meant that they were deprived of civil rights, including the right to draw a pension, unemployment, or health benefits. Another statistic makes it clear that Jews were specifically targeted: in 1926, 44.6% of all *lishentsy* in the Ukraine were Jews, although their share in the total population was only 5.43%. Even with the Stalin Constitution of 1936, when rights, at least according to the letter of the law, were restored to almost everybody, 4–11% of the Jews remained in this status. In the main commercial and

Antisemitism in Russia and the Soviet Union

industrial centers, those private entrepreneurs still allowed in Soviet law until 1928, the so-called NEP-men, were subjected to raids and arrests, often carried out with great public fanfare. Because the population at large and the lower cadres of the party tended to identify Jews with NEP-men, they more than others suffered from these attacks on private trade and business. Expropriation of private property hit everybody, but, once again, Jews were hit particularly hard.

In short, the state's economic policies and its repression of classes deemed unproductive weighed heavily upon the Jews. In 1926, 20.6% had no specified occupation, and close to 10% were unemployed. Contemporary observers considered the small market town or *shtetl* worse off than before the revolution. In order to destroy the Jewish bourgeoisie once and for all, the *shtetl* was left to die. "The scissors crisis [the deliberate setting of agricultural prices at too low a level] will with all...historical necessity rob the poor Jewish masses of any means to earn a living and will destroy the *shtetl*," a Yevsektsiya publication declared approvingly. By the end of the 1920s, drastically raised taxes, confiscations and persecutions, competition, and the refusal to provide goods or raw materials destroyed the economic basis of craftsmen and small traders. Many sought refuge by moving into agriculture, only to leave it again for other work. By the end of the 1930s, the Yevsektsiya prophecy had come true; the *shtetl* had disappeared as a meaningful social formation.

Until industry could employ more people, agrarianization took its place in the regime's plans for Jews. This strategy appealed to some Jews because agrarian settlement, they hoped, meant the chance to attain the status of a recognized national group. A sense of urgency gripped those who thought this way, because impending industrialization and social change threatened to destroy the basis for a special Jewish identity. Mikhail Kalinin, the titular head of state, played to this desire when he declared:

A great task lies ahead for the Jewish people—to preserve its nationality, but for this it is necessary to turn an important part of the Jewish population into a...compact agricultural population, which should comprise at least a few hundred thousand. Only under such circumstances can the Jewish mass hope for the further existence of its nationality.

A Jewish territory, the precondition for a Jewish national Soviet republic, did not materialize in either the southern Ukraine or the Crimea, although many Jews were settled there. The surrogate for these was established in Far Eastern Birobidjan, motivated also by the need to improve the geo-strategic position of the Soviet Union in the area. But it failed for many reasons, including Jewish unwillingness to settle in such a remote, undeveloped area. Meanwhile, collectivization and integration of the Jewish colonies in Ukraine and the Crimea into "international" collective farms (1928) destroyed their national character and had the effect of making factory work more attractive to Jews. The share of Jewish

184 *Heinz-Dietrich Löwe*

farmers declined from 11.1% in the late 1920s to 5.8% in 1939. During World War II, the Nazis destroyed the still sizable Jewish colonies on the Crimea and murdered most of their inhabitants.

As industrialization took hold in the 1930s, the proletarianization of the Jewish population made substantial progress. Even so, Jews remained under-represented in certain fields of endeavor, for instance in the railroad system and in the mining industries. For a variety of complicated causes, including a grassroots antisemitism tolerated and even often shared by officials, proletarianization of Jews was finally a transient phenomenon. Only in the middle of the 1930s did the percentage of manual or wage laborers stand higher than that of salaried or white-collar employees among Jews, and then only slightly. Soon the numbers of the salaried rose above those of wage earners. This trend continued after the war, making Jews almost exclusively middle class and an important element of the Soviet middle classes in general.

The Bolshevik project to reconstruct Jewish society depended on the Jewish socialist intelligentsia. Its members had roots in various pre-revolutionary movements, partly labor Zionist and partly internationalist, such as the former Bundists. The latter had, since the turn of the century, developed a new national Jewish identity, as had broad elements of the rest of Jewish society. Cognizant of these developments, Bolshevik leaders, in their first decade of rule, introduced new cultural components to satisfy Jewish aspirations in a Soviet setting. But the drive to win Jewish allegiance in this way abated during the 1930s; the Yiddish-language school system, as previously mentioned, was wound down, Yiddish literature was more tightly controlled and specifically forbidden to glorify the Jewish past. Yiddish cultural life and the Jewish theater also declined.

Once again, the government's alternation between light- and heavy-handed policies makes it difficult to be precise about its intentions. Did the Bolsheviks originally seek to foster creation of a Soviet Jewish culture? Or was the objective always complete assimilation? In this context the suppression in 1930 of the three-volume *Malaia Sovetskaia Entsiklopediia* (*Small Soviet Encyclopedia*) suggests a decisive turning point toward complete assimilation. The suppression may have been in response to the detailed entries in it for "Jews" and "Jewish history." Jewish history was presented as a continuum, and due recognition was given the many languages and literatures of the Jews. Another article spoke at length about Jewish political parties—the bourgeois parties of the tsarist era included—and the social-democratic Bund was, contrary to the official view, described as a socialist revolutionary workers' party. The destruction of this encyclopedia, already set in type and ready for printing, was symbolic. Jews in Russia were being denied a separate intellectual home in Soviet thinking, or a place in the Soviet hierarchy of nations.

Although the government's growing hostility was fairly clear, the strength of antisemitism in Soviet society is more difficult to gauge. Our perception

Antisemitism in Russia and the Soviet Union 185

depends almost totally on the reaction of the regime to expressions of popular antisemitism. Official campaigns against it reflected Bolshevik political motives and ideological mindset, but not necessarily antisemitism's actual strength. Antisemitism was attacked intermittently during the 1920s and early 1930s, but the attacks then ceased. Reports of antisemitism nearly disappeared from the controlled press. The authorities may have concluded that hostility to Jews could be a useful tool in sovietizing Jewish society, as well as an inevitable part of the struggle against the NEP-men and Jewish middlemen. The prominence of Jews in trade was seen as provoking popular antisemitism, reflecting social conflicts typical of capitalism. Fighting antisemitism, therefore, was not a high priority, since it would vanish along with capitalism. By the end of the 1920s, the OGPU (secret police) was inclined to view antisemitism as a reflection of anti-Sovietism. This enabled Bolshevik leaders to define two forms of antisemitism, one dangerous—the result of agitation by class enemies—and the other less dangerous, even pardonable, because it came from unenlightened, misled workers betraying "a natural class-hatred against the Jewish NEP-man."

The authorities reinforced these antisemitic sentiments. The highly visible attacks on private trade, especially in Moscow and Leningrad, often targeted Jewish traders, reminiscent of the scandalous raid by tsarist authorities on the Moscow stock exchange in 1916. The high percentage of Jewish *lishentsy* (that is, those disenfranchised in the Soviet state) after the revolution may also have been interpreted by the public as sanctioning antisemitic feelings. Also extremely ambiguous in its effects must have been the tendency of Soviet officials to explain antisemitism in a way that strengthened old stereotypes. E. A. Preobrazhensky, a leading party theoretician, explained antisemitism in *Pravda* (March 17, 1927) as an effort by the bourgeoisie to discard an element of itself. This came close to classifying all Jews as a hostile bourgeois element.

Official publications explained the low employment of Jews on the railway system (clearly a reflection of antisemitic sentiments among railroad workers) as a perfectly understandable result of the latter's frequent confrontation with Jewish speculators on trains and in stations. *Der Emes* (*The Truth*), the central Communist Yiddish-language newspaper, contributed to the perpetuation of antisemitic stereotypes by attacking Jewish religious institutions. Traditional Jewish organizations, it charged, were local branches of world Jewry; those Jews attending synagogues were NEP-men and their families; the Moscow Choral synagogue (of Reformed Judaism) was no more than a trading center, a stock exchange. Jewish noses figured prominently in the paper's caricatures.

Meanwhile, official policies that had enabled most Jews to become members of the Soviet middle class also fed antisemitic stereotypes among ordinary Russians, confirming their long-held belief that Jews avoided hard manual labor. Beliefs spread as well that Jews had become the main beneficiaries of the regime, visible in its elites as party members, state and industrial employees, and the Soviet intelligentsia. The *Protocols of the Elders of Zion* still circulated, and simple

186   *Heinz-Dietrich Löwe*

people sometimes gossiped about a Jewish conspiracy to take power in the Soviet Union and the rest of the world. The Jews were accused of occupying positions of authority everywhere and then filling them with their kin and friends. E. Yaroslavsky, one of Stalin's most loyal *aparatchiki*, explained in 1929 that not only Russian but also Jewish nationalism had to be fought. The regime apparently did not care that its actions strengthened old prejudices. Its overriding concern was the class struggle, but the accusatory language it habitually employed brought its fight against speculation, NEP-men, and the Jewish petty bourgeoisie close to forms of racism.

From World War II to Stalin's Death: Attacks on Jewish Cultural Elites and Nationalism

Antisemitism increased markedly during the war against Nazism, first among common people, then within the regime, which readily bowed to pressure from below. In 1942, it began to take stock of Jews active in cultural life and dismissed large numbers of them. This campaign was not public and hardly ever openly justified. Linda Stern, a scientist and convinced Communist from Switzerland, when ordered to fire two Jewish staff members from her scientific journal, was told that "Hitler has leaflets distributed everywhere saying Jews are occupying important positions all over the Soviet Union, and this is a slight to our honor." The regime refused to publish newspaper reports about the bravery of Jews in the Red Army, among the partisans, and, more importantly, kept silent about the Jews as special victims of Nazi extermination policies. The rising tide of antisemitic sentiment among the Soviet public and the widespread slander of Jews as profiteers and military shirkers were thus met with official silence. In the absence of rebuttals of these slurs, however, the situation often turned nasty for Jews lining up for bare necessities or arriving in far-away cities after being evacuated. When Jews later tried to return to their homes in formerly Nazi-occupied territories, they often met with hostility, sometimes leading to pogroms, such as the one in Kiev in September 1945.

Average Soviet readers never got any information on Nazi extermination measures against Jews. Soviet press releases only spoke of "peaceful Soviet citizens," not specifically of Jews as victims. Neither Nazi racism, which targeted Jews in particular, nor the methodical character of the killings was reported during the war or the following decade. The Soviet authorities presented Auschwitz as an extermination camp of the Slavic people. Only those educated readers who combed the press and specialized journals could form some idea of the exceptional character of the persecution of the Jews. The psychological impact on the Jews of this denial of their sufferings was made even worse by the regime's continuous repression of spontaneous attempts to commemorate the Jewish dead. The victims' attempt to vent their frustration through the only channel open to them, the Jewish Anti-Fascist Committee (JAC), proved unsuccessful.

Antisemitism in Russia and the Soviet Union 187

The suppression of the *Black Book*, detailing Nazi massacres of Jews, added to a growing sense among Jews in Soviet Russia of the regime's callous disregard for their fate. Under these conditions many Jews turned back to their roots, setting in motion a strong Jewish national revival.

The authorities took note of this development and reacted harshly. The Council for the Religious Cults under the Council of Ministers of the USSR reported a considerable increase in nationalistic tendencies among Jews; "Soviet Zionists" refused to acknowledge that the Jewish Question had long been solved within the Soviet Union. They had turned synagogues into a place of "national concentration." Local Soviet authorities were thus instructed to observe the activities of Jewish communities, to restrict traditional welfare activities, to disband burial societies, and to oppose customs that "spur on nationalistic feelings." When, in October 1948, during the high holy days, thousands of Jews rallied around Moscow's central synagogue to honor Golda Meir, the first Israeli ambassador, the authorities became especially alarmed at the signs of Jewish disaffection.

Renewed attacks against "nationalist deviations" were the government's response. Minority writers were accused of nationalist or—worse still—of bourgeois-nationalist deviations, of belittling Soviet achievements, and denying the progressive character of Soviet society. Politburo member Andrei Zhdanov criticized Jewish wartime literature for its parochialism because "the German-fascist murders of the Jewish population are depicted as isolated and not integrated with the Hitlerite killings of Soviet people in general." Jewish writers, accused of giving politically idealized impressions of the old Jewish way of life, were ordered to abandon their "limited national" framework and to write instead about the social processes of wider Soviet society. Some were singled out for "Jewish exclusiveness," for constantly referring to the Holocaust as a special Jewish martyrology, and for overtly propagating Zionist ideas.

Jewish writers, poets, playwrights, and historians were asked to sever themselves unequivocally from their cultural and historic past. In 1949, Soviet Jews, especially those prominent in the administration, sciences, and cultural life, became the main targets in the unfolding campaign against "cosmopolitanism," linked to their supposed groveling before the West and their belittling of Russian culture and achievements. The campaign peaked with the dissolution of the Jewish Anti-Fascist Committee and with a number of trials on charges of nationalist deviation. In one trial twenty-three men, activists of the JAC and Jewish writers, among them David Bergelson, Itzik Fefer, and Perets Markish, were condemned to death and executed; many more disappeared in prisons and the Gulag. Yet others were convicted of espionage for the United States and medical murder. This last charge involved mostly Jewish doctors in the so-called Doctors' Plot. As Stalin explained to the Politburo in December 1952: "Every Jewish nationalist is the agent of the American intelligence service. Jewish nationalists think that their nation was saved by the USA ... They think they are indebted to the Americans. Among doctors, there are many Jewish nationalists." A few days later the decision to organize a show trial was made, the grounds announced by a *Pravda* article on January 13, 1953, "Vicious Spies and Killers under the Mask of Academic Physicians." This antisemitic witch hunt had already spread to the Soviet satellites of the Eastern Bloc. As a consequence of the Prague trials against Rudolf Slánský and other party functionaries, thirteen former Czechoslovak Communist leaders (eleven of whom were Jewish) were executed. Similar trials were conducted or prepared in other communist countries.

The campaign against the Jews and Zionism tried to destroy any surviving traces of a separate Jewish culture in the Soviet Union by physically liquidating its leading representatives. By killing or jailing the foremost Jewish "cosmopolitans," the USSR could simultaneously be isolated and safeguarded from the West. In all likelihood, the Doctors' Plot was to serve as the starting shot for another massive wave of terror comparable to that of the late 1930s. It did not materialize, however, because of Stalin's death on March 5, 1953.

This prolonged hostile scrutiny of Jews fed an explosive antisemitic mood in the public at large, and this particular legacy of late Stalinism was to linger on long after his death. However, no documentary proof has been found for the widespread contemporary rumors of an impending deportation of the Jews.

From Khrushchev to Brezhnev: Economic Trials and Anti-Zionist Campaigns

Stalin's successors quickly ended the worst features of this nightmare. But Nikita Khrushchev, often perceived in the West as a reformer, for some time acted as an apt pupil of his master, especially in the matter of the Jews. A heavy-handed anti-religious campaign was resumed, the national prerogatives of non-Russians were withdrawn, and national cultures were repressed. Khrushchev still insisted that the Jewish Question had been solved by assimilation and that the Jews themselves did not want anything else. For him assimilation was inevitable and progressive. Mikhail Suslov, for decades to come the "grey cardinal" of Soviet ideology, seconded his leader: "we have no intention to revive a dead culture."

There were nonetheless some slight relaxations to be observed in the post-Stalin era. In 1957, a yeshiva was officially permitted, and Yiddish books reappeared two years later. But the antisemitic tone of governmental policy continued unabated, sustained by numerous campaigns between 1958 and 1966 against economic crimes. In 1961 alone, 110 managers were condemned to death, 60 of them Jews. The press dwelt on this point and leveled familiar accusations. Jews worshipped the golden calf and used synagogues for their speculations. *De facto* rather than *de jure* discrimination led to an undeclared *numerus clausus* in universities and scientific institutes. In the campaign against alleged Jewish superstition and obscurantism, the blood libel resurfaced once again, this time

Antisemitism in Russia and the Soviet Union 189

in a central Asian publication. The official disclaimer could not prevent the pogroms linked to this fable that broke out in 1961 and 1962 in Uzbekistan and Turkestan.

Despite Soviet support for the founding of the state of Israel, anti-Zionist campaigns became the hallmark of official policy. Attacks on Zionist racism and comparisons with the Nazis had already become common currency by the late 1940s. The Suez War of 1956 intensified this tendency. However, foreign policy considerations always played second fiddle to concerns about domestic conditions. One of these clearly was the fight against the growing desire of Soviet Jews to emigrate. The development of a Zionist underground prompted the unleashing of a steadily more menacing anti-Zionist crusade. Trofim Kichko's 1963 antisemitic book *Judaism without Embellishment*, published by the Ukrainian Academy of Sciences, was a notable step in this direction. He revived practically all prerevolutionary prejudices: the Talmud taught Jews to detest all non-Jews, especially the simple people; Judaism was no more than a recipe for capitalist exploitation; and so forth. As in Stalin's day, anti-Zionism clearly retained its anti-Western characteristics. New, however, was the accusation that Zionists and Nazis had cooperated closely all through World War II.

After the 1967 Arab-Israeli war, Kichko produced a new book (with a print run of 60,000), which blamed the Torah for alleged Israeli war crimes and declared Zionism to be the spearhead of imperialism and international capitalism. With Yuri Ivanov's book *Beware, Zionism* (1969, with a print run of 75,000) and innumerable publications of this genre by various authors, the last restraints had fallen away. There was an international Jewish conspiracy to conquer the world—everyone knew this; Zionists already dominated the mass media and the financial markets; Zionism was the most important enemy of the Soviet system, a new form of racist exclusionism; antisemitism, remarkably, was a tool of the Zionists, who had instigated the pogroms of the tsarist era. The press retroactively justified those pogroms as the self-defense of the common people against Jewish exploitation. The government's hostile reaction to Yevgeny Yevtushenko's poem *Babi Yar* (1961) and Anatoly Rybakov's novel *Heavy Sands* (1979), which treated Jewish suffering under the Nazis and the regime's distortion of that history, left no doubt that it was still risky to mention the Jews as special victims of Nazi extermination policies.

In the 1970s, the equivalence of Zionism and Nazism reached new extremes. The biblical concept of the Chosen People was transformed into a racially based aspiration for world domination on the part of the Jews. The official organ for party workers, *Agitator*, printed an article by the well-known anti-Zionist hack, Yevgeny Yevseev, a nephew of an influential Central Committee secretary. Finally, even the Soviet Academy of Sciences published a book that repeated the main tenets of the *Protocols of the Elders of Zion*.

The claims that Jews were responsible for many of the country's problems were accompanied by directly discriminatory measures. The number of

190   *Heinz-Dietrich Löwe*

Jewish university students declined from 94,000 in 1965 to 66,900 in 1976. The authorities closed numerous private religious classes and interfered in the activities of the journal *Jews in the USSR*, harassing the Jewish intelligentsia that had gathered around it. The KGB frequently beat up Jewish *"refuseniks"* (those refused an exit visa from the USSR). Prominent dissident Anatolii Shcharanskii (now Natan Sharansky) went to prison on charges of espionage. Following a circular logic all its own, the regime responded to the growing desire of Jews to emigrate from the Soviet Union by intensifying the very measures responsible for that desire. The anti-Zionist campaign continued intermittently until the breakdown of the Soviet Union.

Antisemitism from *Perestroika* to the Present

Toward the end of his life Leonid Brezhnev attempted to rein in Soviet antisemitism, as the growing demand for emigration and an economic slump added to the problems of Soviet domestic politics. The momentum of the campaign could not be broken, however, and some of the worst antisemitic diatribes appeared in 1983, after Brezhnev's death. Only with the advent of Mikhail Gorbachev's *perestroika* did it become possible to challenge antisemites in the courts, but even then the results were mixed. Gorbachev himself was reluctant to come to the defense of the Jews because he might then give credibility to opponents of his reforms. Antisemitism had become one of their most frequently employed weapons; for them, Soviet Jewish *kosmopolity* and left liberals were behind Gorbachev's reform efforts.

When the Soviet Union collapsed in 1991, antisemitism did not simply disappear. The loss of political direction and the decline in personal security that followed the breakdown of the Soviet empire fostered the return to prerevolutionary ideologies, a trend already under way before the collapse. An elaborate neo-Slavophilism emerged, maintaining that Russia was a civilization with its own path of development. The Christian religion was central to nationality. Russians possessed a more harmonious personality than the machine-men of the West, and Russia had developed historically in a communitarian economic system, different from and superior to the West with its cult of money. Western men live in a society under the rule of law, Russians in a society of truth. The strength of this Slavophile revival manifested itself in certain trends, for example, the exclusion of Jewish writers—held not to be authentically Russian—from anthologies of Russian literature and culture.

Antisemitism during and after *perestroika* also fed on more contemporary sources than Slavophilism. Exponents of the so-called village prose, such as Valentin Rasputin, faulted the Soviet system for the impoverishment of the Soviet and post-Soviet village. Rasputin, along with many others, the majority of whom were former party functionaries involved in the literary scene rather than writers of quality, have created a discourse that sees Soviet history in terms

Antisemitism in Russia and the Soviet Union 191

of a Masonic-Jewish, anti-Russian genocide. Another contemporary source invested in the promulgation of antisemitism has been the military press. In 1993, *Sovetskaia Rossiia* once again deployed the blood-libel accusation, which *Pravda* picked up in May of that year, maintaining that the Hasidim practice ritual murder. The extreme right-wing press regularly has run similar stories. In 1998, *Nashe Otechestvo (Our Fatherland)*, a patriotic Petersburg newspaper run by a former military man, celebrated the fiftieth anniversary of the state of Israel with the following statement: "It is really very simple; 1998 is the 50th anniversary of Israel. This means that the number of ritual murders of *goyim* must sharply rise." The group around Igor Shafarevich sees russophobia in any Westernizing attitude, and some of his associates accuse the Jews of having brought alcohol to Russia to weaken the Russian national character. The notorious Leningrad chemistry teacher Nina Andreeva, representing the neo-Stalinist wing of the Communist Party of the Soviet Union, denounced Gorbachev and his supporters as left-liberal socialists, overt or covert cosmopolitans, and internationalists—all buzzwords for Jews.

The leader of the reconstituted Communist Party of the Russian Federation (CPRF), Gennady Zyuganov, grounded his ideological hodgepodge of neo-Stalinism, anti-Zionism, anti-Judaism, and anti-Westernism with his book *I Believe in Russia* (1995):

The...influence of the Jewish Diaspora on...the culture and ideology of the Western world is growing...by the hour. The Jewish Diaspora, which traditionally controlled the financial life of Europe, has become...the owner of the controlling stocks of all economic systems of Western civilization. The goals of "chosenness," a predestination for world leadership and exclusivity, are so much a part Jewish religious dogma that they have begun to exert a profound influence over Western consciousness. Their messianic arrogance is...showing itself in ever more powerful forms.

When restraint is imperative, Zyuganov, as many other antisemites, uses the code word *kosmopolitizm* to express antisemitic and anti-Western prejudices.

The increasingly visible publicist Alexander Dugin, influenced by the European neo-Right, satisfies his anti-Western proclivities with his own, highly idiosyncratic version of Eurasianism (*evrazizm*), a doctrine that allows him to distance himself from his earlier even more chauvinist and antisemitic origins. Dugin was an early member of *Pamyat* as well as the National-Bolsheviks of Eduard Limonov, and he composed the program of Zyuganov's CPRF; he is also an expert for the Duma commission on geopolitics, adviser to one-time communist president of the Duma, Zeleznev, and rumored to be close to the Kremlin. In his view, in Jewish metaphysics the creation is separated from the Creator and set against him. This is the cause of the Jews' alienation, their diaspora existence, and clannishness. Alienation of the individual from the community and the universe, typical of modern times, paved the way for worldwide liberalism and all subversive theories, characteristic of the contemporary world dominated by the West, "that damned place, the empire of Antichrist." Dugin's worldview is permeated by, as he puts it, an eschatological awareness of the global struggle between "Atlanticism," composed of the maritime powers, and Eurasianism, or the continental powers, with Russia occupying the most important place among them. For him the maritime existence represents the extreme form of nomadism, typical of the Jewish Diaspora. The commercial character of the atlanticist arch-enemy stems from "Semitic" tribes, and is alien to the Eurasians because commercial elements were unknown to the class structure of the traditional Indo-European peoples. The most common antisemitic stereotypes are seldom directly present in Dugin's writings, but his language and rhetoric are familiar enough to most Russians to resonate in an antisemitic way.

Since the fall of the Soviet Union, dozens of chauvinistic and antisemitic parties have appeared and soon disappeared, most ridden by splits and counter-splits. Electorally quite successful for a time was the chauvinist Liberal Democratic Party of Vladimir Zhirinovsky, himself the son of a Jewish father.

Among the plethora of right-wing and antisemitic parties in the post-Soviet era, the one that attracted most attention in the Western media was Pamyat. Its proclamation to President Boris Yeltsin clearly characterizes the worldview of its membership:

Your Jewish entourage... has already made good use of you and doesn't need you anymore. You will share the destiny of Napoleon, Hitler, etc. who were Zionist-maintained dictators... The aim of international Zionism is to seize power worldwide. For this reason Zionists struggle against national and religious traditions of other nations, and for this purpose they devised the Freemasonic concept of cosmopolitanism.

There is nothing original in the antisemitism of the radical Right. Prerevolutionary and Soviet prejudices are still visible, and the rhetoric that accompanies their use is also familiar. However, the overtly racist elements to be found on the Right today are stronger than ever before, and many groups clearly borrow from Nazi models. Neo-Stalinism is also popular in a number of organizations. The only distinguishing belief systems that divide one group from another are neo-paganism, sometimes veiled although clearly present, as in the case of Dugin, and a widespread monarchism. Traditional Christian antisemitism remains strong, at times even popping up in the utterances of the neo-paganists.

Racist attitudes are widespread. A majority of the people believe that national characteristics are bestowed by God. On the whole, hatred for other nationalities is strong, against Chechens and Gypsies (51% of the population), Azerbaijanis (32%), Arabs (22%), Americans (19%), and Jews (13%). The anti-Jewish feeling does not seem particularly high at first sight, but when combined with popular notions of other traits, not necessarily pegged to nationality, Jews score much higher. In another poll, for example, Jews come up as the least hospitable, least reliable, and most cunning (43.9% believed this to be true), also most secretive (20.1%), least willing to help others, most egoistic and miserly (12.1 and

24.4%, respectively), least industrious (only 12.7% of the Russians see them as work-loving), and the most power-hungry (14.8%) of all peoples. Jews scored second highest among those people regarded as most rational, trailing only the English in this characteristic. But, taking into consideration that only 2.5% of Russians polled thought that Russians were most rational, it may be fair to assume that rationality is not a highly valued human virtue. Russians regard themselves instead as open, warm-hearted, and spontaneous; the Jews are the opposite—cool, formalistic, rationalistic, calculating, and secretive. Obviously, Jews, to very many Russians, are the quintessential domestic and international Other. This is the base of popular sentiment upon which the Russian national-istic elites and the many fringe groups discussed above hope to build their move-ments. Antisemitism is vital to their appeal.

The present and future of antisemitism in Russia are difficult to assess. Racist violence is frequent in today's Russia, but it does not often target Jews. Given the relatively small number of Jews in Russia, however, this may be a bit of an optical illusion. Harassing Jews and attacks on synagogues or yeshivas do, in fact, occur regularly. Right-wing demonstrators verbally attack them. In November 2005, for example, a rally in Moscow called for "purging Russia of the kikes' yoke." The public showed itself opposed to another right-wing march in 2005, with 52% of the Russians polled reacting negatively (24%—distinctly negatively); still, one-third remained unconcerned. Of late, the authorities have taken stronger measures against right-wing demonstrations (as well as against legiti-mate protesters of government policy); the relevant laws have also been strength-ened accordingly. International respectability, rather than protecting the rights and lives of Jews, seems to be the government's paramount concern. What the future holds for Russia's Jews remains unclear.

RECOMMENDED READINGS

General Works

Baron, Salo W., *The Russian Jew under Tsars and Soviets*, 2nd edn (New York: Schocken Books, 1987).

Gitelman, Zvi, *A Century of Ambivalence: The Jews of Russia and the Soviet Union, 1881 to the Present* (New York: Schocken Books, 1988).

Slezkine, Yuri, *The Jewish Century* (Princeton, NJ: Princeton University Press, 2004).

Prerevolutionary Times

Aronson, I. Michael, "Russian Commissions on the Jewish Question in the 1880s," *East European Quarterly* 14(1) (1980): 59–75.

Dolbilov, Mikhail, "Russifying Bureaucracy and the Politics of Jewish Education in the Russian Empire's Northwest Region (1860s–1870s)," *Acta Slavica Iaponica* 24 (2007): 112–43.

194 Heinz-Dietrich Löwe

Dubnow, Simon, *History of the Jews in Russia and Poland: from the Earliest Times to the Present Day*, 3 vols, trans. I. Friedlaender (Philadelphia: Jewish Publication Society of America, 1916–20).

Klier, John D., *Russia Gathers Her Jews. The Origins of the Jewish Question in Russia, 1772–1825* (DeKalb, IL: Northern Illinois University Press, 1986).

——*Imperial Russia's Jewish Question, 1855–1881* (Cambridge: Cambridge University Press, 1995).

Lohr, Eric, "The Russian Army and the Jews. Mass Deportation, Hostages, and Violence during World War I," *Russian Review* 60(3) (2001): 404–19.

Löwe, Heinz-Dietrich, *The Tsars and the Jews: Reform, Reaction, and Anti-Semitism 1772–1917* (Chur, Switzerland: Harwood, 1993).

——"Political Symbols and Rituals of the Russian Radical Right, 1900–1914," *Slavonic and East European Review* 76(3) (1998): 441–66.

——"Poles, Jews and Tartars: Religion, Ethnicity, and Social Structure in Tsarist Nationality Policies," *Jewish Social Studies* 6(3) (2000): 52–96.

Murav, Harriet, "The Beilis Ritual Murder Trial and the Culture of Apocalypse," *Cardozo Studies in Law and Literature* 12(2) (2000): 243–63.

Petrovsky-Shtern, Yohanan, "The 'Jewish Policy' of the Late Imperial War Ministry: The Impact of the Russian Right," *Kritika. Explorations in Russian and Eurasian History* 3(2) (2002): 217–54.

Pipes, Richard, "Catherine II and the Jews: The Origins of the Pale of Settlement," *Soviet Jewish Affairs* 5(2) (1975): 3–20.

Rogger, Hans, *Jewish Policies and Right-Wing Politics in Imperial Russia* (London: Macmillan, 1986).

Springer, Arnold, "Gavriil Derzhavin's Jewish Reform Project of 1800," *Canadian-American Slavic Studies* 10(1) (1976): 1–24.

Stanislawsky, Michael, *Tsar Nicholas and the Jews: The Transformation of Jewish Society in Russia 1825–1855* (Philadelphia: Jewish Publication Society of America, 1983).

Tager, Alexander S., *The Decay of Tsarism: The Beiliss Trial* (Philadelphia: Jewish Publication Society of America, 1935).

Pogroms

Aronson, I. Michael, *Troubled Waters: The Origins of the 1881 Anti-Jewish Pogroms in Russia* (Pittsburgh: University of Pittsburgh Press, 1990).

Budnitskii, O. V., "Jews, Pogroms, and the White Movement: A Historiographical Critique," *Kritika. Explorations in Russian and Eurasian History* 2(4) (2001): 751–72.

Judge, Edward H., *Easter in Kishinev: Anatomy of a Pogrom* (New York: New York University Press, 1992).

Klier, John D., and Shlomo Lambroza (eds), *Pogroms: Anti-Jewish Violence in Modern Russian History* (Cambridge: Cambridge University Press, 1992).

Löwe, Heinz-Dietrich, "Pogroms in Russia: Explanations, Comparisons, Suggestions," *Jewish Social Studies* 11(1) (2004): 16–24.

Staliunas, Darius, "Anti-Jewish Disturbances in the North-Western Provinces in the Early 1880s," *East European Jewish Affairs* 34/2 (2004): 119–38.

Soviet Times

Altshuler, Mordechai, "Jewish Holocaust Commemoration Activity in the USSR under Stalin," *Yad Vashem Studies* 30 (2002): 271–96.

Freedman, Theodore (ed.), *Anti-Semitism in the Soviet Union: Its Roots and Consequences* (New York: Freedom Library Press of the Anti-Defamation League of B'nai B'rith, 1984).

Kochan, Lionel, *The Jews in Soviet Russia since 1917*, 2nd edn (London: Oxford University Press, 1972).

Korey, William, *The Soviet Cage: Anti-Semitism in Russia* (New York: Viking Press, 1973).

Kostyrchenko, Gennadi, *Out of the Red Shadows: Anti-Semitism in Stalin's Russia* (Amherst, NY: Prometheus Books, 1995).

Löwe, Heinz-Dietrich, "The Holocaust in the Soviet Press," in Frank Grüner, Urs Heftrich, Heinz-Dietrich Löwe (eds), *Zerstörer des Schweigens: Formen künstlerischer Erinnerung an die nationalsozialistische Rassen- und Vernichtungspolitik in Osteuropa* (Wien-Köln: Bohlau, 2006), 33–55.

Pinkus, Benjamin, *The Soviet Government and the Jews 1948–1967: A Documented Study* (Cambridge: Cambridge University Press, 1986).

—— *The Jews of the Soviet Union: The History of a National Minority* (Cambridge: Cambridge University Press, 1988).

Redlich, Shimon (ed.), *War, Holocaust and Stalinism: A Documented Study of the Jewish Anti-Fascist Committee in the USSR* (Luxembourg: Harwood Academic, 1995).

Ro'i, Yaakov, "The Jewish Religion in the Soviet Union after World War II," in *Jews and Jewish Life in Russia and the Soviet Union* (Ilford, Essex: Frank Cass, 1995), 264–89.

Schwarz, Solomon M., *The Jews in the Soviet Union* (Syracuse: Syracuse University Press, 1951).

Post-Soviet Times

Brym, Robert J., and Andrei Degtyarev, "Anti-Semitism in Moscow. Results of an October 1992 Survey," *Slavic Review* 52(1) (1993): 1–12.

Korey, William, *Russian Antisemitism, Pamyat, and the Demonology of Zionism* (Chur, Switzerland: Harwood Academic, 1995).

Narskii, Igor S., and Marshall Shatz, "The Right-Wing Parties: Historiographical Limitations and Perspectives," *Kritika. Explorations in Russian and Eurasian History* 5(1) (2004): 179–84.

Rossman, Vadim, *Russian Intellectual Antisemitism in the Post-Communist Era* (Lincoln: University of Nebraska Press, 2002).

Sedgwick, Mark J., "Neo-Eurasianism in Russia," in *Against the Modern World: Traditionalism and the Secret Intellectual History of the Twentieth Century* (Oxford: Oxford University Press, 2004), 221–40.

Spier, Howard, "Pamyat: An Appeal to the Russian People," *Soviet Jewish Affairs* 1 (1988): 60–71.

12

Antisemitism in the Nazi Era

Doris L. Bergen

To describe antisemitism in the Nazi era might seem to be a simple matter. During World War II, under Hitler's leadership, Germans and their accomplices around Europe murdered 6 million Jews. They destroyed Jewish communities that dated back to ancient Rome and almost completely eliminated the Jewish presence from Amsterdam to Athens, Zagreb to Zhytomyr. The Nazis had other victims, but they unleashed their fullest fury against the Jews, whom they hunted across every border, into every hiding place, in a systematic, total drive for annihilation. What other than deep, widespread, deadly hatred of Jews could account for such persistent and rampant slaughter?

This logic notwithstanding, even contemporaries had difficulty assessing the level of antisemitism within Nazi Germany and analyzing how it connected to institutionalized attack and mass murder. The combination of familiar prejudices with the unprecedented scope and ruthlessness of the Nazi assault on Jews confounded understanding. Under Hitler's leadership, anti-Jewish attitudes became concrete actions against Jews, sanctioned and indeed mandated by the state and enforced by its courts, its police, and its bureaucrats. This transformation—from antisemitism as an idea to antisemitism as policy and practice—proved disorienting for even the most astute observers.

Victor Klemperer, a professor of French literature in Dresden, provides a case in point. Klemperer, the son of a rabbi, converted to Protestant Christianity, married a Gentile, won the Iron Cross for service in World War I, and identified fully with German culture. Under Nazi law, however, he counted as a Jew. In his detailed and insightful diary, one of the issues that preoccupied him was what he referred to as the *vox populi*. What did "ordinary Germans"—that is, the non-Jewish Germans around him—think of Jews? What did they make of Nazi anti-Jewish measures? How antisemitic were they? Between 1933 and 1945, Klemperer went back and forth on these questions, often within the same diary entry, unable to make up his mind. Yet he understood one thing from the outset: hatred of Jews was the center of Hitler's worldview, and the Nazi rise to power spelled disaster for Jews everywhere.

Antisemitism in the Nazi Era

In his infamous speech of October 1943 to SS leaders in Posen, Heinrich Himmler gave voice to the centrality of annihilatory antisemitism to Nazi German practices of conquest and domination. At the same time Himmler raised questions about how ideological commitments linked to mass murder. Everyone present knew what he was talking about, he told an audience of hardened killers:

The extermination of the Jewish people. It is one of those things which are easy to talk about. "The Jewish people will be exterminated," says every party comrade, "It's clear, it's in our program. Elimination of the Jews, extermination and we'll do it." And then they come along, the worthy eighty million Germans, and each one of them produces his decent Jew. It's clear the others are swine, but this one is a fine Jew. Not one of those who talk like that has watched it happening, not one of them has been through it.
(Noakes and Pridham 2001, 3:617)

To strengthen his listeners' resolve, Himmler offered a grab bag of antisemitic possibilities. Jews had caused the defeat of Germany in World War I, he warned; they were behind the Allied air raids on German cities; they were "bacteria," "Bolsheviks," masters of disguise, and sexual predators. Himmler introduced only one original point, but it was a crucial innovation that extended antisemitism from living Jews to the dead. The task was almost done now, he reassured his men: only a few Jews were left. By October 1943 that boast was true, at least for Europe. Yet the Jews remained a threat, Himmler argued, because any mercy shown would endanger later generations of "Aryan" Germans. And even the piles of Jewish corpses threatened to turn the killers soft with remorse or weak with horror unless they kept in sight the mortal danger posed by "the eternal Jew." In Himmler's system, antisemitism constituted more than a reason to kill Jews; it offered a justification for killers after the fact.

Scholars of National Socialism and the Holocaust have paid surprisingly little attention to antisemitism. There is a noticeable disjuncture between the popular and commonsensical assumption that antisemitism was the direct and indeed only motive for the genocide of Jews, and scholarly analyses, which look elsewhere for the forces that drove Nazism. In 1996, Daniel Goldhagen's attempt to bring these positions together produced a bestseller (*Hitler's Willing Executioners*), but Goldhagen remained an outsider to the academic establishment. Saul Friedländer's prize-winning study, *Nazi Germany and the Jews*, posits "redemptive antisemitism" as the center of Nazi ideology and practice. Even here, antisemitism, paradoxically, plays a more prominent role in the first volume, which deals with Germany from 1933 to 1939, than it does in Volume 2, *The Years of Extermination, 1939–1945*. Raul Hilberg's monumental work, *The Destruction of the European Jews*, opens with reflections on the continuities of anti-Jewish stereotypes and behaviors from the medieval period to World War II but returns to that theme only rarely in the hundreds of pages that follow. The ubiquity of

198 *Doris L. Bergen*

antisemitism in the Holocaust, combined with its explosive force, seems to defy analysis and push scholars to look elsewhere for perpetrators' motives: to political, sociological, and psychological factors, from peer pressure to opportunism, greed, disorientation, and careerism.

In this discussion I take a different tack from the linear equation often assumed (extreme antisemitism → Nazism → Holocaust) to consider instead how antisemitism functioned within the Nazi system of destruction. Here antisemitism must be understood as not only a set of convictions and rituals but as specific policies and practices that targeted Judaism and Jews, individually and collectively. We can identify three stages of Nazi antisemitism, each of them anchored in a certain chronological period yet building on and subsuming earlier developments, and each playing a particular role in the persecution and murder of Jews. The first category deals with antisemitism as ideology, that is, antisemitism as a motivating force and an input into processes of persecution. Here the focus is on the period prior to 1933, that is, before Adolf Hitler became chancellor of Germany.

The second category can be called "antisemitism in power." Not only was antisemitism a component part of the Nazi worldview, but once Hitler came to power, antisemitism itself was shaped through processes of institutionalization, legalization, implementation, and destruction that occurred from 1933 to 1945. In this period, antisemitism spread rapidly, through propaganda and education but also through official measures and actions that implicated ever more individuals and groups of people in attacks on Jews and gave them vested interests in upholding a system that sought to eliminate Jews, whether or not the Gentiles involved shared that goal. The third category, antisemitism as a product of the Holocaust, follows from the second. Violence against Jews produced and promoted particular forms of hatred, resentment, and destruction (including erasure and denial) that began during the Holocaust and continued to exist and mutate after it ended with the defeat and collapse of Nazi Germany in 1945.

ANTISEMITISM AND NAZI IDEOLOGY:
MOTIVATIONS AND INPUTS

Antisemitism constituted the core of Hitler's worldview and the center of National Socialist ideology from the party's formation in 1919. For Hitler the two notions of race and space—racial purification and spatial expansion—were inextricably intertwined. To achieve the world dominance it supposedly deserved, the "Aryan" race, Hitler reasoned in Social Darwinist fashion, had to be in a constant state of increase. Such reproduction required land, and conquest of territory meant war. In Hitler's eyes, because the Jewish race was the mortal enemy of the Aryans, any war would be or become a war against the Jews. Indeed, by Nazi logic, other enemies were either puppets and dupes of or masks for International Jewry. For Hitler and others who shared his views, the notion that Germany had lost the Great War because of a "stab in the back" from a treacherous homefront led by cowardly Jews meant that driving Jews out was necessary in order to win the wars to come.

Saul Friedländer's conception of "redemptive antisemitism" is useful for attempting to understand Hitler's radical antisemitism. According to Hitler, defeating something called "the Jew" was the only way to save Germany from disaster. Characteristic of redemptive antisemitism was a religious zeal that linked fighting Jews and destroying so-called Jewish influence to the struggle against evil. In *Mein Kampf*, Hitler claimed that when he attacked the Jew he was doing God's work. At the same time, redemptive antisemitism built on racialist notions: Jewishness, it assumed, was in the blood and could not be removed or undone through religious conversion, legal emancipation, or cultural assimilation. Indeed, proponents of racial antisemitism reviled those processes as masks that concealed the Jewish threat so it could catch its victims off guard. Redemptive antisemitism also sounded a note of urgency. It was almost too late, Hitler and like-minded orators intoned, for the Aryan race to save itself from the corrupting forces that had already defiled its bloodstream. Only rapid and violent action, they insisted, could stop the Jew.

An amalgam and accumulation of many forms of Jew-hatred, redemptive antisemitism appealed to people with a wide variety of agendas. It was not necessary to buy into the entire package to find common ground with Nazism. The legacies of older, narrower kinds of antisemitism provided points of contact to Nazism's redemptive brand that both borrowed from and fed on them. Christian anti-Judaism was one such pre-existing form. The notion that Jews were children of the devil who had betrayed and crucified Jesus prepared the way for the accusation that Jews were perfidious traitors to the fatherland. The image of Jews as enemies of Christianity merged with charges of Jews as the masterminds behind atheist communism.

Political, economic, and social stereotypes about Jews that predated the emergence of National Socialism meshed with Nazi antisemitism as did cultural anxieties and sexual fears. Starting in the 1920s, Julius Streicher's newspaper *Der Stürmer* and other propaganda instruments played on images of the Jew as the racially inferior male predator, the ugly yet fantastically fertile female, and the devious temptress who led unsuspecting Aryans to their doom. These sexualized figures echoed and reflected racist and imperialist thinking at the same time as they connected different sets of target populations in mutually reinforcing stereotypes. Jews were blamed for spreading homosexuality and profiting from a gay subculture that purportedly undermined German strength. People suspicious of Gypsies pointed out that, like Jews, Gypsies had no homeland, perhaps the result of a divine curse that somehow revealed their innate criminality.

The antisemitism preached in Nazi speeches and tracts was rife with contradictions. Jews, antisemites insinuated, had invented Christianity to make their

200 Doris L. Bergen

enemies meek and weak; yet it was Jews, they charged, who killed Jesus and assaulted Christians everywhere. Nazi antisemitism depicted Jews as at once oversexed and weak and androgynous (effeminate men, masculine women). To Nazi antisemites, Jews were both capitalists and communists; congenitally inferior yet capable of mounting a diabolically clever conspiracy to rule the world; never able to conceal their true essence yet hiding everywhere.

Instead of weakening the power of Nazi antisemitism, such contradictions strengthened it. They provided an infinite number of places to connect with hatred and fear of Jews, according to an individual's anxieties and desires. They rendered Nazi antisemitism simultaneously amorphous yet absolutely vivid and specific. All these conflicting images came together in representations of Jews as germs and bacteria—small, invisible things that are nevertheless deadly—and rats: ubiquitous, dirty, ugly, contemptible, cunning, and menacing. Also common was depiction of the Jew as hiding behind a mask or veil that needed only to be torn away by some astute observer—propaganda master Joseph Goebbels was the supreme example—to reveal the Jewish peril lurking behind it.

Antisemitism provided an organizing principle for Nazism, an adhesive that connected various components of the party's platform. How would Nazis end the encirclement of Germany by international enemies? By exposing the Jews who plotted to keep Germany from its proper place in the world. How would Nazism address domestic challenges including unemployment, poverty, and public indecency? By removing Jews from public life, of course. What was the "positive Christianity" that Nazism officially espoused? A Christianity purged of all Jewish elements.

Antisemitism was central to Nazism as an ideology and a program, but it does not seem to have played a major role in bringing Hitler to power. Here we see an imbalance that draws attention to the ways power would transform antisemitism after 1933. Hitler never concealed his antisemitism, but he did downplay it until he came to power, except when the opportunity presented itself to score points with a particular audience. He needed respectability, and prior to 1933, radical antisemitism was not good form in respectable German circles.

By all accounts, Hitler was a true believer in the redemptive antisemitism he espoused, not merely a charismatic manipulator of popular sentiment. Indeed, he and his associates had to work to educate the German public about the purported danger that Jews and Judaism posed to the Aryan race. As Nazi antisemites learned after 1933, their strongest ally in this task was power itself. Power enabled implementation of antisemitic ideas that before 1933 had been little more than brutal fantasies. The fall from power ended Hitler's reign but did not change his mind. In April 1945, in a bunker under Berlin, as he prepared to end his life, Hitler wrote his last testament, blaming the Jews for the war and all its miseries and admonishing the Germans to uphold the racial laws.

ANTISEMITISM AS A WEAPON OF SOCIAL DEATH

Power institutionalized Nazi antisemitism and diffused it throughout society in ways that merged its extraordinary force and vehemence with the ordinary, even banal manifestations of everyday life. In the first six years of National Socialist rule in Germany, a series of laws and regulations isolated German Jews and produced what historian Marion Kaplan has called their "social death."

On January 30, 1933, Hitler became Chancellor of Germany. Initially he did not command a majority in the Reichstag; his cabinet included only two other members of the Nazi Party, and non-Nazis occupied key positions as president and vice-chancellor. Nevertheless, Hitler still found ways to target Jews. The number of German Jews was small: in 1933, approximately 500,000 Jews constituted less than 1% of the whole population. Disproportionately present in some highly visible areas of the economy—publishing, medicine, the performing arts—German Jews were noticeably under-represented in the higher ranks of the military, judiciary, government bureaucracy, police, and agriculture. In April 1933, in an effort to highlight the Jewish presence in the economy and ostracize German Jews, the Nazi leadership proclaimed a boycott of Jewish businesses.

This first public act of organized antisemitism turned out to be a failure, or at least a disappointment to Hitler and Minister of Enlightenment and Propaganda Joseph Goebbels. Old-fashioned antisemitism alone, it turned out, was not strong enough to counter non-Jewish Germans' habits of consumption. Even some Stormtroopers and Nazi Party members violated the boycott to frequent shops convenient for them. In any case, what constituted a Jewish business? If the issue was Jewish ownership, what about Aryan employees? What about enterprises owned jointly by Jews and non-Jews? To Nazi leaders, the April 1933 boycott revealed how tightly Jews were woven into the fabric of German economic life and proved the need to isolate Jews before mounting a direct attack.

Those lessons informed the next step, which also occurred in April 1933. Nazi authorities introduced a law to remove Jews from the German civil service. This measure met with much more success. Non-Jews, the regime learned, preferred anti-Jewish measures that they perceived as improving their lives over those that inconvenienced them. Firing Jewish civil servants, from lowly clerks to high-profile professionals, opened up positions for non-Jewish Germans, or at least held out the promise of doing so, and provided opportunities for self-serving initiatives that sometimes went beyond the law. Ambitious university professors targeted unpopular colleagues by denouncing them as converts from Judaism to Christianity or married to Jewish women and requested that they too be expelled from their posts. The civil service law, euphemistically labeled the Law for the Restoration of the Professional Civil Service, was a crucial step in transforming antisemitism from an attitude that required members of the public to share Nazi ideals into a wide range of actions that did not.

The subsequent five years brought countless measures large and small that built up the pressure on German Jews and cut them off from the Gentiles around them. The Nuremberg Laws of 1935 forbade marriage between Jews and so-called Aryans and criminalized sexual relations between them, banned people who counted as Jews from flying the national flag or hiring Aryan women under the age of forty-five to work in their homes, and stripped Jews of most of the rights and protections of German citizenship. Subsequent regulations defined as Jews those who had three or four grandparents of the Jewish religion.

These stipulations sparked a wave of investigations and prosecutions. Even Christians who harbored no particular ill will toward Jews discovered it was dangerous to associate with them. Displays of affection or friendship could result in charges of *Rassenschande*—race defilement—or in public humiliation. Policemen, lawyers, and judges solicited detailed testimonies from men and women accused of violating laws against sexual contact between people who found themselves deemed members of different races, even though they lived side by side, spoke the same language, and looked more or less the same. Convictions meant long sentences in prison or concentration camps, and even acquittals left reputations damaged and careers shattered. Stormtroopers and other thugs harassed and abused Jews and non-Jews suspected of violating the race laws, by beating them up or forcing them to stand in the street wearing sandwich boards with degrading messages.

This combination of official measures and public bullying proved poisonous for Jews and uncomfortable for their Gentile relatives and friends. An endless stream of restrictions and prohibitions heaped injustices, indignities, and hardships one on top of the other and further separated Jews from their neighbors. Jews were forbidden from using public swimming pools; owning radios, telephones, and typewriters; attending school, practicing medicine, wearing dirndls and lederhosen, shopping other than at specified times, and giving the "Heil Hitler!" greeting. Hundreds of such prohibitions tormented and stigmatized Jews by translating antisemitic ideas into everyday routines that required no effort whatsoever from most non-Jewish Germans.

The Christian churches played a significant role in furthering and legitimating isolation of Jews. Nazi law required Germans in a wide range of professional and even volunteer positions to prove their "Aryan blood" by establishing the religion of their forebears, and records of baptism into the Roman Catholic or Protestant churches were the only way to do so. There is no evidence that the priests, pastors, and church workers who spent long hours combing through dusty tomes and copying out names and dates of births, baptisms, and marriages were hardcore Nazi antisemites. Probably most of them were just doing a job. But their work was essential for identifying and marginalizing Jews. Meanwhile, the eagerness of Christian leaders, Roman Catholic and Protestant, to maintain good relations with the state added to a dynamic that made the churches effective normalizers of Nazi antisemitism.

Some church people took a more proactive role. Calling themselves the "Stormtroopers of Christ," a predominantly Protestant group known as the "German Christian" movement attacked every aspect of Christianity related to Judaism. Members rejected parts or all of the Old Testament, revised the New Testament, and denied that Jesus was a Jew. Because the German Christians considered Jewishness to be racial, they refused to accept conversions from Judaism to Christianity as valid. A sign displayed in Westphalia in 1935 stated their position with crude clarity: "Baptism may be quite useful, but it doesn't straighten any noses."

At the national and local levels, German Christian spokespeople and activists were obsessed with Christians of Jewish background and used every means to harass them, their families, and their few supporters. In many congregations, German Christians organized campaigns, including physical assault, against pastors, members of church councils, musicians, and parishioners who had Jewish ancestors, were married to Jews, or expressed empathy with the plight of Jews in Germany. For all their enthusiasm, the German Christians were not mere pawns of Nazism, and sometimes they initiated measures not mandated by the state. In late 1933, they demanded removal of all pastors of Jewish ancestry from Protestant pulpits, going beyond what even Hitler's regime was willing to risk. In some cases, Aryan Protestants came to the aid of their fellow-church people, but implicitly and even explicitly, many Christians outside the movement endorsed German Christian goals, if not their methods.

By early 1939, Nazi aggression had pushed almost half of Germany's Jews out of the country. Yet antisemitism continued to intensify. Many Aryan Germans who acquired homes, businesses, jobs, or promotions thanks to the expropriation or emigration of Jewish Germans discovered compelling reasons to hate Jews or at least to support policies against them. The widespread perception of Jews as fabulously wealthy meant even Gentiles who had not yet profited from persecution and expulsion could hope to do so and worried that criticism of the regime might cost them their share of the spoils. Given these circumstances, debates about how antisemitic ordinary Germans were can miss the point. The Nazis in power offered potent incentives for people to behave like antisemites even if they did not share that worldview.

In late 1938, as Hitler and his inner circle planned the dismemberment of Czechoslovakia and the invasion of Poland, both of which followed in 1939, they also engineered a massive assault on the Jews of the German Reich, whose numbers had been newly enlarged by the annexation of Austria. This offensive culminated in the *Kristallnacht* pogrom of November 9–10, 1938. Hitler's regime benefited in numerous ways from this putatively spontaneous but carefully coordinated attack on Jews, Jewish property, and sites of Jewish worship and communal life. Impatient Nazis satisfied their thirst for violent action. German

204 *Doris L. Bergen*

Gentiles, initially uncomfortable with the brutal tactics of their government, found that paying rock-bottom prices for property from Jews eager to get out of the country fostered a new loyalty to the Nazi system.

Still, many Germans grumbled about public disorder, and international observers decried the level of violence in Hitler's Germany. Why were Hitler and Goebbels, generally so keen to maintain a positive image at home and abroad, willing to take this public relations risk? One reason was their desire to force Jews out of Germany before going to war. By Nazi logic, every Jew gone meant one less traitor who would stab Germany in the back.

This line of reasoning exposes the self-fulfilling logic of Nazi antisemitism. The more than 200,000 Jews who fled Germany between 1933 and 1939 settled where they could, elsewhere on the European continent, or in Britain and its dominions, the United States, Palestine, China, the Caribbean, India, or Africa. Nazi conspiracy theorists claimed that from those new homes Jews would plot against Germany and lead an international effort to destroy the Aryan race. By making it impossible for Jews to live in Germany but simultaneously increasing their numbers abroad, Nazi Germans fed their own paranoia about international enemies and lent urgency to the emerging conviction that what was needed was total destruction of the Jewish threat.

ANTISEMITISM AS WARTIME DUTY

From the outset Nazi ideology and practice linked attacks on Jews with preparation for war. In March 1935, Hitler announced full German rearmament, including the draft. Within weeks, German Jews were banned from military service. This exclusion implied that Jews were dishonorable, unfit to be soldiers, and in league with Germany's enemies. In 1936, a wave of propaganda prepared Germans for involvement in the Spanish Civil War by painting defenders of the Spanish Republic as bloodthirsty atheists, anarchists, communists, and Jews. This reversal of realities—presenting Jews as if they were vicious aggressors rather than victims of Hitler's Germany—became a hallmark of Nazi antisemitism at war.

Even before Hitler's war began, the assault on the Jews was under way. "Europe cannot find peace until the Jewish Question has been solved," Hitler told the Reichstag on January 30, 1939, less than three months after thugs torched synagogues and pillaged the homes and businesses of Jews all over Germany. War, Hitler had already decided, would start that year. "In the course of my life I have very often been a prophet," he proclaimed, "and have usually been ridiculed for it." Now, he concluded, things were different:

Today I will once more be a prophet: if the international Jewish financiers in and outside Europe should succeed in plunging the nations once more into a world war, then the

Antisemitism in the Nazi Era 205

result will not be the bolshevizing of the earth, and thus the victory of Jewry, but the annihilation of the Jewish race in Europe! (Noakes and Pridham 2001, 3:441)

Later Goebbels and others often quoted this prophecy, which they consistently misdated to coincide with the German invasion of Poland on September 1, 1939. That "mistake" revealed a sleight-of-hand, an attempt to cast Hitler's words as self-defense, a response to attack, rather than a declaration of murderous intent.

War raised the stakes of Nazi antisemitism in every possible way. Most obviously, it multiplied almost tenfold the number of Jews under German rule. The conquest of Poland in September 1939 put approximately 2 million Polish Jews in German hands (after June 1941, the number rose to 3 million), and Nazi ideology plus years of antisemitic rhetoric and action inside Germany made those Jews targets against whom anything and everything was permitted. To the Germans in Poland, Jews embodied both the racial threat to Aryan blood and a major obstacle to German order.

Malleable stereotypes meant Jews were easily linked to other opponents and targets. High-level German policies and letters from Wehrmacht soldiers alike conflated Poles and Jews as Asiatic barbarians, filthy, barely human, and unworthy of consideration. Insinuations that Poles and Jews fought dirty and shot from concealed positions led to assaults on civilians, including the taking of hostages, ransom, rape, theft, murder, and destruction of synagogues, on the pretext that snipers operated from inside them. In autumn 1939, the Germans' first priority may have been destroying the Polish intelligentsia (Gentile and Jewish), but attacks also singled out Jews, especially those who looked distinctive, in particular Orthodox men.

German practices in conquered Poland reinforced notions of Jews as dangerous and created new proof of Jewish inferiority. Ghettoization of Jews began in late 1939. According to the official line, Jews had to be confined to preserve German safety and prevent the spread of disease. In fact, ghettoization facilitated stealing Jewish property and drove a wedge between Polish Jews and non-Jews. Although the German leadership hoped to capitalize on antisemitism in Poland, it did not trust the Poles and preferred to pit Polish Gentiles and Jews against one another. Like other Nazi antisemitic measures, ghettoization functioned as a self-fulfilling prophecy. Locked up under conditions of terrible shortage—of food, housing, sanitation, and everything else needed to live—Jews in the ghettos of occupied Poland sank into desperation. Starving, begging, dressed in rags, and dying in the street, they embodied the opposite of the Aryan ideal. No wonder Germans shot movies in the ghettos, most famously, *The Eternal Jew*, which juxtaposed images of swarming rats with crowds of emaciated Jews.

During wartime as before, antisemitism connected Nazi prejudices and policies and provided coherence where there was none. After the German and Soviet foreign ministers signed a Non-Aggression Pact between their countries in

August 1939, antisemitism remained the only constant in Nazi ideology. Hitler's deal with Stalin blocked anti-communist statements and actions (for the time being), but the notion of a Jewish conspiracy survived his total about-face. Meanwhile, stepped-up violence against Jews became the accepted way to solve problems. When Himmler's Race and Settlement authorities began bringing ethnic Germans from eastern Europe "home into the Reich," that is, resettling them in occupied Poland, they ran into major difficulties. Where could they house the hundreds of thousands—eventually to be millions—of people they had lured in with promises of prosperity and comfort? Their answers invariably targeted Jews. In Łódź, SS men went door-to-door through Jewish neighborhoods, demanding people leave their homes within hours. In Germany, when municipalities ran short of money, they cut Jews off from public assistance, even before the central government in Berlin requested they do so. Antisemitism enabled ambitious Germans to "work toward the Führer" while serving their own schemes, and Nazi propaganda made clear the advantages of such behavior.

During the war, anti-Jewish violence merged with attacks on other enemies. In late 1939, Nazi Germans began systematically killing disabled people inside the German Reich. As the historian Henry Friedlander has shown, Nazi genocide originated in this euphemistically labeled Euthanasia Program. Here Nazi leaders learned how to recruit and train professional killers, exploit existing institutions, develop means of killing large numbers of people, and dispose of their bodies. Antisemitism did not drive these murders, but it remained apparent. Proponents of this sort of killing accused Jewish doctors of having purposely weakened the German race by encouraging softness toward people deemed handicapped. And even the cursory examinations that identified prospective victims singled out patients defined as non-Aryan for killing.

In 1940, the Germans invaded France. There too the war brought mass killing, this time of black French soldiers. In May and June 1940, Germans captured thousands of French African soldiers and killed most of them immediately. White French soldiers did not face the same treatment. Racism and old imperialist accusations played a role, as did a propaganda campaign urging Germans to show no mercy to these supposed defilers of white womanhood. Echoes of anti-Jewish charges were audible here, too. A reminder that Jews as the ruthless enemies of Germany had caused defeat in World War I thereby laying open the fatherland to occupation by soldiers of color was employed as a warning for the present. The same charge that had been used against Jews and Poles in 1939—that they were cowardly sneaks who shot from concealed positions and then mutilated the bodies of their victims—reemerged in 1940 against black French soldiers, again as a justification for Germans to indulge in mass killing.

As Hannah Arendt pointed out in *Eichmann in Jerusalem*, the perpetrators of Nazi crimes were not abnormal. Under the Nazi system as elsewhere, it was normal to obey the laws, support the national war effort, and protect one's self-interest—in other words, to do one's duty. Yet doing those normal things made people part of the machinery of destruction. A German soldier did not have to be a fanatic antisemite to help herd Jews into a ghetto. Nor did his wife's enjoyment of the silver candlesticks he sent her require any particular hatred of Jews. Nazi antisemitism was pervasive but it was neither unavoidable nor imposed on innocent non-Jews. Still, to resist doing one's duty in the matter of antisemitism required awareness and courage.

ANTISEMITISM AS ANNIHILATION

By the middle of 1941, Nazi Germans were systematically murdering Jews. Special killing squads followed the Wehrmacht into Soviet territory where they rounded up Jews of all ages and killed them, usually by shooting them into mass graves. These actions, carried out by the so-called *Einsatzgruppen*, the German Order Police, and non-German auxiliaries, also targeted non-Jews—Roma and Sinti (Gypsies), high-ranking Communists, and inmates of mental hospitals— but most of the 1 million victims they amassed by the end of 1941 were Jews.

In *Ordinary Men*, his study of a reserve police battalion, Christopher Browning argues that antisemitism was not a major motivation for this group of German killers. But how can we know for certain? Most of the available sources are postwar trial records. Defendants can be expected to say what they think puts them in the most favorable light, and even if they were not lying, who can reconstruct their own complicated motives years after the fact? Antisemitism may well have functioned as a script to make the killers' job easier and to justify it after the fact, even if it was not the sole or prime motivation.

After the invasion of the Soviet Union in June 1941, antisemitic themes became even more prevalent in German propaganda as Goebbels and his underlings found endless grist for their mills in the notion of a Jewish-Bolshevik conspiracy. When the war was going well for Germany, propaganda trumpeted the impending defeat of the diabolical foe. When military setbacks started coming, they only served to prove how fearsome the Jewish enemy was. Against the ally of the hammer and sickle and the power that pulled the strings of the puppets, Churchill and Roosevelt, the most extreme measures had become imperative. In this view of the world, no Jew was innocent, and any appearance of harmlessness was just another cunning ploy. This ideology and the war it fueled created a deathtrap for Jews. The police regulation of September 1941 requiring all those inside the German Reich who were defined as Jews to wear a Star of David badge rein-forced the obvious: stigmatized as enemies, Jews everywhere were open targets. Systematic transports of Jews from Germany and western Europe for killing in the East began the next month.

Nazi antisemitism was not only pervasive, it was contagious. As the Germans advanced into territories occupied by the Soviet Union and further into Soviet lands, they sparked pogroms against Jews, exploiting local resentments for their own purposes. Some indigenous antisemites needed little goading. In the summer of 1941, in Lithuania and parts of eastern Poland, persecution of Jews exploded into massacres that destroyed entire communities. In July 1941, Polish Gentiles in Jedwabne killed hundreds of their Jewish neighbors. Only a handful of Jews survived, all of them rescued by one Polish woman. Almost 75% of the 200,000 Jews of Lithuania were murdered in the first three months of German occupation, many of them by Lithuanian militia and police under the direction of the Lithuanian Provisional Government. Inside Romania, Germany's ally, authorities forced Jews across the border into Ukraine, where they were slaughtered in the killing fields of Transnistria. For Poles, Lithuanians, Ukrainians, and others who had endured Soviet rule, attacking Jews provided a way to take revenge for their suffering, even though Jews had shared all the terrors and abuses of Stalinism. At the same time, assaulting Jews gained German approval and distracted attention from non-Jews who themselves had collaborated with the Soviets. For Romanians and people in Slovakia, Croatia, Italy, and Hungary, attacks on Jews became a way to curry favor with the Germans and to position themselves for present and future rewards.

For Germans and non-Germans, annihilatory antisemitism acted like a magnet, pulling initiatives of all kinds in the same direction. Material rewards awaited those who killed Jews and supported the killing through their work. Peer pressure encouraged participation. Promotions and the approval of superiors came to those who showed particular initiative and effectiveness in destroying Jews. Antisemitism did not compete with those other motivations but rather fused with them and bound them together in a deadly consensus.

In 1942, at the height of German military success, the killing of Jews reached its peak. Nazi Germans also murdered hundreds of thousands of Gypsies in the ghettos and killing centers established to destroy Jews. In 1943, although German power began slowly to wane, killing of Jews did not ease up. Instead German forces concentrated in the western Soviet Union (Belarus) and Poland executed the so-called second sweep, hunting down those Jews who remained in work camps, in hiding, and in rump ghettos and killing them on the spot. To Nazi killers, increasing evidence of Jewish resistance only confirmed their fears of Jewish "bandits" in cahoots with Germany's enemies. At the same time, practices of humiliating and dehumanizing their victims fed the killers' contempt of Jews as little more than beasts who deserved to die. The monstrous scope of the killing meant many Germans grew accustomed to seeing Jews as corpses who, if they were not yet dead, soon would be. That image bled into a stereotype of the passive Jew who almost asked for death and sometimes literally did. Such notions, feeding upon the ongoing destruction, facilitated the killing of Jews. Perhaps even twinges of discomfort, like those evident in Himmler's October

1943 speech, added to the killers' desire to see the Jews eradicated. Who wants living reminders of their own bad conscience?

Himmler's speech points to another component of Nazi antisemitism in the stage of annihilation: guilt, and related to it, shame. For all their brutalization, most of the killers and their accomplices remained "normal" people who longed for the comforts of family life and thought of themselves, to use Himmler's word, as "decent." How could they cover over the guilt of killing old people, women, children, and men who had done nothing to them? Here the antisemitic inversion came into play, with its accusations of Jews as evil personified, conspirators against everything German and good. As the Holocaust intensified, anti-Jewish propaganda retreated from open representations of hatred, such as in *The Eternal Jew* and similar films, and instead used negative images linked to self-defense. This was the antisemitism of a bad conscience, calibrated to justify participation in atrocities without admitting their nature and extent.

By the last stage of the war, killing Jews had become normal for people from many parts of Europe. As German forces retreated westward after Stalingrad and eastward after D-Day, administrators and guards at camps and killing centers began to evacuate the remaining prisoners and march them toward territories still in German hands. Daniel Goldhagen contends that these death marches prove the antisemitic zeal of Germans who, even in the face of defeat, refused to surrender their victims. Gerhard Weinberg offers another explanation: self-preservation. By the end of 1944, the safest place any German could be, Allied bombs notwithstanding, was inside the admittedly rapidly shrinking area under German control. Columns of starving, half-dead Jews and other prisoners represented tickets toward home. Without them, a German man would be sent to the front. To refuse that perilous duty meant to desert, and German military authorities shot some 30,000 German men accused of desertion and defeatism, most of them in the last months of the war.

Goldhagen's and Weinberg's arguments need not be mutually exclusive if we consider the nature of Nazi antisemitism. By the time of the death marches, antisemitism was utterly familiar, inseparable from other aspects of life: the German war effort, cowardice, careerism, common sense. It was not that "ordinary Germans" were merely silent or indifferent to Jews. Under conditions of institutionalized, annihilatory antisemitism, indifference was not an option, even when choosing a topic for a doctoral dissertation or a name for a child. Who between 1933 and 1945 in Germany would call their girl Sara?

ANTISEMITISM AS A PRODUCT OF THE HOLOCAUST

Defeat and collapse of Nazi Germany, it is often pointed out, discredited antisemitism. At the same time, however, aspects of Nazi antisemitism survived the Holocaust and even thrived under postwar conditions. For individuals and

Doris L. Bergen

communities who had benefited from the disappearance of Jews by taking their property and positions, antisemitism offered a way for justifying and normalizing those acts. The Jews had asked for it, the reasoning went: they were too rich, they failed to assimilate, they had not resisted. Hatred of Jews and postwar violence against Jewish survivors served to drive them out and remove painful reminders of the complicity and failure of non-Jews. Politicians used postwar antisemitism, too: Communists eager to consolidate power in eastern Europe refused to acknowledge Jewish suffering under German occupation in order to highlight their own martyrs and win over local populations. Opponents of Zionism accused Jews of profiting from victimization in order to grab restitution payments to finance creation of a Jewish state.

In his book *Fear*, Jan Gross examines postwar antisemitism in Poland. Three million Polish Jews were murdered in the Holocaust, and only a few hundred thousand remained on Polish soil in May 1945, when the Allies declared victory in Europe. Less than two years later, most of that remnant was gone too, hounded out by violent neighbors, hostile local administrators, indifferent authorities, and ineffectual elites. The July 1946 pogrom in Kielce was the most dramatic postwar attack on Jews, but it was neither unforeseen nor unique.

The situation in Poland stands out because of the size of the prewar Jewish population, the totality of its destruction between 1939 and 1945, and the final erasure in the years following the war. But comparable phenomena occurred elsewhere. In her memoir *Under a Cruel Star*, Heda Kovály describes the antagonism she faced as a Jewish survivor in Prague. Victor Klemperer, who lived in Dresden under Soviet occupation and then in East Germany until he died in 1960, was one of few Jews who was in a position to test the postwar waters in Germany. His decision not to reveal the existence of his diary suggests that he knew it would not be well received. Outside Europe too, survivors often met with suspicion, accusations of failure, denial, and indifference.

The massive violence and destruction of the Holocaust left a stigma on Judaism and Jews. In the face of radical evil and unbearable loss, observers, including some Jews, found comfort in the sense that anyone who suffered such catastrophe must somehow be to blame. One of the cruel legacies of the Holocaust is an image of Jews as eternal victims, who not only attract suffering but profit from it. Though sometimes mixed with philosemitic declarations of admiration and fascination, this notion constitutes another form of antisemitism.

RECOMMENDED READINGS

Arendt, Hannah, *Eichmann in Jerusalem: A Report on the Banality of Evil* (New York: Viking, 1963).

Bankier, David, *The Germans and the Final Solution: Public Opinion under Nazism* (Cambridge, MA: Basil Blackwell, 1992).

Antisemitism in the Nazi Era

Bergen, D., *Twisted Cross: The German Christian Movement in the Third Reich* (Chapel Hill: University of North Carolina Press, 1996).

Browning, Christopher, *Ordinary Men: Reserve Police Battalion 101 and the Final Solution in Poland* (New York: HarperCollins, 1992).

Bukey, Evan, *Hitler's Austria* (Chapel Hill: University of North Carolina Press, 2000).

Friedländer, Saul, *Nazi Germany and the Jews*, vol. 1: *The Years of Persecution, 1933–1939*; vol. 2: *The Years of Extermination* (New York: HarperCollins, 1997, 2007).

Friedlander, Henry, *The Origins of Nazi Genocide: From Euthanasia to the Final Solution* (Chapel Hill/London: University of North Carolina Press, 1995).

Goldhagen, Daniel J., *Hitler's Willing Executioners: Ordinary Germans and the Holocaust* (New York: Knopf, 1996).

Gross, Jan, *Fear: Anti-Semitism in Poland after Auschwitz: An Essay in Historical Interpretation* (New York: Random House, 2006).

Herf, Jeffrey, *The Jewish Enemy: Nazi Propaganda during World War II and the Holocaust* (Cambridge, MA: Belknap Press of Harvard University Press, 2006).

Hilberg, Raul, *The Destruction of the European Jews*, rev. edn (New Haven: Yale University Press, 2003).

Kaplan, Marion, *Between Dignity and Despair: Jewish Life in Nazi Germany* (New York: Oxford University Press, 1998).

Klemperer, Victor, *I Will Bear Witness: A Diary of the Nazi Years, 1933–1945*, 2 vols (New York: Random House, 1998).

Kovály, Heda Margolius, *Under a Cruel Star: A Life in Prague 1941–1968* (New York: Holmes and Meier, 1997).

Noakes, J., and G. Pridham (eds), *Nazism: A Documentary Reader*, vol. 3: *Foreign Policy, War and Racial Extermination* (Exeter: University of Exeter Press, 1988, rev. edn 2001).

Steinweis, Alan, *Studying the Jew: Scholarly Antisemitism in Nazi Germany* (Cambridge, MA: Harvard University Press, 2006).

Szobar, Patricia, "Telling Sexual Stories in the Nazi Courts of Law: Race Defilement in Germany, 1933 to 1945," in Dagmar Herzog (ed.), *Sexuality and German Fascism* (New York: Berghahn, 2005), 131–63.

Weinberg, Gerhard, *Germany, Hitler, and World War II* (New York: Cambridge University Press, 1995).

13

Anti-Judaism and Antisemitism in the Arab and Islamic World Prior to 1948

Norman A. Stillman

There is general agreement that the antisemitism found in the Arab and Islamic world today is a relatively recent phenomenon, at least as defined rigorously. Like nationalism, socialism, fascism, and other modern intellectual and political movements, antisemitism is a European import of fairly recent vintage into the Muslim world. But Jew-hatred based on race (especially the "Semitic" race), or on the demonization of Jews, did not have the substantial roots in Islamic civilization that it did in Christendom. There has been, on the other hand, no lack of negative attitudes to Jews among Muslims, going back to the earliest period of Islam.

TRADITIONAL ISLAMIC ANTI-JUDAISM

Some of the fundamental notions about Jews and Judaism are enshrined in the Qur'an (Koran) itself, which for Muslims is the verbatim word of Allah vouchsafed to the Prophet Muhammad by the Angel Gabriel. Thus, as in Christianity, certain negative attitudes toward Jews have the authority of sacred writ. Unlike the New Testament, the Qur'an has both positive and negative things to say about Jews. However, the positive statements come from the early part of Muhammad's career, while he was still in pagan Mecca (610–22), and are mainly in the context of biblical history and lore. In these passages, both the historical Israelites and contemporary Jews are referred to as *Banu Isra'il* (Children of Israel). The *Banu Isra'il* are mentioned as the recipients of earlier divine revelation, and Moses is the archetypical prophet, seen as an obvious parallel to Muhammad. Along with receiving the gift of the Torah, the Israelites are depicted as recipients of divine favor: "Indeed, we gave the Children of Israel the Scripture, authority, and prophecy. We sustained them with good things and favored them above all earthly creatures" (Sura XLV:16, there are 114 Suras or sections in the Qur'an).

Antisemitism in the Arab and Islamic World — 213

These words reflect Muhammad's generally positive view of the earlier monotheistic faiths when he began preaching to his polytheist kinsmen and neighbors. However, his attitudes underwent a radical change after he emigrated from Mecca to Medina in 622. There, the Prophet came into daily face-to-face contact with a large, educated Jewish community. Rather than finding encouragement of the sort he seems to have had from occasional Jews that he had met in the past, he encountered contradiction, ridicule, and rejection from the Jewish scholars in Medina. Thereafter, he came to adopt a radically more negative view of the "people of the Book" (*ahl al-Kitab*), who had received earlier scriptures. Muhammad's negative attitude toward Jews was already beginning to evolve during his last years in Mecca, as he became more aware of the antipathy between Jews and Christians and the disagreements and strife amongst members of the same religion.

In the verses revealed in Medina, Jews are for the first time referred to as *Yahud* (Jews), *Hud* (also Jews), and *alladhina hadu* (those who are Jewish). These designations are generally negative. The Yahud are associated with interconfessional strife and rivalry (II:113). They believe that they alone are beloved of God, and only they will achieve salvation (II:111). They blasphemously claim that Ezra is the son of God, as Christians claim Jesus is (IX:30) and that God's hand is fettered (V:64). They "pervert words from their meanings" (IV:44), have committed wrongdoing—for which God has "forbidden some good things that were previously permitted them" (IV:160). Jews listen for the sake of mendacity (V:41), and some of them who are guilty of usury will receive "a painful doom" (IV:161). Because of the Jews' disobedience to God and their many transgressions "wretchedness and baseness were stamped upon them, and they were visited with wrath from Allah" (II:61). Of all the negative passages about Jews in the Qur'an, perhaps the one with the most lasting consequence is that, together with the polytheists, they are "the most vehement of men in enmity to those who believe," whereas Christians are declared to be "the closest of them ... to those who believe" (V:82).

The belief that Jews (and the Christians) had tampered with (*tahrif*) and made substitutions (*tabdil*) or changes (*taghyir*) to their own scriptures became an article of later Islamic dogma. This accusation was raised again and again in the polemical literature that developed in the Middle Ages and continued down to modern times. The depiction of the Jews as particularly untrustworthy and malevolent was not only sanctified in the Qur'an but expanded and amplified in the *Hadith* (the canonical prophetic tradition), in the hagiographic literature dealing with the life of the Prophet (the *Sira* and the *Maghazi*), and in qur'anic exegesis (*Tafsir*). As in the Qur'an, both the terms *Banu Isra'il* and *Yahud* continue to be used in that traditional literature, with the former having the broader meanings of both ancient Israelites and contemporary Jews. The designation *Yahud* has now become common, and the term appears in contexts that are frequently negative, as in Muhammad's encounters with the Jewish tribes in Medina and with the inhabitants of the oasis of Khaybar, all of which are related in the greatest of detail in the Sira and the Maghazi.

For example, the rabbis of the Jews in Medina are singled out as "men whose malice and enmity were aimed at the Apostle of God" (Ibn Hisham, Sira I, 516). Jews in this literature appear not only as malicious, but deceitful (e.g., Al-Waqidi, 363 ff), cowardly, and totally lacking resolve (Ibn Hisham, II, 55, 236). Still, they lack demonic qualities attributed to them in patristic and medieval Christian literature. Similarly, there is nothing comparable in scope to the Christian preoccupation with Jews and Judaism in the Muslim traditional corpus (except perhaps in the narratives concerning Muhammad's encounters with Medinese Jewry). With a few exceptions, the Jews in the Sira and the Maghazi are not even portrayed as villains of imposing dimensions. Their debased qualities stand in marked contrast to Muslim heroism, and in general conform to the qur'anic image of Jewish "wretchedness and baseness."

The Qur'an, Hadith, and the hagiographic literature established negative stereotypes of Jews that would continue through the succeeding fourteen Islamic centuries in Islamic literature and lore. However, a number of important factors mitigated the full force of that negative portrait. Muhammad never questioned the basic validity of the Jewish religion, and the original recognition accorded monotheists during his years in Mecca was never abrogated. Judaism and Christianity, as well as Zoroastrianism, remained licit or lawfully permitted religions. They were to be fought against only until they submitted to Muslim rule, as humble tribute bearers in accordance with the qur'anic injunction "until they pay the tribute out of hand and are humbled" (IX:29). So long as they accepted this humble status they were not only to be tolerated but were entitled to the protection of the Muslim commonwealth; hence their legal designation as protégés (*ahl al-dhimma*).

Nonetheless, the general attitude to Jews throughout the Middle Ages and into modern times was often condescending, even more than to Christians. For example, the ninth-century essayist al-Jahiz observed that the Muslim masses perceived Christians as being "more sincere than the Jews, closer [to Muslims] in affection, less treacherous, less unbelieving, and deserving of a lighter punishment" (Finkel 1926, 13–14). But despite what may have been the greater social prejudice in early Islam toward Jews, Islamic law made no formal distinction between them and other tolerated non-Muslims. Administrative decrees meant to interpret the Sharia's rules for differentiating non-Muslims from Muslims sometimes also stipulated differentiation as to the badge or garment color for members of each of the various dhimmi communities. But from a strictly constitutional point of view, all tolerated non-Muslims were subsumed under the same legal category of *ahl al-dhimma*. That the Jews shared this status with the far more numerous and conspicuous Christians and Zoroastrians mitigated any specifically anti-Jewish sentiments into a broader prejudice against dhimmis. Furthermore, Jews did not have to bear the onus of suspicion harbored toward some Christian communities—becoming more intense from the period of the Crusades onward—that they were friendly toward the European powers and thus a potential fifth column. This relatively less suspicious attitude to Jews was

Antisemitism in the Arab and Islamic World

to change for the worse in the modern era, with mercantile penetration and colonial rule.

Only when Jews did not conform to the humble role prescribed for them, and when they were perceived as having transgressed the bounds of proper conduct as stipulated in Islamic law, were specifically anti-Jewish sentiments stirred up and all the worst negative stereotypes confirmed (as when a Jew rose too high in the bureaucracy and did not conduct himself in an appropriately humble manner). Much of the anti-Jewish agitation in Islamic history occurred at just such times of perceived Jewish rise and explicitly drew upon the images that had been sanctified in Scripture and religious lore. Anti-Jewish satires circulated widely when the Jewish Tustari brothers, Abu Sacd and Abu Nasr, were at the height of their power and influence in Fatimid Egypt (1036–47). An anti-Jewish satire, disseminated prior to their assassination, proclaimed:

> The Jews of this time have attained their utmost hopes
> and have come to rule
> Honor is theirs, wealth is theirs too
>
> .   .   .   .   .   .
>
> People of Egypt, I have good advice for you:
> Turn Jew, for Heaven itself has become Jewish (Massé 1919, 32).

An even more pointedly rabble-rousing anti-Jewish poem circulated in the days leading up to the murder of the Jewish vizier of Zirid Granada and the massacre of the entire Jewish community in 1066. The poem refers to the Jewish official as "the vilest ape among these miscreants" and calls the Jews a "bastard brood" and "outcast dogs." The poem also compares Jews to rodents, and incites the ruler to:

> Slaughter him as an offering
> Sacrifice him, for he is a fat ram
> And do not spare his people
> For they have amassed every precious thing (Stillman 1979, 214–16).

In these and similar cases, popular animus overflowed into violence not only against the individual Jewish official but to the entire Jewish community. Again, however, such specifically anti-Jewish manifestations of violence were exceptional. The Geniza documents, a collection of almost 200,000 Jewish manuscript fragments found in a synagogue in Egypt, show that medieval Jews were aware of collective hostility toward their community, specifically as Jews, and referred to it by the Judeo-Arabic word *sin'uth* (hatred); the casual Jew-baiter, in contrast, was called by the more standard Hebrew *sōnē* (hater). But Jew-hatred and Jew-baiting were on the whole "local and sporadic, rather than general and endemic" (Goitein 1971, 283).

Medieval Muslim theologians, whether Sunni or Shi'i (Shiite), devoted only a small part of their polemics to Judaism. There was not much comparable in Islam in quantity—and only rarely in sheer vitriol—to the *Adversus Iudaeos*

216   *Norman A. Stillman*

literature of the Christian Church. Most of the exposés of the falseness of Judaism seem to have been written by Jewish converts to Islam, such as in al-Samaw'al al-Maghribi's *Silencing the Jews* (twelfth century); these were men who were anxious to prove their neophyte zeal by exposing the errors of their former faith. An important exception was the eleventh-century Andalusian theologian Ibn Hazm's *Epistle against the Jew Ibn Naghrella*. His hostility none-theless seemed to be prompted by Jews who held high office rather than by strictly theological issues.

In the later Middle Ages, particularly during the Mamluk period in Egypt and Syria (1250–1517), there was a noticeable increase in anti-dhimmi propa-ganda literature. Polemical treatises of the thirteenth and fourteenth centuries, such as al-Jawbari's *Kashf al-Asrar* (*Unveiled Secrets*) and al-Wasiti's *Radd alā Ahl al-Dhimma* (*Refutation of the People of the Pact*), contained horror stories concerning dhimmi physicians and Muslim patients. Al-Wasiti credits the great Jewish philosopher, Moses Maimonides, with having concluded that Jews could legitimately use the blood of Gentiles. Other religious handbooks of the period echo such attitudes. The theme of the malevolent dhimmi doctors—especially Jewish doctors—became widespread in later Arabic literature. However, the anti-Judaism of these works is mixed together with anti-Christian material. Furthermore, in marked contrast to these polemics there were some admirably dispassionate descriptions of Jews and Judaism in the histories and compendia of religions and beliefs by Muslim scholars.

Unlike the situation in Christian Europe, Jews appear only peripherally in the folklore of the Islamic world, although perhaps more in the Maghreb (northwest Africa, excluding Egypt) than the Levant (the eastern Mediterranean), since the Jewish proportion in the general population was greater in North Africa and also because there were no indigenous Christians remaining after the Almohad period. Maghrebi proverbs and folktales portray Jews as irredeemably sly, untrustworthy, and occasionally malevolent. A proverb found in various versions throughout North Africa warns: "Do not trust a Jew even if he has been a Muslim for the past forty years." A Moroccan proverb states that "When a Jew cheats a Muslim, he is happy that entire day." Tales of Jews who abuse Muslim women until dispatched by a Muslim hero are found in both Middle Eastern and North African lore. On the other hand, there are examples of more positive images in which Jews are depicted as useful individuals and even at times better than indi-vidual Muslims (in Westermarck 1930, 130–1).

MODERN ANTISEMITISM

Modern antisemitic ideas of European origin made their first appearance in the Middle East among the Arabic-speaking Christians of Syria. Despite their own problems with the Muslim majority, the Christian Syrians shared a common

Antisemitism in the Arab and Islamic World   217

heritage with Arab Muslims and, despite their social disabilities as dhimmis, they considered themselves part of Arab culture and society. In fact, the Syrian Christians created the renascence of the Arabic language and literature known as the *Nahda* (revival) in the second half of the nineteenth century. Like other non-Muslims, they maintained close commercial and cultural relations with the European nations making ever stronger inroads into the region. The Syrian Christians shared not only the Muslims' traditional contempt for Jews but also appropriated modern European antisemitic notions from French traders and missionaries.

The eastern churches had long propagated the belief that the Jews were deicides and a people cursed by God. However, they did not have in their storehouse of anti-Jewish lore such European horror stories as the host desecration or the blood libel. The classic European notion that Jews kidnapped and sacrificed Christian children first appeared in the Muslim world among Christians in Aleppo, Syria, during the seventeenth century and was current there into the mid-eighteenth. It only gained widespread circulation after the notorious Damascus Affair of 1840. On February 5 of that year, an Italian Capuchin friar and his native servant disappeared in Damascus. The local Christians, supported and possibly instigated by the French consul, accused the Jews of having murdered the two men in order to obtain blood for the coming Passover. The consul brought in the Muslim authorities, and a Jewish barber was arrested. He subsequently made a confession under torture, implicating seven communal leaders, who were also arrested and tortured. Two died under interrogation, one saved himself by converting to Islam, and the others also confessed. Sixty-three Jewish children were taken hostage by the pasha in order to force their parents to reveal the whereabouts of the martyrs' blood.

The Damascus Affair became a *cause célèbre* among European and American Jews as well as liberal Gentiles. The governments of England and Austria intervened on behalf of the Jews, and a delegation headed by Sir Moses Montefiore and Adolphe Crémieux went to the Levant to intercede with the pasha of Egypt (the actual ruler of Syria at the time) and the Ottoman sultan. The latter issued a *firman* (decree) that explicitly denounced the blood libel.

Nonetheless, following the Damascus Affair the blood libel began to take root in the popular imagination of the Middle East. Accusations of ritual murder were repeatedly leveled against Jews throughout the nineteenth century in Syria, Palestine, and Egypt, all of which had large Christian populations. Most of the accusations came from the Christians, although in 1844, just a few years after the beginning of the Damascus Affair, Muslims in Cairo accused the Jews of murdering a Christian for his blood. On this occasion, however, the ruler, Muhammad Ali, quickly intervened to prevent violence and to see that justice was done. In 1847, local Maronite Christians raised the blood libel against the Jews in the Lebanese village of Dayr al-Qamar, and in that same year the Greek Orthodox Christians in Jerusalem accused the Jews of attempting to murder a

218   *Norman A. Stillman*

Christian child for ritual purposes. These incidents did not explode into violence, but outbreaks of the blood libel did result in localized persecutions of Jews, especially in Egypt, between the years 1870 and 1892. The town of Damanhur, near Alexandria, was the site of several such incidents between 1873 and 1877. And the blood libel was again raised in Damascus in 1890. The frequency of blood libels in Egypt may also be attributed to the well-developed print media there. One of the early Arabic classics of blood-libel literature, Habib Faris's *al-Dhaba'ih al-Bashariyya al-Talmudiyya* (*Talmudic Human Sacrifices*) was first published in Cairo in 1890 and was reprinted there as late as 1962.

Neither medieval Christian European fantasies nor the modern political and racial antisemitic ideas taking shape in the early nineteenth century made much headway among Muslims in the Arab world at that time. However, during the last three decades of the nineteenth century antisemitic literature in the European mold, written in Arabic, began to appear among the Syro-Lebanese Christians who were under strong French cultural influence. Apparently, just as the French were the principal purveyors of traditional European antisemitic beliefs in the first half of the nineteenth century, so they were the chief disseminators of the newer form of antisemitism during the last decades of the second half. (It should be recalled that France was the intellectual center of antisemitism in western Europe at the time.) Most of these early antisemitic works were published in Beirut and were translations of European tracts, as for example, Najib al-Hajj's *Fi Zawaya Khabaya, aw Kashf Asrar al-Yahud* (*Clandestine Things in the Corners, or Secrets of the Jews Unmasked*, Beirut, 1893), an adaptation of Georges Corneilhan's *Juifs et opportunistes: le judaïsme en Egypte et Syrie* (1889). Antisemitic literature originally composed in Arabic developed slowly during this period and was still largely confined to Christian writers.

Nevertheless, these early works laid the foundation for a more extensive literature of this genre in the twentieth century, when a radical change took place in the general Arab perception of Jews. Its eventual impact was also aided by the fact that these same Christian writers and translators were part of the above-mentioned *Nahda* cultural movement. Many of the leading Arabic-language newspapers were owned and edited by Levantine Christians. They were active not only in Greater Syria, but in Egypt as well, the modernizing center of the Arab world at the time. It was in Egypt that one of the two most influential works of European antisemitic literature for Arab readers made its appearance, in translation, in 1899: August Rohling's *The Talmud Jew* (1871, originally in German; the Arabic translation was made from its French edition). The book was reprinted several times throughout the twentieth century as Arab authors increasingly made the connection between supposed talmudic teachings and Zionism.

The other influential European antisemitic work, translated into Arabic, was the *Protocols of the Elders of Zion*. Arab nationalists in Palestine and Iraq were already citing the book in the early 1920s, as Arab attitudes toward Jews began

Antisemitism in the Arab and Islamic World

to harden following World War I (and particularly after the Balfour Declaration and the establishment of the Palestinian Mandate under Great Britain). A complete Arabic translation entitled *Muamarat al-Yahudiyya ala 'l-Shuub* (*The Jewish Conspiracy against the Nations*) by the Lebanese Maronite priest Antun Yamin was published in Cairo in 1925. This was the first of a long line of Arabic editions and translations of the *Protocols*. The book has been an enduring best-seller, praised and recommended by political leaders. It is widely available in bookstores from Casablanca to Baghdad to this day.

* * *

During the 1930s, the ties between the Arab world and the Third Reich helped to familiarize educated Arab elites with the vocabulary of modern European antisemitism. As Polish historian Lukasz Hirszowicz observed, the conflict between the Jews and Arabs in Palestine was "as if made to order for the needs and aims of Nazi propaganda" (27). The racist ideology of later Italian Fascism and of Nazism appealed to Arab nationalists, particularly in Syria. Sami al-Jundi, who was a young Syrian nationalist in the 1930s and later a Baath Party leader, recalled in his memoirs that "We were racialists. We were fascinated by Nazism, reading its books and the sources of its thought, especially Nietzsche's *Thus Spake Zarathustra*, Fichte's *Addresses to the German Nation*, and H. S. Chamberlain's *Foundations of the Nineteenth Century*" (27). He and his friends considered trans-lating *Mein Kampf* into Arabic, but Hitler's manifesto was first published in Arabic translation by Kāmil Marwa (Beirut, 1935). The book was soon available in a variety of translations in both the Middle East and North Africa, usually with the anti-Arab passages carefully expurgated—the notion that antisemitism might include not only the Jews but the Arabs, another Semitic people, remained an issue in some quarters.

Pan-Islamic and Pan-Arab paramilitary groups, such as the Green Shirts of Misr al-Fatat, the Phalanxes of the Muslim Brotherhood, the Iron Shirts of the Syrian National Bloc, the Muthanna Club, and the Futuwwa in Iraq, consciously emulated European fascist models. In addition to their uniforms, martial displays, leadership cults, and a marked propensity for violence, many of these groups adopted the Judeophobic rhetoric of their European heroes in their own publications, especially after the Palestinian Arab Revolt of 1936. Ahmad Husayn, the founder and leader of Misr al-Fatat (Young Egypt) echoed the invective found in Nazi publications in his movement's newspaper *Jaridat Misr al-Fatat*. In a front-page article published on July 27, 1939, he wrote "They [the Jews] are the secret of this moral desolation which has become general throughout the Arab and Islamic worlds. . . . Search for the Jew behind every depravity." This kind of vituperation laces Sami Shawkat's book, containing his speeches to Iraqi teachers, entitled *Hadhi Ahdafuna, Man Amana biha fa-Huwa minna* (*These Are Our Aims, Who Believes in Them Is One of Us*, 1939).

When World War II broke out, the sympathies of many in the Arab and Islamic world lay with the enemies of their British and French enemies: Nazi

220 *Norman A. Stillman*

Germany and Italy. In Egypt, the anti-Jewish hostility that had come to the fore in the late 1930s was suppressed by the declared state of emergency, backed up by British tanks. German and Italian propaganda capitalized on popular discontent in Egypt, blaming the shortages and high prices on the Jews who were acting as British agents. Antisemitism reached its highest levels in Iraq, where the Palestinian Mufti Hajj Amin al-Husseini, an ardent antisemite, had taken refuge in 1940. The coup that toppled the pro-British government of Iraq in March 1941 brought to power a pro-Nazi regime headed by Rashid Ali al-Gaylani, some of whose leading members were by then well-known Jew-baiters. In May 1941, Iraq became an ally of the Axis, and the Jewish population of Iraq was considered to be a fifth column.

When the pro-Nazi government fled the country with the approach of British troops to the outskirts of Baghdad, a pogrom against the Jews of the capital broke out and lasted for two days. In the *Farhud*, as it came to be known, 179 Jewish men, women, and children were murdered; 242 children were left orphans, 586 businesses were sacked, and 911 buildings that housed more than 12,000 people were pillaged. The estimated loss of property totaled £680,000. Anti-Jewish violence on this scale was unprecedented in the area. It was, however, to be emulated at the end of the war when large-scale riots broke out in Egypt and Tripolitania in November 1945, with smaller outbreaks in Syria. More anti-Jewish rioting would occur two years later following the vote of the United Nations in favor of the partition of Palestine into Jewish and Arab states.

As will be further described in the final chapter, the birth of the state of Israel, the Palestinian refugee problem, and the resounding military defeats of 1948, 1956, and 1967 hardened and embittered Arab attitudes toward Jews generally. All of the libels and canards of European antisemitism now took on a greater resonance than ever and became commonly accepted in both elite and popular circles. Antisemitic literature in Arabic grew exponentially, always drawing upon the intellectual and literary foundations of the nineteenth and first half of the twentieth centuries. This imported ideology was combined in a more or less integrated fashion with the most negative aspects of traditional Islamic anti-Judaism.

RECOMMENDED READINGS

Adang, Camilla, *Muslim Writers on Judaism and the Hebrew Bible from Ibn Rabban to Ibn Hazm* (Leiden: Brill, 1996).
Finkel, Joshua (ed.), *Kitab al-Raddala 'l-Nasara* (Cairo: al-matbaca al-calafiyya, 1926).
Goitein, S. D., *A Mediterranean Society*, vol. 2 (Berkeley/Los Angeles: University of California Press, 1971).
Hirszowicz, Lukasz, *The Third Reich and the Arab East* (Toronto: Toronto University Press, 1966).

Ibn Hisham, *Sira* (Cairo, 1955).

Ibn Muyassar, *Ta'rikh Misr*, ed. H. Massé (Cairo, 1919).

Jundi, Sami, *al-Baath* (Beirut: Dar al-Nahar, 1969).

Perlmann, M., "The Medieval Polemics between Islam and Judaism," in S. D. Goitein (ed.), *Religion in a Religious Age* (Cambridge, MA: Association for Jewish Studies, 1974), 103–38.

Stillman, Norman A., *The Jews of Arab Lands: A History and Source Book* (Philadelphia: Jewish Publication Society, 1979).

—— *The Jews of Arab Lands in Modern Times* (Philadelphia: Jewish Publication Society, 1991).

—— "New Attitudes toward the Jew in the Arab World," *Jewish Social Studies* 37 (1975): 197–204.

—— "Antisemitism in the Contemporary Arab World," in M. Curtis (ed.), *Antisemitism in the Contemporary World* (Boulder, Co/London: Westview, 1986), 70–85.

Westermarck, E., *Wit and Wisdom in Morocco* (London: G. Routledge and Sons, 1930).

14

Antisemitism in Eastern Europe (Excluding Russia and the Soviet Empire) Since 1848

István Deák

An alien from outer space, alighting in eastern Europe in 1848, then returning one hundred and sixty years later, would find a radical change in the political geography of the area. Instead of three looming empires—the Russian, the Habsburg, and the Ottoman—dominating the entire region from the Baltic Sea in the north to the Adriatic and the Black Sea in the south, the current visitor would find sixteen sovereign states dividing eastern Europe among themselves.

There would be other surprises. Besides signs of dazzling technological advances, the visiting alien would learn that city dwellers in northern and central eastern Europe no longer tend to speak German—or, in the southeast, Greek—but have adopted languages that, back in 1848, were often regarded as no more than the vernacular of peasants. Moreover, there would be no more than traces of the old ethnic diversity—that fabulous mosaic of cultures that then characterized every principality and province within the three empires.

As to the religious practices of this same territorial spread, it is true that by 1848 devotion had long been in decline, especially among the educated classes. Sincere religiosity is even less common today but, just as in 1848, the churches continue to exercise some influence in politics. Meanwhile, the religious affiliation of those in the countryside had become the religion of the urban inhabitants. In brief, the countryside had conquered the city.

It is most likely that the principal political link between 1848 and that of today is the persistent cult of fatherland, nation, and nationality. That link can be further underscored with the widespread preoccupation, then as today, with the presence of Jews. And well may we ask: Why is this so? In such countries of eastern Europe where Jews constituted a sizable proportion of the total population, such concerns were somewhat understandable. Unfathomably, it also marks such countries today where one can grow up without ever laying eyes on or recognizing a Jew. In Poland, where once the population included millions of Jews, there are now a few thousand. Yet the Jewish Question still preoccupies the public.

Antisemitism in Eastern Europe 223

If only one could precisely define who is a Jew! Earlier, before the emancipation of Jews in the second half of the nineteenth century, costume, habits, culture, occupation, religion, and language made such identification quite easy. Today nothing clearly defines a Jew. Religion only confuses matters because many families of Jewish origin have converted to Christianity or are without religion. Ethnicity is even less helpful because during the past one hundred sixty-odd years, millions of Jews embraced the nationality of the most powerful ethnic group around them. Race is also nearly useless because many people of Jewish origin show no Semitic physical characteristics. The Jews themselves are no help in this matter because many, especially among the educated and the successful, have long tended to keep their Jewish descent a secret. The most conspicuous examples of this were the Communist leaders in eastern Europe, not one of whom ever publicly alluded to his Jewish background—not even if his own parents had perished during the Holocaust, or even if the killers had been his fellow-nationals and not the German Nazis. Yet in Communist times everyone knew who among the Party leaders was of Jewish origin, a fact of which the Communist leaders themselves were very much aware. Ultimately, therefore, Jewishness is a personal feeling, but it is also imposed by outsiders.

In 1848, Jews were unevenly distributed in the region, constituting between 3% and 10% of the population in what is today Lithuania, Poland, Slovakia, Hungary, Ukraine, Romania, and Moldova, and a smaller proportion in what is today the Czech Republic, Slovenia, and southeastern Europe. Such unevenness also prevails today, with Jews, or such persons whom others perceive as Jews, forming about 1% of the population in Hungary and far less elsewhere.

The dazzling rise and tragic fall of east European Jewry took place during the one hundred sixty years we are examining here. Between 1848 and the beginning of World War I, Jews expanded into hitherto forbidden areas, thus coming to constitute up to one-third of the population in some major cities. They also created, managed, or owned much of the region's industry, financial institutions, and businesses, as well as constituting the majority of medical doctors, lawyers, journalists, and scientists. Moreover, Jews were making inroads into such previously non-Jewish positions as landownership, public service, politics, the administration, public education, the judiciary, and the military. Following World War I, this phenomenal progress was stopped and then was gradually eroded by antisemitic administrations and public opinion, culminating in the genocide of World War II and the subsequent emigration of the great majority of Jewish survivors. Today Jews do not play a crucial role in the politics, economy, and culture of eastern Europe, except in the feverish imagination of antisemites.

It will be the task of this chapter to try to explain how antisemitism fits into the above complex stories. First, however, we must tackle the question of which countries and peoples we are talking about. The meaning given to the very term *Eastern Europe* depends on the author using the term and the period in question. The three Baltic countries, for instance, included in this account formed parts

224 *István Deák*

of Russia until 1918 and existed as sovereign states only in the dreams of the Estonian, Latvian, and Lithuanian nationalists. But then these countries made themselves independent and, although absorbed by the Soviet Union in 1940, they recovered their sovereignty following the dissolution of the Soviet Union. In the Baltic states, the presence of Jews varied greatly: Estonians had few Jews in their midst; Latvians had many more; and Lithuanians shared space with about 200,000 Jews.

There is nothing more natural than to speak of Poland, the Poles, and the Polish Jews, yet there was officially no Poland from 1795 to 1815, again from 1867 to 1918, and finally from 1939 to 1944. When the country officially existed, it varied in size and, after 1944, in location: Today's Poland is situated hundreds of miles to the west of the Poland of the interwar years. At times when there was no Poland, the common tie of Polish speakers was their Catholic religion, which made many wonder whether a non-Catholic could ever be considered a Pole. The answer in modern Poland was that whereas Protestants and Eastern Christians could generally be so considered, Jews would less often be accepted.

Prague lies to the west of Vienna, but it would be absurd to count today's Austrian Republic as belonging to eastern Europe. Still, we include the Czech Republic because, until 1990, Czechoslovakia had been a part of the Soviet Bloc. Note that Jews in the Kingdom of Bohemia, the ancestor of today's Czech Republic, mostly spoke German, which in the age of nationalism caused the Czechs to accuse them of treason, while the local Germans suspected the Jews of sympathizing with the Czech cause. Slovakia, which once constituted the second half of the now defunct Czechoslovak Republic, had been, before 1918, within the Hungarian Kingdom. Jews in what is today Slovakia spoke Hungarian or Yiddish, which caused the Slovaks to treat them with suspicion, while in the post-World War I period, Hungarians tended to see the Jews of Slovakia as traitors. And it is true that the Czechoslovak census law allowed Jews to declare Jewish as their nationality, which the majority did, in part so as to please the government in Prague, which wanted the Jews of Slovakia to be counted as neither Slovaks nor Hungarians.

As for Hungary, it was, until 1918, three times the size of what it is today, and it had nearly three times as many inhabitants. Following World War I, the Jews formerly within its boundaries, nearly a million strong, automatically became Hungarian, Czechoslovak, Romanian, South Slav, or Austrian citizens; yet none of these nations, least of all the Hungarian, looked at the Hungarian Jews with any particular kindness.

Unlike Hungary, a very old kingdom, independent Romania came into official existence in 1878. However, during the preceding several centuries there already existed such Romanian-inhabited principalities as Moldavia, Walachia, and Bessarabia, which were under either Ottoman or Russian suzerainty. In addition, Romanian speakers formed the majority in the principalities of Transylvania and Bukovina, which belonged to Hungary and Austria, respectively.

In 1918, the Romanian state united all these and more lands, each harboring a great number of non-Romanians who now became Greater Romania's ethnic minorities. Among the latter were nearly 800,000 Jews, many of whom spoke Yiddish; others spoke Romanian, Hungarian, German, or Russian. In Romania, both the public and the state administration were highly suspicious of the Jews, the majority of whom suffered from a dual curse, that of being simultaneously Jews and Hungarians, or of being treated as potential collaborators with Russian Communism.

Finally, south of Romania and Hungary the proportion of Jews has been traditionally lower than that further north, which helped to prevent the development of a strong popular antisemitism. But there were other reasons as well. Under Ottoman rule, for instance, all non-Muslims were treated as equally inferior to the Muslims. Also, Jews in the Balkans were not in competition with non-Jews for the most rewarding businesses and occupations. Many Balkan Slavs perceived Greeks and Armenians as a greater economic menace. For whatever reason, there have always been relatively fewer antisemitic fanatics in what is today Serbia, Bulgaria, Macedonia, Bosnia-Herzegovina, Kosovo, Albania, and Greece. Only in Croatia were there many antisemites, and in that regard it is interesting that predominantly Catholic Croatia had not been a part of the Ottoman empire; it was, until 1918, under the Hungarian Crown and through it, under Habsburg rule. In sum, antisemitism in eastern Europe was a problem that haunted mainly Poland, Lithuania, Ukraine, Romania, and the lands of the Habsburg Monarchy.

When did antisemitism arise in eastern Europe? The phenomenon is at least as old as Christianity; Jews were Christ-killers, it was held, who took the blood of Christian children to make matzos, and who stabbed the Holy Eucharist at every opportunity. In addition, Jews were charged in clerical propaganda and popular imagination with every conceivable sin afflicting humanity. Yet Jews were also perceived as the people of the book who had sinned grievously by not recognizing the Messiah when they saw Him, but who should nevertheless be tolerated as living testimonies of the righteousness of the Christian religion. All in all, Jews were tolerated in Christian Europe, whereas pagans and Muslims were not.

Over the centuries, the vast majority of European Jews congregated in Poland–Lithuania, Prussia, and the Habsburgs' eastern possessions. Jews—and Huguenots as well as other religious dissenters—who had been expelled from western Europe were accepted in the East as potentially valuable sources of revenue. A few select Jewish families became *Hofjuden* or Court Jews and were seen as valuable servants of the imperial or royal treasury. Many more Jews entered the service of great landowners as innkeepers, dues collectors, craftsmen, and shopkeepers. This unofficial alliance between the Jews and the Polish–Lithuanian, Hungarian, Transylvanian, and Croatian landowning aristocracy was all the more striking because most other Jews were still greatly restricted in their movements and occupations.

The first great change came when the Habsburg emperor Joseph II (1765 as emperor, 1780 as king of Hungary) issued toleration patents that allowed Jews to settle wherever they wished and to take up any profession. In return, Jews were expected to pay taxes as individuals, not as a collectivity, and to perform military service. Moreover, in order to make themselves accessible to census takers, Jews were given German-sounding family names. All this met with strong but finally unsuccessful opposition by conservatives in the administration and the military as well as by Orthodox Jews.

The Habsburg government's plan gradually to emancipate and to integrate the Jews was supported by reformers among the nobility, who hoped to make society more prosperous and simultaneously more national. The reformers hoped to elevate the lower classes to the level of the nobles, but without thereby undermining their own leading role. The mostly illiterate peasantry, who made up 80–90% of the Habsburg Monarchy's or Poland's society, and who knew yet little of nation and nationality, could not be counted on for the task of rapid modernization. Nor could the reformers very much count on the mostly German-speaking burghers in the cities, who wanted to protect their privileges and had no wish to adapt to the local nationality. (It should be noted that the Habsburg Monarchy extended from the Swiss border deep into what is today Ukraine, as well as from southern Poland to the Adriatic. People in it spoke eleven major and many minor languages. More importantly, the Habsburg lands were divided into several kingdoms, principalities and other historical-political units, none of which had anything to do with ethno-linguistic boundaries, but most of which were dominated by a landowning nobility that was about to discover the attractions of nationalism—German, Hungarian, Czech, Polish, Croatian, Serbian, Italian, Romanian, etc.)

The best candidates for reform were the Jews, whose most enlightened elements were eager to improve their condition and, concomitantly, to embrace the regional culture. In view of both the Vienna court's and the reforming nobility's goal of turning the Jews into useful subjects, the question was which protagonist would be more successful. Thus began the rise of the Jews, accompanied by hitherto undreamed of successes as, for instance, the commissioning of a handful of un-baptized Jews as cavalry officers during the Napoleonic wars. But these changes also caused the Habsburg authorities to suspect the Jews of siding with the nationalist movements, and the Hungarian, Czech, and Polish political leaders to suspect the Jews of selling out to Vienna. Overall, however, these were dizzying times when the best of government and society worked for the integration of Jews, and even conservatives wanted no more than to slow down what they themselves saw as an inevitable process.

The revolutions of 1848 in the Habsburg Monarchy aimed at administrative, judicial, social, ethnic, and political transformation. Inevitably, the various goals set by liberals, radicals, and socialists, as well as by nationalists (primarily German, Hungarian, Czech, and Slovak), thwarted each other. The resulting bloody

Antisemitism in Eastern Europe 227

confrontation between centrist and particularistic forces was complemented by ethnic wars. For the first time in the region people killed each other not for religion or because the other was a landowner or a rebellious peasant but because the other was of the wrong nationality. In this manifold struggle, Jews could be found in many camps. In Hungary, for instance, a good number of Jews joined Louis Kossuth's insurrectionist army, whether as enlisted men or as members of the officer corps (mostly medical). The Jewish soldiers were driven by enthusiasm for the Hungarian cause, which included the promise of complete emancipation. But, as mentioned earlier, the Habsburg government's plans were not fundamentally different from those of the insurrectionists, and even though the Austrian occupation authorities later fined several Jewish communities for support of the Hungarian rebellion, Emperor-King Francis [Franz] Joseph (ruled 1848–1916) revealingly used these monies for the creation of Jewish educational institutions.

The revolutions of 1848 also brought the first modern-age pogroms in the territory of the Habsburg Monarchy, mostly by urban apprentices and journeymen, who worried about Jewish competition. All were quickly subdued by imperial troops and newly created national guards.

Whereas the road toward the emancipation of Jews promised to be relatively smooth in the Habsburg Monarchy, progress was far from easy in the diverse Polish lands. In Russian Poland especially, which included Warsaw, some Jews had enthusiastically joined the democratic Polish revolts of 1831 and 1863, which were subdued in blood, and caused the already prejudiced Russian authorities to look at the Polish Jews with utter suspicion. Under Tsar Alexander II (ruled 1855–81) many reforms that might have benefited the Polish Jews as well were introduced, but when the tsar was murdered by radicals, among whom were a few Jews, the Russian establishment turned against them with extraordinary fury.

Whether the age of pogroms that began was spontaneous or the work of the authorities is much disputed. In any case, the pogroms intensified Jewish emigration to the new world and into the Habsburg Monarchy. This, in turn, created unease among the Austro-Hungarian Jewry, who felt that, without the arrival of these backward *Galizianer* or *Ostjuden*, integration into Gentile society would have been much smoother. In Poland itself, public opinion, both Polish and Jewish, changed fundamentally in the second half of the nineteenth century; those who had been confident that the assimilation of the Jews would be only a question of time felt more and more that Jewish interests and Polish interests were irreconcilable (Weeks 2006, 3).

In truth, even in Austria-Hungary things were not entirely satisfactory (Hungary had become an equal partner with the rest of the Habsburg possessions in 1867). While the emancipation of the Jews was established in 1867, six years later the stock market crashed, and some Jewish banking houses emerged unscathed while many amateurish non-Jewish speculators suffered ruin. By the early 1880s, a collection of wildly antisemitic journalists, politicians, and political parties made an appearance in Vienna, Budapest, and Prague. In 1882, a blood-libel accusation

228   *István Deák*

emerged at Tiszaeszlár, a small village in east central Hungary. The case was that of a young peasant girl who had disappeared without a trace, causing the villagers to accuse the local Jews of ritual murder. Dozens of very poor Jews were arrested, and a part of the national press as well as the public demanded the severest punishment. Yet in the subsequent trial, the prosecutor himself demanded the acquittal of the defendants, which was granted. This provoked several pogroms, none of which led to killings. Thus the Tiszaeszlár affair came to a satisfactory conclusion from a Jewish point of view, as would most other blood-libel trials that subsequently appeared in Germany, Poland, Austria-Hungary, and Russia. Only in one case, that of Leopold Hilsner in Moravia, in today's Czech Republic, was the defendant found guilty—not for ritual murder, however, but for the ordinary murder that he had most likely committed. The outcomes of the blood-libel trials suggest that the motivation of pogroms was never pure Jew-hatred. Instead, panic among poor people turned against the Jews, as the only local "others." At times, the authorities assisted the pogromists and anti-Jewish demonstrators.

Although the outright antisemitic parties disappeared within a few years, anti-Jewish agitation did not come to an end. Shrill clerical protests against liberalism, capitalism, secularism, modernism, urban immorality, and corruption merged with the fear by little people, such as artisans, that they would be absorbed by the new giant factories and department stores. There was also the perceived threat of the ever-rising, mostly Marxist workers' parties. New Christian Social mass parties appeared that advocated municipal and social reform, while charging the Jews with being corrupters of society, destructive aliens who ought to be ordered out of the country.

The discontent of the urban lower middle classes and of the peasantry was not completely without substance, since it was indeed difficult for a non-Jew without skills and experience to compete with Jewish artisans and shopkeepers, or for a non-Jewish university student of lesser noble or peasant stock to do better at the university than his Jewish colleagues who had come from households in which speaking several languages, reading books, and arguing theory had been tradition.

Whatever the threats to their security and welfare, integrated Jews were able to enjoy the decades before World War I, seeing themselves as valuable and appreciated citizens of the Mosaic persuasion. Austro-Hungarian governmental officials regularly attended major Jewish holiday celebrations; when traveling, Emperor-King Francis Joseph never missed an opportunity to visit one or more synagogues, there humbly to receive the blessings of the rabbis.

In contrast, in 1903, the Hungarian-born Theodor Herzl, founder of the modern Zionist movement, gave the following warning to a Jewish member of the Hungarian parliament:

The hand of fate shall also seize Hungarian Jewry. And the later this occurs, and the stronger this Jewry becomes, the more cruel and hard shall be the blow, which shall be delivered with greater savagery. There is no escape.   (in Braham 1994, 37)

Antisemitism in Eastern Europe   229

What did Herzl know or see that others did not? Not much; his warnings were based more on premonition and insight than experience. The Hungarian Jewish elite rejected Herzl's warnings and indeed all Zionist ideas. Since the complete "reception" of Judaism in 1895, of the three mutually hostile Jewish religious congregations (orthodox, status quo, and neolog), both the Hungarian state and the Jewish elite considered Judaism a denomination just like any other. Only the Gentile public did not share this view completely.

Undoubtedly, Hungary's case was in some regards atypical in the extent to which its elites welcomed emancipated Jews. Not without reason did the Austrian Christian Social leader Karl Lueger refer to the Hungarian capital as Judapest. In Poland, Roman Dmowski, the founder and leader of the vast National Democratic Party (Endecja), was highly successful with his extreme antisemitic propaganda. The Hungarian leadership needed the Jews not only for the economy but also to boost the proportion of Hungarians in a country where Hungarian speakers formed a minority. Dmowski perceived no comparable use for a Jewish or for any other ethnic minority. Unlike his rival, Jozef Pilsudski, who dreamed of recreating a multinational Polish–Lithuanian Commonwealth, Dmowski worked for a smaller Poland that was only for Poles. His turned out to be the attitude that eventually prevailed: The equivalent of his slogan, "Poland for the Poles," was subsequently adopted by every east European country, resulting finally in full-scale ethnic cleansing.

So long as the liberal or conservative east European governments resisted such a measure, the "un-mixing of peoples," as Nazi leader Heinrich Himmler later put it, could not start. However, the un-mixing began, even without governmental fiat, as a consequence of a world war. To many Europeans, above all workers and Jews, World War I initially brought the promise of complete equality, legitimized by common sacrifice. And, indeed, to provide a telling example, during the war more than one-fifth of the Dual Monarchy's reserve officer corps consisted of Jews (Deák 1990, 172–8, *passim*). Developments in that regard were less positive in the Prussian, Russian, or Romanian armies, but in Austria-Hungary large numbers of Jewish officers, including baptized and non-baptized generals, served with great loyalty (such was true also in Italy). Antisemitism was not tolerated by those in charge of the Austro-Hungarian army, and indeed by those at the head of most other European armies. However, in politics, the press, and public opinion, antisemitism experienced a quick revival for the simple reason that scapegoats had to be found for the sufferings of war. To the customary accusations were now added the charges of treason, spying, black marketing, and shirking.

War's end brought a series of national and social revolutions, as well as ethnic clashes, amounting in many places to ethnic cleansing. The subsequent flow of refugees consisted in a large part of Jews, hundreds of thousands of whom had fled the tsarist armies or had been driven west by the pogroms perpetrated by Polish, Ukrainian, and White Russian soldiers. Yet the war's end, 1918–19, also brought hope for many Jews in Russia, Hungary, Austria, and Bavaria, since socialist governments, made up largely of Jews, affirmed their complete impartiality in matters of ethnicity, race, and religion.

The absolute majority of the people's commissars in Hungary's Bolshevik revolution were of Jewish origin; as in Russia, command positions in an east European country were now held by Jews. But, in fact, few Hungarian Jews embraced Béla Kun's Communist regime. In any case, it lasted only 133 days and was then overthrown by the Romanian army, with the support of France. Still, Jews everywhere would pay a terrible price for the Hungarian Bolshevik experiment. The presence of such a Communist regime, as well as its perceived Jewish characteristics, frightened people everywhere. The counterrevolutionary propaganda image of the Bolshevik monster with a crooked nose, clutching a bloody knife between his teeth while raping an innocent blonde, inundated the world and was used to legitimize every subsequent massacre of Jews. The Polish term *zydokomuna*, Jewish Communism, had its equivalent in every language and is still very much in use.

The interwar years brought different varieties of strong-arm and later, fascist-type regimes to eastern Europe. Many, but by far not all, made antisemitism the alpha and omega of their politics. It was a strong feature of governmental policy in semi-dictatorial Poland, Hungary, Romania, and Bulgaria but was less shrill or nearly absent in the semi-dictatorial Baltic countries, Yugoslavia, Albania, and Greece. Within democratic Czechoslovakia, antisemitism was embraced mainly by Czech, German, and Slovak nationalists. The leading political parties in Hungary, Romania, and Poland were similarly antisemitic in inclination, especially as they felt the need to compete with the parties on the far Right in proving themselves firm on the Jewish Question.

More even than the governments, much of the public was passionately hostile to Jews in the interwar years. Many of the charges were not new; racism and Social Darwinism had been well known before the war. But agitators now enlarged the list of alleged Jewish crimes, among them warmongering, defeatism, pacifism, the spreading of Russian Bolshevik and American capitalist ideologies, creating inflation, and, later, bringing about the Great Depression. In defeated Hungary, Austria, and Germany, Jews were said to have stabbed the undefeated army in the back. In Romania, Czechoslovakia, and Poland, which had emerged with greatly expanded territories from the war, Jews were accused of siding with defeated Germany, Austria, and Hungary.

Yet it would be wrong to suppose that the development of antisemitism was linear and incremental. All through the interwar years, and even during World War II, east European governments were watching each other as well as the major powers, primarily Fascist Italy, to see how far they ought to go in adopting anti-Jewish measures. On the one hand, there was the need to satisfy Nazi Germany and the radical agitators at home; on the other hand, there was the expected disapproval, first of France and Great Britain, and later of the

Antisemitism in Eastern Europe 231

United States. There was also the danger of causing a social upheaval that might not stop with the despoliation of Jews. The latter argument proved crucial to the armory of conservative aristocrats everywhere in opposing further anti-Jewish measures. Finally, genuine humanitarian concerns prevailed from time to time in the Jewish policy of the Hungarian, Romanian, and Bulgarian governments.

During World War II, governments hoped to balance the national budget by seizing the property of Jews, which in the case of Hungary amounted to one-fourth of the national wealth, whereas Jews constituted around 6% of the population. The government of Hungary hoped, by seizing all Jewish property and deporting the Jews to Auschwitz in 1944, to balance the tumbling Hungarian budget. Unfortunately for that government, much of the Jewish wealth had been dissipated and, in any case, the Red Army soon occupied Hungary (Kádár 2004; Kádár and Vági 2004).

The unfolding of the Holocaust in eastern Europe fit into the above patterns. Hungary, Romania, Bulgaria, Croatia, and Slovakia were allies of Nazi Germany, and possessed their own government, administration, and army; they thus were able to decide if and when to enter the anti-Soviet military campaign and what to do with their Jews. Every German ally used the Jews as bargaining chips in their relations with the Third Reich, the western Allies, and each other. Even such German-occupied countries as the Czech Protectorate and Greece—not to speak of France, Denmark, and Norway—had their own governments and thus some leeway in pursuing their Jewish policy.

In Romania, Marshal Ion Antonescu's regime at first engaged in its own genocide, with perhaps 300,000 Jewish victims, but then stubbornly refused to send the rest of the Romanian Jews to Auschwitz. This change in policy came even before the annihilation of German and Romanian troops at the Battle of Stalingrad in the winter of 1942–3. By 1944, Romania was ironically serving as a refuge for Jews fleeing from abroad. No less ironically, three months after Hungary had been militarily occupied by Germany in March 1944, and after nearly half a million Jews had been dispatched to Auschwitz, the Hungarian leadership refused to surrender to the Germans the nearly 200,000 Jews in Budapest, as well as the forced Jewish laborers in Hungarian army service. And, again, the antisemitic Bulgarian government delivered every single Jew in the Bulgarian-occupied parts of Greece and Yugoslavia to the Nazis but would not give them a single Bulgarian Jew. In this resistance, the Bulgarian government was supported by much of the political elite and the public.

The Germans never granted sovereignty to the three Baltic countries, but popular sympathy was mainly on the side of the Germans (and against the Soviets), and thus a large number of Estonian, Latvian, and Lithuanian volunteers served the Germans as SS soldiers and as concentration camp guards. In Poland, the only country in Hitler's Europe that never engaged in political or military collaboration with Nazi Germany, many Poles were antisemitic enough to give the Germans a helping hand in catching fugitive Jews. Moreover, Polish villagers perpetrated major pogroms in those parts of Poland that between 1939 and 1941 had been under Soviet occupation—and in which many Poles attributed their sufferings to the rule of the *zydokomuna*, the Jewish Communists. It was not uncommon for otherwise heroic Polish anti-Nazi resisters to shoot down Jewish refugees—or even Jewish anti-Nazi partisans (or Ukrainian, Lithuanian, and Belorussian anti-Nazi partisans): a vivid testimony to the desire of most Poles to live, after the war, in a purely Polish country.

There are no worthwhile public opinion polls regarding wartime antisemitism in eastern Europe. The shifting popularity of such extreme rightist movements as the Romanian Iron Guard and the Hungarian Arrow Cross proves little because many people supported these radical movements less out of antisemitic motives (shared by the governing conservative-nationalist parties) than for reasons of social discontent. In the east European countries officially allied to Germany, the population left the final decisions regarding the Jews largely to the authorities; Jews were left in peace or brutally harassed, depending on government orders. Deportations were an orderly affair, executed under German guidance by the Hungarian, Czech, Slovak, and Croatian police and administrations. Romania, as noted, acted on its own in regard to the Jewish Question. Where chaos reigned, as in the Baltic countries, in Poland, and in Ukraine in the summer of 1941, volunteers massacred Jews without waiting for the Germans.

The eagerness of the population from Estonia down to Bulgaria and Greece to inherit the property, jobs, offices, shops, factories, businesses, and lands owned or managed by Jews amounted to a social revolution that continued unabated under Communist rule. Considering that the population showed no compunction at the end of the war in taking over the property of the German minority in Poland, Czechoslovakia, Hungary, Yugoslavia, and Romania, it is difficult to say whether the looting of Jewish property during the war ought to be attributed primarily to antisemitism or simply to a desire for better living conditions.

Closely connected to the appropriation of Jewish property was the attempt to get rid of the Jews themselves; yet here again it is not clear how much of it can be explained by antisemitism. After all, in the last year of the war, while Jews were still dying by the hundreds of thousands in German camps, the new democratic east European governments and the public began to expel, in some cases kill, German civilians, driving perhaps a total of 13 million from their homes. Czechs, Poles, and Yugoslavs committed worse atrocities against their former German compatriots than they had against the Jews (Zayas 2006, 151–2). The main motivations in all these cases were greed and the desire to create "pure" nation states, a task that is still unfinished.

One reason that Jews returning from the camps or from hiding were received with hostility nearly everywhere was the desire for ethnic purity. The other reason was, of course, the reluctance of the new owners to give back all that they had acquired, from managerial posts down to silver spoons. Thus, there were many east European pogroms, minor and major, the most infamous at Kielce in

Poland in July 1946, where about forty Jews were killed with some assistance by the local authorities and the police. The perpetrators at Kielce and elsewhere were mainly industrial workers and peasants. One must not forget, however, that non-Jewish Poles, too, had been the victims of endless atrocities committed by both the Germans and the Soviets; the Poles were now taking revenge on whomever they could. To claim that there were only an insignificant number of persons of Jewish origin among the Polish, or Hungarian, or Romanian Communist policemen and torturers is as false as to say that east Europeans had been innocent of the Holocaust during the war. (Many Poles feel that their sufferings also deserve the name Holocaust, and, in truth, about 3 million non-Jewish Poles perished during the war whether as soldiers, underground fighters, or victims of Soviet and German persecution.) Pogroms with fewer victims also took place in the rest of eastern Europe, and Jewish returnees were sometimes mistreated in western Europe as well.

The poverty of eastern Europe, the step-by-step Soviet-Communist takeover, the creation of Israel, and the pogroms (whether real or merely feared) led to a massive Jewish emigration from eastern Europe, at least until the Stalinist regimes closed all borders around 1949. Yet as late as 1968, the Polish Communist regime's anti-Zionist propaganda and antisemitic measures precipitated a new Jewish emigration to the West, often by Jews who had been personally involved in Stalinist terror.

The Communist regimes tended to sweep Holocaust issues under the rug with the argument that these old-regime crimes would not occur again. Governmental anti-Zionism often served as a substitute for antisemitism, but it was practiced unevenly, taking a serious turn only at the time of the great purge trials in the late 1940s and early 1950s, when scores of prominent Jewish Communists and non-Communist Zionists were tortured, tried, and executed as spies for Israel. Official anti-Zionism flared up each time that nationalist elements came to the fore in the party leadership or when the Soviet Union ordered such a campaign, but the consequences were no longer so lethal. In subsequent years, anti-Zionism became a formality in many countries, nearly ignored by the Hungarians and Romanians, but practiced more loudly by the East German Communist leadership.

We know little about popular antisemitism in the Stalinist or early post-Stalinist period, when official lies obfuscated every conceivable issue. Beginning in 1953, popular uprisings erupted against the Soviet presence and Communist rule, which should have given an opportunity for popular antisemitism to resurface. Yet only a handful of such incidents occurred in East Germany in 1953, in Hungary in 1956, in Czechoslovakia in the spring of 1968, and in Poland during the struggle of the Solidarity movement. It has been alleged that, in 1956, Polish factory workers threatened to kill Jews but, in general, anti-Jewish activity in Poland was more a concern of the party leadership than the general public.

The departure of the Jews from eastern Europe in modern times might well have been a natural process had it not been hastened by the erupting nationalist movements and especially the Holocaust. Jews had moved to eastern Europe centuries before because there was nowhere else to go; in modern times they used the opportunity offered by capitalist development to move west, to countries where life promised to be better. Similarly, it is likely that many Germans would have left voluntarily for the more prosperous West. The Holocaust and the expulsions caused all power and all the wealth to pass into local hands, but they also left behind a moral, political, and cultural void that east Europeans have not yet completely filled.

Antisemitism has not disappeared in eastern Europe. Witness the feverish activity of the presently minor far-right parties there. Witness, too, some of the far larger conservative-nationalist parties, which recruit followers by obscurely hinting at Jewish crimes and treason, while refusing to condemn the far-right groups. This type of right-of-center politics is common today not only in Hungary, where there are still Jews active in politics, the media, and culture, but also in Poland where there are fewer actual Jews than there are young Gentiles enthusiastically cultivating Jewish music and culture. Even in Bulgaria, whose prewar population of only 50,000 Jews mostly left for Israel after the war, today some nationalist parties appeal to the public with surreptitious antisemitism.

Without the foresight and generosity of east European kings, princes, and nobles, Jews in the Middle Ages and early modern times would have found no refuge anywhere in Europe. Without the benevolence of Habsburg rulers and the liberal idealism of reforming nobles, the rise and integration of the Jews into modernizing eastern Europe would have been far more difficult. As it happened, Jews served as the locomotives of the economy, as heralds of modern culture, and as instruments of integration into the locally dominant nationality. But after World War I, the silent contract between princes and nobles, on the one hand, and the Jewish elites, on the other, came to an end. The newly created nation states had less and less use for princes, nobles, and Jews. Meanwhile, the new middle class, often of peasant origin, regarded the Jews as foreign competitors and encouraged the state to intervene against them. A unique opportunity to solve the problem arose when the German Nazis engaged in the so-called Final Solution of the Jewish Question. The Nazi killing program did not completely achieve its goals, but it allowed the east Europeans to rid themselves of most Jews and then of most Germans. The result of these and other ethnic purges was a more ethnically pure eastern Europe, although also one nearly bankrupt morally, where a part of the frustrated and disappointed population continues to harbor antisemitic—and anti-foreign—sentiments. One can only hope that a majority of east Europeans will put their faith more in the European Union, less in cultivating their hatreds.

Antisemitism in Eastern Europe 235

RECOMMENDED READINGS

Bankier, David (ed.), *The Jews Are Coming Back: The Return of the Jews to Their Countries of Origin after World War II* (New York: Berghahn Books, 2005).

Braham, Randolph L., "The Holocaust in Hungary: A Retrospective Analysis," in *The Nazis' Last Victims: The Holocaust in Hungary*, with Scott Miller (Detroit: Wayne State University Press, 1998).

—— *The Politics of Genocide: The Holocaust in Hungary*, 2 vols, 2nd edn (Boulder, CO: Social Science Monographs, 1994).

Carp, Matatias, *Holocaust in Romania: Facts and Documents on the Annihilation of Romania's Jews, 1940–1944*, ed. Andrew L. Simon, trans. Sean Murphy (Safety Harbor, FL: Simon Publications, 2000).

Cherry, Robert, and Annamaria Orla-Bukowska (eds), *Rethinking Poles and Jews: Troubled Past, Brighter Future* (Lanham, MD: Rowman and Littlefield, 2007).

Deák, István, *Beyond Nationalism: A Social and Political History of the Habsburg Officer Corps, 1848–1918* (New York: Oxford University Press, 1990).

Georgescu, Vlad, *The Romanians: A History*, ed. Matei Calinescu, trans. Alexandra Bley-Vroman (Columbus, OH: Ohio State University Press, 1991).

Gross, Jan. T., *Neighbors: The Destruction of the Jewish Community in Jedwabne, Poland* (Princeton: Princeton University Press, 2001).

Handler, Andrew, *Blood Libel at Tiszaeszlár* (Boulder, CO/New York: East European Monographs, 1980).

Kádár, Gábor, "Rationality or Irrationality? The Annihilation of Hungarian Jews," *Hungarian Quarterly* 45(174) (Summer 2004): 32–54.

—— and Zoltán Vági, *Self-financing Genocide: The Gold Train, the Becher Case and the Wealth of Hungarian Jews*, trans. Enikö Koncz and Jim Tucker (Budapest: Central European University Press, 2004).

Lukas, Richard C., *Forgotten Holocaust: The Poles under German Occupation, 1939–1944* (Lexington: University Press of Kentucky, 1996).

Mendelsohn, Ezra, *The Jews of East Central Europe between the World Wars* (Bloomington: Indiana University Press, 1983).

Michlic, Joanna Bata, *Poland's Threatening Other: The Image of the Jew from 1880 to the Present* (Lincoln: University of Nebraska Press, 2006).

Moskovich, Wolf et al. (eds), *Jews and Anti-Semitism in the Balkans* (Jerusalem–Ljubljana: Scientific Research Center of the Slovenian Academy of Sciences and Arts, 2004).

Naimark, Norman M., *Fires of Hatred: Ethnic Cleansing in Twentieth Century Europe* (Cambridge, MA: Harvard University Press, 1991).

Patai, Raphael, *The Jews of Hungary: History, Culture, Psychology* (Detroit: Wayne State University Press, 1996).

Pietrowski, Tadeusz, *Poland's Holocaust: Ethnic Strife, Collaboration with Occupying Forces and Genocide in the Second Republic, 1918–1947* (Jefferson, NC: McFarland, 1998).

Polonsky, Antony, and Joanna B. Michlic (eds), *The Neighbors Respond: The Controversy over the Jedwabne Massacre in Poland* (Princeton: Princeton University Press, 2004).

236   *István Deák*

Todorov, Tzvetan, *The Fragility of Goodness: Why Bulgaria's Jews Survived the Holocaust* (Princeton: Princeton University Press, 1999).

Volovici, Leon, *Nationalist Ideology and Antisemitism: The Case of Romanian Intellectuals in the 1930s*, trans. Charles Kormos (Oxford: Pergamon Press, 1991).

Weeks, Theodore R., *From Assimilation to Antisemitism: The "Jewish Question" in Poland, 1850–1914* (De Kalb, IL: Northern Illinois University Press, 2006).

Zayas, Alfred-Maurice de, *A Terrible Revenge: The Ethnic Cleansing of the East European Germans, 1944–1950* (New York: Palgrave Macmillan, 2006).

15

Israel and Antisemitism

Meir Litvak and Esther Webman

Zionism and subsequently the state of Israel have faced ideological and political opposition since their inception. This opposition has often been translated in the Arab and Muslim worlds into enmity toward the Jews and Judaism, in antisemitic terms. Antisemitism was not the root cause of the Arab-Israeli conflict but has been exacerbated by it, aggravating its representations and serving as an additional tool for the delegitimization and dehumanization of the Other—Zionism and Israel. The demonization of the Jew in modern Arabic writings went "further than it had ever done in Western literature, with the exception of Germany during the period of Nazi rule" (Lewis 1986, 201). Anti-Jewish beliefs were created and shaped in the social-cultural reality of the Middle East, becoming over the years organic to various Arab and Islamic worldviews and interwoven in their discourses (Yadlin 1990, 54). Even broader universal processes, such as globalization or democratization came to be associated with the Jews and the animosity toward them was expressed in antisemitic terms.

The stand taken against Israel and Zionism, advocating their obliteration, actually derives from the national territorial struggle but is buttressed by traditional Islamic references. These not only disparage the Jews for what they do but also attribute to them a series of inherently negative features, giving rise to a deeper, irreconcilable hatred. Islamic fundamentalism has given further impetus to this trend, radicalizing the demonization of Israel, and rationalizing the prospect of eradicating the Jews. Outside the Middle East, opposition to Zionism and criticism of the state of Israel have often, though not always, served as a respectable cover for latent antisemitism, as manifested particularly in the early twenty-first century.

At any rate, denying Jews the right to self-determination, dehumanizing and demonizing Israel as well as singling it out as the source of evil, while employing blatant double standards in judging its conduct, go beyond legitimate criticism and have been the hallmark of "the new anti-Semitism," exacerbated by the Palestinian-Israeli armed confrontation of 2000. Antisemites tended to attack throughout history what they perceived to be the most salient manifestation of the Jews or Judaism. In the more distant past it was their religion, subsequently

238   *Meir Litvak and Esther Webman*

their supposed racial attributes, and in more recent times their nationalism represented by Zionism. What has been termed the new antisemitism has, in fact, characterized Middle Eastern antisemitism since the establishment of Israel. The virulence of the antisemitic utterances in Arab discourse exceeds the negative attitudes toward the West, even though the latter is considered to be a greater political and cultural challenge. The very existence of Western countries is not delegitimized, as is the case with Israel, despite the Islamists' stated goal to Islamize them. Whereas the Western public at large is not dehumanized and demonized, the Jews both as individuals and as a nation are portrayed as inherently and eternally evil.

FROM THE END OF WORLD WAR II
TO THE SIX DAY WAR

A marked rise in anti-Jewish utterances in Arab public discourse took place in the immediate post-World War II era as a result of the Jewish-Arab struggle over the future of Palestine and the pressing problem of Jewish Holocaust survivors seeking refuge in Palestine. The conflict elicited a fierce public debate about Zionism, its nature, ideology, history, and political aspirations, which has not ceased to this day. Tackling Zionism was perceived as an existential national challenge. It replaced fascist imperialism and racist Nazism in the Arab anti-colonialist and national thought, leading to a rising preoccupation with the Jews and evoking a whole range of images and stereotypes of the Jew, the eternal Other. The controversy over Zionism and Zionists increasingly blurred the distinction between them and Judaism or the Jews. "We have erased from our vocabulary the term Zionist and non-Zionist," admitted an Egyptian writer already in 1946, "because the political conflict turned into a conflict between Arabs and Jews" (*al-Risala*, March 25, 1946). Whatever sympathetic understanding that had existed for the plight of the Jews was replaced by growing animosity, seen in attempts to minimize Jewish suffering during the war, and even to justify the Holocaust as an understandable German reaction to Jewish treason.

The birth of Israel in 1948 and the Arab defeat in the war launched against it were perceived by many Muslims as contradicting the right course of history and divine order, since God had ordained that Jews were to remain subordinate to Muslims. Zionism's success became a glaring symbol of the deeper crisis of the Muslim world. And since Islam's modern crisis was unprecedented, Islam's new Jewish problem appeared to be of even greater dimensions than had been Muhammad's predicament in his encounter with the Jews of Medina. The polemics against the Jews and the Children of Israel in the Qur'an (Koran) "serve as a basis for the negative reconstruction of the Jewish character," and provide "an explanation for the Zionist successes, the offense in Palestine, and the political and economic Jewish domination in other parts of the world"

Israel and Antisemitism 239

(Taji-Farouki 1998, 15). Rather than forthrightly facing their own internal weaknesses, Arab regimes and writers have preferred to describe the Jews as an all-powerful group that manipulates international organizations and foreign powers. Hence, in addition to demonizing the enemy, antisemitic language has helped to rationalize Arab military and technological inferiority vis-à-vis Israel.

Social psychologist Daniel Bar-Tal has shown that societies involved in intractable conflicts develop suitable psychological traits that enable them to cope with the conflict. The beliefs that support the development of these psychological traits include a conviction about the justice of one's cause and delegitimization of the adversary. Put together, these beliefs constitute an ethos that supports the continuation of the conflict and are reflected in language, stereotypes, images, myths, and collective memory (351–65). Consequently, Arab antisemitism was promoted up to the 1967 War from above by governments for political mobilization but was also expressed from below, reflecting popular beliefs. It has never been confined to the political fringes but has been shared by mainstream popular writers, academics, and politicians from leftists to radical Islamists. Rising hostility toward Jews was a major reason for the massive Jewish exodus from Arab countries after 1948.

By adopting Western classical antisemitic motifs, such as the blood libel and the allegations of Jewish designs to control the world, and buttressing them with Islamic anti-Jewish precepts, Arab antisemitism developed its own authenticity and uniqueness. An example of this combination is a statement in a Friday sermon delivered by Anwar al-Sadat, then member of the Revolutionary Council, in November 1955, in which he alluded to the Muslim hatred of the Jews since the time of the Prophet, accusing them of falsifying the Torah, violating agreements, killing the prophets, striving to control the world, and greed (*Al-Ahram*, November 26, 1955). The first three motifs are derived from Islamic sources, whereas the last two are typical of Western antisemitism.

The spreading use of Nazi-era language to depict Israel, Zionism, and the Jews was an additional trait of Arab antisemitism. The *Protocols of the Elders of Zion*, which had already appeared in Arabic in the 1920s, was given new translations into Arabic, Persian, and Urdu, and by 1970 appeared in nine editions (and over 60 by 2007). The *Protocols,* describing Jewish designs to take over the world, provided an explanation for the hatred that the various nations felt toward the Jews in the past and justification for the need to take drastic measures against the Zionists in the future. Even those well aware that the *Protocols* were a forgery continued to make use of them, arguing that their authenticity was unimportant since their agendas were coming to pass.

Left-wing thought, which was particularly influential during this period, associated the Jews with the ugliest aspects of capitalism, as had many leftists in Europe until the 1930s. The Egyptian Marxist Fathi al-Ramli claimed that the Jews were persecuted not for religious reasons but rather because they were the vanguard of the exploitative system in capitalist societies. The persecutions were

240   *Meir Litvak and Esther Webman*

the natural outcome of the hatred that the masses harbored against their exploiters (113–14). Some of them maintained that the Zionist movement played a central role in advancing antisemitism by urging the Jews to preserve their distinct identity in European societies. Zionism, they claimed, spoke of Jewish racial purity, but such arguments were compatible with the antisemites' views of the Jews as aliens in the countries where they lived. Leftists rejected the notion that the Jews constituted a nation; many, especially Communists, adopted the equation of Zionism with Nazism, and insisted on the difference between Zionism and Judaism. Yet, after the mid-1950s they also resorted to representing Zionism in antisemitic terms.

As elsewhere, the Middle Eastern version of antisemitism contained many contradictions, primary among them the claim, alluded to earlier, that the Jews are not a modern people at all, since they lack any of the objective attributes of modern nationhood. Rather, they are an amalgam of disparate groups with nothing in common among them except their religion. The Jews cannot even be considered Semites; they are rather a mixture of various peoples who, throughout history, took up Jewish religion and culture. At the same time and somewhat contradictorily, it was argued that all Jews throughout the world share basic characteristics and aspirations, and that they have striven to attain their goals throughout the centuries under a unified worldwide leadership. Arabs often rejected Zionist arguments by claiming that modern Jews were completely unrelated to the ancient Israelites, and were, in fact, descendants of the Turkish-Khazar people. Yet, these "non-Jewish" Jews allegedly carried the negative traits of the Israelites, and were continuing the war that the Jews of seventh-century Arabia had waged against the Prophet Muhammad (Webman 2005, 318).

TRANSFORMATIONS AND CONTINUITIES: THE IMPACT OF THE SIX DAY WAR

The swift Israeli victory over the Arab armies in June 1967 dealt an additional blow to Arab self-esteem and generated unrest that continued to be channeled against Israel, Zionism, and the Jews. Israel's image turned overnight from a weak country whose further existence was in doubt into an all-powerful state. This change in perception was also evident in Arab caricatures. Prior to the war, caricatures presented Israel and Israelis as miserable and despicable creatures who were about to be punished by proud self-confident Arabs. After the 1967 defeat, the Israeli image changed into a menacing brutal Nazi-type oppressor (Webman 2003, 118–19). This shift required satisfactory explanation, leading to the further entrenchment of conspiracy theories and demonization of Zionism and the Jews.

A similar change in the perception of Israel and Zionism occurred in Europe. The passage of time since 1945 and the continued Israeli occupation of the West

Bank and Gaza eroded Israel's image as a refuge for persecuted Jews, transforming it to that of an expansionist state, with the Palestinians increasingly portrayed as its hapless victims. The shift of Israel's image from a David to a Goliath enabled many Europeans to free themselves from the burden of guilt over their conduct toward the Jews during World War II, and allowed dormant anti-Jewish sentiments to resurface under the guise of opposition to Israeli policies or to Zionism (Wistrich 1985, 10 ff). A corollary development was the rise in anti-Israeli propaganda, with antisemitic undertones, that flowed into the Middle East.

The convergence of anti-Israeli sentiment in the Middle East with European leftist anti-imperialist sentiment culminated in 1975 in the adoption of UN Resolution 3379, equating Zionism with racism. Since the UN Charter called for the eradication of racism, the implication for Zionism was quite clear. European antisemitism further assumed a political dimension following the 1982 Israeli invasion of Lebanon, particularly the Sabra and Shatila massacres (perpetrated by Christian militias), as it intensified opposition to Israel, its policies, and even its existence (Wistrich 1976, 12 ff).

The European Left, particularly its radical elements, gradually shifted from a social program of working-class liberation into a view of competing camps, in which the central divide is between the oppressed and oppressor nations of the world. This view, which has been characteristically labeled internationalist, raised anti-imperialism to an absolute principle. As Israel became increasingly perceived as a key site of the imperialist system, the European Left came to see Zionism as the epitome of all that is bad in the world, rejecting the right of Jews to have a state of their own and regarding the existing state of Israel as a manifestation of narrow nationalism and racism (Hirsh 2007, 9–10).

ISLAMIST ANTISEMITISM

The 1967 war served as a catalyst for the rise of Islamist movements as major players and as alternatives to nationalist Arab elites and governments. This rise was given further impetus by the 1979 Iranian Revolution. Unlike Arab states after 1967, Iran endorsed antisemitism as part of its anti-Zionist program (Litvak 2006). Since then, the Islamists have become the main bearers of ever harsher antisemitic pronouncements, and antisemitism became a major component of the Islamist worldview. Unlike its state-sponsored predecessors, Islamist antisemitism emerged from below and is more deeply rooted. The modern Islamist animosity exceeds anti-Jewish attitudes in traditional Islam, since historically Muslims regarded Christianity as a greater threat than Judaism. However, because of the conflict with Israel, Judaism has become the Islamists' prime enemy.

242   *Meir Litvak and Esther Webman*

Unlike mainstream nationalists and leftists, Islamist movements perceive the Arab-Israeli conflict as essentially one between Muslims and Jews everywhere, and even more between Islam and Judaism. In view of the identity crisis of Islam in modern times there has been a growing tendency to use the past to give meaning to the present. The resentment toward the Jews of the early Islamic period has been translated into an intense Islamic Judeophobia, inciting religious and political activism. While Islamists reject Western cultural influence as destructive to authentic Islamic culture, they have not hesitated to borrow anti-Zionist and anti-Jewish themes from the West in the service of their cause. The Hamas Charter, for instance, provides a picture of the Jews and Judaism that is transparently based on the *Protocols of the Elders of Zion* (Webman 1994, 17–22, 35–6).

Another factor that has shaped Islamist antisemitism is the quest for authenticity or the redefinition of Muslim identity. This process has involved an intensified literalist and uncritical reading of earlier Islamic history. Such a reading has led to the reopening and the need to settle competing historical accounts between Islam and other religions. This approach has involved revisiting medieval polemics with the Jews, emphasizing the sins they had allegedly committed against Muslims since the early days of Islam, particularly their treachery against the Prophet Muhammad. It also revived the long-standing image of Judaism as a harsh and restrictive religion, compared to the more tolerant and humane Islam (Sivan 1990).

Consequently, Islamists view the conflict in the Middle East as the culmination of a thousand-year conflict between Islam and Judaism, as well as between Islam and Western civilization—between divine law and man-made laws. Israel is identified with the West and considered its arm in the region, to assure continued control. At the same time Zionism is described as manipulating the West against Islam. It is a war between good, personified by the Muslims, who represent the Party of God (*Hizballah*), against "evil incarnated … the party of Satan"(*hizb al-shaytan*) represented by the Jews (*Filastin al-Muslima*, April 1990).

Jews have been depicted as traitors, warmongers, violators of agreements, killers of prophets, blood-suckers, "descendants of apes and pigs" (based on a number of Qur'anic verses, which state that some Jews were turned into apes and pigs by God, as a punishment for violating the Sabbath), disseminators of corruption on earth and "enemies of God and humanity." Rejecting any distinction between Judaism and Zionism, Islamists assert that Zionism is a racist movement and ideology responsible for translating aggressive Jewish religious tenets into a belligerent reality (Litvak 1998, 150–2; Webman 1994, 1–16). According to this interpretation, the clash is irreconcilable, and the destruction of Israel is not only predetermined by the Qur'an but also necessary in order to save humanity and civilization.

Islamist antisemitism has reached a point of openly advocating genocide. The Jews, by insisting on maintaining the state of Israel and by rejecting the Islamist

Israel and Antisemitism 243

peace offer to live as a protected minority under Islamic rule, have forfeited their right to exist under the historical Pact of Umar. While most Sunni Islamist movements have relegated the messianic elements of Islam to a secondary level, Hamas has lent eschatological meaning to the elimination of the Jews, which it claims is a prerequisite for fulfilling God's promise to establish His rule on earth (*Hamas Charter*, articles 13, 9, and 7). Various Islamist writers have taken a position, summarized by one that "people will know that the extermination of Jews is good for the inhabitants of the world," and that "humanity will be relieved of their presence, since subsequently, not one Jew will remain alive" (Holtzman and Schlossberg 2002, 156). Yet, despite the implicit racist undertones, Islamist antisemitism is not racially motivated, and Islamists allow an outlet to the Jews if they convert to Islam, an option which did not exist under Nazism.

THE HOLOCAUST

Another major development in the evolution of Arab and Muslim antisemitism has been an increasing preoccupation with the Holocaust. Earlier discussion of the Holocaust by Arabs dealt very little, if at all, with the events of that mass murder itself. Arab authors were not interested in the processes that led to the Nazi decision to exterminate the Jews and hardly ever referred to the actual acts of mass extermination. Rather, several attitudes evolved, influenced by those in the West, that range on a spectrum from short-lived empathy at the end of World War II, through denial, and finally to justification. The immediate context of the Holocaust in Arab political debate was the establishment of the state of Israel and its efforts to gain legitimacy. Zionist leaders are (and continue to be) perceived as cynically using the Holocaust—and even inventing it as a means of financial and psychological extortion, by cultivating the sense of guilt in the West. A characteristic Arab attitude to the Holocaust emerged already by 1945, when the plight of Holocaust survivors had direct repercussions on the escalating confrontation in Palestine. Arabs viewed World War II as a war between rival European imperialist camps, in which the Arab world had no direct connection or interest. Likewise, they viewed the Holocaust as an event that did not involve them, since it was perpetrated in Europe by Europeans. Yet Arabs had to suffer the consequences, with the loss of Palestine and the displacement of the Palestinians (Litvak and Webman 2009, 1–22).

In the Arab discussion of the 1952 German-Israeli reparations agreement the main theme was the Zionist-Israeli exploitation of the Holocaust, whereas the more prevalent themes during the 1960–2 Eichmann Affair was the alleged Nazi-Zionist cooperation and the equation of Zionism with Nazism. Contacts between Zionist activists and Nazi officials indeed took place during the 1930s up to the war period in order to save as many Jews as possible from the claws of the Nazi regime, and not out of any support or identification with it. The 1933

Transfer (*Ha'avara*) Agreement, signed between the Jewish Agency and the German government, facilitated the emigration of approximately 55,000 Jews from Germany to Palestine. However, these contacts ceased completely once the war broke out and the Zionist leadership mobilized its meager resources to support the British war effort.

The "Holocaust myth," a prominent theme in Arab discussion of Europe's Jews, has been transparently aimed at undermining the moral-historical basis of Zionism and the legitimacy of the Jewish state. Distorting Jewish history and offending the human dignity of the Jews by presenting their worst tragedy as a scam, Holocaust denial had obvious connections to and borrowings from existing imagery about the Jews in Europe. That borrowing has been especially blatant since the early 1980s, in the wake of the first Lebanon war, when the Jews were believed to have forfeited their status as victims by victimizing the Palestinians. Similarly, Israel was believed to have lost its right to exist because of the high human price that existence requires.

The intensification of the denial theme in the Arab treatment of the Holocaust was also related to the growing significance of the Holocaust not only in Israeli identity but in Western reevaluations of the past. As in the West, Arab denial was articulated in several ways. One was total denial of the event, as if nothing had happened to the Jews during World War II, and depiction of that alleged event as a Jewish-Zionist hoax designed to extort funds and political support from the West, particularly Germany. Another approach was to acknowledge the deaths of Jews—a few hundred thousand at the most—as part of the overall loss of civilian life during the war due to hunger, diseases, and random Nazi terrorism. But a specific Nazi policy to exterminate the Jews was denied, and the number of Jewish deaths minimized. Middle Eastern deniers adopt the arguments of Western neo-Nazis and antisemites in order to provide a pseudo-scientific value to their arguments, particularly as these Westerners seemingly claimed to hold objective views on the Arab-Israeli conflict.

Unlike the West, where Holocaust denial is confined to a tiny faction of the radical Right that lacks respectability, in the Arab world it is practiced by the intellectual and political mainstream, including prominent politicians, senior religious leaders, academics, and journalists. Holocaust deniers are able to promote their views in the major media, including leading newspapers and TV channels. Iran has stood out, since many of its senior leaders, from Supreme Leader Ali Khamanei to President Mahmud Ahmadinejad, have publicly denied the Holocaust. Moreover, Iran gave asylum to several notorious Western deniers, who had been convicted of Holocaust denial in their home countries, such as the Swiss Jürgen Graff in 1998, and the Austrian Wolfgang Fröhlich in 2000. Iran's active involvement in Holocaust denial culminated in 2006, with the organization of an international Holocaust cartoon contest, an exhibition of the winning cartoons, and in convening an allegedly scholarly conference, which brought together notorious Western and Arab deniers "to establish the facts of the Holocaust."

Israel and Antisemitism 245

The justification motif, which sometimes appeared simultaneously with denial, was prevalent well into the 1970s, when the conflict with Israel was at its peak. The Holocaust was described as a link in a chain of similar catastrophes that befell the Jews throughout their history, all of them legitimate responses to Jewish treachery and misconduct. The justification of Hitler's action fell into three categories. First were pseudo-historical descriptions of the activities of the Jews in Germany throughout history. Second, short-term explanations were offered, focusing on the period preceding the war, most notably the allegation that the Jews stabbed Germany in the back during World War I, or that Hitler merely reacted to the Jewish declaration of war against Germany in 1939. And finally, there were retroactive justifications based on alleged conduct by the state of Israel. Justification did not disappear even during periods of improved political atmosphere, in the wake of the 1979 Israeli-Egyptian peace or the peace process of the 1990s, although expressions of it were less frequent. It reemerged with the outbreak of the Palestinian-Israeli confrontation in September 2000 (Litvak and Webman 2009, 195–216).

A corollary theme was the equation of Zionism or Judaism with Nazi ideology, most notably articulated in Mamduh al-Shaykh's statement that "Zionism is nothing but Nazism with a Jewish face, while Nazism is actually Zionism with a secular look." Some Arab writers contended that Zionism was "one of Nazism's ancestors" since its racism is rooted in the Torah, while others insisted that the very claim of the Jews, that they constitute one nation is essentially a Nazi idea. Arab writers were presumably aware of the particularly painful effect of such an equation on the Israeli psyche, in view of the past suffering of the Jews at the hands of the Nazis. Again, this accusation sought to transform victims into perpetrators, implicitly threatening them with the ultimate fate of the Nazis (Litvak and Webman 2009, 217–44).

ANTISEMITISM AND POLITICS

The Israeli peace accords with Egypt and Jordan and the peace process with the Palestinians did not lead to the disappearance of Middle Eastern antisemitism. The official state positions toward Israel were contradicted by the prevalent attitudes in the Arab media and public, which continued to be extremely critical of Israel. Opposition to the peace process and to normalizing relations with Israel was often articulated in antisemitic terms. Calls by Israel for regional economic cooperation were dismissed as Jewish plans to dominate the Middle East economically. Newspaper articles attacked what were described as Jewish greed and Israel's intentions to dominate the region. Jewish religious legacy was attacked as full of fallacies and myths, fanaticism, and racial superiority, constituting a real danger to peace.

246   *Meir Litvak and Esther Webman*

The blood-libel theme has been repeated in numerous books, articles, and TV series or discussions since the early 1950s (Yadlin 1989; *Antisemitism Worldwide 1996/97*, 184–5; *1998/99*, 227–9, 232; *1999/2000*, 186–92). Several pseudo-scholarly articles that recounted the story and accused the Jews of sacrificing human beings for ritual purposes cited the Nazi weekly newspaper *Der Stürmer* as one of their sources. Most notable was the bestselling (nine editions) book *The Matzo of Zion*, first published in 1985 by then Syrian Defense Minister Mustafa Tlas, who states in the preface that "the Jew can kill you and take your blood in order to make his Zionist bread." In 2006, the story was repeated on fourteen separate websites.

In Egypt, where the antisemitic discourse was especially prominent, it apparently served as an outlet for many intellectuals to express their frustration over Egypt's failure to achieve national and regional grandeur, epitomized in its compromise with Israel. A seemingly tacit deal emerged between the government and the intellectuals, which allowed the latter to turn their pens against Israel, the Jews, and the USA, in return for avoiding criticism of the government's domestic failures (Ajami 1998, 253–312). Egyptian Islamists cited Jewish hostility to the Prophet in their attack on normalization, stressing that the Arabs are facing the most dangerous and malicious enemy, depicted by the Qur'an as a rancorous, aggressive, and dishonest tribe that does not respect agreements and cannot be trusted (*Antisemitism Worldwide 1996/97*, 186–8; *1999/2000*, 182–3).

Following the collapse of the Soviet Union, frustration over the gloomy state of the Arabs on the world stage led to the introduction of strong antisemitic motifs in the discussion of globalization and the new world order. In addition to the unresolved Arab-Israeli conflict, antisemitism has been progressively woven into the ongoing debate between the agents of change (involving liberalization, democratization, and peace in the Middle East), and the nationalists and Islamists, who reject those processes and continue to see the Jews or Zionism as the driving force behind them. Globalization has been perceived as a threat to the Arab and Muslim worlds not only because of its possible effect on their social cohesiveness but also on its relation to the Arab-Israeli conflict (*Antisemitism Worldwide 1999/2000*; Webman 2006, 190). Arab public opinion, according to the liberal Tunisian philosopher Mezri Haddad, "has found in antisemitism the perfect catalyst for all its narcissistic wounds and social, economic, and political frustrations" (Memri 2006, Special Dispatch 1362).

The outbreak of violence between Israel and the Palestinians in September 2000 (the al-Aqsa Intifada) following the failure of peace negotiations in July brought an upsurge in the antisemitic pronouncements and incidents. Muslim youths rather than right-wing extremists were behind most of the violent incidents against Jews in Europe. Radical Islamist incitement emanating from Arab countries by satellite TV, audio cassettes, and the Internet, in addition to European-based radical preachers calling for violence against the Jews, inflamed the existing anger over the Middle Eastern situation. Frustration over their lack

Israel and Antisemitism 247

of integration in European societies and envy at the more successful Jews added to Muslims' animosity. Such feelings received additional legitimacy by the growing criticism of Israel in Europe (Webman 2002, 37–59).

Most authors in the Middle East chose to ignore in their discussions of the new wave of antisemitism in Europe the violent attacks on Jews perpetrated by Muslim youths, whereas they drew satisfaction from the criticism of Israel. What has been happening in Europe, according to Lebanese Shi'i spiritual leader, Muhammad Husayn Fadlallah, signifies the failure of the brainwashing campaign of the pro-Israel or Jewish-controlled media to deceive Europeans (*Al-Safir*; October 21, 2003).

The radicalization of antisemitic discourse spread beyond the confines of political and journalistic debates. Apart from the imminent threat to Jews worldwide, as part of the Islamists' war against the West and particularly the USA, familiar antisemitic themes prevailed: The equation of Zionism with racism and Nazism; the glorification of suicide attacks against Israeli civilian targets and Jewish targets worldwide; Holocaust denial; and recourse to fantastic charges or discredited sources, such as the blood libel and the *Protocols of the Elders of Zion*.

The events of September 11, 2001, and the ensuing wars in Afghanistan and Iraq exposed a strong linkage between antisemitism and anti-Americanism. After September 11th, the allegation was widely made that American support for Israel, revealing Jewish control of the American government and media, was the main motive for this terrorist act. Again somewhat contradictorily, the search for likely perpetrators and conspirators naturally led to a Jewish connection; a host of arguments appeared linking Jews, Zionism, and the Israeli Mossad to the attacks. They were presented as "the act of the great Jewish Zionist mastermind that controls the world's economy, media and politics." The goal of the allegedly Jewish-directed operation was to coerce the United States and NATO "to submit even more to Jewish Zionist ideology" by cultivating fears of "Islamic terrorism" and instigating a war against Islam. An Egyptian commentator wrote that the explanation for the attacks was straight out of the *Protocols of the Elders of Zion*, which exhorts the Jews to destroy the world in order to control it (Webman 2002, 53). September 11th and subsequent events had a similar impact on European views, strengthening the confluence between anti-Zionism and antisemitism, and between Muslim and European views.

CONCLUSION

Antisemitism is obviously not the root cause of the Arab-Israeli conflict, but it certainly has exacerbated it. Borrowing themes from Western antisemitic writings, Arab-Islamic antisemitism also had indigenous roots. The end product was a peculiar symbiosis of Christian and Islamic themes. Although waves of

248   *Meir Litvak and Esther Webman*

antisemitic manifestations have escalated and receded in relation to political events and developments, antisemitism in the Arab world is increasingly becoming a constant in Arab thought and is linked, as in other places in the world, to broader processes. The hardening of rhetoric and the culture of hate cherished over the years reflect a prevailing mood in the Arab world in relation to Israel, the USA, and many aspects of Western civilization.

Antisemitism is not only more prevalent in the Middle East than in any other part of the world but is also a state policy in Iran. It enjoys open governmental tolerance if not tacit support in other countries. It has acquired pseudo-academic legitimacy in intellectual circles. It goes much further than traditional Islamic prejudice against Jews, in both scope and virulence, reflecting a sense of crisis and frustration among wide sections of Arab and Muslim societies. Moreover, Islamist antisemitism is persistent in its calls to exterminate the Jews, breaking a taboo established since the Holocaust and posing the most threatening danger to world Jewry since Nazism. While one cannot underestimate the Islamists' real danger, when discussing Middle Eastern antisemitism one should not ignore the fact that there are other voices. Though marginal and mostly emanating from Arabs and Muslims residing in the West, they challenge and criticize antisemitism as well as the Islamist discourse of violence and terrorism, seeing both as part of the overall deterioration of Arab and Muslim societies.

The politicization of Middle Eastern antisemitism and the active role of governments until 1967 has led some scholars to assume that it had not taken deep cultural roots and would subside once a political solution to the Arab-Israeli conflict would be achieved (Lewis 1986, 258; Harkabi 1973, 227). While such may have been true in the past, it seems now antisemitism has become entrenched in the political culture of the Middle East, following the continuous antisemitic allegations against the Jews in a wide variety of media, its articulation as an integral part of broader Islamist discourse, and the continued sense of crisis in the Muslim world. In such a delusional atmosphere the agreements between Israel and some Arab states, which were motivated by pragmatism, have not developed into a genuine peace between peoples. Only a profound change in perceptions and attitudes could lead to reconciliation and acceptance.

RECOMMENDED READINGS

Ajami, Fouad, "The Orphaned Peace," in *Dream Palaces of the Arabs: A Generation's Odyssey* (New York: Pantheon, 1998).
Antisemitism Worldwide 1996–2008. Available at http://www.tau.ac.il/Anti-Semitism
Bar-Tal, Daniel, "From Intractable Conflict through Conflict Resolution to Reconciliation: Psychological Analysis," *Political Psychology* 21(2) (June 2000): 351–65.
"The Hamas Charter." Available at http://www.mideastweb.org/hamas.htm
Harkabi, Yehoshafat, *Arab Attitudes to Israel* (London: Vallentine, 1973).

Hirsh, David, *Anti-Zionism and Antisemitism: Cosmopolitan Reflections* (New Haven: Yale Initiative for the Interdisciplinary Study of Antisemitism Working Paper Series, 2007).

Holtzman, Livnat, and Eliezer Schlossberg, "The Modern Religious Polemic between Muslims and Jews as Reflected in the Book Haqaiq Quraniyya Hawla al-Qadiyya al-Filastiniyya," *Historia* 10 (2002): 129–66. [In Hebrew]

Lewis, Bernard, *Semites and Antisemites* (New York and London: Norton, 1986).

Litvak, Meir, "The Islamic Republic of Iran and the Holocaust: Anti-Zionism and anti-Semitism," *Journal of Israeli History* 25 (2006): 245–66.

——"The Islamization of the Israeli-Arab Conflict: the Case of Hamas," *Middle Eastern Studies* 23(1) (1998): 148–63.

——and Esther Webman, *From Empathy to Denial: Arab Responses to the Holocaust* (London/New York: Hurst and Columbia University Press, 2009).

Nettler, Ronald L., *Past Trials and Present Tribulations: A Muslim Fundamentalist's View of the Jews* (Oxford: Pergamon Press, 1987).

Ramli, Fathi al-, *al-Sahyuniyya a'la marahil al-isti'mar* (Cairo: Wikalat al-Sahafa al-Afriqiya, 1956).

Sivan, Emmanuel, "Islamic Fundamentalism, Antisemitism and Anti-Zionism," in Robert Wistrich (ed.), *Anti-Zionism and Antisemitism in the Contemporary World* (London: Macmillan, 1990), 74–84.

Stav, Arie, *Peace: The Arabian Caricature: a Study of Anti-Semitic Imagery* (Tel Aviv: Gefen, 2000). [In Hebrew]

Taji-Farouki, Suha. "A Contemporary Construction of the Jews in the Qur'an: A Review of Muhammad Sayyid Tantawi's Banu Isra'il fi al-Qur'an wa al-Sunna and ʿAfif ʿAbd al-Fattah Tabbara's al-Yahud fi al-Qur'an," in Ron Nettler and Suha Taji-Farouki (eds), *Muslim-Jewish Encounters: Intellectual Tradition and Modern Politics* (Oxford: Harwood Academic, 1998).

Webman, Esther, "Antisemitic Images in the Rhetoric of the Arab-Israeli Conflict," *Kesher* 33 (May 2003): 116–21. [In Hebrew]

——*Anti-Semitic Motifs in the Ideology of Hizballah and Hamas* (Tel Aviv: Project for the Study of Anti-Semitism, Tel Aviv University, 1994).

——"Anti-Semitic Manifestations Worldwide as a Corollary of the al-Aqsa Intifada," in Dina Porat and Roni Stauber (eds), *Anti-Semitism Worldwide, 2000/01* (Tel Aviv, 2002), 37–59.

——"Antizionism, Antisemitism and Criticism of Israel—The Arab Perspective," *Tel Aviver Jahrbuch für deutsche Geschichte* 33 (2005): 306–29.

——"Arab Perceptions of Globalization," in Meir Litvak (ed.), *Middle Eastern Societies and the West: Accommodation or Clash of Civilizations?* (Tel Aviv: Dayan Center for Middle Eastern Studies, 2006), 177–98.

Wistrich, Robert S., *Anti-Zionism as an Expression of anti-Semitism in Recent Times* (Jerusalem: Shazar Center, 1985). [In Hebrew]

——*Muslim Anti-Semitism: A Clear and Present Danger* (New York: American Jewish Committee, 2002).

——*The Myth of Zionist Racism* (London: World Union of Jewish Students, 1976).

Yadlin, Rivka, *An Arrogant Oppressive Spirit: Anti-Zionism as Anti-Judaism in Egypt* (New York: Pergamon Press, 1989).

——"On the Boundaries of Meaning of Antisemitic Texts," *Gesher* 121 (1990). [In Hebrew]

Conclusion: Not the Final Word

Let no one be surprised that the issues our contributors were asked to address have not been completely resolved. Easy answers are the stock in trade of antisemites, not those who seek to understand the hatred that has so possessed them. The nature of the scholarly enterprise is constant, open-ended inquiry. In that spirit some cautious conclusions are presented below, a few ways of thinking about the history and the future of Jew-hatred that may prove productive.

The Introduction refers to how elusive defining antisemitism appears, and all our authors grapple with that problem, implicitly or explicitly. In his masterful survey of eastern Europe, István Deák offers some concrete and revealing examples of how difficult it was to define Jewishness. Identifying antisemites and antisemitism is no easier. Possibly, the sole unanimous conclusion of this collection of essays is that intelligent and informed people can disagree about the meaning of antisemitism. Yet the task of definition is a necessary one. Otherwise, we risk being saddled with a term that has become nearly meaningless and thus mostly useless, or even an obstacle to understanding. We have a genuine need for a *less* inclusive formulation, one that rests on some careful distinctions.

Albert Lindemann makes a case for the existence of a generalized Jewish question before the surfacing of what we commonly think of as the more time-specific "Jewish Question," that is, the debates beginning in the late eighteenth century dealing with the issues arising from the need to find a new place for the Jews in diverse states and societies. The pre-existing Jewish question set the terms of these debates and influenced the thinking of those who deliberated on the status of Jews. However, the same case cannot be made for an "antisemitism before antisemitism." The rapid diffusion of the new term in the 1880s and 1890s cannot have been an accident; it meant something new. Contemporaries must have felt the need for a new term to describe something different that was developing in the relations between Jews and non-Jews. This "something" could not be adequately conveyed by the old terminology: Jew-hatred, Jew-baiting, Judeophobia, and their permutations. Hence the remarkably rapid and widespread embrace of *antisemitism*. The appearance of organized antisemitism first in Germany and then elsewhere in Europe and where Europeans had settled in the world was patently a response to the rise of the Jews, whether or not accompanied by their formal legal emancipation. Organizations with antisemitic agendas arose as a reaction by non-Jews to the specter of Jewish domination. Using the

Conclusion: Not the Final Word   251

term to describe anti-Jewish animosity much before the last quarter of the nineteenth century, when this particular fear became prominent, is problematic and misleading. It suggests an unbroken line of development in the way Jews were regarded and acted upon by others from ancient times to the present. But there is ample evidence of a significantly new departure that the neologism was meant to express.

However, nearly half of the contributions to this anthology on the history of antisemitism treat pre-nineteenth century Jew-hatred. Why has so much space been devoted to the years before "antisemitism proper" came into existence? And how did anti-Jewish prejudice, violence, and persecution before 1879 differ from what came afterward? Certainly, it would be odd if antisemitism bore no relation to traditional thinking about Jews and how to deal with them.

One salient characteristic of antisemitism, setting it apart from earlier varieties of Jew-hatred, is its implicit call for action. Anti-Jewish prejudice, snobbery, or contempt did not always lead to anti-Jewish actions (as touched upon in the Introduction). In wartime Poland individuals who were well known for their opposition to Jews at times worked heroically for their rescue. In Vichy France, on the other hand, political figures with no prior record of animosity toward Jews participated decisively in their deportation and murder. Feelings about Jews—even the absence of such feelings—are no sure guide for defining antisemitism. Antisemitism, in contrast to anti-Jewish prejudice, implied deeds, more precisely programs involving action against them. Whether one regards antisemitism as a free-standing, all-embracing explanation of the world or merely one element in a complex of modern hostilities (Volkov 2006) or as a leavening agent, capable of energizing all sorts of other, usually political, issues (Massing 1949), the activist dimension of the ideology is central and apparent. A solution of the Jewish Question required deeds, not just words or feelings.

Of course, Jews had been subjected to harsh treatment long before the advent of organized antisemitism. However, persecution, especially in its violent forms, had been episodic rather than continuous, and long periods of European history yield no evidence of anti-Jewish violence. Even after oppression became more marked and the periodic explosions of physical abuse more frequent from the end of the eleventh century, relations between Jews and those among whom they lived normally remained more peaceful than not. Later antisemites, Hitler prominent among them, identified their forebears' lack of sustained, rational anti-Jewish action as one of the great historical failings of purely emotional Jew-hatred. When antisemitism entered the political culture of European states in the last decades of the nineteenth century, its exponents intended for it to remain in place until the battle against Jewry had been won, a struggle they expected would last years, possibly centuries. True to its activist origins, organized antisemitism has never altogether disappeared from the lives of many nations and peoples.

The need for activism was self-evident to those who identified themselves as antisemites. A radically altered relationship between Jews and non-Jews dictated that action against the Jewish enemy could no longer be random or sporadic. Jews had become too influential, too wealthy, too aggressive to be fought off with the occasional pogrom or ineffective restrictions on their freedom. Wilhelm Marr specifically warned his contemporaries that "A cultural and historical phenomenon like this is no soap bubble to be popped with a cheap 'Hep-Hep!'" (in Levy 1991, 82). What made disciplined and continuous action against Jewry so imperative was the conviction that Jews stood on the cusp of world domination. While Germans, Austrians, Frenchmen, and others had blithely gone about their business, Jews had been surreptitiously gathering strength, infiltrating key institutions, and undermining the values that had held communities together. No longer was the Jewish Question a matter of what to do about the Jews; it had become "What will the Jews do about us if their power goes unchecked?"

When this fantasy of enormous Jewish power became the possession of enough individuals to float a movement is difficult to pinpoint. Jonathan Karp calls attention to its harbingers as early as the seventeenth century, when Jews were seen by some as already able to exploit their international connections to obtain decisive economic leverage. But the more common view was one of contempt for a physically and morally inferior tribe of strangers. Even in antiquity, as Benjamin Isaac argues, they were often viewed as uniquely sinister, bizarre, and untrustworthy. During the Middle Ages they engaged in exploitative economic activities and became inextricably associated with the malign influence of money. They might even be tools of the devil. From the second century CE, Christian thinkers, according to Philip Cunningham, passionately rejected Judaism's claims to the truth; more than a thousand years later, in Ralph Keen's interpretation of the Reformation era, Christian anti-Judaism stemming from the Jews' repudiation of true messianic redemption still drew the boundaries between Jews and all Christian denominations. By modern times, the Jews' religion was for most of their neighbors no more than an exotic set of rituals, performed in outlandish languages and empty of true meaning. But this store of negativity notwithstanding, there is little evidence to suggest that before the last half of the nineteenth century many non-Jews considered Jews to be enormously powerful, the real masters of political, economic, and cultural life. The Hep-Hep Riots of 1819, the wave of central European pogroms that Marr referred to derisively, reflected the premodern conception of the Jews and the problems posed by their existence. Jews had to be kept within the traditional confines defined by centuries of separation and subordination. Talk of their emancipation, linked to the fear that they might gain rights and privileges they did not deserve, was enough to provoke a wave of popular violence against their property, but rarely their persons.

The Hep-Hep Riots can be considered a brief remedial action, meant to intimidate uppity Jews, reminding them with force about the limitations that

Conclusion: Not the Final Word 253

governed their lives. By the late nineteenth century, however, Marr was far from the only observer to recognize the inadequacy of such reactions to Jewish provocation. The relentless rise of the Jews in the course of the century fed the growing apprehension of their neighbors and overwhelmed the voice of reason. Sooner rather than later, every antisemitic movement drew its energy from a vastly exaggerated conception of Jewish power, now seen as so imperiling that it had to be fought to the bitter end. This belief in the power of the Jews, more than any other characteristic, set antisemitism apart from the centuries of Jew-hatred that preceded it. To this day it continues to differentiate antisemites from the casually prejudiced.

This is not to suggest that the earlier centuries of hatred and persecution were an inconsequential prelude to antisemitism. The negative stereotypes in theology, literature, the arts, and folklore made it axiomatic Jewish power would also be seen as threatening or, at the very least, highly improper. Christians and lapsed Christians still stood in the shadow of St. Augustine's doctrine of witness, analyzed by Alex Novikoff. Augustine taught that Jews should go on living but that their dispersed and degraded condition was fitting testimony to the superiority of the Christian faith. Jews thriving and triumphant rather than suffering and subservient violated a culturally embedded expectation. When Hungarians, at the close of the nineteenth century, noticed that half their physicians and nearly half their lawyers were Jews, many could not simply accept this as the well-earned reward for hard work by the sons of peddlers and petty traders. They knew the Jews too well to believe that nothing more than honest competition had produced such a result, and they also knew that something was ominously amiss in a world where this could happen. Jews and non-Jews, after all, did not meet at the end of the nineteenth century as open-minded neutrals, ready to form opinions about each other based on empirical observation. The dominant majority was already predisposed to see Jews as suspect, possibly dangerous, aliens. Antisemites went further, identifying them as agents of a multifarious evil, whom they were compelled to fight.

Before the nineteenth century, non-Jews had witnessed dramatic Jewish success stories, but these were the achievements of individuals, remarkable yet exceptional by their very nature; they caused wonderment, but their very rarity made them relatively unthreatening to the familiar order of existence. By contrast, dealing with what seemed like the unstoppable progress of a far-flung alien population group, no matter how exaggerated and immune to counter evidence this perception was, posed a particularly modern problem. To solve that problem required taking of action against Jewish power, using means that had not been earlier available or had not yet reached their full potential.

In the context of the late nineteenth century, this led almost everywhere into national politics and political organization. Where this option existed before the emergence of organized antisemitism, it had been at times employed effectively, as in the instance cited by William Rubinstein of the Jewish Naturalization Act

(Jew Bill of 1753) in England and the anti-Jewish agitation that overturned it. Where parliaments existed, they were places to air concerns about the possible negative consequences of Jewish emancipation, but while the arguments against it were grounded in the traditional anti-Jewish stereotypes, they normally did not voice concerns about Jews as already enormously powerful beings. With the emergence of organized antisemitism in the 1880s, parliamentary bodies assumed a different and far more significant role.

In Germany, Hungary, Austria, and France antisemites formed political parties, won a smattering of seats in the national, state, and municipal parliaments, and managed by these means to gain public attention for their cause. Although antisemites proved thoroughly ineffective legislators, failing in all their attempts to curb the rise of the Jews or to deliver on their many other promises, they could not be prevented from broadcasting their anti-Jewish message more widely and more effectively than ever before. National politics commanded the attention of citizens and magnified the importance of that message. The systematic politicalization of the Jewish Question ought to be seen, therefore, as another distinguishing facet of antisemitism, not to be found in earlier times.

Parliaments proved useful as tools of publicity, but mere notoriety did not often translate into political mobilization. Before the rise of the Nazis, the antisemitic parties in almost every instance failed to expand their followings, even after their dramatic appearances and promising debuts. As described in Chapter 8, many disappeared by 1914 or were on the point of doing so. However, formal political parties were not necessarily the best way to combat the enemy or spread knowledge of the cause. Another modern tool, not available to earlier antagonists of Jews, at least not in its fully developed form, was the mass media. Antisemitism is a prime example of a media-driven phenomenon, one that might not have survived without the constant diffusion of newspapers, cheap books, and caricatures.

It was not the antisemites' own newspapers that proved instrumental in this advance. They were mostly dismal failures, speaking only to the already committed and unable to compete with the mass circulation dailies. But the causes and concerns of antisemites became newsworthy, even for the more respectable national press; antisemites proved adept at making news, but they were obviously aided by the turmoil and near-constant crises of modern times, as well as the inherited suspicions about Jews so widely visible in the population. Modern press coverage decisively altered the dynamics of Jew-hatred. In bygone eras, without the press and other modern means of communication, outbreaks had remained localized. Violence could and did spread, although it often took months or years. The Hep-Hep Riots of 1819, for example, unfolded over two full months. Two generations later, the Dreyfus case, as Richard Golsan argues, quickly became a national and international, not a merely local, affair. It was sustained for years by avowedly antisemitic newspapers and by those whose

Conclusion: Not the Final Word   255

politics were more difficult to define. In the process, the public in France and beyond received a massive infusion of antisemitic rhetoric, graphic images, and conspiratorial theories. It was the press that also drove and made possible the first truly national pogrom in history. The Night of Broken Glass (November Pogrom), devastating to Jewish existence in Germany, took place in a single night in scores of locales, not as a slowly developing chain reaction of copycat riots, but as an orchestrated event, organized by telephone, interpreted, publicized, and fully exploited by the controlled press (Steinweis 2009). A comparison of the November Pogrom of 1938 to the waves of riots taking place over two years (1881–2) in the Russian empire, as appraised by Heinz-Dietrich Löwe, shows the augmented power of the media in fomenting antisemitic action, especially when governmentally directed.

Antisemitism, in summary, is best understood as a modern historical phenomenon. It owes much to the expressions of Jew-hatred in earlier centuries, borrowing from traditional anti-Jewish stereotypes to form the content of its ideology and adapting its many ancient accusations to fit modern conditions. Rather than creating radically new ways of thinking about Jews, antisemites interpreted current Jewish behavior in conformity with and according to culturally familiar patterns. This was the crucial contribution of the past to the theory and practice of antisemitism; antisemitism's prehistory, therefore, deserves the extended analysis it receives in this anthology.

However, modern antisemitism distinctly departed from historical precedent by insisting on the life-and-death necessity of organizing long-term, unremitting action against Jews. Antisemites were moved to act because they were passionately convinced that the power relations governing Jews and non-Jews for nearly two millennia had been reversed. Jews had already achieved a terrifying degree of power over non-Jews and were now closing in on ultimate victory. This being so, it was imperative for antisemites to institutionalize their struggle in parties, propaganda associations, newspapers, learned journals, and grassroots reform clubs, employing every modern means at their disposal, the better to act in a sustained and disciplined way against the most ruthless of enemies. As Wilhelm Marr depicted it, this was a war decreed by Nature itself (Levy 1991, 77–9).

* * *

But why the Jews? Antisemites, once again, had a glib answer for this question. Jews, and Jews alone, have engendered antisemitism wherever they have entered history. They were hated by all peoples they lived among—and rightly so! Fond of the "where there's smoke, there's fire" cliché, antisemites thought that the lengthy history of Jew-hatred in and of itself proved their point. Can it have been just bad luck that so many different peoples in so many places lashed out against Jews?

Once again, a simplistic response to a by-no-means simple problem. The record of Jewish communities in India and China seems to have been conflict-free, producing very little "history." Until relatively recently, the treatment of Jews in the Muslim world, in terms of political status, legal discrimination, and occasional violence, was not much different from that met with by other non-believers. As Norman Stillman recounts, Jews have usually been marginal to the major concerns of Islamic civilization. They were of peripheral importance to its theologians, thinkers, and public figures. The endless fascination with their allegedly harmful traits and enthrallment with their nefarious conspiracies are far more typical of the Christian West than of Islam before the twentieth century.

Leaving aside the tendency of antisemites to convince themselves of what they have a great stake in believing, the implicit question is legitimate: what, if anything, did actual Jewish behavior have to do with engendering antisemitism? A legitimate question but also emotionally fraught. When raised in the larger context of overall responsibility for the development of political antisemitism in the late nineteenth century and in full knowledge of the Nazi genocide, the mere broaching of the question of Jewish responsibility has provoked angry reactions. Many observers, Jews and non-Jews, have responded that antisemitism has absolutely nothing to do with the actions or attitudes of real Jews, that it is a Gentile problem. One will learn nothing of value about Jews by listening to antisemites, and that even to suggest otherwise is to blame the victim and give comfort to the enemy.

One trouble with such a formulation is that it implicitly invites us not to think in any serious way about the purposes, functions, practitioners, promoters, or even the content of Jew-hatred. Antisemites and at least a portion of their victims would not see the point of the present anthology. As far as they are concerned, the questions have all been answered—or should not be asked in the first place. Yet, perched precariously between these two sterile extremes can be found those who hope to achieve a more rational grasp of the problem: why did Jews become the targets of mass movements dedicated to their ruin? And what, if anything, in their conduct can account for this response? (For example, Todd Endelman in Berger 1986, III–12.)

Obviously, any generalization that purports to describe the behavior of the totality of Jews is bound to collapse under close scrutiny. Never in their history have they been without deep divisions in every one of the vital concerns of Jewish life. By the time political antisemitism appeared in Europe, "Jewry" embraced extraordinarily variegated groupings, many at war with one another. The monolithic construct of the Jews, so essential to the worldview of antisemites, simply did not and does not exist. It describes no reality. To speak of the responsibility of the Jews, therefore, instead of individual Jews, justly raises the suspicion that prejudice is at work.

On the other hand, this may be too easy a refutation of the proposition that Jews in particular times or places have had something to do with provoking strong reactions to their behavior, real or alleged. It ignores or unfairly designates all generalized criticism of Jews as overtly or, even worse, covertly antisemitic,

Conclusion: Not the Final Word 257

even when it comes from people who denounce the antisemites, reject their programmatic solutions of the Jewish Question, and have a record of championing Jewish rights. Because it can easily be shown that some or many Jews did not behave the way antisemites claim all Jews act does not mean that the charges are worthy of no serious attention. Jewish behavior in general may be an empty abstraction, but there is nonetheless the behavior of a sufficiently large number of Jews to make a case that they are in some sense responsible for given social, cultural, political, or economic ills. Seeing a connection between a poorly defined Jewishness and the behavior of large numbers of Jews may be unfair, but it is not always, and from every source, the product of blind malice. Adam Sutcliffe's caution that Jewish–Gentile relations ought not be reduced to a friend-or-foe pattern but rather be seen as one of "ambivalent complexity" is particularly apt in this context. Ethnic generalizations are notoriously imprecise, unjust, and ought, in a perfect world, be outlawed, but they are the common currency of social discourse, including that of Jews as well as non-Jews. It is not automatically a sign of antisemitism to attempt a critical evaluation of the behavior of Jews in general, even if the evaluation cannot take every individual exception into account—and even if the outcome of such assessment betrays irritation or censoriousness. After all, no other ethnic groups, whether subjected to violence and hatred or not, get an exemption from the generalizing tendencies of others.

The contention that Jews are totally innocent of the accusations leveled against them has led to the only conception of antisemitism that such a view can support: Jews have been the victims of scapegoating throughout their history. Every new visitation of infamy is thus seen as a link in the long chain of such instances, differing only in scale and in the particular agents of doom. Many religiously observant Jews find it somehow comforting to think of antisemitism as eternal and unchanging, giving their suffering of the moment its place in a sad but familiar continuum. By denying any Jewish responsibility, even an inadvertent one, for the wrath of the Gentiles, they seem not to realize the danger that their suffering may be trivialized. As Hannah Arendt asked a half-century ago, why could not any group serve equally well as the eternal scapegoat? (5). Why only the Jews, especially if, as must be maintained, it makes no difference what Jews actually do? The more secularly inclined can also indulge in a blanket denial of connections between what Jews do and the hostility they experience. They speak of the mob's displaced social protest or the projection of guilt onto a culturally available (Jewish) target, or they declare enmity to be the symptom of some psychic illness, again having nothing to do with Jews. Although devoid of theology, such explanations still hinge on the Jew as a scapegoat, the idea now poorly disguised in social scientific garb, but equally unable to answer the question, "Why the Jews?" (Langmuir 1990, 322).

The overblown generalizations of the antisemites invite total dismissal of their charges. Yet a great many Europeans who cannot fairly be described as antisemitic—including many, as mentioned in the Introduction, who are considered heroes to

258   *Albert S. Lindemann and Richard S. Levy*

most Jews—thought of Jews as the cause of one disturbing development or another. Unless one sees a mysterious mass psychosis at work, as opposed to widely varying degrees of anti-Jewish prejudice, the problem remains: why were early indictments like those of Wilhelm Marr, Edouard Drumont, and Georg von Schönerer so widely believed or found creditable at all? Certainly, there was evidence "against the Jews," at least as far as some individuals and population groups were concerned, especially if one is not too fastidious about the term "evidence."

Several Jews had been prominent among those who defrauded gullible investors in the Crash of 1873. In Vienna and Berlin, Jews created the mass circulation daily newspaper, putting many old-style journalists out of work, who then blamed the Jewish-run press for coarsening political discourse and exerting an unhealthy influence over public opinion. In central Europe Jews owned department stores that put small retailers out of business—and, some thought, made women into slaves of ever-changing fashion. Jews were often strongly overrepresented in the leadership of subversive movements, especially in Imperial Russia, and then as agents of the Comintern. One could easily find Jewish names prominently involved in the white-slavery trade, in pornography, and organizations calling for changes in sexual mores—endeavors bound to offend a great many people. But, of course, this is a selective reading of the evidence. More Jews were victims of the Crash of 1873 than its beneficiaries. The overwhelming majority of Jews abhorred and feared the Bolsheviks. Department stores were a boon to consumers, and masses of daily newspaper readers learned about the wider world concerning which they had no other access. Why this counter evidence had relatively little effect on the attitudes of many non-Jews is central to the larger question being discussed here.

Taking into consideration the difficulty of establishing or debunking the reality of antisemitic charges and nonetheless attempting to account for a popular movement that was propelled by these charges, most historians resort to an argument based on plausibility. After all, neither statistics nor objective social reality nor careful sifting of the data was what mattered most in bringing the Jewish Question into the arena of political agitation. Perception—subjective, conditioned, anecdotal, and by nature imprecise—counted for a great deal in the creation of the political movement targeting Jews. It may have been unjust or exaggerated for Gentile Germans, Russians, or Frenchmen to see Jews as an inimical force in their nations, but was it wholly implausible? There are many possible answers to this question. That none of them are completely satisfying suggests plausibility as an interpretive tool, valuable though it is, ought to be applied with care.

Plausibility, not philosophically complicated definitions of truth, helps most people navigate through the world. But the word can be made to bear a great load of subjectivity, and, even when used honestly, it falls far short of *rationally certain, objectively true, empirically verifiable*. The distance between what most

Conclusion: Not the Final Word 259

people regard as plausible and what can be proved to be true can be great, indeed. To be fair, part of the explanation for the general rush to judgment against Jews, promoted by organized antisemitism and observable from the 1870s, had to do with a lack of sophistication in the handling of evidence at all levels of society. The techniques of critical evaluation were not the common possession of populations that had relatively little experience of political discourse and suddenly found themselves bombarded by rhetoric of all sorts, and not just about the Jewish Question. Looking back from our vantage point to the 1870s, we can see how easily some of the newly enfranchised convinced themselves of the plausibility of anti-Jewish attacks, especially when they conformed to expectations, prejudices, or interests. With only a little prompting, too many were able to find plausibility wherever they wished.

There is another objection to putting too much explanatory weight on the plausibility of Jewish guilt in the eyes of the public. It is patronizing (as well as exculpating). Would it have seriously overtaxed the intelligence of ordinary newspaper readers to have expected them to come to the reasonable conclusion that Jews did not control all the money in the world? Evidence to the contrary was available and abundant. Why did more of them not see that along with the Rothschilds and Warburgs there were also Morgans and Carnegies and "Jews without money" all around them? Did Lithuanian militiamen, when murdering grandmothers, rabbis, infants, and other innocents in 1941, really find it plausible that they were striking a blow against Judeo-Bolshevism? These examples, representative of countless others, indicate some of the limits of the plausibility argument. That ordinary people were so easily persuaded had less to do with plausibility or the documented misdeeds of Jews than with the deep felt need to have prejudices vindicated. Plausibility was assessed through a filter of preconceived notions concerning Jews that were too firmly established to be easily shaken off or even much troubled by contrary evidence. Jewish evil may well have been plausible to a great many people, but it should not have been.

* * *

In closing, it is useful to ask what the history of Jew-hatred and antisemitism surveyed here has to tell us about the future. Historians are notoriously poor fortune tellers. The variables and the imponderables they deal with, their imperfect understanding of past and present, argue in favor of humility when plotting the prospects of our subject.

At least in the West in the twenty-first century, institutionalized antisemitism advancing programmatic solutions of the Jewish Question has become harder and harder to find. Organizations surviving into the present labor in obscurity, without the customary platforms or step-by-step processes promising to disempower the Jews. The eliminationist or operational aspects of classical antisemitism—dismantling of legal safeguards, segregation, expulsion, murder— seem to have evaporated. Although long familiar antisemitic defamations are still diffused through newspapers, books, graphic images, verbal and written

260   *Albert S. Lindemann and Richard S. Levy*

insults, the few still functioning groups devote themselves to the education of their neighbors about the Jewish peril, their hopes of defeating Jewish power put off to an eschatological future. One hears little these days from the Institute of Historical Review (the Holocaust deniers' node). The American Nazi Party operates out of a PO box in Westlake, Michigan. British poets, Italian cartoonists, Portuguese Nobel laureates, and academics from many lands have compared Nazis and Jews, Palestine and Auschwitz, but then they go back to their regular jobs. Their criticism is not clearly part of a larger program calling for the disempowerment of "World Jewry"; they are not the spokesmen for antisemitic organizations. Most, in fact, angrily deny any sympathy for antisemitism. Those who have no such scruples, for example, David Irving, Matt Hale, and Ernst Zündel are in and out of prison. David Duke, accused of defrauding his own supporters, received an honorary doctorate in history from the Interregional Academy of Personnel Management of the Ukraine but otherwise seems doomed to wander about Europe and the Middle East. Yet prudence counsels against a premature celebration of antisemitism's demise. Acts of terror by radical rightists are still committed in its name, and Jews can still be numbered among their victims.

Some students of antisemitism see no grounds for optimism at all. The Internet, they warn, has changed everything. Its instant accessibility and global reach have handed antisemites unimaginably larger audiences than ever before. Communication is now so swift and simple that they do not need cumbersome organizational structures or terrestrial addresses in order to recruit new followers and carry the war to the enemy. This, however, may be too alarmist a view of the Internet's potential as a political weapon. It may well serve antisemites, but it serves their opponents just as well and perhaps better. The most widely circulated antisemitic text of all time, the *Protocols of the Elders of Zion*—the fabricated account of an arcane Jewish conspiracy to enslave the Gentile world, many times debunked but seemingly immortal—is downloadable in many versions from the Internet. Devotees have long known where to get it. But those who have merely heard of the document and who have not decided one way or another about the Jewish Question might, it is feared, be inclined to seek it out and have their minds poisoned in the process. A curious person, conducting an Internet keyword search of "*Protocols of the Elders of Zion*" will be confronted by approximately 200,000 hits. Seven of the ten sites displayed on the first page of results, he or she will soon discover, are devoted to exposing and explaining the myth, the fraudulent nature of the document, the motives of its promulgators, its plagiarized sources, and destructive historical impact. Antisemites using the Internet may find it easier and cheaper to get their message out but only at the cost of having it contested, their claims contradicted, and their immediate access to would-be followers effectively interrupted. The Internet may not, in fact, be the powerful tool of mobilization that many fear. Just possibly, it may inoculate the curious rather than infect them.

Conclusion: Not the Final Word   261

If traditional organized antisemitism as developed and practiced by Europeans and their offspring is not dead, it seems certainly to be in eclipse. Its decline has gone almost unnoticed, however, because the vacuum it is in the process of leaving behind has been more than filled by antisemitism in the Muslim world, including the Islamic Diaspora in Europe. Antisemitism's future, it seems likely, will unfold there. In recent years, the verbal and physical assaults on Jews disturbing the peace in Europe appear to have few local causes. In this respect, there is far less evidence to support a plausibility thesis than there was in the 1870s or 1920s. The best explanation for the upsurge in antisemitism in a number of European countries, whether a long-term trend or simply an episode, is to be found in the politics of the Middle East, with the Israeli-Palestinian conflict at its center.

The desecration of Jewish cemeteries and synagogues, defacing graffiti, and attack on Jews in Europe are hardly new phenomena. What is new are the major perpetrators of these deeds. The acts of violence in most European countries and the rising incidence of hate crimes there directed against Jews have been carried out mostly by Muslim youths, the exception being, interestingly, Germany where it is still largely the province of neo-Nazis, skinheads, and radical rightists (http://www.tau.ac.il/Anti-Semitism/statistics/statistics.htm). How much of this is simple thuggery and how much of it is ideologically inspired is difficult to measure. The anger, desperation, and disaffection of young Muslims in Parisian suburbs have obvious sociological and economic roots. It is harder to explain their frequent targeting of Jews, however, without referencing a raw antisemitic ideology disseminated by radical clerics and reinforced by Arab-language media. The violence seems hit or miss, lacking organization, without any clear agenda designed to disempower the Jews. It is nonetheless threatening to develop the infrastructure that might make it more effective.

Antisemitism's shift in gravity from the Christian West to the Muslim world carries with it a number of disturbingly unique features. As Doris Bergen shows with regard to the Third Reich, antisemitism's potential for harm is vastly enhanced when it is organized by government. Not only can the regime marshal the resources of the state against Jews at home and abroad, but it can legitimize and promote the anti-Jewish behavior of ordinary citizens, making them into antisemites in effect, even if they normally give little thought to the Jewish Question. When antisemites received the open or tacit support of government for their endeavors in Hungary, Lithuania, Poland, and elsewhere during the 1920s and 1930s, they were able to realize long-held ambitions, disenfranchising and impoverishing whole Jewish communities. In Nazi-dominated Europe, they were able to perpetrate genocide. Throughout the history of organized antisemitism in Europe, state support for its goals and methods was intermittent and in many places non-existent, even in the worst of times. The overt and sustained support accorded antisemitism by governments in the Muslim world is, in pronounced contrast, the rule rather than the exception. The importance of this fact is difficult to overstress.

262   *Albert S. Lindemann and Richard S. Levy*

In fact, as Litvak and Webman document persuasively, antisemitic indoctrination of ordinary Muslims has been largely the work of the secular and religious elite, including the political leadership. This, too, departs from the historical pattern. In Europe, small and usually marginal political groups attempted to disseminate their message and fashion a constituency. Boosted by crises of one kind or another, they were sometimes able to move from the fringe to the center of political life, gathering to their cause highly placed backers or cynical opportunists. Even in Germany, however, the antisemites themselves were most conscious of their inability to reach out to a mass following, let alone to convert ordinarily prejudiced fellow-citizens into active antisemites. In stark contrast, there is considerable evidence suggesting that indoctrination of "the man in the street" in many parts of the Muslim world has succeeded to a degree unprecedented in the history of organized antisemitism. The record of the *Protocols of the Elders of Zion* in the Muslim world will help clarify this point.

For the first time in its hundred-year history, the *Protocols* is far more likely to be printed, quoted, and deployed for political purposes in the Middle East and in the Islamic Diaspora than in Europe or the Americas. Starting in the 1950s, the leaders of Egypt, Kuwait, Saudi Arabia, and Syria sponsored Arabic translations of the text and then oversaw their extensive distribution. Their motives were transparent. The book served as an alibi, the reason for defeat at the hands of the Israelis or numerous other policy failures; these were the fault of a world-wide Jewish conspiracy. It was not just Israel but all-powerful world Jewry, whose capacity for evil was depicted in the *Protocols*, that waged war against Islam. Governments and authoritative figures thus gave their official blessing to this fraud. As the *Protocols* retreated out of the mainstream in the West, Muslim leaders and movements with and without state resources at their command took up the slack. In 2003, Mahathir Mohamad, prime minister of Malaysia, dissociated himself from Henry Ford's version of the *Protocols* even as his own party distributed free copies. Article 32 of the Hamas Charter directly cites the *Protocols* as proof of a Zionist imperialist plan of conquest "from the Nile to the Euphrates." Even in its American and European heyday in the 1920s and 1930s, when the *Protocols* achieved a sizable following and won influential promoters, it never enjoyed the nearly universal approval of state and religious authority, or of the political and intellectual elites, that it now has in the Middle East.

Historically, the *Protocols of the Elders of Zion* has always been somewhat limited in its effectiveness as a tool of mass mobilization. It has been cited and used as an authority by leaders of the mob but rarely read by the mob itself. It is a difficult and unrewarding read, it must be said, full of esoteric material and obscure references that have very little meaning for ordinary people. Arab-language television has overcome this hindrance with the 41-episode *Knight without a Horse*, loosely but recognizably based on the *Protocols*. The dramatization makes few intellectual demands upon its audience while beaming the message of Jewish conspiracy directly into Arab homes. The *Diaspora*, a more

Conclusion: Not the Final Word 263

recent Syrian-produced series, depicts Jews engaged in an elaborate plot to subjugate the entire world; it has been rerun numerous times in recent years on Arab-language satellite TV and has been aired by *Hizballah* in Iran, and in 2006, during Ramadan, on Jordanian TV, to what was estimated to be a very large audience. The series presents itself as an accurate and factual account of the "Secret Zionist World Government," whose members caused the Russian Revolution, the world wars, encouraged the Nazi murder of Jews, and engineered the use of atomic bombs on Japan. Such programming, government sanctioned in most every case, makes antisemitic imagery and the familiar claims about Jewish malevolence effortlessly, entertainingly available.

With few Muslim voices raised against the irrationality of antisemitism and a growing sense of grievance among the billion who follow the faith, with an ever more sophisticated media prepared to saturate the public with anti-Jewish imagery as never before, with the tacit or overt support of the leadership elite for many forms of Jew-hatred, it is difficult to believe that antisemitism will any time soon be overcome.

RECOMMENDED READINGS

Arendt, Hannah, *The Origins of Totalitarianism* (New York: Meridian Books, 1951).

Berger, David (ed.), *History and Hate: The Dimensions of Anti-Semitism* (Philadelphia: Jewish Publication Society of America, 1986).

Katz, Jacob, "Misreadings of Anti-Semitism," *Commentary* (July 1983): 39–44.

Langmuir, Gavin I., *Toward a Definition of Antisemitism* (Berkeley: University of California Press, 1990).

Levy, Richard S. (ed.), *Antisemitism in the Modern World: An Anthology of Texts* (Lexington, MA: D. C. Heath, 1991).

Massing, Paul W., *Rehearsal for Destruction: A Study of Political Anti-Semitism in Imperial Germany* (New York: Harper, 1949).

Steinweis, Alan, *Kristallnacht 1938* (Cambridge MA: Belknap Press of Harvard University Press, 2009).

Volkov, Shulamit, *Germans, Jews, and Antisemites: Trials in Emancipation* (Cambridge: Cambridge University Press, 2006).

Glossary of Terms

Abraham   Biblical character (*c.*2000 BCE) revered as the first patriarch, chosen by God, and father of the Hebrew people through Isaac (son) and Jacob (grandson); revered also by Muslims.

Adversus Iudaeos or *Adversus Judaeos*   A genre of Christian polemical writings specifically directed against Jews and Judaism, originating in the first century and continuing into modern times.

Alexandria   Major city in ancient times on the Egyptian coast, founded by Alexander the Great; long a cultural center for both Jews and Greeks, especially famous for its library. Site of anti-Jewish riots in 38 CE.

Amalek (Amalekites)   Arch foe of Israel, one whose memory should be obliterated; the Amalekites attacked the Israelites as they were wandering in the wilderness and remained their foes to the time of the Kingdom of David.

Anti-Zionism   Both a principled rejection of the central tenets of Zionism, in particular that Jews represent a separate people with rights to their own sovereign state, and the much more broadly applied opposition to all things Jewish—has become a synonym for antisemitism.

Ashkenazim   Collective designation for the Jews of western, central, and, later, eastern Europe; Yiddish remained the lingua franca of the majority of the Ashkenazim into the nineteenth century. See Sephardim.

Aryan and *Aryan race*   Once used neutrally to describe common language groups, *Aryan*, when combined with *race*, became a political concept. The Nazis, who claimed superiority of the Aryan race, never adequately defined it, and the term proved extremely elastic in its application.

Augustine of Hippo   See *Doctrine of the Jewish Witness*.

Auto-da-fé (in Portuguese) or *auto-de-fee* (in Spanish)   Literally "act of faith"; the public performance of penance for heretics condemned by the Inquisition. In popular usage (and inaccurately), this usually involved burning at the stake.

Balfour Declaration (November 1917)   Formal pronouncement named for the then foreign secretary, Lord Balfour, stated that the British government "view[ed] with favor the establishment in Palestine of a national home for the Jewish people, ... it being clearly understood that nothing shall be done which may prejudice the civil and religious rights of existing non-Jewish communities in Palestine."

Bar Kokhba Revolt (132–6 CE)   Last of the Jewish revolts against Roman rule. Although initially successful, it was eventually crushed. Jews mourn the failure of the revolt on Tisha B'Av at the Western Wall.

Glossary of Terms 265

BCE   "Before the Common Era"; term preferred by many writers, as distinguished from BC ("Before Christ"). Similarly, CE ("Common Era") is preferred to AD ("Anno Domini," "year of Our Lord"), by non-Christians.

Black Hundreds   See *Union of the Russian People.*

Blood Libel   See *Ritual Murder.*

Bolshevik (Bolshevism)   Initially a faction of the Russian Social Democratic Workers' Party ("bolshevik" = "majoritarian"), finally broke away completely and in 1919 adopted the name "Communist" after assuming power in Russia in the autumn of 1917; differed from Western Marxist or social democratic parties by a stronger emphasis on elitist-dictatorial rule.

Bund, Jewish (All-Russian Jewish Workers' Party)   Founded in Vilna in 1897, it championed Jewish autonomy in eastern Europe, a pronouncedly secular Yiddish culture, and socialism. It was staunchly anti-Zionist.

Canaan (Canaanites)   Land (and peoples) in ancient times between the Jordan River and the Mediterranean, from Syria to Egypt; conquered by Joshua and the Israelites; special warnings against the "idolatrous" people of this land and prohibitions in their regard (e.g., intermarriage) become part of Judaism.

Canon Law   Originally signifying a law passed by a church council, has become the body of ecclesiastical legislation by which various churches are governed.

CE   See *BCE.*

Chmielnicki Massacres (1648–54)   Killing of thousands of Jews accompanied the rebellion against the landlords of the Polish-Lithuanian Commonwealth, led by Bogdan Chmielnicki, the military commander of the Zaporozhian Cossacks.

Christian Social(ism)   Number of movements, notably in Germany and Austria, that tried to reconcile Christian ethics and modern laissez-faire economics; it frequently resorted to antisemitic cures for social-economic problems.

Church Councils   "Legally convened assemblies of ecclesiastical dignitaries and theological experts for the purpose of discussing and regulating matters of church doctrine and discipline" (*Catholic Encyclopedia*). The first council took place in Nicaea in 325.

Circumcision   Religious rite widely practiced by both Jews and Muslims entailing removal of the foreskin from the penis.

Civic Improvement of the Jews, On the (1781)   Classic of the German Enlightenment, written by Christian Wilhelm von Dohm; it advocated the emancipation of the Jews as a measure to improve their ability to exercise the rights and responsibilities of modern citizenship.

266 *Glossary of Terms*

Conversos   "New Christians," converts from Judaism (Marranos) or Islam (Moriscos) in fourteenth- and fifteenth-century Iberia. Both were often suspected of continuing to practice their original religions in secret.

Court Jews   Making use of family and international connections to other Jews, acted as financiers, provisioners, and diplomats for nobles and princes during the seventeenth and eighteenth centuries. They and their dependents enjoyed a privileged status, were exempted from the harsh restrictions placed on the general Jewish population, and sometimes amassed great personal wealth.

Crusades   Series of campaigns between the eleventh and fourteenth centuries to recover the Holy Land from the Muslims; the Crusaders at times attacked Jewish communities in Europe.

Deicide   Literally, "god killing," the accusation that Jews, in the Crucifixion of Christ, tried to kill God and retained a fanatical hatred of Christ's followers. See also *Host Desecration*.

Diaspora   From the Greek for *scattering*; the dispersion of Jews outside ancient Israel, dating from their first exile to Babylonia in the sixth century BCE. See *Galut*.

Dietary Laws (Kashrut)   Body of laws governing what is fitting for Jews to eat (kosher), originating in the Book of Leviticus and elaborated upon by rabbinic authorities over the centuries. The explanation for various prohibitions remains unclear and has been subject of ongoing debates.

Doctrine of Jewish Witness   Influential argument advanced by Augustine of Hippo at the end of the fourth century that said Jews and Judaism should be allowed to survive in the Christian world in order to bear witness, in their debased state, to the superior truth of Christianity.

Dreyfus Affair   Protracted case involving a Jewish officer of the French general staff, Alfred Dreyfus, who was convicted, partly on the basis of dubious evidence, of selling military secrets to Germany (1894). The struggle to obtain justice for him ultimately resulted in his exoneration and rehabilitation in 1906, but France remained passionately divided among Dreyfusards and anti-Dreyfusards.

Dual (or Austro-Hungarian) Monarchy   Formed in 1867, combining Austrian and Hungarian lands under the Habsburg Emperor (Kaiser), Franz Joseph; dissolved in 1919.

Emancipation, Jewish   Freeing of Europe's Jews from a multitude of legal restrictions on movement, habitation, and occupation, taking well over a century in some countries, during which time the pros and cons of bestowing equality of status on them were vigorously debated. Whether to integrate the Jews into modern societies, as well as how to go about doing so, became the substance of the "Jewish Question."

Glossary of Terms 267

Esau   Biblical figure, brother of Jacob, son of Rebecca and Isaac, considered the archetypical non-Jew, forefather of the Other Nations (goyim).

Final Solution (of the Jewish Question)   Nazi euphemism for the genocide of the Jews.

Freemasonry   Widespread international humanitarian association dedicated to the advancement of enlightened ideas, tolerance, and cooperation. Secular Jews were attracted to it, and it became an object of suspicion. Freemasons have alternately been accused of using Jews for nefarious purposes, or being used by them as pawns in a world conspiracy aimed at Jewish domination.

Galut   Hebrew term for "exile" or Diaspora, the dispersal of the Jews from their Promised Land. See *Zionism.*

Gentile   From related Greek and Roman words, roughly equivalent to the Hebrew *goy* (nation or people).

Ghetto   Compulsory, segregated, and enclosed Jewish quarters; term originated in Venice from the early sixteenth century, although voluntary and involuntary walled and gated areas for Jewish habitation were known well before this time.

Goy (pl. goyim)   Hebrew for "nation" (or, in the plural, "the Other Nations"), the rough equivalent of "Gentile" or non-Jew.

Haman   Villain of the Book of Esther and the holiday of Purim; associated with the Amalekites and came to symbolize the most extreme antisemites into modern times.

Hamas   ("Zeal" in Arabic) a politico-religious organization founded in Gaza at the time of the First Intifada (1987). Its charter calls for the elimination of the state of Israel and declares that its struggle against that state is "extremely wide-ranging and grave."

Hasidism   Pietistic movement of Jewish orthodoxy originating in the second half of the eighteenth century in eastern Europe.

Hebraism, Christian   Study of the Hebrew language by Christians, often under the guidance of Jewish scholars, stimulated by the Renaissance and Reformation interest in original texts.

Hizballah (Party of God), also Hizbollah   Shiite organization providing social, educational, and medical services in Lebanon, where it arose in response to Israel's invasion in 1982. It has been condemned as a practitioner and supporter of terrorism.

Holocaust Denial, Negationism, and Revisionism   Efforts to deny that the Holocaust occurred or to diminish radically the number of Jews who were killed during it. These claims are linked to the charge that the Holocaust is a hoax perpetrated by Jews to manipulate non-Jews. Few if any reputable scholars pay serious attention to these efforts, but a few prominent figures in Europe, on both

268   *Glossary of Terms*

the political Right and Left, have been attracted to denying or radically revising accepted accounts of the Holocaust. In Arab and Islamic lands Holocaust denial is far more widely accepted.

Host Desecration   From the thirteenth century, the allegation that Jews (as well as other unbelievers) stole the holy wafer, tortured, defiled, and mocked it, thus symbolically reenacting the Crucifixion. Such accusations often resulted in trials, executions, and expulsions.

Inquisition   Office of the Latin Christian Church charged with the investigation and elimination of heterodox beliefs; the Inquisition was especially active against Jews, *conversos*, and Judaizing tendencies (usually having to do with the denial of Christ's divinity) within the church during the fifteenth and sixteenth centuries in the Iberian peninsula and the New World.

International Jew, The (1920–2)   Set of pamphlets published as an inexpensive four-volume book under the auspices of the American automobile maker, Henry Ford; did much to popularize and legitimize the *Protocols of the Elders of Zion*. Its German translation played a significant role in Nazi antisemitic propaganda efforts, and its Arabic translation is now widely distributed in the Middle East.

Intifada   From the Arabic, meaning "shaking off," though its more familiar meaning in English is "uprising" or "resistance to tyranny." Its most familiar applications are to the First Intifada, a Palestinian uprising against Israeli rule from 1987 to 1993; and the Second Intifada, beginning in September 2000.

Isaac   Biblical figure, one of the Patriarchs, son of Abraham, father of Esau and Jacob.

Jacob   Biblical figure, son of Isaac and Rebecca, twin brother of Esau, assumed the name "Israel" and is considered the forefather of the Jews or Israelites.

Jews and Their Lies, On the *(1543)*   Martin Luther's most influential antisemitic work. Its call for confiscation of Jewish property, forced labor for Jews, or expulsion recommended the work to the Nazis, who made it widely available during the Third Reich.

Joshua   Biblical figure, appointed by Moses as his successor, commander of the Israelites in their conquest of Canaan.

Judaizing   See *Inquisition*.

Judeo-Bolshevism   Assertion that communism is a tool of the Jews, part of their conspiracy to gain world domination. The large number and prominence of Jews in the Communist parties of most European countries, especially Soviet Russia, fed this accusation.

Kabbalah   Mystical form of Judaism with ancient roots and religio-racist elements. Among its many schools of interpretation, the most important is devoted to the teachings of Rabbi Isaac Luria (1534–72).

Glossary of Terms 269

Kielce Pogrom   Deadliest in postwar Poland, took place on July 4, 1946, when townspeople attacked Jewish survivors of the Holocaust who had returned to their homes; motives are still a matter of dispute, but charges of ritual murder played a role in the killing of at least 36 Jews, and inaction on the part of the authorities contributed to the toll.

Konitz Ritual Murder   With the help of professional antisemites, suspicion in the murder of a high-school student in this small German town in March 1900 soon focused on the resident Jews. The subsequent investigation and trial of the town's kosher butcher led to the most serious bout of civil violence in the history of the German empire. Troops had to be summoned to restore order.

Kosher slaughtering   See *Shekhita*.

Kristallnacht   See *Night of Broken Glass*.

Lateran Council, Fourth (1215)   Definitive statement on Jewish status in the Middle Ages. The Great Council convened by Pope Innocent III strictly regulated Jewish money-lending, decreed distinctive dress for Jews, and forbade them to appear in public during Christian holidays. Jews were also prohibited from exercising authority over Christians.

Manetho   Egyptian priest and historian, writing from the late fourth to early third century BCE. He provided a counter-narrative of the Egyptian Captivity. His works are known only through references in the writings of later authors.

Marrano   ("Pig" in Spanish), applied in the Iberian Peninsula to New Christians or *conversos* who continued to practice Judaism in secret (crypto-Jews). The equivalent for the Muslims was *Morisco* ("little Moor" in Spanish).

Matzos   "Bread of affliction" used in the Passover ceremony to commemorate the flight from Egypt.

Mein Kampf (My Struggle)   Hitler's account of his life, dictated while in prison in 1924 and published in two parts in 1925 and 1926. Although extraordinarily widely circulated, the book is often referred to as an example of the unread bestseller.

Merchant of Venice   See *Shylock*.

National Socialist German Workers' Party (NSDAP, or Nazi Party)   Hitler's vehicle to power, grew from humble beginnings after World War I to number over 8.5 million members by 1945. It sought to control every aspect of its members' lives, from the cradle to the grave, and remold their outlooks.

Neo-Nazism   Broadly applied designation for post-World War II groups and movements seeking to revive all or some of Nazism's ideological tenets—fascism, antisemitism, racism, white supremacy, etc.

Night of Broken Glass (Reichskristallnacht)   A nationwide pogrom staged by Hitler's stormtroopers on the night of November 9–10, 1938. Its name derives

270 *Glossary of Terms*

from the smashing of thousands of Jewish-owned shop windows. Two hundred fifty synagogues were set afire, 91 Jews were killed, and nearly 30,000 Jewish men were sent to concentration camps.

NSDAP See *National Socialist German Workers' Party.*

Numerus Clausus (quota system) Limitation of Jewish students to a fixed percentage of college, university, and professional school enrollments. It was, officially or unofficially in effect in many countries, including the United States, in the nineteenth and twentieth centuries.

Nuremberg Laws 1935 Set of laws that disenfranchised German Jews making them into state subjects rather than citizens; it outlawed sexual relations between Aryans and non-Aryans, and, in successive supplementary decrees, attempted to provide a legal definition of who was a Jew (mostly in terms of ancestry).

Orthodox As it pertains to Jews, those who rejected Reform Judaism in the nineteenth century, insisting on strict adherence to what was believed were traditional practices and beliefs. For Christians the term refers to the Eastern Orthodox faith (Greek and Russian branches), differing from Catholicism most notably by rejecting the authority of the Roman pontiff.

Ostjuden (East European Jews) Pejorative label for Jewish immigrants from Yiddish-speaking eastern Europe. East European Jews, fleeing poverty and oppression, were regarded as repellant or subversive figures; they were the target of ardent anti-immigration propaganda wherever they appeared in significant numbers.

Pale of Settlement Western areas of the Russian Empire in which permanent settlement of Russia's Jews was legally confined and in which the majority of Europe's Jews lived. "Pale" in this instance means "fence" (cf. palisade) or border. Most of the Pale of Settlement included areas taken by Russia in the partitions of Poland in the late eighteenth century (illustrated in maps pp. x, xi).

Pan-Germanism Racist-nationalist ideology embraced by parties and pressure groups in Germany and Austria that demanded the uniting of all German-speakers in Europe into one state.

Pharaoh God-king of ancient Egypt; Rameses II may have been the (second) pharaoh of the account in the Book of Exodus (13th–14th century BCE).

Philosemitism Interest in and respect for aspects of Jewish culture, religion, or history; in principle the opposite of antisemitism, although the charge has often been made that many figures known to history as philosemitic in fact harbored antisemitic sentiments.

Pogrom Russian for "riot" or "destruction." The word became widely familiar in Western Europe and the United States because of the riots against Jews in Russia from the 1880s to the early 1920s, although it was (and is still) used for riots against other minorities.

Glossary of Terms

271

Protocols of the Elders of Zion   First published in Russia in 1903; describes an arcane Jewish-Masonic conspiracy directed toward the enslavement of non-Jews. Purporting to be a series of twenty-four protocols in which a mythical Chief Sage of Zion lays out the philosophy and method of the conspiracy, this widely circulated and frequently translated work has been exposed as a hoax, plagiarized from a number of sources, and ascribed to Jewish authors.

Purity of Blood (Spanish: limpieza de sangre)   Concept that served as basis for mid-fifteenth century laws in the Iberian Peninsula which were the result of suspicions regarding the sincerity of Jewish and Muslim conversions to Christianity. Based on ancestry or "blood," rather than religion, the laws were invoked to deny public office to *conversos*. Some observers see these laws as reflecting a premodern form of racial antisemitism.

Ritual Murder   Accusations first appearing in the mid-twelfth century and continuing into modern times, claiming that Jews murder Christians—most often children—in order to collect their blood for a variety of ritual purposes. In the Middle Ages, charges of ritual murder often led to mass reprisals, judicial executions, and expulsions. In modern times, ritual-murder accusations frequently developed into widely publicized, sensational court cases.

Rothschilds   Famous family of bankers and financiers, with branches in nearly every capital of Europe; they were often believed to exercise clandestine power over the destinies of Europe's states.

Sephardim   From the Hebrew for "Spanish"; Jews and their descendants expelled from the Iberian Peninsula at the end of the fifteenth century, migrating to North Africa, Turkey, and Greece. A second migration took them to France, the Netherlands, and the New World. By the nineteenth century the Sephardim were far fewer in numbers than the Ashkenazim.

Shekhita   Traditional religious manner in which animals are to be slaughtered in order to be fit (kosher) for Jews to eat. Charges have often been made that shekhita is unnecessarily cruel to animals, and laws forbidding it on that basis have been passed.

Shylock   Fictional villain of Shakespeare's *Merchant of Venice*. The name has taken on an independent existence as one of the most powerful anti-Jewish stereotypes, standing for heartless vengeance and misanthropy.

Shtetl   From the Yiddish, meaning "little town"; the market towns of eastern Europe, as distinguished from the peasant villages, usually had significant numbers of Jewish inhabitants. (The proper Yiddish plural is *shtetlakh*, although the anglicized plural "shtetls" is commonly seen.)

Socialism (socialist, social democrat)   Broad movement in the late nineteenth and early twentieth centuries, calling for the abolition or massive regulation of capitalism and private ownership of the means of production, to be replaced by planned production and a more equitable distribution of goods and social

272 *Glossary of Terms*

ownership of the means of production. In 1919–21 the socialists split into democratic socialist and communist movements.

Stürmer, Der ("The Attacker")   Weekly newspaper edited by Julius Streicher, known for an extremely crude form of antisemitism, often bordering on pornography, during the Weimar Republic and Third Reich.

Talmud   "Learning" in Hebrew; comprehensive term for a vast body of commentaries on the Bible and other aspects of Jewish life and laws; two versions exist, the Jerusalem or Palestinian (4th century) and Babylonian (5th century).

Union of the Russian People   Violent reactionary, chauvinist, tsarist, and antisemitic political organization founded in St. Petersburg in 1905 and thereafter spreading throughout the Russian empire. The Union comprised numerous radical rightist organizations, such as the Black Hundreds (a loose term often used for the Union), and drew its membership from the urban lower middle class, landowners, clergymen, and intelligentsia.

Usury   Originally the taking of interest on loans, the term came to describe the levying of excessive and exploitative interest rates. Forbidden to Christians, usury was permitted to Jews during the Middle Ages (and practiced by some Christians as well) and was a source of the popular hostility to Jews.

Vichy   Resort town in central France that became the headquarters of the collaborationist regime of Marshal Philippe Pétain, from 1940 until 1944. Vichy gave its name to this entire period of French wartime history. Vichy authorities cooperated with the Nazi occupiers in the carrying out of the Final Solution.

Victory of Jewry over Germandom (1879)   Best-selling book by Wilhelm Marr portrayed past and present as the result of an all-but-completed, racially driven Jewish war of conquest. Its twelfth edition advertised the formation of an Antisemites' League, one of the earliest uses of the word antisemite for political purposes.

Yellow Star   Physical marker imposed upon Jews by the Nazis at various times in Germany and occupied Europe. This form of identification was meant as a humiliating reminder of medieval indicators for Jews, such as the yellow badge, pointed hats, and striped clothing.

Zionism   Form of modern Jewish nationalism that emerged in the late nineteenth century. Political Zionism, perhaps the best known of its diverse expressions, sought the establishment of a modern Jewish nation-state.

Index

Abelard, Peter (1079–1142) 71
Absolutism 84, 89–90
  Enlightened 107, 166–7, 180
Abulafia, Anna Sapir 77
Acre Prison 157
Acton, Lord (John Emerich Edward
    Dalberg-Acton, 1834–1902) 3, 12
Addresses to the German Nation
  see Fichte, J. G.
Adversus Iudaeos or *Adversus Judaeos*
    as a genre 68, 71, 215, 264
Afghanistan 247
Africa 204, 216, 219, 271
  see also South Africa
African-Americans 161
Against the Inveterate Obstinacy of the Jews
  see Peter the Venerable
Agatharchides (active 2nd century BCE) 37, 43
Agobard of Lyons (*c.*779–840) 66–8
Agrarian League 129–30
Ahasverus, the Wandering Jew 46
Ahmadinejad, Mahmud (b. 1956) 244
Akiva, Rabbi (*c.*50–*c.*135 CE) 110
Aksakov, Ivan (1823–1886) 172
  see also Slavophilism
Alaric (*c.*370–410) 63
Albania 225, 230
Aleppo 217
Alexander II, Tsar (1818–1881) 170, 172, 178
  assassination of 172, 177, 227
Alexander of Macedon, the Great (356–323
    BCE) 34, 264
Alexandria 22, 218, 264
  anti-Jewish authors and traditions of 34–7,
    45–6
  violence in 45
  see also Exodus, counter-narrative;
    pogroms
Alfonsi, Peter (*c.*1062–1110) 71
Algeria 137
  see also Crémieux Decree
Aliens Act, Britain (1905) 154
Almohad 216
Alsace 144
  Jews in 116–8
Amalek (Amalekites) 12, 264
American Jewish Committee 160
American Nazi Party 260
Amsterdam 89, 104, 105, 196

Ancona 97–8
Anjou and Maine
  see expulsions of Jews
Andreeva, Nina 191
Anglican Church 151, 153, 154
Anschluss (1938) 134, 203
Anselm of Bec (*c.*1033–1109) 70
Anti-Americanism 156, 247
Antichrist 66–7, 192
Antiochus Sidetes (r. 138–129 BCE) 36, 45
Anti-Semite and Jew (1944)
  see Sartre, Jean-Paul
Antisemites' Petition (1881) 129
anti-Trinitarianism 100
anti-Zionism 210, 237–8, 241, 247, 264
  and anti-Western feeling 189
  British 156
  equivalence of Zionism and Nazism 189,
    239–43, 245, 247–8, 260
  Jewish 228–9, 265
  of the Left 32, 156, 161, 240–1
  Muslim 161, 218, 237–9, 245, 247, 262–3
  Russian 174, 191
  Soviet 181–2, 186–92
  in the Soviet Bloc 229, 233
Antonescu, Ion (1882–1946) 231
Antwerp 95
Apartheid 163
Apion (*c.*25 BCE – *c.*45–48 CE) 35, 36, 38, 45
apocalypticism 48
Apollonius Molon (active 1st century
    BCE) 36–7
Arabia 113, 240
Arab-Israeli War of 1967 *or* Six Day War 189,
    238–40
Arab language and literature 73, 113, 215–20,
    237–9, 262, 268
Aragon 73
Arendt, Hannah (1906–1975) 113, 257
  Eichmann in Jerusalem 14, 206
Aristotle (384–322 BCE) 37
Arrow Cross, Hungarian 232
Aryan 35, 197–206, 264, 270
Ashkenazic Jewry, 79, 116, 118, 264 [plural
    noun: Ashkenazim]
Asia Minor 36, 41, 54
Athens 196
Atlanticism 192
  see also Eurasianism

274   *Index*

Augustine of Hippo (354–430) 63, 67
   City of God 63–4
   and doctrine of Jewish witness 64–5, 66,
     122, 225, 253, 266
Augustus, Roman Emperor (63 BCE –14 CE)
   35, 40–3
Auschwitz 186, 231, 260
Australia 152, 162–3
Austria 123–6, 128, 132–4, 203, 224, 230, 266,
   270
   antisemitic parties in 126, 131–4, 254, 265
   Jewish emancipation in 28–9, 123, 227, 252
   Jews in Habsburg lands 29, 100, 102, 107,
     121–2, 125, 133, 217, 224, 227–9
   see also Christian Social Party; Hitler,
     Adolf; Lueger, Karl; Schönerer, Georg
     von
Austria-Hungary *or* Dual Monarchy
   see Austria; Hungary

B'nai B'rith 159
Baath Party 219
Babi Yar (1961)
   see Yevtushenko, Yevgeny
Babylonian Captivity 18, 127
Balfour Declaration 155, 219, 264
baptism 68, 175, 202–3, 226
   forced 66, 67, 69
   see also conversion
Bar Kokhba (Simon ben Kosba, d. 135 CE) 54
   Bar Kokhba revolt 44, 54, 264
Bardèche, Maurice (1909–1998) 137–8, 142
Barnato, Barney (b. Barnet Isaacs, 1851–
   1897) 154
Baron, Salo (1895–1989) 77
Barrès, Maurice (1862–1923) 143
Bar-Tal, Daniel 239
Bauer, Bruno (1809–1882) 125
Beilis, Menahem Mendel (1874–1934) 176
   see also Ritual Murder accusations
Beit, Alfred (1853–1906) 154
Belarus 167, 181, 208, 230
Bell, Francis (1851–1936) 162
Bergelson, David (1884–1952) 187
Bernard of Clairvaux (1090–1153) 69
Bessarabia 224
Beware, Zionism (1969)
   see Ivanov, Yuri
Bielohlawek, Hermann (1861–1918) 132–3
Birnbaum, Pierre 143, 144
Birobidjan, Jewish Autonomous Oblast
   of 183
Bismarck, Otto von (1815–1898) 129, 133
Bithynia 41
*Black Book, The: The Nazi Crime Against the
   Jewish People* 187
Black Death 101

Black Hundreds
   see Union of the Russian People
Blanche of Castile (1188–1252) 73
Blood Libel 7, 225
   in antiquity 46
   in the Middle Ages 74, 81
   in the early modern era 94, 104, 112, 153,
     227–8,
   in modern times 176, 188, 191
   in the Middle East 216–8, 227–8, 239,
     246–7
   see also Ritual Murder accusations
Blum, Léon (1872–1950) 147
Blumenbach, J. F. (1752–1840) 114–15
Boers 163
   Boer or South African War (1899–1902)
     154
Bohemia 224
Bolsheviks 179, 181, 184–5, 265
   see also Russian Revolution (1917);
     Judeo-Bolshevism
Bordeaux 149
Bosnia-Herzegovina 225
Boulangist Movement 143
boycott 160, 163, 201
Brafman, Jakob (c.1825–1879) 171
Brazil 104
Brezhnev, Leonid (1906–1982) 188–90
British Broadcasting Corporation (BBC) 156
British Union of Fascists 155
Browning, Christopher 207
Budennyi, Semen Mikhailovich (1883–
   1973) 179
Bukovina 224
Bulgaria 225, 230, 231, 232, 234
Bund (The All-Russian Jewish Workers'
   Party) 181, 182, 184, 265
Butmi, G. V. (1856–1918?) 175
Butmi, N. A. 175
Byrnes, Robert F. (1918–1997) 139

Caesaria 58
Cairo 217–19
Calvin, John (1509–1564) 87
   Calvinism 86, 88–9, 100, 104
cameralism 102
Cameron, William John (1878–1955) 159–60
Camus, Renaud (b. 1946) 137–8
Canada 152, 161–3
   French-speaking Canada 161
cannibalism, Jewish 7, 35, 37, 45, 46, 76
canon law 60, 67, 72, 81, 265
cantonist system 169–70
Carpentras 138
caricature 185, 240, 254
Cassius Dio (164– c.235) 41, 45
Cassius Longinus (active 1st century CE) 41

Index

Castile 72, 73
Catherine II, Empress of Russia, the Great (1729–1796) 167–8
Catholic Faith Against the Jews, On the
  see Isidore of Seville
Cayenne 103
Céline, Louis-Ferdinand (1894–1961) 137
Celsus (active late 2nd century CE) 36, 39, 57
Center Party, German 130, 133
Chabad
  see Hasidism
Chaeremon (active 1st century CE) 35, 45
chamber serfdom (*servi camerae*) 101
Chamberlain, Houston Stewart (1855–1927) 219
Charlemagne, Holy Roman Emperor (742–814) 67
Charles II, King of England (1630–1685) 153
Charles V, Holy Roman Emperor (1500–1558) 95
Chaucer, Geoffrey (c.1343–1400) 150
Chazan, Robert 77
Chmielnicki, Bogdan (c.1595–1657) 12, 23, 99–100, 178, 265
chosen people 9–11, 20, 23, 35, 48, 189, 191
  God's new chosen people (Christians) 59, 122, 151, 159
  Verus Israel (true Israel) 96–7
Christ
  see Jesus of Nazareth
Christ killers
  see Jesus of Nazareth, Jews and Crucifixion of
Christian Social Party (Austria) 123, 125, 132–3, 229, 265
  see also Lueger, Karl; Vogelsang, Karl von
Christian State 172
Chrysostom, John (c.347–407) 12, 44
church councils 265
  Elvira (c.306) 60
  Seville (624) 67
  Toledo, Fourth (633) 67
  Lateran, Fourth (1215) 72, 98, 269
  Oxford (1222) 72
Church Fathers 63, 79, 86
Churchill, Winston (1874–1965) 14–15, 207
Cicero (106–43 BCE) 38–40
circumcision 39–40, 43–4, 51–4, 85–6, 181, 265
City of God
  see Augustine of Hippo
Civic Improvement of the Jews, On the (1781)
  see Dohm, Christian Wilhelm von
Clandestine Things in the Corners, or Secrets of the Jews Unmasked (1893)
  see Hajj, Najib
Class, Heinrich (1868–1953) 124

Cleomedes 38
Clermont-Tonnere, Count Stanislas de (1757–1792) 116
Cobbett, William (1763–1835) 155
Cohen, Jeremy 77
Colbert, Jean-Baptiste (1619–1683) 103
collectivization, Soviet 181, 183
Collins, Anthony (1676–1729) 109
Cologne 69
Communism 199, 207, 272
  and antisemitism 30, 200, 210, 223, 230, 233, 240
  Soviet 179–91, 233
  see also anti-Zionism; Bolsheviks; Judeo-Bolshevism
Communist Party of the Russian Federation (CPRF) 191
Communist Party of the Soviet Union (CPSU) 179–90, 191
  see also Bolsheviks
confessionalization 89, 91
Conservative Party (British) 153, 156, 157
Conservative Party (German) 129–30
Constantine, Roman Emperor (c.272–337) 60, 63
  anti-Jewish views of 38
conversion 6, 17, 34, 43, 66–7, 75, 81, 86, 90, 97, 117, 199, 201, 203
  forced 18, 64–69, 84, 169–70
  to Christianity 6, 64, 66–7, 71, 73, 75, 81–2, 84, 94–7, 143, 166, 169–70, 196, 223, 271
  see also Baptism; Alfonsi, Peter; Brafman, Jakob; Disraeli, Benjamin; Donin, Nicholas; Marx, Karl; Pfefferkorn, Johann
  to Islam 216–17, 243
  Jewish resistance to 84, 86
  to Judaism 18, 39–43, 45, 51–2, 54, 67
converso 81, 84, 91, 94–6, 266, 268, 269, 271
  see also *Marranos*; Spain
Corneilhan, Georges 218
Cossacks 99, 171, 265
Council for the Religious Cults (USSR) 187
Counter-Reformation 98, 100
Court Jews 102, 122, 225, 266
Crash of 1873 (*Krach*) 123, 128, 131, 227, 258
Creagh, Father John (1870–1947) 163
Crémieux Decree (1870) 137
Crémieux, Adolphe (1796–1880) 217
Crimea 183–4
Crispin, Gilbert (c.1055–1117) 70–1
Croatia 208, 225, 226, 231, 232
Croix de Feu 146
Cromwell, Oliver (1599–1658)
  Cromwellian Protectorate 153
  and readmission of Jews 104, 152–3

276 *Index*

Crucifixion
  see Jesus of Nazareth, Jews and Crucifixion of
Crusades 69–70, 79, 214, 266
  First (1095–1099) 68–9
  Second (1147–1149) 69
  Third (1187–1192) 69
  Shepherds' (1251, 1320) 69
  Albigensian (1209–1229) 73
Czechoslovakia 188, 203, 223–4, 230, 233
  Czech Protectorate 231–2
  Czech Republic 224
  see also Bohemia; Moravia; Slovakia

Damascus Affair (1840) 217
  see also Ritual Murder accusations
Damocritus (probably 1st century BCE) 35
D-Day 209
De Gaulle, Charles (1890–1970) 140
De Valera, Eamon (1882–1975) 163–4
Dearborn Independent
  see Ford, Henry
Decalogue 84
Declaration of the Rights of Man 136
deicide
  see Jesus of Nazareth, Jews and Crucifixion of
deism 109–11
demonization 6, 8, 11, 24, 32, 85, 161, 212, 214, 237, 240
Denikin, Anton (1872–1947) 179
Denmark 231
Derzhavin, Gavril (1743–1816) 168
desecration 138, 261
Destruction of the European Jews, The (1961)
  see Hilberg, Raul
dhimmi 214, 216–17, 243
Dialogue between a Philosopher, a Jew and a Christian
  see Abelard, Peter
Dialogue with Trypho
  see Justin Martyr
Dialogues Against Jews
  see Alfonsi, Peter
Diary of a Writer (1873–1881)
  see Dostoevsky, Fyodor
Diaspora 266
  Diaspora [Arab language television series] 262–3
  German 103
  Islamic 138, 156, 161, 246–7 261–2
  Jewish 48, 50–1, 56, 61, 64, 79–80, 83–7, 91, 97, 115, 191–2
Diderot, Denis (1713–1784) 111
dietary laws (*kashrut*) 39, 42, 51, 176, 181, 266
Diodorus Siculus (active 1st century BCE) 36
Disputation between a Christian and a Pagan
  see Crispin, Gilbert

Disputation between a Jew and Christian
  see Crispin, Gilbert
Disraeli, Benjamin (1804–1881) 29–30, 153–4
Dmowski, Roman (1864–1939) 229
  see also National Democratic Party, Polish
Doctors' Plot, Jewish 187–8
doctrine of Jewish witness
  see Augustine of Hippo
Dohm, Christian Wilhelm von (1751–1820) 30, 114–17, 166, 265
Dominican Order 73–4, 82
Domitian, Roman Emperor (51–96) 41, 53
Domus Conversorum (House of Converts) 75
Donatists 65
Donin, Nicholas (active mid-13th century) 73–4
Dostoevsky, Fyodor (1821–1881) 26, 172
Dresden 196, 210
Dreyfus Affair 14, 30, 144–5, 254–5, 266
  in French politics 136–43, 145–6, 266
  in the analysis of Jean-Paul Sartre 143, 145
  see also Drumont, Edouard; Picquart, Georges
Dreyfus, Mathieu (1857–1930) 144
Drumont, Edouard (1844–1917) 144, 258
  and the Dreyfus Affair 144–5
  La France juive (1886) 137
Dugin, Alexander (b. 1962) 191–2
Duke, David (b. 1950) 260
Duma 175–6
  outlawing of kosher slaughtering 176
  post-Soviet 191

East Germany
  see Germany
Edict of Tolerance (1782) 107
Edward I, King of England (1239–1307) 75
Egypt 37, 45, 109, 264
  Ancient 20–3, 265, 269, 270
  Hellenistic 34–6, 45
  Fatimid 215
  Mamluk 216
  Modern 217, 218–20, 238–9, 245–7, 262
  see also Exodus, counter-narrative; Manetho
Eichmann, Adolf (1906–1962) 14–15, 206, 243
Einsatzgruppen 207
Eisenmenger, Johann Andreas (1654–1704) 112
  see also Rohling, August; Talmud
Elect No Jews! (1879)
  see Marr, Wilhelm
Elizabeth I, Queen of England (1533–1603) 150
emancipation, Jewish 18, 25–6, 103, 114–19, 169, 178, 223, 265, 266
  and origins of antisemitic movement 123–9, 250
  in France 27, 107, 116–17, 136–7, 143, 166

Index

277

in Germany and Austria 8–9, 29, 112–16, 123–6, 128, 133–4, 199, 226–7, 229, 250
in Russian Empire 27–8, 170–7, 178, 227
see also Dohm, Christian Wilhelm von; Grégoire, Henri-Baptiste; Herder, J. G.; Jew Bill of 1753; Jewish Question; Michaelis, J. D.; Napoleon; Nuremberg Laws; philosemitism
Emicho, Count (active late 11th century) 68
emigration
see migrations, Jewish
Encyclopédie (1751–1772)
see Diderot, Denis
Endecja
see National Democratic Party, Polish
England 26, 28–9, 103, 155, 157
medieval 69, 71–2, 74–6, 79, 96, 150
early modern 94, 96, 103–4, 151–2
in the Age of Enlightenment 112, 115, 153
19th century 121, 151–3, 155–7
20th century 155–6
see also expulsions of Jews; *Protocols of the Elders of Zion*; Ritual Murder accusations
English Civil War 152
Enlightenment, Age of 24, 90–1, 96, 103, 105, 107–19, 265
Epistle against the Jew Ibn Naghrella
see Hazm, Ibn
Epstein, Jacob (1880–1959) 152
Essay on Customs (1756)
see Voltaire
Esther, Book of 12, 22, 267
Estonia 224, 231–2
Eternal Jew, The (Der Ewige Jude, 1940) 205, 209
ethnic cleansing 229, 232, 234
eugenics 126
Eurasianism 191–2
see also Atlanticism
European Union 234
Euthanasia Program 206
Exodus 19–21, 23, 270
counter-narrative 21–2, 35, 45, 108
expulsions of Jews 2–3, 18, 32, 75, 79, 81, 90, 94, 98, 128, 225, 259, 268, 271
Terracina (591) 65
France (13th century) 75
England (1290) 75–6, 79, 96, 150
Royal lands of the French king (1306, 1394) 75–6
as result of the Black Death (1348) 79, 101
Iberian peninsula (1492, 1497) 75–6, 79, 81, 88, 105, 271
Vienna (1671) 98
Louisiana (1723) 103

Russia
medieval 166
imperial era 168–9, 173, 176, 229
World War I 176, 179
Germany
Reformation era 89, 101
Third Reich 199, 203–4, 268
post-World War II 234
see also Exodus; migrations, Jewish
Ezra, the Prophet 11, 18, 213

Fadlallah, Muhammad Husayn (b. 1935) 247
Farhud (1941) 220
see also pogroms
Faris, Habib
see *Talmudic Human Sacrifices*
fascism 1, 139, 146–7, 155–6, 161, 212, 219, 269
Fatat, Misr al- 219
Fear (2006)
see Gross, Jan
Fefer, Itzik (1900–1952) 187
Fichte, J. G. (1762–1814) 219
Final Solution
see Holocaust
First Fleet (1788) 162
Flavius Clemens (*c.*150 – *c.*215) 41
Ford, Henry (1863–1947) 262, 268
and the *Dearborn Independent* 159, 160
and *International Jew, The* 159
Foundations of the Nineteenth Century
see Chamberlain, Houston Stewart
Fourier, Charles (1772–1837) 139
France
in the Middle Ages 69–72, 75
early modern 103
revolutionary and Napoleonic 27, 108, 116–19, 136
post-emancipation 121, 136–40, 143–5
Vichy 140–3, 147–8, 231, 251, 272
post-World War II 142, 148–9
and Muslim minority 138, 261
see also Dreyfus Affair; emancipation, Jewish; expulsions of Jews; Holocaust; Jewish Question
Franciscan Order 73, 95
Francistes 146
Franco, Francisco (1892–1975) 145–6
Frank, Leo (1884–1915) 159–60
Frankfurt am Main 122
Franz Joseph, Emperor of Austria–Hungary (1830–1916) 29, 132, 227, 266
Frederick I, Holy Roman Emperor (1122–1190) 69
Frederick II, King of Prussia, the Great (1713–1786) 103
Frederick William I, the Great Elector of Brandenburg (1620–1688) 102

278 *Index*

freemasonry 267
  as ally or tool of Jews 175, 191–2, 267
  see also *Protocols of the Elders of Zion*
French Antilles 103
French Revolution
  see France; emancipation, Jewish
Friedlander, Henry 206
Friedländer, Saul 8, 197
  and redemptive antisemitism 199–200
Fritsch, Theodor (1852–1933) 131, 134
Fröhlich, Wolfgang 244
Futuwwa 219

Galilee 49, 53
Gaul 67
Gaylani, Rashid Ali al- (1892–1965) 220
Gaza 241, 267
Geneva 86, 88
Geniza documents 215
genocide 36, 137, 142, 191, 197, 206, 223, 231,
    242, 256, 261, 267
George, David Lloyd see *Lloyd George, David*
German Christian Movement 200–3
Germania
  see Tacitus, Cornelius
Germany 17–18, 26, 29, 39, 89, 136
  medieval 66, 69, 72, 74, 80, 101
  early modern 85–9, 98–9, 101–3
  18th and 19th century 112–13, 123
  Imperial 28, 29–30, 121–35, 144, 172, 199,
      206, 228, 250–4, 265, 269–70
  Weimar 30, 157, 199–200, 268, 272
  Nazi 12–13, 31, 130, 134–5, 139, 147–8, 155–6,
      162, 187, 196–210, 219, 230–1, 243–5, 255,
      268–70
  post-World War II 210, 232–4, 243–5, 261
  see also emancipation, Jewish; Holocaust;
      Jewish Question
ghetto 98, 153
ghettoization 205, 207–8
Gide, André (1869–1951) 147
Giono, Jean (1895–1970) 147
Giraudoux, Jean (1882–1944) 147
Gladstone, William E. (1809–1898) 154
Glagau, Otto (1834–1892) 125
globalization 105, 237, 246
Glorious Revolution (1688) 152
Goebbels, Joseph (1887–1945) 200, 201, 204–7
Goldhagen, Daniel J. 12, 197, 209
Gorbachev, Mikhail (b. 1939) 190–1
Gospels 51–7
  see also Crucifixion
Graff, Jürgen (b. 1951) 244
Granada 215
Grant, Ulysses S. (1822–1885) 166
Great Britain
  see England

Great Revolt (66–70 CE)
Great Sanhedrin 118
Greece
  Hellenistic period 34, 36–42, 45, 56
  modern 225, 230–2
Greek Orthodox church 217–18
Green Shirts
  see Young Egypt
Grégoire, Henri-Baptiste, Abbé (1750–
      1831) 116–17, 143
Gregory I, Pope, the Great (540–604) 65, 72
Gregory IX, Pope (c.1150–1241) 73
Gross, Jan 210
  Fear (2006)
Guadeloupe 103
Gulag 187
Guyana 104
Gypsies (Roma and Sinti) 7, 192, 199, 207

Habsburg dynasty 131
Habsburg Empire
  see Austria
Haddad, Mezri 246
Hadith 213–14
  see also Qur'an
Hajj, Najib al- 218
Hale, Matt (b. 1971) 260
Halevi, Yehuda (1075–1141) 71
Haman 7, 12–13, 267
Hamas Charter 242–3, 262, 267
Hamburg 126–7
Hanover 102
Hanover, Nathan (d. 1663) 99
Harding, Warren G. (1865–1923) 160
Harrington, James (1611–1677) 104, 115
Hasidism 168, 191, 267
  Chabad 180
Hasmonaean dynasty 39
Hazm, Ibn (994–1064) 152, 216
Heavy Sands (1979)
  see Rybakov, Anatoly
Hebraism, Christian 94, 104, 109, 112–13,
      267
Hecataeus of Abdera (active end of the 4th
      century BCE) 36
Hecataeus of Miletus (c.550– c.476 BCE) 35
heder 181
Hegel, G. W. F. (1770–1831) 21
Hegelians, Young 127
Hell, François (d. 1794) 116
Henry III, King of England (1207–1272) 72
Henry, Hubert Joseph (1846–1898) 144–5
Hep-Hep Riots (1819) 252, 254
Herder, J. G. (1744–1803) 112–14
Herzl, Theodor (1860–1904) 4, 228–9
Hess, Jonathan 114
Hesse 130

Index

279

Hilberg, Raul (1926–2007) 197
Hilsner, Leopold (1876–1928) 228
see also Ritual Murder accusations,
Moravia
Himmelfarb, Milton 13
Himmler, Heinrich (1900–1945) 197, 206,
229
Posen speech (1943) 197, 208–9
Hirszowicz, Lukasz (1920–1993) 209
Hitler, Adolf (1889–1945)
antisemitism of 13, 15–16, 124, 186, 196,
198–200, 251
attitudes toward 137, 147, 155–6, 160, 164,
192, 196, 219, 245
Austrian experience of 16, 131–2, 269
and the Holocaust 13, 196, 204–5
Mein Kampf 160, 199, 219, 269
and the problem of evil 12–13
rise to power of 198–200, 269
Hitler's Willing Executioners (1996)
see Goldhagen, Daniel J.
Hizballah 242, 263, 267
Hobson, J. A. (1858–1940) 154
Holbach, Baron d' (1723–1789) 109
Holland
see Netherlands
Holocaust 3, 12, 17, 77, 197–8, 223, 256
in eastern Europe 207–8, 223, 231–4
in France 137–8, 142, 148, 272
in Germany 13, 197–210, 261, 267
in the Middle East 238, 243–5
in Poland 206, 208, 269
in the USSR 186–7, 189, 207–8
in the United States 161
aftermath of 198, 209–10, 236
deportations 140, 148–9, 207–8, 231–2, 251
role of antisemitism in 197–209, 231–4, 261
see also ghettoization
Holocaust Denial, Negationism, and
Revisionism 6, 137, 243–5, 260, 267–8
Holy Roman Empire 80
Honorius III, Pope (1148–1227) 72
Horace (65–8 BCE) 40, 43
host desecration 7, 75, 217, 225, 266, 268
House of Commons 152–3
House of Lords 153
Howard, Michael 157
Huet, Pierre-Daniel (1630–1721) 109
Hugh of Lincoln (1246–1255) 150
see Ritual Murder accusations
Huguenots 103, 225
Hungary 28, 208, 223–34, 254, 261
Husayn, Ahmad (1879–1957) 219
Husseini, Mufti Hajj Amin al- (1895–
1974) 220
Hyman, Paula 136, 146
Hyndman, H. M. (1842–1921) 154

I Believe in Russia
see Zyuganov, Gennady
Iberian Peninsula 79–81, 88–90, 105, 268
see also expulsions of Jews; migrations,
Jewish; Portugal; Spain
immigration
see migrations, Jewish
Infamous Decree 118
see also Napoleon
Innocent III, Pope (1160/61–1216) 72–3,
269
Inquisition 73, 77, 91, 264, 268, 269
see also Spain
International Jew, The
see Ford, Henry
Internet
see mass media
Intifada (1987–1993) 268
Intifada, al-Aqsa (2000–) 237, 245–6, 268
Iran
antisemitic policies of 244, 248, 263
Revolution (1979) 241
Iraq 218–20, 247
Ireland 18, 104, 157–8, 162–3
Irish Free State 163–4
Irgun 156
Iron Guard, Romanian 232
Iron Shirts 209
Irving, David (b. 1938) 260
see also Holocaust Denial, Negationism,
and Revisionism
Isaacs, Isaac (1855–1948) 155
Isaacs, Rufus (1860–1935) 162
Isidore of Seville (*c.*560–636) 66–7
On the Catholic Faith Against the Jews 67
Islam 6, 18–20, 24, 31–2, 68, 71–3, 95, 138, 219,
239, 243, 256, 264–9
anti-Jewish literature in 215–16, 218–19,
239, 256
anti-Judaism in 212–16, 220, 238, 242, 246
see also Hadith
and emergence of antisemitism 8, 32, 77,
212, 216–19, 256
Islamist antisemitism 237–8, 239, 241–6,
248, 261–2, 267
status of Jews in 8, 214–15, 217, 256
see also anti-Zionism; *dhimmi*; Diaspora,
Islamic; Hadith; Qur'an
Israel, ancient 20–3, 264, 268
Christian theological views of 47–62, 66,
97, 113–14, 159, 265–6
see also Exodus
Israel, state of 19, 156, 163, 187, 189, 233
and antisemitism 31, 138, 156, 191, 233,
237–48, 261–2; 267
demonization of 32, 161, 237–40
relations to Arabs 32–3, 138, 220, 268

280 *Index*

Israel, state of (*cont.*)
  see also anti-Zionism; Islam; Six Day War;
    Zionism
Italy 117, 229
  ancient 38, 43
  Renaissance 82, 98, 100
  Fascist 139, 146, 155, 208, 220, 230
Ivanov, Yuri 189

Japan 28, 174, 263
Jawbari, Umar al- (active early 13th
    century) 216
Je suis partout 137
Jean-Baptiste de Boyer, Marquis d'Argens
    (1704–1771) 111, 117
Jedwabne
  see pogroms
Jerusalem 37, 48–51, 58, 86–7, 217–18
  destruction of 42–3, 47, 52, 54, 58–9
Jesuit Order 103
Jesus of Nazareth 49–50, 53, 86, 213
  Jewishness of 6, 49–50, 51, 57, 85, 203
  Jews and Crucifixion of 6–7, 47, 49, 50, 53–9,
    61–2, 68, 151, 172, 199–200, 225, 266
  Jews' enmity toward 24, 59, 67–8, 74–6, 81,
    112
  and Nazism 199–200, 203
  as opponent of Judaism 47
  see also Gospels
Jew Bill (Jewish Naturalisation Bill, 1753) 153,
    253–4
  see also emancipation, Jewish
Jew of Malta (1589)
  see Marlowe, Christopher
Jewish Agency 244
Jewish Anti-Fascist Committee (JAC) 186–7
Jewish badge
  see yellow star
Jewish Conspiracy against the Nations, The
    (1925)
  see Yamin, Antun
Jewish Letters (1735–1738)
  see Jean-Baptiste de Boyer, Marquis
    d'Argens
Jewish Notables, Assembly of (1806) 27, 118
Jewish Question 2, 17–33, 119, 266, 267, 250,
    259–61, 266, 267
  in eastern Europe 222, 230, 232, 234
  in the English-speaking world 27, 152
  in France 27, 136–47
  in Germany and Austria 29–30, 124–34,
    204, 251–2, 254, 257–9, 267
  in Russia and the Soviet Union 27–8, 30,
    166–7, 187–88
  see emancipation, Jewish; Russia
Jewish Question, On the (1844)
  see Marx, Karl

Jews and Their Lies, On the (1543) 86, 89, 96,
    101, 268
  see also Luther, Martin
Jiménez de Rada, Bishop Rodrigo
    (1170–1247) 72
Job, Book of 66
John I, King of England (1167–1216) 75
John, the Evangelist 49, 55
  see also Gospels
Jordan, Kingdom of 245, 263
Jordan River 265
Joseph II, Emperor of Austria (1741–1790) 107,
    226
Josephus, Flavius (*c.*37–100 CE) 21, 35–8
  see also Apion
Journey to the End of the Night
  see Céline, Louis-Ferdinand
Jud Süss (Joseph Süss Oppenheimer,
    1692–1738) 102
  see also Court Jews
Judea 35, 44, 49, 79
Judaism Exposed (1700, 1710)
  see Eisenmenger, Johann Andreas
Judaism without Embellishment (1963)
  see Kichko, Trofim
Judaizing (Judaizers) 57, 83–4, 94, 97–8, 109,
    268
Judeo-Bolshevism 30, 159, 197, 204–5, 207, 230,
    232, 259, 263, 268
  see also Russian Revolution (1917)
Judeophobia 79, 242, 250
*Juifs et opportunistes: le judaïsme en Egypte et
    Syrie* (1889)
  see Corneilhan, Georges
Julian, Roman Emperor (332–363) 36
Julius III, Pope (1487–1555) 97
Julius, Anthony 4, 8
Julius Caesar (100–44 BCE) 41
Jundi, Sami al- (b. 1924) 219
Justin Martyr (*c.*100– *c.*163) 58
Juvenal (67–140) 40–1

Kabbalah 82, 94, 268
kahal 167–9, 172
Kahal, On the (1869)
  see Brafman, Jakob
Kalinin, Mikhail (1875–1946) 183
Kant, Immanuel (1724–1804) 117
Kaplan, Alice 137
Kaplan, Marion 201
Kaplan, Yosef 96
Kennicott, Benjamin (1718–1783) 112
KGB (Committee for State Security) 182, 190
Khamanei, Ali (b. 1939) 244
Khazar kingdom 71, 240
  see Halevi, Yehudah
Khrushchev, Nikita (1894–1971) 188

Index   281

Kichko, Trofim 189
Kielce
  see pogroms
Kiev 169, 176, 186
  see also pogroms
Klemperer, Victor (1881–1960) 196, 210
Know-Nothing Party 157–8
Koran
  see Qur'an
kosher slaughtering (*shekhita*) 112, 176, 181,
  269, 271
  see also dietary laws; Ritual Murder
    accusations
Kosovo 225
Kossuth, Louis (1802–1894) 227
Kovaly, Heda 210
Kun, Béla (1886–1936) 230
Kuwait 262

La France juive (1886)
  see Drumont, Edouard
La gerbe 137
La hora de todos
  see Quevedo, Francisco de
Labour Party (British) 152, 155, 156
Lacombe Lucien (1974)
  see Malle, Louis
Langmuir, Gavin (1924–2005) 76–7
Laski, Harold (1893–1950) 152
Lateran Council, Fourth
  see church councils
Latvia 224, 231
Lazare, Bernard (1865–1903) 25
Le Pen, Jean-Marie (b. 1928) 137
Lebanon 217–19, 241, 244, 267
Lectures on Romans (1517)
  see Luther, Martin
Lectures on the Sacred Poetry of the Hebrews
  (1753)
  see Lowth, Robert
Lenin, Vladimir Ilyich (1870–1924) 179
Leningrad 185, 191
  see also St. Petersburg
Lessing, Gotthold Ephraim (1729–1781) 111,
  117
Levant 216–8
Lewis, Bernard 8–9, 14
Liberal Democratic Party, Russian 192
  see also Zhirinovsky, Vladimir
liberalism 1, 9, 26, 29, 131, 133, 153, 156, 175,
  191–2, 217, 226, 228–9
  and opposition to antisemitism 130, 133, 150,
    158, 164, 246
  Jewish association with 18, 122–3, 125, 132–3,
    152, 172, 175, 190–1, 234
Limerick boycott 163
Limonov, Eduard (b. 1943) 191

Lindemann, Albert 121, 250
Linz Program (1882) 131
Lithuania 99–100, 167–8, 181, 208, 223–5, 229,
  231–2, 265
Livorno 97, 104
Lloyd George, David (1863–1945) 155
Loans, Jacob ben Jehiel (d. 1506) 82
Locke, John (1632–1704) 104
Łódź 206
London 70, 75, 95, 104, 110, 151–4, 157
Lopez, Roderigo (d. 1593) 150–1
Lorraine 144
Louis I, King of France and Holy Roman
  Emperor, the Pious (768–840) 67
Louis IX, King of France, Saint (1214–
  1270) 72–3
Louis XIV, King of France (1638–1715) 102–3
Louisiana 103, 159
Lowell, A. Laurence (1856–1943) 160
Lowth, Robert (1710–1787) 112–14
Lueger, Karl (1848–1910) 29, 124–5, 132–4, 229
Luke, the Evangelist 54
  see also Gospels
Luther, Martin (1483–1546) 12, 23, 82–90, 96,
  101, 268
Lysimachus (360–281 BCE) 35

McCarthy Era 161
Macedonia 225
Machiavelli, Niccolò (1469–1527) 95
Maecenas, Caius (*c.*70–8 BCE) 41
Maghazi 213–14
Maghreb 216
Maghribi al-Samaw'al, Ibn Yahya 216
Maimonides, Moses (1135–1204) 216
Mainz 68–70
Makhno, Nestor (1889–1934) 179
Malle, Louis (1932–1995) 148
Mamluk 216
Manetho (active early 3rd century BCE) 21–3,
  35, 269
Manicheans *or* Manichaeans 65, 141, 144
Marchandeau Law 148
Marconi Scandal 155
Mark, the Evangelist 51
  see also Gospels
Markish, Perets (1895–1952) 187
Marlowe, Christopher (1564–1593) 95–6
Maronite Christians 217, 219
Marr, Wilhelm (1819–1904) 25, 8–9, 123–6,
  128, 252–3, 255, 258
  and *The Victory of Jewry over Germandom*
    (1879) 127–8, 272
Marrano 266, 269
  see also Spain
Marshall, Louis (1856–1929) 160
Marsham, John (1602–1685) 109

282 Index

Martí, Ramón (active last half of the 13th century) 73
Daggers of Faith (1278)
Martial (*c.*40–114 CE) 43
Martinique 103
Marx, Karl (1818–1883) 13
 antisemitism of 30, 139
 and *On the Jewish Question* (1844) 30
Masada 69
mass media 192, 218, 246, 254, 255, 258, 263
 antisemitism in 156, 218, 244–5, 248, 254, 259–61
 exclusion of Jews from 148, 186, 190, 202
 film 205
 Internet 246, 260
 newspapers 122, 128–31, 133, 137, 155–6, 159–60, 185, 191, 199, 218–19, 244–6, 254, 272
 power of Jews in 121, 137, 189, 234, 247, 258
 radio 137, 202
 television 244, 246, 262–3
 see also France, Vichy; Nazi Party; Russia, Soviet
Matthew, the Evangelist 51, 53–4, 57
 see also Gospels
Matzo of Zion, The
 see Tlas, Mustafa
Mecca 212–14
Medina 213, 238
Mein Kampf
 see Hitler, Adolf
Meir, Golda (1898–1978) 187
Melbourne 162
Melito of Sardis, Bishop (d. 180) 57–8
Mendelssohn, Moses (1729–1786) 25, 111
Mensheviks 28
mercantilism 94–105
Merchant of Venice
 see Shakespeare, William
Michaelis, Johann David (1717–1791) 113
 opposition to Jewish emancipation 114, 117
 and race 114–15
Middle East 74, 216–17, 219, 237–48, 260–2, 268
migrations, Jewish
 in antiquity 2, 19–23, 266–7, 270
 as source of antisemitism 4, 28, 122, 129, 137, 144–6, 154, 158, 270
 from Arab lands 239
 from central and eastern Europe 28, 98–9, 146, 154, 158, 163, 203–4, 223, 227, 229, 233–4, 270
 from Iberian Peninsula 79, 90, 104, 271
 from Nazi Germany 156, 162, 203, 244
 from the USSR 187, 190
 to eastern Europe 79, 98–9, 101

to western and central Europe 67, 76, 81–2, 122, 129, 144–6, 156, 163, 229, 271
 overseas 90, 158, 162–3, 204, 227
 see also Diaspora, Jewish; expulsions of Jews
Milice 148
Miliukov, Pavel (1859–1943) 175
Miliutin, Dmitry (1816–1912) 171
Mill, John Stuart (1806–1873) 13, 26
Mirror to the Jews (1862)
 see Marr, Wilhelm
misanthropy, Jewish 35–7, 39–40, 115, 127, 189, 271
Misr al-Fatat
 see Young Egypt
Moldavia 224
Moldova 223
Monash, Sir John (1865–1931) 162
Montefiore, Moses (1784–1885) 217
Montesquieu, Baron Charles-Louis de Secondat (1689–1755) 111
Moore, R. I. 77
Moravia 228
Mordecai 22
Mosaic Law (1770–1775)
 see Michaelis, Johann David
Moscovy 100
Moscow 167, 173, 176, 179, 185, 187, 193
Moses 48, 268
 in Graeco-Roman literature 35–6, 38, 40
 in Christian thought 57, 59
 in Islam 212
 in the Enlightenment 109, 111, 114
Mosley, Oswald (1896–1980) 155–6
Mossad 247
Muhammad (*c.*570/571–632) 212–14, 238–9, 242, 246
Muhammad Ali, Khedive (1769–1849) 217
Munich agreements 147
Muslim Brotherhood 219
Muslims
 see Islam
Muthanna Club 219

Nahda (revival) 217–18
Napoleon I (Napoléon Bonaparte, 1769–1821) 27, 29, 192
 and Jewish emancipation 27, 107, 117–9
Nashe Otechestvo (Our Fatherland) 191
Nasi, Joseph, Duke of Naxos (1524–1579) 95–6
Nathan the Wise (1779)
 see Lessing, Gotthold Ephraim
National Democratic Party, Polish (Endecja) 229
Natural Varieties of Mankind, On the (1775)
 see Blumenbach, J. F.

Index   283

NATO (North Atlantic Treaty Organization) 247
Nazi Germany and the Jews (1997–2007)
  see Friedländer, Saul
Nazi Party (National Socialist German
    Workers' Party)
  historical precedents for 137
  program of 197–200
  propaganda of 198–200, 246, 268
  rise to power of 15, 130, 196, 198, 200–1, 269
Nazism 13, 30–1, 204, 206, 243, 269
  antisemitism of 13, 15, 123, 163, 197–210,
    246, 268
  and Christianity 200–3
  collaboration with 137–8, 142, 146–9, 206,
    219–20, 230–2, 272
  resistance to 148, 156, 164, 186, 230–2, 238
  see also Hitler, Adolf; Holocaust; Nazi
    Party; Vichy
Nazi–Soviet Pact *see* Non-Aggression Pact of
    1939
Neo-Nazism 192, 260, 269
Neo-Stalinism 191–2
  see also Stalin, Josef
NEP (New Economic Policy)
  NEP-men 183, 185–6
Nero, Roman Emperor (37–68) 52
Netherlands 88, 103, 104, 111, 115, 271
New Christians 94, 96–8, 228, 266, 269
  see also *converso*; *Marrano*; Spain
New Deal 158
New Testament 23, 49, 51–2, 54, 56–8, 61, 80,
    82, 109, 203, 212
  see also Gospels
New Zealand 152, 162–3
newspapers
  see mass media
Nicholas I, Tsar (1796–1855) 168–9, 171
Nicholas II, Tsar (1868–1918) 175, 179
Nicholas III, Pope (c.1216–1277) 73
Niebuhr, Carsten (1733–1815) 113
Nietzsche, Friedrich (1844–1900) 26, 219
Night of Broken Glass
  see pogroms
Nobel Peace Prize 2, 10, 260
Non-Aggression Pact of 1939, Nazi–
    Soviet 205–6
Normandy 70, 75
North German Confederation
  see Germany
Norway 231
Novoe Vremia (New Time) 174
numerus clausus 270
  Russia 173
  USSR 188–90
  United States 160, 270
Nuremberg Laws (1935) 148, 202, 270

Odessa 175
  see also pogroms
Odo of Chateauroux (c.1190–1273) 74
Old Testament
  see Torah
One Christian Against Six Jews (1776)
  see Voltaire
Ophuls, Marcel (b. 1927) 148
Oppeheimer, Joseph Süss ("Jud Süss")
  see Court Jews
Ordinary Men
  see Browning, Christopher
Origen (c.185–254) 58–9
Ostjuden (east European Jews) 28, 79–80, 100,
    122, 223, 227, 270
  see also migrations, Jewish
Ottoman Empire 97, 217, 222, 224–5

Pact of Umar 243
Pale of Settlement 167–70, 173–4, 176–7, 270
Palestine 204
  ancient 37, 80
  Arab opposition to Jewish presence
    in 217–19, 220, 243–6
  partition of 220
  and sovereignty conflicts 138, 155, 156, 220,
    237–8
  and world opinion 32, 155–6, 161, 240–1
  see also migrations, Jewish; anti-Zionism;
    Zionism
Pamyat 191–2
papacy 65, 66, 83
  papal states 97
Papon, Maurice (1910–2007) 149
Paris 73, 74, 118, 121, 138, 144
Paris, University of 72, 74, 146, 261
Parti Populaire Français 146
Party of God
  see Hizballah
Passover 20, 23, 49, 58, 74, 217, 269
  see also Exodus
Paul IV, Pope (1476–1559) 97, 98
Paul of Tarsus, the Apostle (c.5– c.67) 47,
    50–2, 56, 82–3, 85
Péguy, Charles (1873–1914) 145
perestroika 190
Persia 7, 22
Persian Letters (1721)
  see Montesquieu, Baron Charles-Louis de
    Secondat
Pétain, Philippe (1856–1951) 137, 148, 272
Peter of Terracina, Bishop (active 6th
    century) 65
Peter the Venerable, Abbot of Cluny
    (c.1092–1156) 71–2
Petliura, Symon (1879–1926) 179
Petronius (c.27–66) 43

284 Index

Pfefferkorn, Johann (*c.*1469– *c.*1522) 82
see also Talmud, banning of
Pharisees 83
Philip II, King of France, Augustus (1165–1223) 75
Philip IV, King of France (1268–1314) 75
Philo of Alexandria (20 BCE –50 CE) 36–7
philosemitism 61, 91, 153, 163, 210, 270
philo-Judaism, Christian 86
philosophes 24, 107, 127
Philosophical Dictionary (1764)
see Voltaire
Philostratus (*c.*150–200) 39
Picquart, Georges (1854–1914) 14, 144–5
Pilsudski, Jozef 229
plague 7, 12, 79, 81
Plamondon, Jacques-Edouard 161
Plehve, V. K. (1846–1904) 174
Pobedonostsev, Konstantin (1827–1907) 172–3
Podolia 99–100
pogroms
in general 69–70, 79, 98, 128, 177–9, 189, 228, 233, 252, 255, 270
Alexandria (38 CE) 40, 45, 264
Rhineland (1096) 69
Second and Third Crusades 69
after Black Death (mid-14th century) 101, 79, 81
Spain (1391) 96
Hep-Hep Riots (1819) 252, 254
Odessa (1821, 1859, and 1871) 177–8
German-speaking Europe (1848) 227
Russia (1881–1882) 172–3, 177–8, 227, 270
Tiszaeszlár (1882) 228
Kishinev (1903) 178
Gomel (1904) 177
Limerick (1904) 163
Odessa (1905) 177
Russia (1905–1906) 173, 177, 179
during Russian Civil War (1917–1920) 177, 179, 229
Night of Broken Glass (1938) 203–4, 255, 269–70
Baghdad (1941) 220
Jedwabne (1941) 208, 232
Kiev (1945) 186
Tripolitania (1945) 220
Kielce (1946) 210, 232–3, 269
Uzbekistan (1961) 189
Turkestan (1962) 189
Poland
Polish-Lithuanian Commonwealth 167, 199, 225
in the medieval and early modern eras 98–102, 105
Partitions of 224, 270
Congress Poland 167

in the 19th and early 20th centuries 223–4, 227, 229
interwar 230, 261
during World War II 203, 205–6, 208, 231–2, 251
post-World War II 210, 222, 224, 232–4, 269
see also migrations, Jewish; pogroms
Pompey (106–48 BCE) 48
Pompidou, Georges (1911–1974) 148
Popular Front 147
populism
American 155, 158, 159
Australian 162
British 154
French 116
German and Austrian 125, 131
Russian 28
Portugal 81, 95, 104
Posen 197
Pravda 185, 188, 191
Preobrazhensky, E. A. (1886–1937) 185
Prioress's Tale (1387)
see Chaucer, Geoffrey
proselytism
see conversion
Protocols of the Elders of Zion 262, 271
in Germany 268
in Great Britain 155
and Henry Ford 159–60, 262, 268
and the Internet 260
in the Middle East 218–19, 239, 242, 247, 260, 262–3
in post-Soviet Russia 192
in the Soviet Union 185–6, 189
on television 260, 262–3
in tsarist Russia 175, 177, 179, 271
Provisional Government (Russia, 1917) 177
Ptolemy I Soter (*c.*367–282 BCE) 37
Purity of Blood Laws (*limpieza de sangre*) 96–7, 271
see also Spain

Quebec 161–2
Quevedo, Francisco de (1580–1645) 97
Quintilian (35–95) 38
Qur'an (Koran) 212–14, 238, 242, 246

racism 115, 139–40, 158, 193, 198, 218
anti-Black 206
anti-Jewish 6, 61, 20, 24, 91–2, 97, 114–15, 126–7, 139–40, 143, 146–7, 160, 186, 192–3, 199–200, 203, 205, 212, 219, 230, 238, 242–3, 272
definitions of 1–2, 9, 32, 34, 61, 115, 237–8, 271
Jewish 32, 189, 240–1, 242, 245, 247
Ramli, Fathi al- 239

Index

Rasputin, Valentin (b. 1937) 190
Recife 104
Reformation 80–92, 97, 98, 151, 156, 252, 267
  Counter-Reformation 98, 100
  see also Calvin, John; Hebraism, Christian;
    Luther, Martin
refuseniks 190
Reichstag 129–31, 133, 201, 204
Reichskristallnacht
  see Night of Broken Glass
reparations, German-Israeli 243
Resistance, French 140, 148
Reuchlin, Johann (1455–1522) 82
  see also Talmud
revolution 12, 16, 30, 63, 152, 229
  of 1848 123–6, 226, 227
  as fomented by or attributed to Jews 28–30,
    125, 155, 159, 172–3, 175, 226–7, 230, 263
  as inimical to Jews 12, 30–1, 63, 117–18, 125,
    134, 155, 173, 175, 179–86, 226–7, 230, 241
  and Jewish emancipation 27, 103, 107,
    116–17, 123, 136, 143, 166, 175, 178–9
  see also Judeo-Bolshevism; pogroms
Rex vs. Osborne (1732) 153
Rhodes, Cecil (1853–1902) 154
Rhodes, Island of 37
Ritual Murder accusations 35, 74–75, 98, 112,
    150, 153, 217–18, 225, 246, 271
  Norwich (1144) 74, 150
  Blois (1171) 74
  Lincoln (1255) 150
  and the Black Death (2nd half of the 14th
    century) 101
  Aleppo (17th century) 217
  Damascus (1840, 1890) 217, 218
  Cairo (1844) 217
  Dayr al-Qamar (1847) 217
  Jerusalem (1847) 217–18
  Damanhur (1873–1877) 218
  Tiszaeszlár (1882) 227–8
  Moravia (Polna, 1900) 228
  Konitz (1900) 269
  Quebec (1910) 161
  Beilis case (1911) 176
  Kielce (1946) 269
  USSR (1961, 1962) 188–89
  Russia (1993, 1998) 191
  see also expulsions of Jews
Rohling, August (1839–1931) 218
Roma and Sinti (Gypsies) 7, 192, 199, 207–8
Rome
  city 38, 39–40, 42–4, 46, 63–4, 72, 74, 82,
    84, 87
  republic 40
  empire 38, 40–1, 43–6, 52–4, 56, 59–60, 63,
    67, 196
Romania 208, 223–5, 230–2

Roosevelt, Franklin Delano (1882–1945) 14,
    158, 207
Rosenberg, Joseph 162
Rosenblatt, Jason 104
Rothschilds 139, 151, 153
Rousseau, Jean-Jacques (1712–1778) 111
Russia
  Imperial 15, 27–31, 100, 154–7, 166–79, 222,
    224, 227, 228, 255, 258, 270, 271, 272
  Civil War era 177–9, 229
  Soviet 164, 166, 179–90, 230, 258, 265, 268
  post-Soviet 74, 190–3
  see also pogroms
Russian Civil War (1917–1921)
  see Russia
Russian Orthodox Church 172, 175–6, 270
Russian Revolution (1905) 175, 177–9, 272
Russian Revolution (1917) 30, 166, 180, 265
Russo-Japanese War 28, 174
Ruth, the Moabite 11
Rutilius Namatianus, Claudius (active early
    5th century CE) 39, 41, 43
Rybakov, Anatoly (1911–1998) 189

Sabbath 10, 37, 43, 87–8, 114, 242
Sabra and Shatila massacres (1982) 241
Sadat, Anwar al- (1918–1981) 239
Saint-Simonians 139
Salomons, David (1797–1873) 153
Salonica 97
Samarin, Yuri (1819–1876) 172
Samuel, Herbert (1870–1963) 155, 157
Sapiro, Aaron (1884–1959) 160
Sartre, Jean-Paul (1905–1980)
  and analysis of the Dreyfus Affair 143–4
  Anti-Semite and Jew (1944) 140–8
Saudi Arabia 262
scapegoatism 13, 81, 229, 257
Schechter, Ronald 108
Schindler, Oskar (1908–1974) 14
Schönerer, Georg von (1842–1921) 125, 131–2,
    258
Second Coming 104
Selden, John (1584–1654) 104
Seleucids 36–7, 45
Seligman, Joseph (1818–1880) 160
Semites 240
Seneca (1–65) 38, 40–1
Sephardic Jewry 71, 80, 88–90, 95, 97, 108, 111,
    116, 151, 153, 271 [plural noun:
    Sephardim]
September 11, 2001 247
Serbia 225, 226
serfdom 100, 101, 170, 178
Sforno, Obadiah (1475–1550) 82
Shafarevich, Igor (b. 1923) 191
Shakespeare, William (1564–1616) 94–5, 269

286   *Index*

Sharansky, Natan (b. 1948) 190
Sharapov, Sergei (1855–1911) 174
Sharia 214
Shawkat, Sami 219
Shaykh, Mamduh al– 245
Shinwell, Emanuel (1884–1986) 152
Shoah
  see Holocaust
shtetl 79, 182–3, 271
Shylock 95–6
Silencing the Jews
  see Maghribi al-Samaw'al, Ibn Yahya
Sinai 2, 20, 24, 27, 85
Singer, Isaac Bashevis (1904–1991) 2
Sisebut, King of the Visigoths (c.565–621) 67
Six Day War 189, 220, 239–41
Slánský, Rudolf (1901–1952)
  Slánský Trial 188
slavery 158
Slavophilism 172, 174, 190
  neo-Slavophilism 190
Slezkine, Yuri 31
Slovakia 208, 223, 224, 226, 230–2
Slovenia 223
Smuts, Jan (1870–1950) 163
Social Darwinism 230
Social Democratic Party (Austria) 133
Social Democratic Party (Germany) 130
socialist movement 127, 131, 133, 179, 226, 271
  and affiliation of Jews 122, 125, 175,
    184, 265
  antisemitic attitudes within 125, 133, 139, 154,
    180, 182
  and opposition to antisemitism 130
solafideism 83
Solidarity movement 233
Solzhenitsyn, Alexander (1918–2008) 1, 14, 16
Sorrow and the Pity, The (1969)
  see Ophuls, Marcel
South Africa 152, 161, 163
Sovetskaia Rossiia (Soviet Russia) 191
Spain 60, 67, 72–3, 75–77, 79–81, 88, 90–1,
  94–7, 105, 145–6, 150, 271
  see also expulsions of Jews
Spanish Civil War 145–6, 204
Spencer, John (1630–1693) 109
Spinoza, Baruch (1632–1677) 90, 108–9
  Theological-Political Treatise (1670)
Spirit of Hebrew Poetry, On the (1782)
  see Herder, J. G.
Spirit of Judaism, The (1770)
  see Holbach, Baron d'
St. Petersburg 173, 177, 179, 272
  see also Leningrad
stab-in-the-back myth 199, 204, 230, 245
Stalin, Josef (1879–1953) 14, 206
  antisemitism of 186–8

and anti-Zionism 179, 186–8, 189, 233
and plans for deportation of Jews 188
Stalingrad 209, 231
star of David
  see yellow star
Stavisky, Sacha (1886–1934) 146
Steed, Henry Wickham *see* Wickham Steed,
  Henry
Stern, Linda 186
Stoecker, Adolf (1835–1909) 124, 130
Stolypin, Pyotr (1862–1911) 175
Strabo (c.63–3 BCE) 35, 37, 43
Strasbourg 118
Streicher, Julius (1885–1946) 272
Stürmer, Der 199, 246, 272
Stuyvesant, Peter (1592–1672) 103–4
Suez Crisis 189
Suleiman the Magnificent, Sultan
  (1494–1566) 95
supersessionism 55–61
Suriname 104
Suslov, Mikhail (1902–1982) 188
Suvorin, Aleksei (1834–1912) 174
Sweden 100
Sydney 162
Synesius, Bishop (c.373–c.414) 38–43
Syria 41, 43, 216–20, 262

Tacitus, Cornelius (55–120 CE) 35–45, 89
Talmud 71, 82, 112, 118, 189, 272
  suppression of 73–4, 82, 98, 168–9
  Talmud Trial (1240) 73
  Talmudic Human Sacrifices (1890) 218
  Talmud Jew, The (1871) 218
  see also Eisenmenger, Johann Andreas;
    Rohling, August
Temple, Second 42, 48, 52
  destruction of (70 CE) 47–8, 52, 53, 56, 57
  Judaism of 53, 82
  and relations to early Christianity 49–51,
    52, 53, 57, 83
  in Protestant thought 83, 85–6, 87
  at the time of Jesus, 48–9, 57
terrorism
  Islamist 247, 248, 267
  Nazi 202, 244, 269–70
  radical rightist 138, 260
  Russian 172, 175
  Soviet 181, 188, 208, 233
  Zionist 156
  see also pogroms
Tertullian (c.160– c.220) 67
The Times of London 26, 155
Theodosius I, Roman Emperor
  (c.346–395) 60, 63
Theological-Political Treatise (1670)
  see Spinoza, Baruch

Index

287

These Are Our Aims, Who Believes in Them is One of Us (1939)
  see Shawkat, Sami
Third Reich
  see Germany; Nazi Party; Nazism
Third Use of the Law 87–8
Thirty Years War 90, 127
Thomas of Monmouth (active second half 12th century) 74
Thus Spake Zarathustra
  see Nietzsche, Friedrich
Tiberius, Roman Emperor (42 BCE –37 CE) 35, 40
Tlas, Mustafa (b. 1932) 246
Toland, John (1670–1722) 109, 111, 115
Toledot Yeshu 59
Tolerance, Edict of (1782) 107, 226
Torah 23, 24, 48, 51–7, 60, 64, 97, 108–9, 112, 151, 153, 189, 203, 212
Tory Party
  see Conservative Party (British)
Touvier, Paul (1915–1996) 149
Transfer (*Ha'avara*) Agreement 244
Transnistria 208
transubstantiation 75
Transylvania 224–5
Treitschke, Heinrich von (1834–1896) 8–9, 121–3
Trent 98
Tripolitania
  see pogroms
Truman, Harry S. (1884–1972) 14–15
Turkestan 189
Turkey 37, 95, 271
Tustari, Abu Nasr (d. after 1047) 215
Tustari, Abu Sacd (d. 1047) 215

Ukraine 99–100, 178–9, 181–3, 189, 208, 223, 225–6, 229, 232, 260
Ulrich von Hutten (1488–1523) 89
Ulster 162–3
UN Resolution No. 3379
  see United Nations
Union of Lublin 99
Union of the Russian People 175–6, 272
United Kingdom
  see England
United Nations 220, 241
United States of America 27, 28, 152, 158, 230
  antisemitism in 5, 155, 157–9, 160–2, 260, 268, 270
  Jewish well-being in 31, 152, 157–8, 204
  support for Israel 31, 161, 247
universal suffrage 131
USSR
  see Russia, Soviet

Unveiled Secrets
  see Jabari, Umar al-
usury 75, 81, 94–5, 101, 151, 213, 252, 272
Uzbekistan 189

Venice 94–8, 267, 269, 271
Versailles 102
Verus Israel 96–7
Vichy
  see France
Victoria, Queen of England (1819–1901) 154
Victory of Jewry over Germandom, The
  see Marr, Wilhelm
Vienna 29, 102, 121–3, 128, 132, 224, 226–7, 258
Vilna 169–71, 265
Visigoths 63, 64–7
Vogel, Julius (1835–1899) 162
Vogelsang, Karl von (1818–1890) 123, 132
Volhynia 99
Voltaire (1694–1778) 24–5
  anti-Jewish views of 108–12, 119, 127

Wagner, Richard (1813–1883) 124, 125
Walachia 224
Wales 155
Wandering Jew
  see Ahasverus
Wasiti, Ahmad ibn Ibrahim al- (d. 1374) 216
Watson, Tom (1856–1922) 159
Weber, Eugen 146
Weinberg, Gerhard 209
West India Company 104
Westminster 70
Westphalia 203
Westphalia, Peace of (1648) 102
Whig Party 153
White Army (Russian) 179, 229
white slavery 258
white supremacy 126, 269
Why God Became Man
  see Anselm of Bec
Wickham Steed, Henry (1871–1956) 26
Wiesel, Elie (b. 1928) 10
Wieviorka, Michel 138
William of Norwich (*c.*1132–1144)
  see Ritual Murder accusations
Wisse, Ruth 5
Witte, Sergei (1849–1915) 174–5
Wittenberg 86–7
World War I 12, 16, 146, 155, 159, 162, 176, 196–7, 206, 229
  Jews as powers behind 206, 245
World War II 156, 163
  and antisemitism 156, 187, 205–6, 219–20, 223, 232, 241, 243–4, 251
Worms 69
Württemberg 82, 102

Index

xenophobia 160
  as a fault of the Jews 36
  of the French 136, 143, 145–6

Yamin, Antun 219
  see also *Protocols of the Elders of Zion*
Yaroslavsky, Emelian (1878–1943) 186
yellow star 72–3, 75, 207, 214, 272
Yeltsin, Boris (1931–2007) 192
yeshiva 188, 193
Yevseev, Yevgeny 189
Yevsektsiya (Jewish section of the Communist
  Party of the Soviet Union) 182–3
Yevtushenko, Yevgeny (b. 1933) 189
Yiddish 10, 122, 154, 184, 224–5, 264–5,
  270–1
  language education 180–1, 184
  literature 184, 188
  newspapers 185
  theater 184
York 69, 150

Young Egypt 219
Yugoslavia 224, 230–2

Zagreb 196
zemstva 171, 173–4
Zhdanov, Andrei (1896–1948) 187
Zhirinovsky, Vladimir (b. 1946) 192
Zhytomyr 196
Zionism 122, 181–2, 272
  ideology of 4, 184, 238, 240, 242, 245
  and philosemitism 163
  politics of 56, 174, 181, 189, 228–9, 238, 243, 272
  suppression of 181, 186–9, 233, 241
  see anti-Zionism
Zyuganov, Gennady (b. 1944) 191
Zola, Émile (1840–1902) 144
Zoroastrianism 214
Zuchowski, Stefan (d. 1716) 100
Zündel, Ernst (b. 1932) 260
  see also Holocaust Denial, Negationism,
    and Revisionism